Paul Rand:

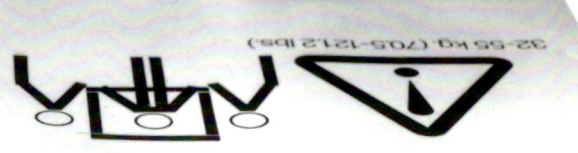

Print advertisement
Think Different ©
Apple, Inc.
1998
Printed with
permission.
Ad Agency:
Chiat Day
Photography:
Peter Arnell

On "art"

Art is an idea that has found its perfect form. A work of art is realized when form and content are in synthesis. The genius of art is when form and function come together. Art is a question of quality, not classification.[1]

On "fine" in fine art

I was talking to somebody yesterday who wanted me to contribute to an exhibit and he said he was going to show fine art and graphic design. I asked him what he meant by fine art and graphic design. Being a painter, he meant he was going to show paintings and graphic design. He used "fine" art to mean painting, so I suggested that he simply call it graphic design, painting, photography, sculpture, film, etc. Categories and genres have been mixed up, creating confusion. The genre of graphic design or painting or photography or sculpture or film, etc., is art. These categories are all art, or could be, depending on the quality and relevance of the work.[2]

On "typography"

When giving a lecture at the Baltimore Museum of Art in April 1994, a young designer asked Paul Rand if he used a lot of typefaces because there are today a lot more typefaces than in the past. Paul Rand replied rhetorically – "How many strings are on a violin? Fantastic music has been made with a few strings and chords. You only need to concern yourself with legibility, readability, appropriateness, suitability, materials, and beauty. All you want to do is to communicate effectively and honestly."[3]

---

[1]. Excerpt from a conversation about art and classification with Franc Nunoo-Quarcoo in June 1996.
[2]. Excerpt from the video *Paul Rand* by Preston McLaren, 2000.
[3]. Excerpt from a lecture delivered to the AIGA Baltimore Chapter at the Baltimore Museum of Art in April 1994.

Issues in Cultural Theory 6
Center for Art and Visual Culture
University of Maryland Baltimore County

Distributed by D.A.P.
Distributed Art Publishers
New York
2003

Paul Rand: Modernist
Design

Franc Nunoo-Quarcoo

to: Marion Swannie Rand

Paul Rand: Modernist Design
is the sixth title in the series
Issues in Cultural Theory.

Generous support for the
publication of *Paul Rand:
Modernist Design* has come
from The National
Endowment for the Arts,
Mossberg Foundation and
Mossberg & Company Inc.,
South Bend, Indiana
46601-3547.
www.mossbergco.com

Published by
The Center for Art
and Visual Culture
University of Maryland
Baltimore County
Baltimore Maryland 21250
www.umbc.edu

Distributed by D.A.P.
Distributed Art Publishers
New York

Copyright
© 2003 by
Franc Nunoo-Quarcoo
franc@umbc.edu

All rights reserved
Published 2003
Printed in the
United States of America

No part of this book may be
reproduced, stored in a retrieval
system, or transmitted in
any form or by any means,
including electronic, mechanical,
photocopying, microfilming,
recording, or otherwise (except
for that copying permitted by
Sections 107 and 108 of the U.S.
Copyright Law and except by
reviewers for the public press)
without written permission
from the copyright bearer and
publisher.

Library of Congress
Control Number
2003103609
ISSN 1521-1223
ISBN 1890761036
4 3 2 1

"Paul Rand" by Allen
Hurlburt is reprinted with
permission of *Communication
Arts,* ©1999 Coyne &
Blanchard, Inc. All rights
reserved. This article first
appeared in the January/
February 1979 issue of
Communication Arts and
was reprinted in the
March/April 1999 issue
of *Communication Arts.*

"Paul Rand: American
Modernist," 1998, by
Jessica Helfand is reprinted
with permission.

The dialogue between Paul
Rand and Rudolph Arnheim
in *Rudolph Arnheim: Revealing
Vision,* 1997, edited by Kent
Kleinman and Leslie Van
Duzer, is reprinted with permission from the University
of Michigan Press, Ann Arbor.

Paul Rand, Artograph 6, edited
by Virginia Smith and Roslyn
Bernstein, is printed with permission from Virginia Smith.

The dialogue between Paul
Rand and Mario Rampone in
Type Talks, Fall 1989, vol. 1,
no. 1, is reprinted with permission from Mario Rampone.

Contents:

10: Preface
12: Introduction and Acknowledgments

17: Essays
69: Tributes
131: Dialogues

199: Plates

357: Timeline
386: Contributors
390: Bibliography

10:   11:

Preface
Maurice Berger, Ph.D.
Curator
The Center for Art
and Visual Culture
University of Maryland
Baltimore County

Fellow
The Vera List Center
for Art and Politics
New School University

- The Center for Art and Visual Culture (CAVC), begun more than a decade ago as the Fine Arts Gallery of the University of Maryland Baltimore County, is committed to analyzing the visual world not just for its optical pleasure, but for its underlying social and cultural meaning. The exhibitions and books it sponsors — one-person, retrospective, thematic, and experimental projects — give voice to artists, subjects, and curatorial approaches often ignored or underrepresented in mainstream museums. If Paul Rand has been discussed widely in the history of twentieth-century design, his broader social and cultural commitments have not always been at the forefront of these discussions.

- Rand was one of the twentieth century's most progressive and far reaching designers, helping to reshape the look of American culture. His endeavors were not purely esthetic or visual. Rather, his designs considered a whole range of intellectual, social, and cultural concerns — from the programs and operations of the organizations and businesses he represented to the effect of design itself on the way we see and understand culture. It is not surprising, then, that the recollections and analysis in this volume reposition Rand both as a visionary designer and thinker.

- It is also fitting that Franc Nunoo-Quarcoo should serve as this volume's designer and principal author. Franc is a visionary of our day — a graphic designer who reaches deeply into the meaning of the text for inspiration. I have never worked with a designer of Franc's intellectual intensity. Before Franc visualizes a book design, he thinks it. He engages in lengthy conversations with the author in an effort to understand the work's subtlest intellectual nuances. And so he produces designs of subtle nuances, both visual and intellectual. Like Rand, he is able to balance elegance with subversion, the cutting edge with an uncanny sense of visual familiarity. This book represents a synthesis of the two designers' visions. It is an extraordinary testament to the power of design to change ideas, perceptions, expectations, and biases about the world around us.

Introduction and Acknowledgments
Franc Nunoo-Quarcoo

- Design not only expresses but creates values. As Nietzsche declares, "Valuing is creating.... Valuation is itself the treasure and jewel of the valued things." Design is thus fundamental to the whole enterprise of living as a means of expression, creation, and appreciation. To appreciate and judge excellent design, we must live with it until its qualities, its meanings, sink deep into our conscious and subconscious mind, and if its appeal is deep and varied enough to be lasting, we can realize its excellence because our lives are being substantially enriched. Design is the language of all humanity – a way of communicating across all the barriers of culture, time, and place.

- *Paul Rand: Modernist Design* illuminates Paul Rand's role as a major figure at the epicenter of twentieth-century design. This book is a compendium of essays, interviews, dialogues, photographic reproductions, contextual timeline, extensive bibliography, and impressions of the great American designer's impact on modern communication practice and theory. My curiosity has regularly been stimulated by Paul Rand's work, writings, and philosophy, and I sense that others are equally curious about this powerfully creative genius. We have too few chances to chronicle how designers work and to truly celebrate their innovations, contributions, and achievements. This is an unparalleled opportunity to describe how one designer gave life to his art, definition to a profession in need of the evocation of enduring quality, and through this endeavor left a noteworthy legacy.

- *Paul Rand: Modernist Design* is organized into four sections: Essays, Tributes, Dialogues, and Timeline. This allows for different ways of discussing and experiencing Rand in context, and from different points of view – the critical, the personal, and the observational. The idea is to offer a complete, layered understanding of Rand's life as a person and as a designer.

- Complex undertakings of this kind rely on enlightened individuals and institutions for their generous support. At the Center for Art and Visual Culture, I recognize David Yager, Distinguished Professor of Visual Arts, and Executive Director, for his friendship and unconditional support of my projects; Symmes Gardner, Affiliate Associate Professor of Visual Arts, and Director, for his demonstrated support and commitment; Dr. Maurice Berger, Curator and Series Editor of the *Issues in Cultural Theory* series, for his advice and support; Antonia LaMotte Gardner, Managing Editor of the *Issues in Cultural Theory* series and editor of this

particular volume, for enhancing the intent of this book with her commitment, sensitive touch, and informed input; Janet Magruder, Business Manager, for attending to logistical concerns critical to this project.
- Grateful acknowledgment is made to the following essayists and interviewers whose significant contributions have greatly enriched both this publication and my own understanding of Paul Rand's accomplishments: Guenet Abraham, Antonio Alcalá, Georgette Ballance, Derek Birdsall, Bob Burns, Philip Burton, Ivan Chermayeff, Kyle Cooper, Helen Federico, Shigeo Fukuda, Nathan Garland, Milton Glaser, Diane Gromala, Gerald Gross, Sarah Gross, Jessica Helfand, Steven Heller, Ken Hiebert, Charles Hillman, Armin Hofmann, the Allen Hurlburt Estate, Takenobu Igarashi, Kent Kleinman and Leslie van Duzer, Julie Klugman, John Maeda, Naoko Matsuzono, Judy Metro, Bez Ocko, Mario Rampone, Marion Rand, Richard Sapper, Virginia Smith, Massimo Vignelli, and Wolfgang Weingart. Each embraced my requests with grace and a positiveness that bespoke their understanding and appreciation of Paul Rand's contribution to art, visual communication, art history, theory, and criticism.
- To my dear friend and mentor, the late Rudoph de Harak, a belated thank you for all your support, the many conversations about the relevance of design and art. Your story is next. Rest in peace.
- At the University of Maryland, Baltimore County, I am grateful to President Freeman Hrabowski; Provost Arthur Johnson; and Dean of Arts and Sciences G. Rickey Welch; Mr. Mark Behm, Vice President for Administrative Affairs; and Mr. Sheldon Caplis, Vice President for Institutional Advancement, for their support of the Center for Art and Visual Culture.
- Externally, I would like to acknowledge the Design Arts Award Program of the National Endowment for the Arts for their support and patience towards this project. My obsession with making sure this book is a worthy addition to the growing critical literature on Paul Rand and art history prolonged its release. I am most grateful and indebted to Messrs. Charles and James Hillman of Mossberg & Company Inc., and the Mossberg Foundation for their most generous and unconditional support of the publication. Both your embrace of and interest in a record of your very good friend Paul Rand's meaningful legacy has resulted in this beautifully manufactured book, a true testament to your insistence on quality, philanthropy, and support of graphic design as a discipline. To Roger

Brown, also at Mossberg & Company, I say, thank you for your kindness, patience, and diligence. To Mr. Mario Rampone, I extend my profound gratitude for your unconditional support of my research and for the important and critical information about your friend Paul Rand. Messrs. Hillman and Rampone collaborated with Paul Rand for decades on many projects (some of which are published in this book), and provided in their interviews critical insights toward a better understanding of Paul Rand, the man and the designer. At Mohawk Paper Mills, I thank Mr. Craig Slemp, Vice President for Marketing and Ms. Renee Vernold, Marketing Assistant for unconditionally donating the paper for the cover of this book.

- To the following friends and colleagues, I extend a sincere appreciation for your support and involvement: Graham Smith, Professor of Art History at the University of St. Andrews, Scotland; Marvin Eisenberg, Professor Emeritus of Art History at the University of Michigan, Ann Arbor; Edward West, Professor of Art at the University of Michigan, Ann Arbor; Nahum Chandler, Professor of the Humanities at Johns Hopkins University; Chris Pullman, Vice President for Design at WGBH Education Foundation; Thomas (NMI) Strong of Strong-Cohen Design in New Haven, Connecticut; George Ciscle, Curator-in-Residence at the Maryland Institute, College of Art; Richard Cleaver, artist; Cheryl Hanba of Main Street Design in Cambridge, Massachusetts; Adam Gross, architect, Ayers, Saint, Gross, Baltimore; Peter Arnell and Tara Grote of The Arnell Group in New York; Professors Hollie Lavenstein, Ellen Handler Spitz, Mark Alice Durant, Teri Rueb, John Sturgeon, and Margaret Re, of UMBC; at Baseline International Typographics journal in Kent, England, I thank Hans Dieter Reichert for translating Armin Hofmann's essay from the German, and for providing a critical forum for chronicling the history of visual communication.
I am also grateful to my very dear friends Ralph and Hiroko Insinger of Cambridge, Massachusetts, for sharing the burden of being readers. I thank Hiroko for translating the essay by Shigeo Fukuda from the Japanese. At the Ginza Graphic Gallery, I thank Yoshio Hirayama, Director, Tsusako Kon, and photographer Mitsumasa Fujitsuka for all their help. I thank my first assistant, Joanna Raczynska, for being there at the very beginning of this project, for exceptional research and superb documentation of materials, for assistance in completing the NEA grant, and for a good

friendship. I am equally thankful to my second assistant and good friend, Naoko Matsuzono, who for the past year, has worn many hats with grace and efficiency. She has my deep appreciation. I am grateful to Gideon Webster, who went beyond the call of duty in answering my many calls for technical help and direction. To Mary Hess, Phyllis Addison and Holly Burke, thank you for all you have done on my behalf. At the Albin O. Kuhn Library at UMBC, I am appreciative of the assistance from Simona Simmons-Hodo, Head of Special Projects, and for her tireless location of research and bibliographic sources and resources on my behalf, and Cynthia Wayne, Curator of the Albin O. Kuhn Library Gallery, for her friendship and invaluable advice concerning many critical issues.

- I am deeply indebted to my friend and photographer Dan Meyers. For all our years of collaboration, Dan has accommodated all my requests, each time providing thoughtful and stunning visual compositions that speak clearly and poetically to the senses. His beautiful photographic compositions of the Rand House, published in this book for the first time, are possibly the most complete and final references of the environment in which Paul Rand lived and created some of the most recognizable visual icons of the mid- to late twentieth century.

- I am grateful to Marion Rand for her understanding, interest, and support of this project. She generously granted me an excellent interview, which is a definite read for anyone interested in knowing about Paul Rand, and also about Marion Rand as an executive at IBM, at the height of modernist design in the middle of the twentieth century. Over the course of this extensive project, she has become a good friend. It all started when she and Paul Rand met with me more than six years ago to listen to my proposal, shortly before his death. In addition to her involved schedule in making sure her husband's legacy is properly archived, she graciously made time for many requests and many visits to her home.

- Finally, to my muse, Maria Phillips, I express my profound appreciation and respect for sacrificing so much in order for me to complete this book. I especially appreciate the little-big things, and that knowing smile when I am about to ask for the proverbial last favor. I am forever thankful to you for understanding, and appreciation of what I do. As the great architect Le Corbusier put it, "Creation is a patient search." One can never do it alone.

16: 17:

Essays:

18: Allen Hurlburt
28: Helen Federico
32: Jessica Helfand
45: Antonio Alcalá
50: Steven Heller
54: Takenobu Igarashi
57: Ivan Chermayeff
61: Milton Glaser
63: Franc Nunoo-Quarcoo

Allen Hurlburt
Paul Rand

- If the word "legend" has any meaning in the graphic arts and if the term "legendary" can be applied with accuracy to the career of any designer, it can certainly be applied to Paul Rand. When I first met him in 1951 at a lunch with Arnold Gingrich, the founding editor of *Esquire* magazine, the legend was already firmly in place. By that time Paul had completed his first career as a designer of media promotion at *Esquire-Coronet* – and as an outstanding cover designer for *Apparel Arts* and *Direction*. He was well along on a second career as an advertising designer at the William Weintraub Agency, which he had joined as art director at its founding. Paul Rand's book *Thoughts on Design,* with reproductions of almost 100 of his designs and some of the best words yet written on graphic design, had been published four years earlier – a publishing event that cemented his international reputation and identified him as a designer of influence from Zürich to Tokyo.

- Paul Rand was only thirty-two years old when he completed *Thoughts on Design,* and he was still in his thirties when we met. My impressions of that meeting are still vivid – the quick, curious, and intensely analytical look in his eyes framed by dark-rimmed glasses; the close-cropped hair above a forehead where a frown always seemed to lurk, ready to pounce on the first banality that had the effrontery to rear its ugly head; all of this over a conservative suit marked by a black knit tie – the trademark of his Madison Avenue days. Paul recalled a time when, in a somewhat less conservative mood, he was wearing a bright red viyella shirt and matching red socks that prompted his friend Saul Steinberg to remark, "That must be the longest underwear I ever saw."

- There was little change since the Madison Avenue period – his hair was certainly grayer after twenty years – his frown was less evident and his glasses had become trifocal; but the eyes continued their curious analysis of anything that had the nerve to cross his field of vision.

The Early Years

- In an interesting way the chronology of Paul Rand's design experience paralleled the development of the modern design movement. In America, unlike Europe where the poster was dominant, new design directions came first to magazine design and media promotion. By the 1940s this emphasis began to shift to advertising design, following the pioneering work already being done at N.W. Ayer in Philadelphia and at Young & Rubicam and Calkins and Holden in New York. At the end of the 1950s, with the rapid growth of national companies into multinational corporations, another shift of emphasis placed the spotlight on coordinated corporate design programs.

- Paul Rand's first career, in media promotion and cover design, ran from 1937 to 1941, his second career, in advertising design, ran from 1941 to 1954, and his third career, in corporate identification, began in 1954. Paralleling these three careers was his consuming interest in design education, and Paul Rand's fourth career as an educator started at Cooper Union in 1942. He taught at Pratt Institute in 1946, and in 1956 he accepted a post at Yale University's graduate school of design, where he held the title of professor of graphic design. He was also an honorary professor of design at Tama University in Tokyo. His essay "Design and the Play Instinct," written in 1965 for the book *Education of Vision* published by George Braziller, still stands as an outstanding statement on design education.
- The Rand apprenticeship in graphic design began in 1935 when he worked for George Switzer, an innovative designer whose package and advertising design helped set the style for modern merchandising. In 1937 Paul launched his first career at *Esquire*. Although he was only occasionally involved in the editorial layout of that magazine, he designed extensive promotion and direct mail material on its behalf and turned out a spectacular series of covers for *Apparel Arts,* a quarterly published in conjunction with *Esquire*. In spite of a schedule that paid no heed to regular working hours or minimum wage scales, he managed in these crucial years to find time to design an impressive array of covers for other magazines, particularly *Direction*. From 1938 on, his work was a regular feature of the exhibitions of the Art Directors Club.

Advertising Design

- Most contemporary designers are aware of Paul Rand's highly successful and often compelling contributions to advertising design. What is not well known is the significant role he played in setting the pattern for future approaches to the advertising concept. Paul was probably the first of a long and distinguished line of art directors to work with and appreciate the unique talent of William Bernbach. It was shortly after Bernbach's stint with the New York World's Fair and several years before he was to become the principal creative force at Doyle Dane Bernbach that he worked briefly with the recently formed Weintraub Agency.

Paul described his first meeting with Bill Bernbach as "akin to Columbus discovering America," and went on to say, "This was my first encounter with a copywriter who understood visual ideas and who didn't come in with a yellow copy pad and a preconceived notion of what the layout should look like."

- A few years later when Bill Bernbach had moved on to the Grey Agency, Paul and Bill were brought together again to create advertising for Ohrbach's, a New York department store. For more than two years they created the now famous series of intensely visual newspaper advertisements. During this period Paul worked at Weintraub and served the Ohrbach account as a design consultant.

- You can't quite say that it all began there, because it was a time when too many things were happening in advertising in too many places, but it is reasonable to assume that from this point on the isolation of the art and copy departments was destined to give way to a closer if not always harmonious working relationship between these two creative forces. The William Weintraub Agency originally consisted of a small staff drawn largely from the business side of *Esquire,* but by 1951 it had a staff of over 100. The agency continued to function under a different name, but it was a far different agency from the one that was built around Paul Rand's talent in 1941 when he was twenty-seven years old.

- During the years when Paul was at the agency, Weintraub served many impressive accounts including Schenley, Revlon, Kaiser, Seaman Brothers, Stafford Mills, and El Producto Cigars. His advertisements for Airwick that combined modern typography with nineteenth-century engravings not only introduced a new product, but also succeeded in turning a local distributor into a nationwide success story overnight.

- Paul spent fourteen years in advertising and left a mark that would last for many more. He was a primary mover in the fusing of visual ideas and persuasive communication. He demonstrated the importance of the art director in advertising and helped break the isolation that once surrounded the art department. He played a key role in establishing the art and copy team as the base for the advertising concept. But perhaps his overriding contribution was the inspiration that his brilliant approach to design brought to generations of future advertising art directors. To me, an even more significant contribution was his sense of responsibility to the reader and his emphasis on quality and good taste. Today this contribution may be more honored in the breach than in the observance in many agencies, but scores of responsible art directors around the world continue to demonstrate that the Rand influence was considerably more than brief moment of an advertising Camelot.

- The final thought of his *Thoughts on Design* is worth repeating: "Even if it is true that commonplace advertising and exhibitions of bad taste are indicative of the mental capacity of the man in the street, the opposing argument is equally valid. Bromidic advertising catering to that bad taste merely perpetuates that mediocrity and denies him one of the most easily accessible means of aesthetic development."

- Rand also pointed out that when an art director translates a literal approach into a "visual message, which is not only arresting and persuasive, but imaginative, dramatic and entertaining as well, he has fulfilled his obligation to his audience, and perhaps he has fulfilled his obligation to more personal standards."

- By the time he decided to leave advertising, Rand had gained considerable experience in the not so gentle art of working with difficult people. It began with David Smart and William Weintraub at *Esquire,* which in its early days was pressure cooker par excellence. He recalled a time when Dave Smart stuffed him with artichokes in his luxurious hotel apartment so that Paul could go back to the loft and work through the night on a special *Esquire* Christmas promotion.

- William Weintraub, himself a legendary accomplished, but unusually tough, salesman, had once tried to convince the Steinway people through an elaborate presentation that by advertising in *Esquire* they could increase the sale of pianos in bordellos. Bill Weintraub was a formidable impresario who you remembered as being taller than he actually was. He appreciated and exploited the commercial value of Paul Rand's talent and taught him how to make and enjoy money, but he was never an easy man to work for. He was a master of the demeaning gesture, and it was sometimes his style to create tension and conflict among his staff in the misguided belief that controversy had something to do with creativity.

- Client relations at the agency were not a bed of roses either, with clients like Revlon's Rosenstiel. In fact, one of the more absurd myths surrounding the Rand legend was the notion that while other art directors were forced to face day-to-day pressures, Paul operated in the splendid isolation of some ivory tower. Nothing could be further from the truth. One of the outstanding, but little-known, attributes to his success was his ability to bridge the gap between creative communication and business needs, and he achieved all of this without any assistance from representatives and without compromising his principles.

- Although he was never at ease with the time-consuming and rarely productive meetings of the board, and he avoided these sessions whenever he could, he was excellent in the all important face-to-face meetings with major management executives, where most of the real decisions are made.

Corporate Identity

- In 1954 when Paul Rand decided that for him Madison Avenue was no longer a two-way street and he resigned from the Weintraub Agency, he was cited as one of the ten best art directors by the Museum of Modern Art. This was the same year in which he received the gold medal from the Art Directors Club for his Morse Code advertisement addressed to David Sarnoff of RCA. Although it didn't result in the agency getting the Radio Corporation account, this memorable advertisement was an appropriate indicator of that point in the Rand career where corporate design began to supersede advertising.

- By the time that Paul started working out of his Weston studio he was well known as a designer of trademarks. He had completed designs for several companies including *Esquire*, Coronet Brandy, Robeson Cutlery, and Smith Kline and French Laboratories. In 1952 he designed a trademark for El Producto cigars and built an advertising campaign around it that was to be part of his first independent corporate design program for the Consolidated Cigar Company. This coordinated campaign included some of the best package designs for such products since the invention of the cigar box.

- In the period between 1954 and 1956, Paul also began work on some children's books in collaboration with his wife, Ann Rand. His daughter Catherine was then only a baby, and the books reflect her father's warmth, his personal identification with play, and the childlike character of much of his design. The first of these books was called *I Know A Lot of Things,* and it was followed one year later by *Sparkle and Spin*.

- By 1955 the fates that continued to play a fortuitous role in channeling the Rand talent toward critical areas of design began to set the stage for his third major design career. Thomas J. Watson, Jr., had come recently to the presidency of the International Business Machines

Corporation, and with his expanding vision of the future for computers in science and word processing, he felt the need to clarify the identity of this somewhat amorphous company. He had already brought in the late Eliot Noyes to reshape the product lines, and the search for a graphic designer to create the corporate image led to Paul Rand. He worked on a graphic design program during the last half of 1955, and a trademark was designed and accepted early in the following year. At the outset it was decided that this program would not be based on rigid standards or some predetermined theme that might date the project and deny it the flexibility that the continuous growth and change of this company demanded. From the beginning the trademark was used with a unique freedom. By making the style of the design the guiding influence over a carefully organized group of international designers, a progressive unity was achieved without the loss of spontaneity and excitement.

- Heading this outstanding design program was a triumvirate of noted designers, as Charles Eames joined Noyes and Rand as consultant on displays, exhibitions, and films. In 1976 when Tom Watson brought the group together at a dinner to mark twenty years of the design program, he pointed out that not only was the selection of designers right, and their design philosophy correct, but in 1956 the time had been right. He had to admit that it might have been impossible for IBM to achieve the same result at a different time in the company's development.

- The work at IBM led to a new program for Westinghouse under the guidance of the same design team. This project began in 1960. During this period Paul also engineered redesign programs for Harcourt Brace in 1957, Colorforms in 1959, United Parcel Service in 1961, and the American Broadcasting Company in 1962. In the 1960s he undertook a major corporate design program for Cummins Engine Company, and he continued to serve this account and his two other major accounts, IBM and Westinghouse, for many years. This meant a heavy workload and an extensive travel schedule, but he still found the time to take on an impressive array of other commissions, including a surprising number for nonprofit organizations that he served without any design fee.

- It would not be fair to cover his career in corporate design without mentioning one of the accounts that didn't quite work out according to plan. In 1966 the Ford Motor Company asked Paul to redesign the quasi-Spencerian script and oval medallion that had adorned Ford automobiles for more than sixty years. After extensive research and considerable design exploration, a new style was worked out, and a handsome printed and bound presentation was prepared in a limited edition for the eventual review by Henry Ford II. After some deliberation, Mr. Ford finally decided that, when it came to the family name, what was good enough for his grandfather was good enough for him.

The Rand Style

- To understand Paul Rand's personal style as an artist, designer, and educator, it may be helpful to take a closer look at his early background. He was born in 1914 in Brooklyn, New York, a remarkably fertile ground for the nurturing of design talent, though no one can say quite why.

- His earliest years were spent living behind the store where his parents ran a shop serving the neighborhood's needs for a wide variety of necessities. He remembers, with some fondness, the early hours of many cold winter mornings when the fresh bread and rolls were delivered. Freshly baked and still hot, they were unceremoniously passed through the convenient window of his room to add their warmth to the foot of his bed.

- There is nothing very unusual about Paul's early educational background, but somewhere along the line he decided that art and design was his calling. Like many of his contemporaries in these nascent years of graphic design, he pretty much shaped his own learning process. At that time art schools were almost totally committed to the fine arts, and only a few were making tentative explorations in the applied art form that was then called commercial art. The pervading philosophy of the time was that students who didn't show sufficient talent at the easel might become illustrators, and if a student's skill as draftsman was inadequate, then perhaps he could be passed off as a commercial artist. Designations like art director and graphic designer were hardly known. There was never any doubt in Paul's mind about becoming a designer, and he took advantage of three of the better schools – Pratt Institute, the Parsons School of Design, and the Art Students League, where he studied with George Grösz, who had been a member of the Dada movement in Berlin after World War I. Paul Rand's intellectual curiosity, and a natural bent for academic scholarship, took him far beyond the meager limits of the schools he attended, and his knowledge of design was rarely matched by design theorists. His lectures at Yale University on Cézanne and other Postimpressionist painters often broke new ground in art history and research.

- Like most American designers who were educated in the early thirties, one of his principal sources of design awareness came from the European design publications that were beginning to find their way into American libraries. Two of the most important were *Gebrauchsgraphik,* from prewar Germany, and *Arts et Metier Graphique,* from Paris. Paul Rand was probably the only private collector with a complete file of *Arts et Metier Graphique.* Rand's personal library included nearly every major book on the modern design movement. He was an early follower of the work and writings of El Lissitzky, the Russian pioneer Constructivist graphic designer, and he had read practically every word written by Theo van Doesberg, a leading design theorist and one of the major influences of the de Stijl movement.

- For him the learning process never ended, and his conscientious concern for knowledge led him from his own studies to the teaching of others. In spite of a heavy work schedule, he had been involved in one way or another in design instruction throughout his career. His course at the Yale University School of Art received international acclaim and his ex-students include the partners of several major design studios on both sides of the ocean, a number of design directors, and the head of the department of graphic design at more than one university.

- Most of the influences that helped shape the Rand style mentioned up to now originated in Europe, and yet his style could never be described as Swiss, German, or French. To explain the uniquely American aspects of his style, it is necessary to turn to another source. This leads us to an interesting group of American industrial and graphic designers who came into prominence in the late twenties. This group was represented by the stylishness of Raymond Loewy and the theatricality of Norman Bel Geddes, but it is also known for the pioneering designs of George Switzer, Paul's first boss, that were to become the foundation for modern package design. This group of designers also included Walter Dorwin Teague, Joseph Sinel, Donald Deskey, and Gustav Jenson, a designer who brought a sense of elegance to graphics, packaging, and industrial design that has rarely been matched. The important contribution to contemporary American design by this still-

The Rand Typography

- Paul always believed that a design is the synthesis of all of its elements and that type is an integral part of the design process. For that reason it is difficult to isolate his typographic approach, which was devoted to the refinement of use rather than eccentricity of selection. He was one of the first designers to use traditional Garamond in a modern design; he used and understood sans serif letterforms long before the invention of Helvetica; he mastered the application of modern faces like Bodoni, Baskerville, and Walbaum to the smooth white surfaces of modern paper; and he was a pioneer in the effective use of typewriter type and stencil letters.
- Probably the Rand typographic credo is best revealed in his comment in *Thoughts on Design:* "By carefully arranging his type areas, spacing, size, and color, the typographer is able to impart to the printed page an aesthetic message which in turn complements the message conveyed by the words. He is able to transmit tactile sensations and intensify and minimize these sensations at will. By concentrating the type area and emphasizing the margin [white space], he reinforces by contrast the textural quality of the type."
- His belief in the simple reality that words are meant to be read and that reading should be a pleasant experience kept his work clear of the pitfalls of merely fashionable solutions. Nowhere in his design will you find the telescoped typography or wall-to-wall copy sometimes identified with current layout. He understood and used the Swiss style of typography, but he was not locked in to its pristine austerity, and he still indented a paragraph or used initial letter where it would aid the design or readability. While he deliberately avoided the bizarre and expressed himself as opposed to "the folly of distorting English letters in the character of Chinese calligraphy because the subject happens to deal with the Orient," his typography was not lacking in innovation. His ABC trademark designed in 1960 received a modification of the san serif style that originated at the Bauhaus and anticipated its more general revival by nearly a decade. He based his IBM trademark on a well-designed but neglected typeface called City Medium, and his Westinghouse trademark introduced an original identifying letterform.

- Paul Rand believed in the creative use of grid structures in his known design and emphasized their value in this teaching "because the making of the grid necessitates analyzing simultaneously all the elements involved, and once the grid is evolved the designer is free to play with pictures, type, paper, ink color and with texture, scale, and contrast." It was this balance of play and constraint, plus his demands on the student for the appropriate and innovative solution, that lay behind his impressive teaching record.

Style and Lifestyle

- Another way to gain some insight into the Rand style was to visit his Weston, Connecticut, home and studio, where he lived behind the store once again. Set on eight rolling acres, the house was built on his own modular design and echoes but does not imitate the asymmetrical order that characterized Japanese domestic architecture. Like an oriental house, it was designed to open outward to enhance its environment. In this instance, it was the New England landscape, which was in turn honored by the walls of native fieldstone that set off the dark-grided white panels and expanses of glass. The Early American aspect was also revealed in the massive stone-faced woodburning fireplace at one end of the living room. Inside, one failed to find the expected pristine modern interior design. Instead there was a pleasant, disarmingly casual arrangement of furniture and an exciting collection of objects that had a special appeal to Paul, including weathervanes, carpenter tools from Japan, and amusing hand-crafted toys.

- Describing Paul Rand's style remains somewhat akin to catching lightning in a bottle. Perhaps the true measure of that style lies in the fact that it was uniquely his. He was one of the few graphic designers whose work can be identified without his signature and whose work has never been successfully imitated in spite of the wide range of commissions he handled over such a long period of time. In an era when contemporary graphics are being progressively homogenized by the pressure of fashion and group involvement, it is still refreshing to encounter Paul Rand's innovative and highly personal style. Laszlo Moholy-Nagy, a pioneer typographer, photographer, and designer of the modern movement and a master at the Bauhaus in Weimar, may have come closest to defining that style when he described Paul as "an idealist and a realist using the language of the poet and the businessman. He thinks in terms of need and function. He is able to analyze his problems, but his fantasy is boundless."

Helen Federico
Working with Paul Rand

- I worked with Paul Rand for seven years at the William H. Weintraub Agency in New York City. I had left the Abbott Kimball Advertising Agency to work under Alexei Brodovitch, the noted graphic designer and art director of *Harper's Bazaar*. He had arranged to be consultant for I. Miller, New York shoe manufacturer/retailer, two afternoons a week; I was to carry through in a full-time job.

- After six months, the Army changed its policy and released forty-year-old draftees. Art Director George Greene returned. Brodovitch felt responsible for finding me another job, and it was arranged for me to be in touch with Paul Rand. I was very excited at the prospect…here was yet another god of the design world and, after a meeting with him at the Weintraub office in 30 Rockefeller Plaza, I was hired to work in the art department. Upset by his contrary, confrontational manner, but thrilled to have been considered worthy of being hired by this greatly talented person, I began to work at the agency in the spring of 1943.

- Paul had brought with him some of the art staff from *Esquire* magazine (of which Weintraub had been co-publisher before founding the agency). Among them were Stanley, a meticulous worker (and part-time bookie); Jabez, a religious fantastic; and Rudi, a talented artist. Many were refugees from Europe for whom Paul felt great empathy. Among them was a poor fellow who had very little understanding of English, was hard of hearing, and was unfamiliar with the ways of the American ad agency. "Iss too dunkel, Kurt," Paul would try to explain, in an unusually gentle way, shouting in order to be heard, if not necessarily understood. In his working relationships with the art department staff, Paul was sometimes gruff, but not meanly critical.

- Paul's small office was next to the larger art room (commonly called the "bullpen") in which five or six of us worked at drawing tables. His office was compact and a reflection of his contemporary design sensibility, refreshingly different from the other ordinary, conventional offices. The art room itself, with its odors of rubber cement and thinner, of chalk and fixative, was (as in every office I have worked in) the gathering place for others in the agency, who seemed to gravitate there, as at the proverbial water-cooler. The more relaxed environment seemed to be conducive to conversation and humor and exchanges of experiences.

- The camera lucida (called, of course, "lucy") was probably our single most useful tool. This small, simple prism set on a rod, clamped to a stationary base, reflects the image in front of it down onto the stationary base surface on which one could draw that image, making it smaller, larger, flopped sides, etc. The Russo Photostat company, an elevator ride away, produced black-and-white images that were used in paste-ups for presentations, sometimes for finished artwork. An airbrush spraying liquid-watercolor was fueled via a tube to a compressed air tank. An outside studio was sometimes used for retouching photographs. Special lettering jobs were sometimes created by Andrew Szoeke. Paul's strong visual memory enabled him to draw with seemingly effortless facility, often using his own drawings, photographs, and photograms for finished art. Very much a hands-on art director, he considered photographers, with a few exceptions, tools for carrying out his ideas. His friend photographer Ewing Krainin ("Butts") worked with Paul on many projects.

- In practice, Paul's layout sketch was worked up into a "comp," short for "comprehensive," by one of the art department staff members for intra-office approval. The comp was then presented to the client. Compared with today's presentation, it was a primitive, almost arrogant way to show a client what he might expect for an advertisement of his product or service. For a comp, a color photograph, for instance, was rendered in flat-sided Nupastels with no attempt at simulating the photo-to-be. A black-and-white photograph was shown with photostats; the hand-lettered headline simulated a specific typeface. Body copy was indicated by ruled lines with, sometimes, wooly-looking scribble in between the lines, accompanied by typewritten text. Layouts for presentation were matted in folders designed by Paul, as were all the agency's letterheads and business forms.

- Paul Rand admired the typography of other cultures. "In my own case...I was apprenticed to George Switzer, who was influenced by French and German typographers. Amongst others, I was directly influenced by Piet Zwart, the Dutchman; El Lissitzky, the Russian; Moholy-Nagy, the Hungarian; Jan Tschichold, the Czech; and Apollinaire, the Pole (calligrammes), not to mention the Chinese and Persians." Letterheads and logotypes were often the first items Weintraub would have him design for a pitch to a prospective client.

- Weintraub was supportive of Paul's work from the *Esquire* days and into the early agency years. At the end of 1944, their contract called for twenty hours a week plus other perks.

- As far as I know, he was the first agency AD to sign ads. His outside work also was proving fruitful as well, particularly with Alfred Knopf for whom he designed many beautiful books. Paul's ability, which he combined with good salesmanship by presenting the client as a maker of good products, shows he had both a simple, exciting look and an intelligent regard for his profession and his market. Some of this he cannily achieved by working closely with agency's writers, charming them and even bulldozing them into writing with brevity with works based on ideas. I recall his often provocative conversations with Bill Bernbach and Frank Zachary, and with Betty Buffe Norgaard, notable copy writers in the early forties, sometimes resulting in dynamic, effective ads.

- There were accounts that Paul had either little interest in or had no time for, and I was assigned to some, finally achieving the title of associate art director. I recall preparing three-dimensional constructions for Dubonnet, one in particular of autumn leaves spattered with toothbrush and ink. I carried the box down to the rotogravure production of the *New York Times,* where I worked with the cameraman, set up the lighting ("from the upper left," always) for the shoot of the ad to be used in the magazine section.

- Paul used a wide range of faces, among them, Scotch Roman and Bulmer, Century Schoolbook, Futura Black, and, of course, the sans serifs. "When in doubt, make it smaller" was one of his type maxims…how this might affect middle-aged close-vision was not then a consideration. Flush left, ragged right, mandatory (legally) in liquor advertising, was one of the banes of our existence, the type size as small as we could get away with. The standard, accepted form of headline, subheadline, body text, logo still prevailed, and Paul did break the mold. He was a pioneer in upturning the rigid order of the ad world's self-imposed structure.

- Paul Rand's example really upgraded the position of the creatives. His stubborn, skillful business acumen and knowledge of his own value, his innovative use of the best of what he'd observed of graphic design from the past, and his own personal, brilliant concepts all contributed to the stature of the creative members of the business. The generation immediately following in his footsteps became heads of ad agencies of note…artists, designers, writers, all led by the example of the boy from Brooklyn. They all owe him thanks. As the agency grew it took on a more ordinary look, giving up its unique, innovative quality. In the attempt to join the "big boys," "heavy hitters" from the establishment were brought into the firm to aid in acquiring bigger accounts, bigger revenues with stupid, ordinary ads. There was more infighting among the principals. Often fervid discussions spilled out into the art room...during one of them, I witnessed a seasoned account man collapse with what may have been his first heart attack.

- Paul's influence waned and Bill Weintraub really lost the battle in which he had become an arbitrator between the opposing philosophies. After the war, the conflict began in earnest. The management won accounts like Revlon, headed by the notoriously difficult Charles Revson; women's underwear, Maidenform; Kaiser & Fraizer automobiles... all of which Paul worked on and, in the case of the latter, produced some innovative and powerful ads. But his concepts were incompatible with the demands of the intransigent old/new guard, and Paul finally refused to work on the hiring of art directors who were assigned those specific accounts. That was the end, I suppose, of that stage of the William Weintraub Agency. I, myself, following the assignment of a banal photoshoot for an ill-conceived campaign in Kaiser's factory near Detroit, decided to leave. I had worked up some of Paul's comps for his freelance clients, such as Ohrbach's, and continued to do so for a brief time after I'd left the agency, in 1950.

Jessica Helfand
Paul Rand:
American Modernist

- Graphic design is the most ubiquitous of all the arts. It responds to needs both personal and public, embraces concerns at once economic and ergonomic, and is informed by numerous disciplines, including art and architecture, philosophy and ethics, literature and language, politics and performance. Graphic design is everywhere, touching everything we do, everything we see, everything we buy: we see it on billboards and in Bibles, on taxi receipts and on web sites, on birth certificates and on gift certificates, on the folded circulars tucked inside jars of aspirin and on the thick pages of children's chubby board books. Graphic design is the boldly directional arrows on street signs and the blurred, frenetic typography on the title sequence to E.R. It is the bright green logo for the New York Jets and the monochromatic front page of the *Wall Street Journal*. It is hang-tags in clothing stores, playbills in theaters, timetables in train stations, postage stamps and cereal box packaging, fascist propaganda posters and junk mail. It is complex combinations of words and pictures, numbers and charts, photographs and illustrations that, in order to succeed, demand the clear thinking of a particularly thoughtful individual who can orchestrate these elements so that they all add up to something distinctive or useful or playful or surprising or subversive or in some way truly memorable. Graphic design is a popular art, a practical art, an applied art, and an ancient art. Simply put, it is the art of visualizing ideas.

- Until the Second World War, graphic design was better known in the United States as commercial art. Performed by printers and typesetters, it was more vocation than profession, more a reflection of the economic realities of a newly industrialized culture than an opportunity to engage the creative expression of an individual or an idea. Unlike the experimentation that characterized design as it was being practiced and taught in Europe in the early years of this century— led by Cubists and Constructivists, pioneers of de Stijl and disciples of the Bauhaus — what we now think of as graphic design was, in this country, driven by the demands of commerce and fueled by the prospect of eliminating the economic hardships that had plagued the nation during the Depression. Commercial art was a service industry motivated by the same honorable objectives that characterized the average consumer: it sought to encourage stability, promote prosperity, and maintain a generally happy, don't-rock-the-boat kind of aesthetic status quo.

- If these were indeed the values extolled by a collective national consciousness, it is perhaps not surprising that a good deal of the design of printed matter dating from the years between the wars was dry, unimaginative, and predictable. It was also cluttered and decorative: the use of ornament became a kind of aesthetic panacea, masking the greater cultural complexities marking this awkward, transitional age. More perplexing still, such ornamentation was at direct odds with the streamlined simplicity that otherwise characterized so much of the artistic expression – including painting, music, and literature – being produced during this same fertile period. Then again, if we consider commercial art not a fine but a popular art, it fails equally as an adequate mirror of social history. With the great exception of World War II propaganda – which as a body of work suggests an altogether different aesthetic, evoking the dramatic urgency of a highly politicized and socially polarized nation – the typical outlets for what would eventually become graphic design were met, in the 1920s and thirties, with little in the way of truly noteworthy activity. It is, in a sense, a puzzling sort of hiccup on the timeline of design history: a period marked at once by great societal change and negligible creative progress.
- But by the early 1930s, a small but accomplished group of American and European expatriate designers began to experiment with new ways to approach the design of commercial printed matter. Combining the experimental formal vocabularies of their European colleagues with the material demands of American commerce, they inaugurated a new visual language that would revolutionize the role of design as both a service and an art. Of this group – which included Lester Beall, Bradbury Thompson, and Alexey Brodovich, among others – none was so accomplished, or would produce as many lasting contributions to this field as Paul Rand, arguably our most celebrated American graphic designer, who died in 1996 at the age of eighty-two.
- More than any other designer of this century, Rand is credited with bringing the modernist design aesthetic to postwar America. Highly influenced by the European modernists – Klee and Picasso, Calder and Miro – Rand's formal vocabulary signalled the advent of a new era. Using photography and montage, cut paper and what would later become known as the New Typography – asymmetrical typography that engaged the eye and activated the page – Rand rallied against

the sentimentality of staid, commercial layouts and introduced a new, modified avant-garde that spoke to the clever ideas and restrained minimalism that he had observed in such European design magazines as the German *Gebrauchsgraphik* and the English *Commercial Art*. To look at Rand's work today – work that dates from half a century ago – is to observe how an idea can be distilled to its most salient form. The style is playful, the message immediate, the communication undeniably direct. The results are engaging, effective, and, indeed, memorable.

- Born in 1914 in Brooklyn, the son of Viennese immigrants and Orthodox Jews, Rand began drawing as a child and went on to attend Pratt Institute, the Parsons School of Design, and the New York Art Students League, where he studied with George Grösz. He opened his own studio in 1935; two years later he was named art director of *Esquire*. Still in his twenties, he suffered a terrible loss when his identical twin brother, a jazz musician, died in an automobile accident; Rand's own divorce and subsequent remarriage followed not long after. During these personally turbulent years Rand remained busy designing layouts for *Apparel Arts* magazine as well as covers for the antifascist magazine *Direction,* where, between 1938 and 1941, he honed his editorial skills experimenting with complex political issues: the Nazi partitioning of Czechoslovakia, for example. In 1941, at the age of twenty-seven, he joined the William H. Weintraub advertising agency, where he would spend the next thirteen years producing ads for, among others, El Producto, Dubonnet, Ohrbach's, and Revlon. Rand was hired as the graphic design consultant for IBM in 1956 (the same year he was hired by Josef Albers to teach in the graduate design program at Yale), where he collaborated with Thomas Watson, Jr., and Eliot Noyes on the famous striped letterforms that are still in use today. Rand was one of the few distinguished practitioners of graphic design who saw fit (or found time) to publish on the subject. A contributing essayist to numerous design publications here and abroad, Rand went on to publish four critically acclaimed books: *Thoughts on Design* (1946); *Paul Rand: A Designer's Art* (1985); *Design, Form and Chaos* (1994), and finally, *From Lascaux to Brooklyn* (1996). Consequently, he was perhaps the only designer of his generation to stake out a truly theoretical position where graphic design is concerned. It is this more than anything else that distinguishes his writing and, indeed, his lasting contribution to the study of graphic design.

- If his work reflected the reductive formal vocabularies of modernist practice, it is also true that his thinking (and writing) mirrored the intellectual curiosity of modernist ideology. Preoccupied by certain recurring themes, Rand's books typically consist of short, staccato-like essays in which he considers the fundamental factors that shape our understanding of visual communication. In each of his books, he scrutinizes the relationship between art and design, between design and aesthetics, and between aesthetics and experience. At length, he examines the role of intuition and ideas, the balance between form and function, and the universal language of geometry. These ideas – which he called the designer's raison d'etre – were fundamental to his inquiry, and perhaps equally fundamental to his lifelong search for creative, intellectual, and spiritual resolution as an artist, a designer, and a Jew.

- Rand believed these topics to be timeless: "My interest has always been in restating the validity of those ideas which, by and large, have guided artists since the time of Polyclitus," he writes. "It is the continuing relevance of these ideals that I mean to emphasize, especially to those who have grown up in a world of punk and graffiti." That these same ideas would resurface in each successive book is puzzling: one wonders whether the arguments were an open expression of Rand's passionate beliefs, or an attempt to validate them in the first place. Certainly the confidence with which he was universally identified – supported not only by the writing, but by the kinds of inflammatory public statements that made him so eminently quotable ("The development of new typefaces is a barometer of the stupidity of our profession.") – would likely lead us to the first conclusion. It is, however, equally true that the fervent devotion with which he applied himself to the practice of design was itself influenced to a considerable degree by the events of his early life. Here, one can imagine how those events – the break with the family, the loss of a brother – were played out in the studio and on the typewriter, and how the promises of modernism – in which the harmony of formal relationships gesture to a higher order, and seek to embrace a purist ideal – might have held, for Rand, a kind of Divine appeal.

- And while Rand's celebration of pure form gestured to an economy of means that might well be characterized as quintessentially modern, his resistance to new, more abstract forms of expression revealed itself repeatedly in his writings, in public lectures, and in interviews, thus branding him, in his final years, as outmoded and conservative. A lifelong advocate of the axiom "less is more," Rand was often criticized for his rejection of a more contemporary design idiom: it is not surprising, perhaps, that for most of his professional life, the words most frequently associated with Rand were "irascible," "ornery," and "curmudgeon." True to form, the dedication in his last book is "To my friends and enemies."

- His resistance to changes in the design profession produced renewed devotion to the principles he held most dear. To this end, the critic in him saw contemporary design practice as a postmodern free-for-all, in which sentiment and subjectivity supplanted logic and clarity of purpose. The teacher in him saw an opportunity to redefine and restate the great lessons of the modernist legacy: his writing has a tireless, autodiagnostic quality, in which he carefully articulates the fundamental components that enable ideas to be made visually manifest. And the artist in him saw the necessity of promoting the same exacting standards that he used not only to evaluate his own work, but to assess the quality of any great work of art. "The quality of the work always precedes everything else," he explained in an interview not long before his death. "And the quality, of course, is my standard."

- Throughout his books, Rand sustained his arguments through repetition and, at times, dogmatic emphasis: consistent with the urgency of his modernist mentors, his literary style mirrored the passionate – if not evangelical – rhetoric of the manifesto. Written primer-style on such topics as "The Beautiful and The Useful," "Design and the Play Instinct," and "Intuition and Ideas," Rand's essays were illustrated extensively by visual examples from his own portfolio and documented with extensive citations from his library. In this view, his arguments were able to gesture with greater intellectual scope, as the ideas themselves were presented within more robust discussions: here, design was examined not as a disenfranchised art form, but as an inherently humanist discipline. The idea that the value of design could be explained and enriched by accompanying notes on philosophy, art criticism, or political discourse thus became Rand's editorial bailiwick. His marginalia was rich with references to John Dewey, Alfred North Whitehead, Bertram

Russell, Henry Bergson, and Henry James. In more targeted appeals, Rand would refer to the writings of Kant and Hegel, the teachings of Leger and Albers, or would add other equally enlightening observations from an exotic sampling of social theorists, architectural critics, and ex-Presidents. (Indeed, in his last book, he quotes Jimmy Carter.) In spite of such breadth – or perhaps because of it – the core of his thinking was always rooted in graphic design.

"To design," Rand writes in *Design, Form and Chaos,* "is much more than simply to assemble, to order, or even to edit: it is to add value and meaning, to illuminate, to simplify, to clarify, to modify, to dignify, to dramatize, to persuade, and perhaps even to amuse. To design is to transform prose into poetry." For Rand, graphic design was poetry. It was rhythym, contrast, balance, proportion, repetition, harmony, and scale, a carefully orchestrated vocabulary of simple form, specific function, and symbolic content. In his vision, a circle could be a globe, an apple, a face, a stop sign: at his hand, a square became a gift-wrapped box (the UPS trademark), an Egyptian frieze (the IDEO trademark), or a child's toy (the Colorforms trademark). Over the course of a career that spanned more than six decades, Rand produced a prolific body of work that included advertising and posters, books and magazines, illustration and – perhaps most important – a host of memorable trademarks for such corporations as ABC, IBM, UPS, and Westinghouse. More than anything, it is for these that he is best remembered, perhaps because they, like the man who created them, lasted so very long.

A trademark is a company's signature, an emblematic stamp of authenticity that establishes its name and firmly communicates the qualities with which it seeks to identify itself publicly. It is circumscribed within the larger notion of positioning a company's personality through its material presence in a culture, and perhaps for this reason falls under the more comprehensive rubric of "Corporate Identity." The process of mediating the relationship between the pragmatic demands of the corporation and the formal requirements of its trademark is the principal task of the designer: for Rand it was an ideal task, and one which showcased his greatest strengths. It demanded at once a serious attention to the value of intuition (visualizing the logo that must be instantly recognized by millions of people) and an equal, if not greater, attention to the importance of intellect (isolating the idea that must be distilled into its most salient, germane form). That said, the success of many (though not all) of these logos may be attributable to a number of factors.

- To begin with, Rand spent more than a decade in advertising, where he developed an acute appreciation for the value of design in the interest of commerce. Working on short deadlines, collaborating with clients and copywriters (while working with the Weintraub Agency, he pioneered the use of the art-and-copy collaborative teams practiced in most agencies today), Rand quickly learned that design could function as a potent strategy tool. This experience did little to lessen his commitment to the importance of art and design: if anything, it reinforced his aesthetic and increasingly modernist leanings. But it also forced him to become ruthlessly pragmatic, even skeptical — qualities that made him particularly well-poised to understand the communications need of corporations: determining what he called "the relevant idea and its formal interpretation." In the wake of his years spent reading, designing, and hacking his way through the advertising battlefields of postwar America, the challenges of corporate identity provided Rand with the ideal framework within which to test the validity of his combined talents and experience.

- Second, Rand was blessed with good clients. He himself never claimed to be particularly good at business (crediting this skill to his wife, Marion), but he made a point of approaching his projects with laser-beam focus. Given the passionate tenor of the ideas expressed in his writings, one can easily imagine Rand playing the aesthetic evangelist, and it is more than likely that he was instrumental in fostering his clients' vested interest in – and appreciation for – the importance of good design. "A company's reputation is very much affected by how it looks and how its products work," he writes in the essay "Good Design is Good Will." "A beautiful object that doesn't work is a reflection on the company's integrity. In the long run, it may not lose only its customers but its good will. Good design will no longer function as the harbinger of good business but as the herald of hypocrisy."

- Hypocrisy was something Rand successfully avoided for the length of his career: consistent with his irascible demeanor, he was brutally honest with himself and everyone around him, including his clients. Steve Jobs reportedly once asked Rand to "design a few logos" for his then-start-up company, NeXT. "If you want a few logos, then ask a few designers,"

Rand barked back. "But if you want me to solve your problem for you, I'll solve your problem for you." Such exchanges were typical of Rand's brusque negotiating style. Equally typical for Rand, but atypical for the industry in general, were the six-figure fees he was able to command for the design of a single trademark.

- Third, Rand had the good fortune to work with clients who stayed in their jobs long enough to ensure the longevity of his creations. This may explain why the more enduring logos commissioned more than thirty years ago – IBM (1956); Colorforms (1959); Westinghouse (1960); UPS (1961); and ABC (1962) for example – have remained virtually unchanged since their inception. Today, however, the peripatetic nature of corporate life makes such sustained activity considerably more difficult to achieve. The way business is conducted has changed in keeping with new management strategies and new multi-disciplinary teams; the way trademarks are used has changed in keeping with new products, activities, and services; and consequently, the very nature of corporate identity itself has evolved over the years as a response to such technological, social, commercial, and bureaucratic fluctuation. The discrepancy between Rand's formally isolationist view of the logo and these complex metamorphoses in business culture and practice may explain in part why some of Rand's later logotypes – The Limited (1988) and Morningstar (1991) for instance – received less favorable public attention and achieved, consequently, less competitive success.

- Certainly there have been, and are, other designers and design firms who have made enormous contributions to the practice of corporate identity. The work of Pentagram, Landor Associates, and Chermayeff and Geismar are among many such firms in the United States whose efforts have been widely recognized and whose role, in addition to the design of the mark itself, has grown to include market research, product positioning, and consumer branding. These firms typically work in teams and in collaboration with clients to determine the applications of an identity across a wide platform that may include, among other things, publications, collateral materials, signage, and packaging. Rand, on the other hand, worked solo, and only with the chief person responsible for making the decisions. He was violently – and quite vocally – opposed to group dynamics of any kind, including focus groups and what he called "design by committee," either of which he believed added an unnecessary layer of complexity to an already difficult process. In this way, he streamlined the workflow dynamic in much the same way that he distilled a design idea: it was a methodology that served him, and his clients, extremely well. In the mid-fifties, Rand produced his most successful logo, the trademark for IBM. Working closely with Eliot Noyes – then IBM's consulting director for design – Rand quickly understood that to be successful, what mattered was a flexible logo that could be interpreted as a system by different designers to suit different needs within the corporation. For Rand, this translated to a kind of modular thinking: taking his philosophical cues from architecture (and in particular, from the writings of Le Corbusier on similar spatial principles in architecture), he experimented with proportion, scale, color, and humor. For the IBM logo, this translated to a basic equation in which the fundamental mark might be duplicated, rotated, colorized, or mutated in such a way as to play the variable against the constant. In 1970, he extended the boundaries of this notion to include an "eye-bee-m" pictogram which has been widely used in posters and promotional materials ever since.

- The trademark itself (commissioned by the conservative Thomas Watson, Jr., largely in response to its great competitor, Olivetti) was based on City Medium, an obscure typeface designed by George Trump in 1930. Rand designed the initial logo in 1956; four years later he added the stripes, in an effort to minimize the discrepancy in character widths between the narrow I and the wider B and M. His inspiration in striping the letterforms came from observing the multi-lined striations on legal documents designed to discourage counterfeiting. By weighting up the stripes, Rand modernized the font, simplified the mark, and gestured to a kind of visual speed one might rightly associate with a technology company. (He also believed stripes had a universal appeal, evoking images including Romanesque architecture and Parisian fashion.) Rand went on to design both a thirteen-line variation and later an eight-line variation, which remains the corporate standard today.

- IBM, however, is perhaps more the exception than the rule. Typically, Rand's programs were logo programs, not identity programs. They were trademark based, not communication based. His marks were simple, modern, geometric abstractions of letterforms, recognizable shapes and symbols. He designed them to work at any scale or at an angle, on the side of a truck or emblazoned on an annual report cover, but they were rarely conceived of as part of larger, more complex communications programs – designed to embrace evolution and permutation over time or across disparate media. To Rand, a modern mark was a simple mark, and the secret to making things last lay in keeping them simple. In keeping them simple, he was indeed able to lay claim to the greatest endurance record of any trademark designer to date: while the Westinghouse logo was retooled five times between 1900 and 1953, Rand's 1960 redesign has remained intact for forty-three years. His 1961 logo for UPS has lasted almost as long (it is, however, now reportedly being redesigned by Pentagram, as is his 1973 logo for Cummins Engines).

- Do these logos succeed where others fail merely because they are simple? Are they better because they are ubiquitous, making us recognize them faster and behave more efficiently as a result? Or do we tire of their inertia, demanding more from identity programs than predictability and sameness? Many classic marks that previously achieved success through widespread recognition – the bell in Bell Telephone, for instance – have been given face-lifts in recent years. These upgraded marks may remain simple in theory, though in practice they reflect more complex uses and are, consequently, of a more idiosyncratic nature. It is interesting, too, to note the degree to which stripes, particularly in the mid-eighties, started to take on a kind of visual identity of their own, gracing marks for such corporate giants such as AT+T (Saul Bass, 1984), Nynex (Lippincott and Margulies, 1984), and the traditionally depicted, though striped, Prudential rock (Lee and Young, 1984).

- Today's identity programs face even greater performance expectations as they compete for attention in a media landscape dominated by increasingly kinetic media. Modernism notwithstanding, a timeless logo is, to some, little more than a tired logo. Consider UPS: fixed and predictable, a beige package trapped inside a heraldic shield on a flat, brown field. Once an emblem of the solid reliability of the U.S. postal system, today it is little more than a gloomy graphic portrait of snail mail – a fact somewhat exacerbated by the clean look and no-nonsense efficiency of its greatest competitor, Federal Express, reborn not long ago as FedEx in a cheery orange-and-purple identity program redesigned by Landor Associates. Or think ABC: compared to NBC's fluttering peacock, or CBS's blinking eye, Rand's

1962 logo is surprisingly static fare for television — a modernist bubble sporting Bauhaus typography, but static nonetheless.

- Clearly, to design a modern mark forty years ago was a very different task. The corporate America into which Rand was introduced in the 1950s and sixties was eager to define itself within the context of a relatively new — and rapidly growing — consumer culture. Rand's penchant for purism gave visual form to the exalted ideals of corporate leaders whose great ambition was to embrace new and complex audiences: this process involved rethinking traditional methods of corporate communication, which, in the years directly following the Second World War, had been largely characterized by unimaginative marketing efforts and unnecessarily decorative design. Given a climate ripe for change, the idea that visual communication could be both powerful and simple was a radical — but fashionably pragmatic — idea.

- More important even than this was his unusual capacity to express an idea verbally. For his corporate clients, Rand habitually prepared detailed reports in which he presented a new trademark as a carefully documented process, illustrating the evolution of his ideas over time and articulating his argument with clarity and purpose. In these eloquently written reports, what was perhaps most striking was his decision to expose the design process. The writing is a lyrical mix of intention, comparison, description, and analogy: here, Rand celebrated the integration of reasoning with the presentation of graphic design. Rather than minimizing the impact of his conclusions, such thoughtful discourse reinforced his visual thinking by positioning his ideas within a broader cultural context. By removing his argument from the immediate corporate climate it was intended primarily to address, and by distancing it from the broader demographic audience it was intended ultimately to reach, he gestured to a larger, more universal world. In the process, Rand used a clear formal vocabulary in precisely the way his mentors would have intended, as an international language: cross-cultural, timeless, and accessible to all. Rand called these reports the "musical accompaniment" to design.

- Looking back on his prolific career, it is paradoxical to think that the man who gave graphic life to such technological giants as IBM (with whom he retained the esteemed position of graphic design consultant for more than thirty-five years); IDEO (the international technology think tank based in Northern California); and Steve Jobs's NeXT should himself have been so averse to the computer. How could Rand, the devout modernist, be so openly resistant to the progressive changes brought about by the machine – the symbolic child of modern industry? It is as though the same geometric forms that embodied the logic of mechanical reproduction, the same formal vocabulary that inspired his mentors and defined the very spirit of modernism, was available to Rand only in theory.

- Such contradictions underscored his entire career, if not his entire life, and they are everywhere present in his writing. Quoting William J. R. Curtis on Le Corbusier in *Good Design is Good Will,* Rand writes: "It is necessary to understand history, and he who understands history knows how to find continuity between that which was, that which is, and that which will be." A moment later he discourages any reference to historical precursorism, and quotes the British philosopher Karl Popper: "The past is only an indication," he writes, "not an explanation." And what of the contradictions in his own personal history? The darling of corporate America for decades, Rand rejected the lure of city life, opting to work alone in his Connecticut home studio for the better part of his career; while he openly claimed to despise academia, he remained a revered member of the Yale faculty for over thirty-five years; and despite the painful consequences of his family's extreme religious standards, he remained an observant Jew for the whole of his life. The orthodoxy that characterized both his relationship to design and his relationship to God was likely an attempt to equalize these polarities, to right the balances, to establish order in the studio as well as in the spirit.

- Yet here too there were contradictory impulses: "Five is better than four, three is better than two," he often announced to his students, claiming that the mind worked harder and received a greater sense of reward when optically resolving asymmetrical relationships on the page. As he grew older, such lessons were taught with even greater passion and emphasis. At the same time, in his own work, the pioneering spirit that led him to push the boundaries of expression on magazine covers and in advertisements in the 1930s and 1940s – the poetic interpretations, the playful juxtapositions – grew decidedly less ambitious. And with each successive book, the editorial organization is looser, the type is larger, and the writing is weaker. Rand's last book, *From Lascaux to Brooklyn*, is in many ways the weakest book of all, and has certainly been the least favorably received. Here, the precision that qualified the earlier essays is missing, the ideas follow a less logical path, and the bibliographic marginalia are an eclectic mix of philosophy, aesthetics, and literature, combined somewhat randomly with Rand's brazen, ex-cathedra statements. But it is in many ways his greatest work: passionate, exuberant, without question a remarkable achievement for anyone at the age of eighty-one. "The impulse to creation knows no exception – fashionable or practical," he writes. "Cosmetics or jewelry, flatware or footwear, hammers or nails – it is the urge to invent, to solve problems, visual or mechanical, that really matters." This is also a fitting final achievement for such an accomplished life: this is Rand going out in a blaze of glory.

Letters…possess some magical quality.
Paul Rand – *Thoughts on Design*

Antonio Alcalá
The
Huge, Heroic
Letterform

- I present a few of Paul Rand's ideas on how type can contribute to a design by highlighting a unique characteristic found in some of his favorite solutions – the huge, heroic letterform.
- In October of 1938, the first article published on the work of Paul Rand appeared in the industry journal *PM*. Sixteen pages are devoted to the then twenty-four-year-old's work. They present a varied assortment of portfolio pieces: ads, booklets, trademarks, posters, and packaging. On the seventh page, however, the parade is momentarily interrupted by four elegant, hand-drawn numbers. That they are the only work presented out of context is itself notable. Their sequence is unexpected 2, 3, 4, 5 (where is the 1?). But it is their large scale that contributes the greatest drama both to the progression of pages and to its own composition. By filling the entire page, Rand deemphasizes the sequence while simultaneously asking the reader to appreciate the formal skills of the artist. Look at the contrast between the thin fragile lines and the bolder strokes. Enjoy the rhythm of the solid black dots. Explore the space between the forms. Paul Rand said, "There are essentially two kinds of typography: the familiar kind for reading, and the other, simply for viewing, like a painting."[1] In this page, with these outsized numbers, Rand announces his interest in modernity, love of and belief in the power of form, and a creative language to promote important ideas of concept and form.
- From 1938 until 1945, Rand designed a series of covers for a publication titled *Direction*. With complete creative control, the series demonstrates the agility of his technique (collage, montage, illustration, photography) and the power of his ideas. Two notable issues incorporating the large-scale letterform date from March 1941 and July 1944. In the first, the author of Rand's *PM* profile contributes the feature article "Art in Industry."
- The article promotes the adoption of modern design and its values into the world of industry. Illustrated using examples of design pioneers (and contemporaries of Rand) such as Cassandre, Bayer, Burtin, Beall, Brodovitch, Jensen, Alto, and Moholy-Nagy, the article makes an appeal Rand must have greatly appreciated. In turn, his cover not only states his support of art in industry, but goes further, boldly proclaiming

his firm conviction in design as the process by which art is made. It is constructed using collage as a new language of modern art. The composition begins and ends with an enormous black sans-serif A stretching from top to bottom and filling most of the page from left to right. Its form is cut from a folded, creased piece of paper. To its side stands a red-brick smokestack with smoke billowing from its top. Formed of the roughest pen and pencil scrawls and an irregularly cut shape, it succinctly and efficiently represents industrial production. It is paired with a smaller, lighter shape made from clipped pieces of a newspaper's financial page. This addition helps to update the smokestack and gives reference to a broader understanding of industry.

In his book *Thoughts on Design,* Rand states that the designer's problem is "to anticipate the spectator's reaction and meet the designer's own plastic needs."[2] To find a common ground between the two, Rand prescribes the modernist solution: develop a symbol creating an image which is "universally comprehensible."[3] He writes further, "A symbol may be depicted as an abstract shape, a geometric figure, a photograph, an illustration, a letter of the alphabet, or a numeral."[4] Rand uses the massive A to symbolize art. Literally and metaphorically, this folded, creased, worn piece of paper, cut into an A, is all that is needed to make art. Additionally, Rand wrote and spoke often of attempting to "defamiliarize the ordinary,"[5] of "seeing things in a way that is unexpected."[6] To do so engages the viewer and invites their participation. Rand takes the most common letter, one that we first learn as very young children, and super-sizes it. It becomes massive! He pushes it right to the front of our picture plane. No longer is it the letter of a primer or an alphabet or even a word. It's a new symbol, a form that begs us to recognize it as art.

- Rand displays both the March 1941 "Art in Industry" and the July 1944, "D-Day" *Direction* covers in *Thoughts on Design* under a brief paragraph that begins, "The isolated letter affords a means of visual expression which other forms of imagery cannot quite duplicate."[7] The emotional power of the D-Day cover is almost tangible. Unlike "Art in Industry," Rand's solution for this cover grows not from the magazine's content (the summer fiction issue), but from the ongoing World War. Less than a month earlier, the allies had launched the D-Day invasion of Europe, signaling the end of the Nazi regime. Rand notes the event with a cover that

46: 47: The Heroic Letterform: Alcalá

brilliantly reflects emotional complexity and somber reportage. Again, the work begins with an oversized letter – a D that almost fills the entire cover. It is pushed to the front of the viewing plane and extends off the cover's left edge. Its form is graceful, with thin, attenuated serifs contrasting the bold vertical strokes. The letter takes on a dual meaning – it is the D for D-Day and also the D for death. Consequently, its elegance creates a counterpoint to the brutality of the event. The massive D dominates the small image of a helmet resting on a swastika-inscribed burial cross. It diminishes the significance of the Nazis while avoiding the usual clichés of propaganda. Rand's composition notes the monumentality of the event and suggests a desire to shout with pride at the enormity of the accomplishment. Limiting the cover's palette to black and white only intensifies its content. As Rand writes of black and white in an essay "Black in the Visual Arts": "They are the raw unadulterated colors of the struggle between life and death."[8]

- These concerns of contrasts in scale, form, and color, which are integral to his use of the large D, are typical of Rand's search for a unification of form and content. Rand revisits the theme of art and the enlarged symbolic A in a catalog cover for an exhibition of twentieth-century art from the Arensberg Collection. Seizing on the fortunate accident of both art and Arensberg beginning with the same letter, Rand makes the enlarged A the key to his design. As Rand later wrote, "This cover is composed of a series of contrasts...The tension between black and white in the cover is heightened by opposing a large area of black to a small area of white. The contrast theme is carried out further by the drastic variation in the size of the letters. The roughness of the edges of the large A emphasizes the sharpness of those smaller A, and the extreme diagonals of the letters are counteracted by the right angles of the book itself."[9] The choice of font provides an additional contrast, as he selects a classic eighteenth-century form to represent a twentieth-century subject. While the A's placement is not pushed forward as in the *Direction* cover, its forcefulness remains by virtue of its large size. Additionally, Rand uses this symbolic letter and cover to tell the viewer that twentieth-century art is not about direct representation and literal illustration, but about meaningful ideas and significant form. The huge isolated A again proclaims his belief that design is a key activity in creating art.

- Rand continued designing book covers using the isolated letterform as focal point through the sixties. F for *The Life of Forms in Art,* i for *six nonlectures,* W for *Wagner as Man and Artist,* and X for *The Road to Xanadu*. A personal favorite from this period is his design for *The Anatomy of a Revolution*. The book is essentially a historic review and academic analysis of revolutions, and Rand prudently avoids an esoteric visual in favor of using a solitary, enormous R. It fills the entire front of the paperback. Once again, its size is unexpected but its meaning is easily deciphered: R is for revolution. It appears bold and strong. To strengthen its symbolic content, the letterform is divided into thirds, suggesting an examination of different facets of a revolution. The red and blue portions hint at flag designs and evoke nationalistic associations. The black might represent tragedy, death, or failure. The photograph presenting either "bombs bursting in air" or celebratory fireworks contributes sound and energy to the composition, two elements crucial to the concept of revolution. Thus Rand successfully transforms the letter R into a dynamic, loud, modern symbol, a focal point from which to capture the viewer and communicate the content.

- From these examples of isolated letterforms one could effortlessly move onward, exploring first Rand's brilliant typographic trademarks. The next step might include examining other powerful designs that rely on a slightly less limited typographic palette. Eventually the investigation could progress all the way through the extensive artistic statements his complete oeuvre provides. In undertaking such a journey, one is guaranteed to discover many more facets to Rand's typography: economy, simplicity, honesty, wit, humor, charm, modesty, intuition, purity, precision, and intelligence. As the range of examined work grows, so too grow the rewards from understanding the artistic genius of Paul Rand.

1. *Type Talks,* Advertising Typographers Association, vol. 1, no. 1, Fall 1989, p. 6.
2. Rand, Paul, *Thoughts on Design,* New York: Wittenborn, 1947, p. 7. Rand rephrases this in his book *A Designer's Art* (New Haven: Yale University Press, 1985) to read "…and to meet his own aesthetic needs."
3. Rand, *Thoughts on Design,* p. 7.
4. Ibid.
5. Rand, *A Designer's Art,* p. 45.
6. Rand, *From Lascaux to Brooklyn,* New Haven: Yale University Press, 1996, p. 45.
7. Rand, *Thoughts on Design,* p. 129.
8. Rand, "Black in the Visual Arts," *Graphic Forms,* Cambridge: Harvard University Press, 1949, p. 39.
9. Ibid., p. 40.

Steven Heller
Randism

- To call Paul Rand shy is to challenge the perception of the man as outspoken and authoritative. Yet shy was indeed one of his most perplexing traits. For much of his career Rand refused to speak in front of audiences that exceeded three people. Other designers routinely stood before assembled multitudes flipping through endless trays of personal slides, but Rand suffered from severe stage fright. The few times that he took to the podium the results were not satisfying, especially for him. However, in his mid-seventies, he made a curious reversal. Spurred by the need to publicize his book *Paul Rand: A Designer's Art,* he agreed to do public speaking with the help of interlocutors, like myself, who peppered him with questions. He found his comfort level and self-confidence, and to his surprise he also garnered large audiences who were disarmed by the candor, insight, and anecdote of what I call Randism.

- Design as practiced by Rand, although rooted in European modernism, was decidedly Randism. Unlike other contemporary American exponents of Cubism, Dada, Contructivism, de Stijl, and the Bauhaus who mimicked these methods, Rand incorporated a modern essence or spirit into his work. He was American, not German, Russian, French, or Dutch. His distinctive elocution made it quite clear that he was a Brooklyn-American – indeed a Jewish-Brooklyn-American. He was not born into the culture that gave birth to Futurism or die Neue Typographie. He was not schooled in the European ways. He practiced drawing in the back of his father's small grocery store, and was influenced by comic strips, advertisements, and *The Saturday Evening Post*. Emerging from an hermetic early childhood he found enlightenment at Macy's Department Store where, in the bookshop, he found two European graphic design magazines, England's *Commercial Art* and Germany's *Gebrauchgraphik*. In these pages he learned about contemporary commercial design and its kinship to the arts, and was introduced to the Bauhaus notion that good design was an integral part of everyday life.

- Once he decided to become an artist/designer he could have fallen into conventional American methods of practice. In fact, his teachers at Pratt did not offer much guidance other than rote methods of lettering and composition. So Rand absorbed the lessons of modernism in his own way, at his own pace, often by trial, error, and luck.

- "I was apprenticed to George Switzer [a progressive

industrial designer in New York], who was influenced by French and German typographers," Rand said about his earliest exposure to avant-garde design. "Among others, I was directly influenced by Piet Zwart, the Dutchman; El Lissitzky, the Russian; Moholy-Nagy, the Hungarian; Jan Tschichold, the Czech; and Apollinaire, the Pole, not to mention the Chinese and Persians." In Rand's early work his inspirations were obvious – that is to anyone in America who knew of these relatively unknown European masters. But before long he found his voice, synthesizing European notions of typography and composition with a uniquely individual, Brooklyn way of conceptualizing.

- As a young man Rand was as nervous about the correctness of his words as he was convinced about the rightness of his design. A desire to be fluent in language caused him to read and re-read critics and philosophers like John Dewey, Alfred North Whitehead, and Roger Fry, among others. He matched his intuitive methods to their reasoned insights, and by quoting them in his later writing on themes such as beauty, aesthetics, function, simplicity, and play, he found a means to articulate his own philosophical underpinnings. Ultimately he used their ideas as armatures on which he built Randism.
- So what makes Randism different from other leading adherents of American modernism? Alvin Lustig and Lester Beall, among them, frequently wrote and lectured on art and craft. But Rand was the first of the young American moderns to publish a book cum manifesto, *Thoughts on Design* (1946). It was the first serious monograph to lay down a theory about producing mass-market advertising. In perceptive declarations that eschewed pedantry, he wed modern dicta (as borrowed from earlier books by Tschichold and Moholy-Nagy) to his own pragmatic methods, as in this rationale about why good design was a virtue in a world where mediocrity was accepted. "Even if it is true that the average man seems most comfortable with the commonplace and familiar, it is equally true that catering to bad taste, which we so readily attribute to the average reader, merely perpetuates that mediocrity and denies the reader one of the most easily accessible means for aesthetic development and eventual enjoyment."
- He also explained how to walk the tightrope of art and function, as in this statement: "Ideally, beauty and utility are mutually generative," he wrote. "In the past, rarely was beauty an end in itself." Rand introduced

theory to a profession whose writing was heretofore predominantly how-to. Nevertheless, he rarely invoked academic jargon.

- During the last decade of his life when he started appearing in public, audiences did not know what to expect. Would he talk over their heads or drone on with show-and-tell monologues? His books and articles offered few clues; they were tightly structured. He did not allow himself the luxury of informality, but rather arduously wrote and rewrote every sentence to achieve correct parsing, leaving his texts reasoned, logical, and terse. Yet in a public forum he was unable to edit himself, nor did he want to. His candor was infectious, like when, at his penultimate lecture at Cooper Union in October 1996, he received an ovation when he answered a question about passion. "I just like things that are playful; I like things that are happy; I like things that will make the client smile." Was this the orthodox modernist who spoke religiously about the rightness of form? Yes. But Rand and Randism had a variety of inflections.

- Rand said "I hate words that are abused, like 'creativity,'" and he eschewed all fashionable slogans. Sure he had pet phrases like "for the birds," which was reserved for expressing mild contempt for bad design. But most of the time he was strident about issues that he felt undercut good design. This critique of trendiness is just one example: "It's something that's superimposed on a problem. It has to do with being part of the scene, or doing what is the latest thing to do." Randism was not a smokescreen; it was a way of propagating the faith – his faith. Moreover, it was a way of educating those who knew little or nothing of design. At times Randism was used as a tool to sell his ideas. Presentations to clients are often an occasion when designers make hocus-pocus. Conversely Rand believed, "A presentation is the musical accompaniment of design. A presentation that lacks an idea cannot hide behind glamorous photos, pizzazz, or ballyhoo." Anyone reading the presentation booklets that he wrote and produced for NeXT, English First, Ford, and a dozen others (reprinted in his three monographs) knows that each is a primer in logo design and visual communication. He meticulously walks the reader through his intellectual and aesthetic process, discussing the false starts and failed tries, until finally revealing the final product as though it was the only logical solution to the problem. "I never make a presentation personally," he explained in *Artograph* (1988).

"I usually send it in the mail…because if it's going to be rejected I don't want to be there. But more importantly, I think that the thing has to stand on its own merits. I've seen skillful presentations made by people doing terrible work….People spend money making presentations with three-dimensional things and lights and theatrical effects, dancing girls and music…."

Rand was arrogant, but Randism was forged from truths that he fervently believed. And he left behind a catalog of tenets about clients, style, and aesthetics that continue to have resonance, including these. "What the designer and his client have in common is a license to practice without a license"; "A style is the consequence of recurrent habits, restraints, or rules invented or inherited, written or overheard, intuitive or preconceived"; and "Simplicity is never a goal: it is a by-product of a good idea and modest expectations."

Paul Rand's life was consumed by work. Randism was the sum total of his accomplishments, the words, deeds, and artifacts that comprise his legacy. But Randism is not a style or method, it does not exist without him. In fact, it is best summed up in his own words in the preface to *Paul Rand: A Designer's Art:*

"My interest has always been in restating the validity of those ideas, which, by and large, have guided artists since the time of Polyclitus. I believe that it is only in the application of those timeless principles that one can even begin to achieve a semblance of quality in one's work. It is the continuing relevance of these ideals that I mean to emphasize, especially to those who have grown up in a world of punk and graffiti."

Takenobu Igarashi
Paul Rand:
Intellectual Conscience
and
Perfection in Design

- Powerful form and perfection are representative characteristics of Paul Rand's design. His sharp vision would not even allow an error of 0.01 millimeter. His firm belief in the horizontal and the vertical, his psychological insight into angles, his understanding of the meaning of shape, and his keen judgment balancing between the positive and the negative – all of these give weight to his design. It was Yusaku Kamekura who first brought out the theory of weight in design. According to Kamekura, every design has its own weight, and this is especially apparent in symbol marks. Beauty and originality alone are not enough for genuine design if it lacks weight. In order to have style and to endure time, Kamekura based his weight theory on the Japanese family crest, whose beauty retains its simple design over hundreds of years. Here, the weight of design can be felt clearly without any need for explanations. Simple arguments – the use of black creates heaviness, for example – are totally irrelevant in this case. Kamekura sympathized with Paul Rand's design especially on this point. The weight theory can also be applied to composition, whether in the field of posters or package design. What Kamekura meant by weight is not simply the visible physical weight, but rather the inevitable elements of meaning and style, which add weight to the clean and aesthetic world of design.

- The artistic quality of Paul Rand's work is not that of personality, common to the art world, but rather that of the scientific world, equipped with rules based on theory. His comment that "{graphic} design is not good design if it is irrelevant" is a good example of his theory. Rand was strongly involved in design education. His approach to design is educational, and he was conscious of this as he spent so many years teaching design. I once had the chance to look at presentation booklets of visual identity programs for Westinghouse and Cummins Engine Company. The basic idea and design were so clearly and beautifully presented in a layout that no explanations were necessary. Paul Rand's intellectual world of design flooded out of these booklets and overwhelmed me. His will to graphically educate his clients in good design could be felt without a doubt. I have heard that he would often send his booklets to his clients without going personally to present and explain his design. This anecdote shows how he himself embodied the perfection of content and his belief in visual communication.

- Minori Nijima, a Japanese designer who studied with Rand at Yale University in the early eighties, expressed what he learned from Paul Rand in these words: "Design is shape or space resulting from the process of setting up the vector to limit the concept inherent in shape." All of the representative works from the 1930s to the mid-1980s are compiled in *Paul Rand: A Designer's Art*. His work can be divided into hard-edged corporate logo design, typographical, editorial, posters, package design, and freehand illustrations. Style and quality are constant throughout his career. Here again, there is similarity with Kamekura. The corporate logo, editorial, poster, and package design were Kamekura's favorite domain. Moreover, some of his logos, and especially his illustrations, have a similarity with Rand's wonderful world of freehand illustration, although I do not know to what extent Kamekura was aware of Rand's work before they met, eventually.
- It sometimes seems to me that Paul Rand's half-century's work had been programmed in advance. I can imagine him dealing with endless requests from clients just as he would attend to his new students, starting with a set of fundamental rules and basic matter, and then perfecting his work with sensitivity and intuition, reviewing it critically, comparing it with his past work so it fits. He probably did not let himself get distracted, and with his strong mental powers, maintained his self-confidence throughout the process of completing his work. Looking at his work over the last fifty years, one notices that there is not a single eccentric idea in his work. Rand's ideas exist along the extension of good sense, refined to perfection at the end. This attitude has something in common with Japanese culture, where value is given to the natural and the ordinary. It is interesting to note that in his book *Paul Rand: A Designer's Art,* Rand uses a photograph of a Japanese tool and even mentions its functionality and its beauty of form in his text.
- There is no doubt about the perfection of Paul Rand's work. On the other hand, his uniform, steady, and direct approach to the method of problem solving in design could be considered boring as well. It is also somehow unnatural that hardly any difference exists between his work in the beginning and at the end of fifty years. As long as design is closely related to the change of time and the developments in industry, it must reflect the age in which we live. Timeless design is an ideal, difficult to attain in the field of graphic

design because it involves communication. The cause lies mostly in factors outside of design. In spite of such consideration, the perfection and the graceful sensitivity of Paul Rand's work is simply amazing.

- With the times, people's interests change, and the position of design in our society is also beginning to change. The diffusion of design and its popularization is a victory for design, but ironically, as a result, design is not always considered as special. Paul Rand's perfect design with its uniform worldview is being questioned in today's fast moving, globalized society. The rise of Eastern spirituality replacing Western rationalism in design is one example. The world we live in is diverse, and nobody can deny the existential value of different cultures. Today, global as well as regional thinking is asked for in design. People are becoming aware that diversity is the more human way. Problem solving through design is now approaching a new difficult stage.

- Paul Rand is a great, and at the same time a lucky, designer, for he was able to develop and express his talent at a favorable time in a privileged country. How to apply this great achievement to the future is the legacy left to us.

Ivan Chermayeff
Hand of Rand

- Paul Rand had a wide array of graphic gifts going for him. They are all obvious and necessary for the creation of exceptionally good work, but very few artists and even fewer designers have had them all to such an extent and at such extraordinarily high levels as Paul Rand. He had these gifts across the board and applied them consistently.
- Paul Rand had a profound, instinctive, unnerving sense of color, form, typography, and visual connections. What's more, Paul Rand had impeccable taste. Paul Rand always started with an appropriate idea before applying his talents. Nothing was left out that was, in his view, necessary, and nothing was excluded that did not contribute in some way to the communication. His great and very personal and thoughtful choices about every ingredient made provocative, interesting, tasty visual meals, abounding with subtle and sensitive Rand seasoning. He used type like salt and pepper, sprinkled in just the right quantities in just the right places.
- The meanings of connection in the arena of graphic design are never a constant array of the same truths, or at least the same truths presented in the same way. The meanings shift, the associations change, according to context. As Rand states, it is difficult to pin down what graphic design is. "It is a moving target and even if very difficult, close to impossible to pin down, it is clear when it happens. It has been accomplished in examples of good work. And good work is persuasive, provocative, and informative."
- Visual connections through collage and assemblage are in profusion in Rand's work. All the elements of form, color, typography, and image are somehow dependent on one another. But they are not necessarily alike stylistically from project to project. The connections in the assembly of elements are subtle. Each aspect of every project is in balance with every other. What happened in Rand's process is that every contributing element presented was seamlessly connected to the whole conception. The manipulation of words and pictures are dealt with for a purpose. The choice of how the words impact the pictures depends on their nature and import. For Rand, the end is the beginning. Where he decided to go and what the route would be would vary according to the terrain and the expected traveler. "Significant form, meaningful ideas, metaphor, wit, humor, and exercises in visual perception" get the emphasis they deserve according to a reasoned judgment. It is, as Rand states, the

designer's job to select and fit material together and make it interesting.

- Rand designed an advertisement for Westinghouse in 1962 about a cardiac pacer they had developed. The central image is both exclamation point and an image of a heart simultaneously. Color bars surround the heart/exclamation point. One can see the cut marks of Rand's scissors; the lively, arresting choice of colors–green, magenta, purple, and yellow around the red heart. The colors set off the spirit of a new product while allowing the red to dominate and the yellow to have the message overprinted for legibility. The type is typewriter, again fresh and immediate. This ad is forty years old as I write and looks like it was done this morning. It is pure Rand. It would be recognized as his upside down, at fifty-five miles an hour.

- Another example: a Knopf cover design of 1958; cut papers, red and blue, with a photograph of H. L. Mencken as the central image, roughly cut to suggest Mencken with a raised finger. All the cut pieces were placed to add movement to the entire, collaged arrangement of loose pieces on the cover. The words were written by Rand's hand and add to the curmudgeonly sense of Mencken's own outrage at the goings on of the world around him expressed in his essays. The shapes cut from paper or photographs in all of Rand's work were always fresh and free, uninhibited and strong. No weak or washy, indecisive, vague forms, whether abstract or illustrative, and all clearly understandable.

- He always found an essential and unmovable visual reminder of the subject matter, sometimes seemingly simple, perhaps a small telling detail – barbed wire, a splash of paint, a brush stroke. The dots and dashes of a Weintraub Agency ad with a telegraphic message to a specialist list of readers. The barbed wire cruciform of a 1940 *Direction* magazine cover at the beginning of the war with dots sprinkled around the entire cover becoming machine-gun bullets. The egg form as a symbol of birth behind the splatter of ink drops – a poster for the International Design Conference in Aspen. Forms, gestures, and symbols collaged together comfortably and naturally. *The Graphic Art of Paul Rand* on a poster for an exhibition of his work in Paul Rand's writing, contrasted, to the cut paper image of a hand with the shape of a top spinning on the index finger, with color stripes on a sleeve repeated in stripes on the top itself. Typical

Paul Rand, timeless and seemingly completed in seconds thirty years ago.

- Rand was also a master typographer. Titles and authors completed the whole assemblage by being integrated and essential to the form and content of the work. Not just there, but intimately keeping the composition in balance and bringing yet another component into play. Lightbulb packages for Westinghouse with very large wattage numbers. Stenciled letters digging their way through mine shafts for *Mine Boy:* a 1956 cover in startling magenta and green within the painted black tunnels. The clown mask for an AIGA cover lets the letters of the institution read through the entire assemblage and is on the provocative edge of legibility.
The large Didot letter D with the image of a German soldier's burial cross in the field of battle brings the assembly of image and type to a poignant, emotionally filled relationship in a *Direction* cover nearing the end of the war, in 1945.

- The contrast of an enlarged dot pattern with a sharply defined rectangle would be arresting all by itself. To have the graphic quality described take place on one arm of a Nazi swastika, an image the viewer discovers and then ties to the war effort of the allies to defeat Nazi Germany, is extraordinary. Even the broken arm becomes a V for victory. So many visual subtleties are at work. I do not know the colors Rand employed in this collage, but undoubtedly they contributed to the message too.

- The collages of letterforms combined with photographic images run through Paul Rand's work and include such diverse fragments as a Swiss chalet, the head of a Minute Man, dancers, eyes, faces, the sea, and the cosmos.

- His color brings other worlds to mind, chocolate, spumoni, candy, Miro, Klee, Schwitters, Calder, and children. One can taste the color or take in its meaning.

- Paul Rand's work is a distillation of the essential elements of any communication fraught with purpose, intelligence, sophistication, and a personal knowledge of art and art history, remarkable in its consistently high level of performance. It is, in fact, hard to explain why or how such standards were searched for and found. Never too much of anything either. A tight, unexpected palette: UPS brown, for instance. Connections through the juxtaposition of forms, silhouetted photographs, observed textures and graphic qualities, splashes and dribbles, lots of handwriting, Garamond, bold condensed sans serif gothic, and often plain typewriter.

- Paul Rand's collages or assemblages of type, shapes, and telling images with judicious color choices complete a work. The end result is provocative and artistic, personal and worldly, on the edge. Above all, communicative and original. Fresh and amazingly consistent.

60: 61: Hand of Rand: Chermayeff

Milton Glaser
Paul Rand
the Illustrator

- In the United States, illustration has a history that could crudely be described as beginning with Eakins and Winslow Homer, continued by Howard Pyle and N. C. Wyeth and family, and finally arriving at Westport, Connecticut, and the *Saturday Evening Post*. During these origins, the conventions of painting and those of illustration were not clearly differentiated from one another. Winslow Homer, for example, considered himself a painter-journalist, and all of his work is a reflection of observable reality. With the advent of modernism, painting and illustration parted company as Picasso, Bracque, Klee, Arp, Duchamp, and countless others attacked the philosophical idea of painting as a way of reproducing the visible world. By and large, illustration was left to shoulder that task alone. Rand would never have described himself as an illustrator; in fact, the word itself might have been the antithesis of his self-definition. Rand's vision was shaped by the advent of modernist thought, where ideas of literal representation had been replaced by an abstract or symbolic vocabulary. When Rand was growing up, illustration was still linked to realistic or academic painting. Illustrators made understandable pictures; designers had a somewhat different role, they organized information. Both activities involve communication, but each discipline employs somewhat different means, most notably the use of abstract formal relationshps and typography as the central elements of the designer's vocabulary. Rand is obviously a superb shape maker and disciplined typographer, but his picture making was also exemplary, within a new tradition.
- A significant part of Rand's sense of drawn form derived from the influence of Paul Klee, whose playfulness and informality using a thin unweighted line came at least in part from the drawings of children. The idea was to recast drawing as an informal expressive tool, in contrast to the skill-based academic principles that embodied the perceived stifling values of the nineteenth century. Rand's drawings in his early advertisements for El Producto Cigars and Ohrbach's, as well as much of his later work in children's books, are emblematic of this way of working. Rand acknowledged Klee as his "master," and the latter influence on Rand's visual vocabulary cannot be overestimated. The impulse to depart from academic drawing that moved Picasso to look for inspiration to Catalan and African art encouraged Rand to use Klee's cultivated innocence as a primary conceptual resource.

I'm also inclined to believe that Rand had to be influenced by comic strips, the most powerful vernacular graphic form around while he was growing up. The sensibility that informs his animal drawings for *Architectural Forum* (1945) and his children's books shares the charm and accessibility of the cartoons he read as a young man.

- Incidentally, the presumption that ideas created in the world of high art could be adapted and used by designers and illustrators for commercial purposes was not as obvious in Rand's early years as it is today. The Russian Constructivists Rodchenko, Malevich, and El Lisitzky showed how it could be done in Russia, and Rand – along with Leo Lionni, Lester Beall, Herbert Bayer, and others – demonstrated the same principle in the United States.

- Another of the most influential factors in Rand's sense of form was the work of Hans Arp. Rand adapted Arp's abstract biomorphic vocabulary to his illustrative needs. Many of Rand's book jackets – *Caligula* by Camus, *The Revelations of Dr. Modesto* by Alan Harrington, and *The Transposed Heads* by Thomas Mann – demonstrate this tendency. Finally, what seems to be the most sustained and pervasive factor of all of Rand's influences were the paper cutouts that Matisse produced toward the end of his life. Matisse's ideas were so pervasive and influential, it is hard to imagine that Rand could be immune to their meaning.

- In any event, cut paper was by far Rand's most compatible medium in his illustrative work. It might be said that almost any illustrator who uses cut paper as a drawing medium seems to owe Matisse a debt. Rand also subscribed to the modernist canon of maintaining the flatness of the picture plane, and because he doesn't employ light and shadow to define form, his color is almost never modulated. His palette is generally restricted to pure primary color relationships. By traditional standards Rand was an unconvincing draftsman, but the advent of modern painting freed him from the historical tradition of naturalistic representation and draftmanship that had defined traditional illustration. The precise demarcations between artist, designer, and illustrator are always difficult to define. In Rand's case, conventional illustration was swept aside as he invented his own definition of what it might be.

Franc Nunoo-Quarcoo
The House on
87 Goodhill Road
Weston
Connecticut

- Henry Thoreau, a man who knew the secrets of living, once wrote: "I sometimes dream of a house, standing in a golden age, of enduring materials, and without gingerbread work, containing all the essentials of a house, and nothing for housekeeping." In 1951 when Paul and Ann Rand designed their house on 87 Goodhill Road, they wanted such a house, too, an enduring, essential house, built for beauty and privacy, security and shelter, peace and an intimacy with its surroundings. They built a house to work and live in, and it proved to be a culmination of his work and life, reflecting his philosophy of form and content. This philosophy is well explained in his his last book, *From Lascaux to Brooklyn.*
- The character of the Rand House is perhaps best exemplified through the Japanese word *shibumi*. Shibumi essentially means austere elegance. The concept of shibumi covers many aesthetic properties. When it is applied to various other properties such as color, design, taste, human character, manner, voice, etc., it designates a subtle, unobtrusive, and deeply moving pattern of beauty, an austere elegant color, sophisticated luster, uncommon balance, and masterful performance. The concept of shibumi has been carefully preserved in the vocabulary of the common people and is often associated with concepts such as the beauty of simplicity, and the beauty of tranquility.
- The design of the Rand House was not accidental. In 1947 he had commissioned European modernist architect Marcel Breuer to design a bungalow in Woodstock, New York, but the project was never realized. Paul Rand's first house, located in Harrison, New York, was designed by Breuer in 1948. The Rand House, set on eight acres in the wooded backcountry of Weston, Connecticut, was inspired by Breuer. It adheres to the Japanese ideal setting for a house: a hill to the north, a brook to the east, a road to the west, facing the south. In describing a visit to Rand's home in 1984, Mildred Friedman (then director of the Walker Arts Center, Minneapolis, and editor of *Design Quarterly*) wrote: "How Rand has brought his particular awareness and sensitivity to things literary and historical into his graphic work was made clear to me on a visit to his Connecticut home. Designed by him and Ann Rand (who studied with Mies van der Rohe) and built in 1951, this low profile, stone and glass house seems absolutely right on this hilly, tree-covered site. The interior of the house is informal, filled with colorful collections of folk art, superb paintings by

Paul Klee, and graphics by Picasso and Pierre Bonnard, whose brilliant 1894 poster, *La Revue Blanche,* dominates one wall. The furnishings have the elegance and strength of classical twentieth-century design, Le Corbusier's black box chairs juxtaposed with brightly painted wood cabinets on cool tile floors. This house belongs to a period of great invention in American art – that in which Rand matured as a designer."

- The compact yet spacious modern home takes issue with Connecticut's rustic environment and traditional New England architecture. The house neither tosses the inhabitants out into the open by too much picture window exposure, nor shuts them off from the outdoors by conventional barriers. The entrance, for example, utilizes natural light in the small court and roof opening to the left, where birch trees stand reaching to the sky. All this, from a reasonable distance creates an illusion reminiscent of a surreal painting by René Magritte. While not a large house, it feels as if it was made to measurement for every interaction and every function. The vista from the living room to the inner court and beyond is breathtaking from sunup to sundown, from season to season. The court, open to the sky, temptingly visible from the other rooms, brings the outdoors in, offers shelter from the wind, and confirms the privacy of a room. The open floor plan lends the house a significant sense of spaciousness.

- There is a strong dualism in the design of the Rand House because of the contrasts of polarities. Despite the formal functionalistic tendencies, the house is rich with organic details, and the use of natural metaphors, forms, materials, and textures are the recurrent themes. Rand confronts romantic ideals with rationalism, natural forms with geometry, the modernist with the vernacular, and thus creates an infinitely rich environment. The dining area is a clearly defined room despite its semi-open connection to the kitchen and long corridor. All the house's functional areas, although well defined, borrow visual space from the open areas and adjoining rooms, and thus create a feeling of spaciousness. The spaces are especially beautiful and in perfect scale with the human body, standing or seated. Rather than replicating the positivist gestalt implied by the early modernists, volume is treated as a neutral background for images, objects, and living. Space is not treated as a tangible substance to be contained, or as some mystical, ameliorative substance that would gradually uplift and transform those who experience it, but as the logical consequence of structure. Rand had long welcomed

87 Goodhill Road: Nunoo-Quarcoo

plants as a natural ornament. This is one way he infused humanism into his interpretation of modernism.

He hung his considerable collection of art in the salon style, a clear move meant to complement the whole rather than respond to the prescriptive style of a clinical modernist interior. Integration of growing things with the architectural elements is achieved through the use of courts, with full-cut openings to the sky.

- The Rand House avoids the clichés of the modernistic, and strives for a warm companionable use of building materials. The geometrical, one-story structure offers on the outside a collection of plane surfaces with a rough texture of native fieldstone. The wood used in the frame is black-stained cypress, the white paneling is Marlite, and the flags for the court and entrance are bluestone. The house is accepting of all types of New England weather.

- There are historical references to Japanese residential architecture and European modernist symbolism in the house, albeit personalized. The first is related to the Japanese attitude toward interior and exterior space. With loving respect for material and detail, uncluttered interiors and sensitive interrelationships with its natural surroundings, Rand made an unpretentious, serene, but comfortable home. In all, it was the compatibility and natural dovetailing of all the elements that made it more than just a house – it made it a home. Not unlike the Japanese house, the Rand House embodies simplicity, serenity, and nature, again, not unlike the best ideals of the best of modernist architecture. The Edo ideals of purity, humility, and oneness with nature that captivated seminal practitioners like Frank Lloyd Wright and Alvar Aalto are evident in every aspect and object in the Rand House. The use of a central court in the Rand House has parallels in classic Japanese residential architecture such as the Katsura Palace, where inside and outside blend into one. This kind of inversion is most successful in the central courtyard looking into the living room and out into the rolling tree-covered back yard and the bordering creek.

- Like many who had been invited to the Rand House, I had first heard about it, imagined it, seen photographs, and anticipated the visit. I was not disappointed. I have since visited many times, each time finding it more a work of art, like the celebrated Eames house in southern California. It was in the autumn of 1954 when Yusaku Kamekura, Rand's Japanese contemporary and friend was invited to visit. He made the thirty-minute train ride from New York's Grand Central Station, observing the transition as the train passed through treeless, colorless, vertical structures, and compact spaces to wooded areas of birch, beech, and oak trees, with colonial-style homes here and there among the trees. The season's red, yellow, and orange foliage colored the area. He arrived at the Westport, Connecticut, station to be greeted by Paul Rand. Together, they arrived at the estate, and Kamekura noted that "having seen many photos of Mr. Rand's house in magazines, I felt I had been there before." He remarked that "the property sloped down to the south, looking mountain-like and beautiful. White trees imparted a translucence to the yellow and red leaves, a kind of wonderland. I could hear the birds singing. Mr. Rand told me the acreage of his property, but I could not comprehend its size. I was stunned as Mr. Rand gestured. It stretched from this tree to that marsh. The acreage was like our Shiga Plateau and Katsura put together. This house was designed with influence from Katsura Palace. From the large windows, black structure and window frames, and white walls, the feeling of Katsura was evident. Justly, it is indeed very fine modern residential architecture."

- Among the forces most instrumental in crystallizing the visual ideas and molding the attitudes and opinions of Paul Rand was de Stijl. Of all the abstract art movements, de Stijl was the most idealistic. Its form stemmed largely from Cubism and its theories from the writings of M.H.J. Schoenmaekers, whose book *The New Image of the World*, was their bible. This perhaps explains why de Stijl was an ethical as well as an aesthetic movement. The forms developed by the de Stijl movement are everywhere in everyday life, architecture, interior design, graphic design, and art. With de Stijl, Dutch artists and architects such as Piet Mondrian, Theo van Doesberg, Vantongerloo, Gerrit Rietveld, Van Hoff, and J.J.P. Oud made a considerable contribution to classical modernism.

- Like these artists and architects, Rand developed an informed and personal vocabulary of form. Rather than depicting a certain subject, he aimed at communicating with the viewer through subtle variations of a few elementary compositional principles, such as horizontal versus vertical, small versus large, light versus dark, and the three primary colors – red, yellow, and blue, and an extended secondary and tertiary palette influenced by the colors he observed in nature. With these limited means of composition, he achieved a staggering number of masterpieces. This interpretation of the vocabulary of form is what Paul Rand understood, adapted and used to stir up and sharpen our perception of the nuances of simple visual phenomena in visual communication.

- That all the ceilings in the Rand House are painted a medium gray, that all the walls are painted white, that the sides of the skylights are painted red (which casts beautiful light, depending on the time of day and season), that the doors and utility panels are painted red or yellow are a direct link to de Stijl. These experiments are as much a part of his built environment as they are of his visual communications work. Both the exterior and interior of the house present an unusual connection to the transitional and later paintings of one of his heroes, Mondrian. The juxtaposition of asymmetrically ordered black-stained cypress frames, clear glass, and white Marlite panels against the rough textures of native Connecticut fieldstone is reminiscent of Mondrian's Cubist *Tableau/Composition* paintings from 1912-15, and the abstract square and lozenge *Tableau/Composition* series from 1920-40.

- Characteristically, Paul Rand did not blindly absorb the Japanese and European modernist aesthetic traditions that informed and influenced him. He assessed and adapted what he knew to be the relevant aspects of these influences into designing his house, making a home and a work environment, making his work, and living a life he found meaningful and useful. It is the inherent sense of play, and simplicity, that characterize Rand's designs, and why they continue to live despite the changing styles and whims of fashion.

- In Paul Rand's visual thinking, the "what" of visual communication is not separate from the "how." A work of art or design, whatever its content, is an organic unity, a concrete structure in which the character of the whole influences the character of the parts. Every typeface applied to the design of a book, every dimensional material applied to architectural and environmental wayfinding, every visual entity, every typographic, illustrative, or photographic element, and even the planning and design of his home and work environment attains meaning and value in context: it is infected through and through by its relations with the other elements and the whole. This implies that the distinction between *form* and *content* (principles of de Stijl) is relative: the content is the elements in relation, the form is the relation among the elements, and the total is an irrefrangible unity.

"Visual thinking" (a term coined by Rudolph Arnheim and the title of his 1969 book, *Visual Thinking*) in the study of aesthetics, practice of art, design, and architecture is a way of storytelling, narration, expression, and communication that reflects comprehension of a wide array of pertinent signifiers and symbols. As a dialogue with the public, it records both the temporal and permanent moments of a culture, conveying meaning and expressing a society's values.

68: 69:

Tributes:

70: Gerald J. Gross
74: Sarah Kerstin Gross
76: Massimo Vignelli
78: Wolfgang Weingart
80: Ken Hiebert
84: Judy Metro
87: Nathan Garland
92: John Maeda
95: Diane Gromala
99: Armin Hofmann
101: Derek Birdsall
102: Georgette Ballance
106: Bob Burns
111: Kyle Cooper
116: Richard Sapper
117: Shigeo Fukuda
119: Philip Burton
123: Julie Klugman
125: Guenet Abraham
127: Naoko Matsuzono

Gerald J. Gross
In the Snow's Silence,
Paul…

- The time: shortly after World War II. The place: New York City. It was December and the city was covered by snowfall so heavy that cars were not to be seen on the streets. The night was lovely for walking, as my wife, Flora, and I trudged forth into the quiesescent snowscape from our Greenwich Village apartment. We had ambled a few blocks, sublimely comfortable in the absolute softness of the snowfall, when we happened to encounter a friend, Eugene Ettenberg, then owner of The Gallery Press, one of the better small print shops in the city. He was accompanied by a companion, and that was when we first met Paul Rand. Gene suggested that we retreat for suitable grog at his nearby apartment. Our discussions with Paul began that evening. They continued throughout the years, until Paul's death in Norwalk, Connecticut.

- Paul's companionship with Gene Ettenberg that first evening was an early example of the close relationships with printers that Paul sustained throughout his career. He valued components of true craftsmanship wherever he found them, and he knew how central the skills of the printer could be in attaining the very quality he demanded of himself as a graphic designer. It was no wonder that Paul was a bibliophile, concentrating on all aspects of the arts and society as they related to his work. Whether it was a first edition of Matisse's *Jazz,* or a new volume by Meyer Shapiro or Erich Fromm, Paul was a keen reader and a scrupulous collector.

- As such, we had both gravitated to the superbly chaotic art book store of Wittenborn & Schultz. In the years before we met Paul, Flora and I often emptied our meager wallets there for a new study of Grünewald or Klee. Robert Motherwell had also been a steady customer. He was able to offer financial support to George and Henry when they decided to publish the ground-breaking series *Documents of Modern Art.* George asked Flora to work on the series as production supervisor and associate editor. And he solicited Paul to produce all the stunning covers for the series. And so Flora began a working relationship with Paul, which developed into their close friendship over the years. The *Documents of Modern Art* stand as a perfect example of Paul's devotion to the content of the work that he was dealing with as graphic designer. Its only rival: his later work for the Bollingen Foundation. With an early interest in good printing, Paul was easily taken with the few book publishers whose volumes gave evidence of such concern. And in respecting the book imprint as he did, he dutifully accepted much lower fees from such sources than he would ever contemplate for commercial work in advertising or packaging.

- Since I was a publisher, Paul would often challenge me as to why certain books even saw the light of publishing day. "What a pile of junk!" could often be his laconic comment. After seeing the books that Paul had designed for Knopf, through our mutual friends Sidney Jacobs and Harry Ford, Flora brought Paul's work to the attention of her close friend Wolfgang Sauerlander of Pantheon Books. It was through Wolfgang that Paul began a thoroughly satisfying relationship with the Bollingen Foundation, for whom he designed about thirty book jackets over the years. That earlier volumes in the Bollingen series had jackets designed by E. McKnight Kauffer made the relationship with Bollingen that much more precious for Paul. Kauffer, like Jan Tschichold, had been one of Paul's formative graphic design heroes. Furthermore, the relationship with Bollingen was particularly satisfying for Paul because the Foundation's administrators, Jack Barrett and Vaun Gillmor, loved his work. Paul, in turn, was often contentedly entrapped by the exhaustive erudition of the Bollingen authors.

- It was a long jump from the distinction of the Bollingen work to the joyous and playful renderings of Paul's artwork in children's books. I still recall a day in Westport, Connecticut, when I met Paul at our favorite hangout, Gold's Delicatessen. His wife Ann had just given birth to Catherine, and Paul was very much the proud papa. Publisher that I was, I took our meeting as the perfect moment to suggest to Paul that he do a book for young children to mark the occasion of Catherine's birth. He shrugged off the idea. Then a few weeks later, he called to say that he had some drawings to show me. On seeing them, I brought the artwork to the attention of Margaret McElderry, the best children's book editor in the industry. She got in direct touch with Paul and, as was her wont, charmed him no end. After *I Know a Lot of Things*, Paul happily collaborated with Margaret on *Sparkle and Spin, Little 1,* and *Listen! Listen!* Ann provided all the texts.

- It was in the same period of the late fifties that a volume dedicated to Paul's work was first published in Japan. When I grew up in the thirties, Japanese products, poorly designed and junky in appearance, were a scourge on the international market. It may have been only after World War II that the Japanese recognized their business need for good design. Clearly, the varied austere qualities in Paul's work struck a sympathetic chord for Japanese sensibilities. Hideo Kobayashi was a young, aggressive publisher who published Paul's work in Japan.

- Given the interest there, he brought Paul to Japan for successful meetings and considerable adulation. As with so many other of his relationships, Paul and Hideo became good friends, with Paul staying in close touch with Hideo until Hideo's death.

- Early on in his career Paul was able to establish the fact that he was a high-ticket designer, a costly hire. His work never came cheap, and in later years I sometimes felt that Paul had earned more from his logo design for Steve Jobs's NeXT than Jobs gained from establishing the company.

- The seeming simplicity of that design, like so many others of Paul's, suggested simple solutions of minimum effort. Yet, as Paul so often made clear, the work evolved over weeks and months. I recall an evening at Paul's home and studio when he was working on the Jobs project. Sundry color panels were scattered over his rug as he engaged Flora in close discussion of certain color values. He had always admired Flora's sense of color, as he saw it come into play both in her dress and home. So, the final, absolutely right value of yellow was chosen there amidst banter and light argument.

- Steve Jobs had chosen Paul (after obtaining IBM's approval for the commission) because of Paul's memorable achievements in guiding IBM over the years. That association with IBM surely stands as an unmatched example of one individual's graphic design impact on a major international corporation. Paul not only gave IBM its everlasting logo. As its ranking graphic design consultant, he assumed the role of cicerone to the entire organization. He was often overseas, engaged in lectures and counsel with IBM staff throughout the world. And apart from handsome remuneration from IBM, Paul was blessed by his eventual marriage to one of IBM's senior executives, Marion Swannie, lifelong sentinel and inestimable helpmate.

- Paul had a deep appreciation of classical music. In the glory days of LPs he and I patronized the same eclectic record merchant. Located in a small well-stocked shop on West 43rd Street, just off Fifth Avenue, Will Lerner was a most knowledgeable enthusiast, quick to ascertain the compelling interests of his best customers. I can still recall the time when I entered his shop and he told me that I had just missed Paul, who had, an hour earlier, ordered the recently issued first complete set of the Bach cantatas, about forty LPs in all.

- These vignettes are but fragments of our relationship with Paul over the years. He was a Thanksgiving dinner member of our family. Later on, he brought Marion to our table. So close to our daughter, Sarah, Paul designed the logo gratis for her catering company (though he was happily paid back in food samples over the years). Always interested in architecture, he was a stern critic for our son, Adam, whose career and national presence is now established. And Paul was certain in urging Flora to return to the workplace when he supported her election as executive director of the American Institute of Graphic Arts in 1976.

- Finally, it is most appropriate to recall Paul's contribution as a teacher. The appointment to Yale University, thanks to Alvin Eisenman, meant a great deal to Paul. He cherished his relationships with his students and all that he was able to accomplish with them at Yale. The simplicity, directness, and sophistication of Paul's design forms brought forth an excitement and a certain sense of commonality not to be found in any designer of his time. His students – at Yale and at Brissago, Switzerland – were indeed the beneficiaries of that singular accomplishment.

Sarah Gross
I
Love
Paul Rand

- I love Paul Rand
- He is with me often, even in his absence. He is a part of me. When I was a little girl, Paul was always present at our Thanksgiving celebrations, which consisted not of immediate family members, but of our extended family of friends that my mother gathered together to celebrate thanks. That group of distinct individuals, artists, authors, book people – characters, everyone one of them – had a profound influence on my life. As a shy, quiet, fragile being, Paul always connected with me. He saw me no matter how silent and invisible I tended to be. That meant the world to me; to this day it does. So all pervasive was his essence: yet there was (it seemed miraculous) still room for me in his dynamic world. With his direct, authentic, cerebral presence, he gracefully affirmed my own sense of self.
- Our visits to Paul and Swannie were special too: the drive up to the house, the circle of brick imbedded in the center of the driveway, the rough natural landscape of the Weston woods out the big glass windows, the ambience of the entrance walkways, the continuity of the stone walls moving in and out of the house, the owl on the roof, the modern furniture, the tree in the middle of the patio, the striped painted door, the orange entrance rug, all the fixtures, the bathrooms, the blue striped dishes, the Klees, the Picassos, Paul's paintings, the library, the Pirelli floors, serious yet whimsical, with purpose. All the visuals…so key to Paul's life. I remember taking a drive with him in his black BMW. There was a black box on the dashboard. "What's that?" I asked – "A cover I made for the Kleenex," he said. Every aspect of Paul's surroundings was acknowledged…. They were in my own family environment too, and in turn for me now.
- My mother and Paul had a unique connection. He valued her opinion on color and vice versa. At times he was a champion for her as well. When you are overflowing with self-trust there is a generosity of spirit. This was so with Paul. My adult relationship with Paul began when I coyly asked him to design a logo for my catering business. I like purple, I told him, and I use a lot of cabbages in my work.
- Returning home from a cross country summer trip, there was a gruff, blunt message on my voice mail – "Your logo is done." In retrieving it, Paul spent time showing me the process of how he came to create it, that there was a face within the cabbage, a subtle hook – a smiley face… Who knew?… Always connect with something recognizable; there is a force generated by familiar repetition. And, "Your logo is only as good as you are," he told me…From then on, every time I stopped by to visit Paul, I learned. In our discussions he continually challenged my thinking by talking about

Mencken, Dewey, IBM, NeXT, Enron, warm bagels left at the foot of his bed when he was a child, his orthodox upbringing. Once I stopped by and he had just finished dovening – Jewish devotional prayer. On rare occasions he was so on my case, questioning my motives about something so directly that I cried – not unusual, I am told. But he was demanding of himself and in so doing he was demanding of all those around him, to be true, to be authentic. He hated the insincere. This is what Paul, with his thick black glasses, the squint of his eyes, the genuine hugs and kisses, pinching of cheeks, sweetie – he would endearingly call me, always mirrored back to me: Who are you? Be true to who you are and trust that. He was passionate about life, design, Judiasm, a continual learner, a voracious reader, a world traveler, and a profound mentor for me.

- I always loved buying Christmas presents for Paul, as he knew me the way I knew him. It was my way of acknowledging him, together with my annual Xmas cookie drop, continuing a tradition my mother had started. When my parents moved to Boston, those grand Thanksgivings as we knew them stopped. One year, I recreated Thanksgiving at my home with Paul and Swannie and my family. Paul and Swannie were a part of my family as we knew it to be. Swannie still is.

- The day Paul died, I got a phone call from Swannie that Paul was in the hospital. I was taken aback, I had no idea he had been ill and that he had been in the hospital for a week! I ran over there immediately. In his striped head cap, he was breathing laboriously. His daughter, Catherine, was there, and I relieved her so she could take a nap. I sat there for quite awhile and then went to Paul, gently hugged and kissed him, and whispered in his ear, "This is Sarah, Paul; this is all okay;…do not worry; if it is time to go, let go into the light; I will be there for Swannie; have a grand journey." Ten minutes later, Paul quietly passed over.

- I am gruff, I am direct, whimsical yet stern, I am demanding of myself and others, headstrong, authentic and present, color is key in my life, design integral, a continual learner. All of this, Paul mirrored back to me in his presence as being true. Paul is still with me and always will be a part of me. I love Paul Rand.

- I feel blessed to have shared this moment of transition with Paul, again affirming the profound connection I have with this significant being in my life. I am also grateful to have Swannie in my life now, to share memories and life as we know it to be in the present, with many moments of missing Paul and in getting to know Catherine and her family a bit more as an adult since our encounters long ago were brief and blurry. One night with Swannie, not too long ago, I went exploring through the house, noticing even more…. books on midrash and Steven Hawkins on his bedroom shelf, a chest full of everything he had gathered from Japan, full of tools, special stamps, paint brushes, odd puzzles, and photos, a drawer of incredible drawings done in the 1950s that are so wonderfully Paul. It was a special evening.

Massimo Vignelli
Paul Rand...
Design Itself

- To me, Paul Rand is the most important American graphic designer of the twentieth century. No one has developed the language of design, set its grammar, articulated the syntaxes, and reached poetry better than he. His incredible sense of appropriateness and lucidity of mind have signaled to generations the boundaries within which one designer can and should operate, beyond which uselessness, mediocrity, and vulgarity quite often make the turf.
- He made the term "commercial artist" obsolete and elevated it to "graphic designer." As an art director, he transcended the grossness of the advertising hard sell into a responsive beacon of cultural involvement. As a teacher, he moved designers and corporations to new levels of intellectual elegance never attained before. Nobody in the whole century achieved such results or had more impact on the design profession.
- Paul Rand was not a designer; he was design itself. From the forties on, his influence became worldwide, and we find traces of his impact on the work of graphic designers in many countries. His sense of purpose, the directness of his message, the elegance of his compositions, and the lucid freshness of his wit became benchmarks against which designers the world over were measuring their work.
- Modernism came to the U.S. the only way Americans could understand it: as a style. Europe, by contrast, is a continent intellectually nourished by a continuous refinement of philosophies, where continuity means development of basic truths (or assumptions) inherited from the past. In Europe, modernism was not a style. It was a movement: an intellectual, cultural, and socially responsible attitude with an operational methodology to investigate and solve problems of any nature.
- Modernism, as imported and divulged by Philip Johnson and Henry Russell-Hitchcock in their legendary 1931 exhibition at MoMA in New York, was basically presented as a style, devoid of its cultural content and social implications. It was a style that followed Art Deco, as Art Deco had followed Beaux Arts, and so on throughout history. It should be no surprise that the same person who introduced the international style (as the modern movement had been renamed to make it more accessible to a capitalist culture) in later years replaced it with a new style called postmodernism, to be replaced a few years later by deconstructivism, and later on by neomodernism, etc.

- Style, like fashion, is a commodity in a consumerist society based on obsolescence: exciting, consumable, and disposable after use. In America, a country developed by the desire and continuous anxiety for newness and diversity, there is neither room nor time for commitments besides change. And change can have its own rewards: liveliness, vitality, and fame, ephemeral as they may be.
- Paul Rand embraced modernism and understood the social mission imbedded in its philosophy. Design is a tool to bring quality of life where crass greed has been before. Advertising, if well designed, can sell just as well. White space is no longer wasted space; copy can be as concise as the images. Impact is aimed at the brain rather than the crotch. Type is elegant, classical or modern, or is handwritten, according to the intent of the message. There is a new semiotic set of values coming to fruition, even before any theory is formulated about it. In Paul Rand's work, modernism is not a style but an attitude: a way of being, an integral part of a poetic mission, a message to the world.
- Rand was also extremely well read. His readings were cultured, not erratic, and focused to achieve a quality in his writing that underscored content. His writings were thus precise, concise, and to the point. No wonder he grew intolerant of mediocrity and superficiality. He knew better than anybody else the struggle for quality, depth, strength, and timelessness. He had no time to waste: life is too short to accomplish one's agenda. At eighty-two, he was about to start a new book before he died. I miss that book.

Wolfgang Weingart
Aphorisms
about
Paul Rand

- In 1968 I started teaching typography at the Basel School of Design, in Switzerland. Paul Rand came once with Armin Hofmann. Down in the basement of the darkroom of the lithography department, I felt honored to meet with an internationally known design personality, from a country that, I thought, had skyscrapers in every village.
- The handshake ritual was combined with a question: "Is this the crazy Weingart, Armin?" I was twenty-seven, and only a few insiders knew me as the "crazy man," but Paul Rand knew everything, all the insiders' secrets.
- Over the next twenty-three years I met students during the Yale Summer Program in Graphic Design, in Brissago, Switzerland. Everyone had a story about their teacher Paul Rand. Since the stories were often quite contradictory, I became more and more intrigued with this unique, mysterious person.
- Philip Burton, one of my first students at the Basel School of Design, was teaching typography and graphic design at Yale, and so, in April 1986, I had the opportunity to teach for a week there, the first-year class. Paul Rand could not attend my opening lecture. Driving his car was becoming an increasing problem because of his eyes.
- But then Burton received a surprising invitation: we were both asked to Rand's house in Weston, Connecticut – which he designed and worked on from 1952 until his death – to give him and his wife Marion a private lecture. The evening was combined with a wonderful dinner, and over the course of the evening all of the stories that I had in my mind about the Rand family became irrelevant. We began a friendship that lasted until November 1996, when he died in Norwalk, near his quiet home surrounded by tall trees.
- We met regularly in the United States or in Switzerland. During his few visits to Basel, we were twice able to take the opportunity to invite him to our school, to bring him and Marion together with my students in the typography classes. These events were highlighted by his intelligent and humorous lectures.
- Through the years we discovered a common love of children's books. Between 1956 and 1970, he illustrated and designed four books for the legendary children's book editor Margaret McEldery at Harcourt Brace and World: *I Know A Lot of Things, Sparkle and Spin, Little 1,* and *Listen! Listen!* The text was always written by his second wife, Ann. I was also creating children's

books, for children in Jordan and Pakistan.
- Tom Bluhm, a student and friend of Paul Rand's for many years, would sometimes visit with me. He would bring me some of the materials that Rand wrote and designed as presentation booklets for different companies. One of the booklets described the development of the logo for Steven Jobs's new company, NeXT Computer, in Palo Alto, California. In these he helped the companies understand his research into different typefaces and their transformation into the definitive mark. I was always impressed with how clear, concise, and complete his explanations were. Even with my bad English, I could understand every sentence.
- Paul Rand was for me one of the strongest, most important warning voices about the future of design and the world we inhabit. His attitude was honest and direct. I believed in what he had to say, and we shared many opinions. He delivered his last lecture (organized by John Maeda) in early November at the Massachusetts Institute of Technology. His lucid and relevant delivery in the packed auditorium was about form and content in art and design, the focus of his last book, *From Lascaux to Brooklyn* (1996).

Ken Hiebert
Perpetual
Modernism

- We thought a lot alike.
  He said once, "We think so much alike it scares me."
- Our friendship stemmed from what we came to share as ideals.
- I was a novice printer-photographer-designer when, in the early fifties, the revolutionary work of Paul Rand penetrated to the Midwest and to my own inner reaches. By the mid-sixties, when I had the great privilege (and burden) of collaborating in developing Rand's identity programs at both Westinghouse and IBM, we had each undergone transformations. I had made my way through the schooling of Armin Hofmann, Emil Ruder, and the Basel milieu; Paul had made his way through the self-schooling that was his mode and forte. In evolving the IBM identity, he had been drawn irrevocably into the world of corporate identity, one of the least ephemeral in graphic design. On the way, designing the books in the Pantheon series seemed to gel the cuteness of the previous handwritten titles into durable and solid, crystal clear typography. Geometry, the most durable of forms, became increasingly the inarguable base. "How can you argue with geometry?" The keen interest in European modernist design and Japanese sensitivity for nature extended to the latest in structural foundations for this design, for grids and systems, and for the pure shape of information itself. The semiotic clarity required had long been Rand's hallmark.
- We met then as individuals who had gone through their own refining fires, I becoming the foil for his restless inquisitiveness and doubts about systems.
- While systems were a serious interest, the artist was at work in all of it: a singular point of view, a process that sought feedback among the visually unschooled (where an honest spontaneous reaction could be expected), knowing for the client what would be best and presenting it as *fait accompli*. When patience with the detail and intricacies of systems was exhausted, the artist superseded. In the mid-nineties, not feeling at home at a party dominated by computer talk, he asked me (rhetorically), "What is all this stuff about graphic design? That's not what I am – I'm a commercial artist." I cringed. What else, after our battle as educators for respectability as designers? But Paul had nothing to lose and was not afraid to say that his sense of art – observation, reflection, play, invention beyond cliché, the work of the hand, and a place in the grand scheme of cultural history – was what was missing these days. Nor was he afraid to voice his commitment

to giving form to the products of commerce. *There* was the possibility of touching the most lives and adding quality and value to them.
- Ideals: In about 1965, he created a poster for Westinghouse titled "Quality." There was nothing presumptuous about the treatment of the word. Stencil-derived letters, playfully arranged, anything but pompous, followed by a declaration of quality as separate from something defined by canons of taste or status, but rather as something felt.
- A second paragraph defined quality as concerned with proportion, the discovery of analogy and contrast, and the transformation and enrichment of the relationship of formal and functional elements.
Who could disagree?
But a third paragraph polarized the ideal against the typical:
"Quality is concerned –
with truth, not deception
with ideas, not techniques
with the enduring, not the ephemeral
with precision, not fussiness
with simplicity, not vacuity
with subtlety, not blatancy
with sensitivity, not sentimentality."
The beauty of this poetic list is that it requires no elucidation. Like most of Rand's writing, it is unveiled, crystal clear. Yet the ostensible clarity hides the subjective judgment it presupposes.
- In an era when graphics of identity are made arbitrarily seductive, cast in a roiling sea of motion, made elusive by distortion, diminished by congestion, their ephemeral entertainment value paramount, they beg evaluation by Paul Rand's standards. But make them hold still, the poverty of insignificance is soon revealed. The feature of visual form-field interaction that can lift the elements of our everyday world to where they join with those that through time had a socially beneficial effect loses out to sensational motion.
- Is his mission to see things for their aesthetic potential at the level of the common and ordinary (as befits a Brooklynite who never lost the brash outward character of the streetwise while his world opened to the treasures not bounded by epochs of time – whether Lascaux, Klee, or the beautiful machinery he saw printing the "god-awful" products of consumerist culture) lost on us? Or has it, against all good intentions, like most artifact products of modernism, become elitist and distant? Or, in fact, has the pioneering

spirit of Rand infused our world with a new consciousness and sense of the value of design? All of these?

- Though the world of commerce embraces design as never before, the products mostly fill the gap of the empty self with prefabricated taste and meaning. Rand found a way to challenge us to assemble and make sense of form, where figure and ground are of equal dynamic significance. The authenticity-seeker retreats to the homely, the coincidental, or to kitsch – to the reality of impurity, both high and low, missing the world of the essential and simple, where the object enhances the sense and depth of self.

- This was Paul Rand's world, and it was increasingly an isolated one. His tenacious defense of the validity of his hard-won point of view was both understandable but also, in its dogmatic certitude, understandably seen as irrelevant.

- Complexity is a new order of things; the ephemeral is a way of life; techniques reign; emptiness, a lack of civility in manners and language, and now sentimentality and retro attitudes flourish. How should quality look, sifted from this tumultuous present? Time will tell; Rand at the end could hardly bear to look at the new realities.

- If I use great music as a measure, to help remove me from the ideological wars, then I see that music is a rhythm of concealing *and* revealing, of technique *and* idea, of the momentary *and* the extended, of intricacy *and* broad strokes, of simplicity, complexity, *and* silence, subtlety *and* blatancy, sensitivity *and* sentimentality, each ascendant over time or layering contrapuntally in ways to give meaning to the other. The either/or third paragraph of the "quality" definition makes no allowance for the expression of these opposing qualities. The first two paragraphs give us the latitude we need. Whether as a manifestation of his discomfort with the last paragraph or simply in the interest of brevity, his later poster defining quality for IBM dated 1990 keeps only the first paragraph with its nondogmatic stance, separating quality from status and depending on an intuitively found and felt image. And reading his tribute to the work of Wolfgang Weingart in Weingart's *My Way to Typography,* Rand had in the end come to tolerate a lot that one might have expected him to reject. Emerson's quote "perpetual modernness is the measure of merit in every work of art" was my choice as maxim for my book *Graphic Design Sources*. While polishing my manuscript, Rand's *From Lascaux to Brooklyn* went to press. Our thoughts had run along the same lines again: Emerson's quote was Rand's choice for a leitmotiv. In deference, I folded it into the text. The proportion was right. The giant deserved it. Upside down and in gray, as a complement to Emerson, is Rand's own statement, "(with few exceptions) there's no such thing as bad content, only bad form." The unstated corollary is that content permits the nature of form, and there will always be a good form possibility for any content. The changing nature of content constantly refreshes form.

- Truth, not deception; ideas, not techniques…
The test was hard to pass. The last poster of mine that he saw, he characterized as typographic trickery. "But Paul, it's true to the content." "Maybe so, but it's not a poster. I couldn't even hang it in my bathroom." The subject of the poster was the button-pressing world of the internet. Someone else would have to find the perpetual modernity of it all.

Judy Metro
Editing
Paul Rand

- I navigated up the hairpin drive at 87 Goodhill Road to find Paul Rand at the top with his back to me. He gestured to the place I should park but went right back to his chore, which turned out to be removing the blossoms on his rhododendron bush. "I'm not a gardener," I said, "but I never saw anyone pull off the blossoms." (I didn't say, With or without such a vengeance.) "Is that going to make it flower double-time next season?"
- He gave a look that made me droop. "It better not. I bought this bush because the flowers were supposed to be white, and they turn out to be purple, which looks terrible against the house. Ruins the whole effect, every year." Wow, I thought. A nipper in the bud.[1]
- I paid this call in the mid-1980s, at the outset of my experience as the editor of three books that Paul published with Yale University Press: *Paul Rand: A Designer's Art* (1985), itself a long-awaited sequel to and reworking of his wonderful 1946 book, *Thoughts on Design*; *Design, Form, and Chaos* (1993); and *From Lascaux to Brooklyn* (1996). Having just read *Thoughts on Design,* I knew Paul was not inclined to offer readers casual or random observations in a take-it-or-leave-it fashion; no, these thoughts on design were careful, deliberate pronouncements intended to stir discussion and debate. Here was a designer who, like most, knew what he liked and didn't, but who also – enviably, it seemed to me – knew what was good and what wasn't. Not incidentally, he was an eloquent writer. The way he composed his thoughts on paper seemed to matter as much to him as how he made things look. And if he color-corrected his house and garden, I thought uneasily that day, what might he do to preserve his parts of speech – and what exactly was my role as his editor?
- I can't say Paul put me at ease. But he did at least indicate in that first meeting that he wanted my help. The project he was abo*ut* to hand over was a mosaic, the pieces of which hadn't found a pattern. My job was to unlock the pattern, which I did satisfactorily, and then to order and edit the parts. Never did my pencil touch a page of manuscript, or even see one! (I'm sure it would have been handwritten, yellow, and legal-sized.) All the editing was performed on typeset galleys, which shuttled like shoreline commuters between me and Paul, then between Paul and Mario Rampone in New York, and then back to me in New Haven – every time either one of us made changes.

- In the publishing ranks we were trained to make changes only while they were free (i.e., *before* typesetting), so this was the closest I'd come to wearing white gloves to work. Meanwhile Paul's attentive and positive response to the substantive editing, and even to the more mundane matters of style and usage, was also taking me by surprise. As Mario produced galley after galley with my changes and Paul's responses, then Paul's new ideas and my responses, it dawned on me that this was teamwork, and that we were both enjoying it. Paul was interested, relaxed, and truly respectful of the editorial process. That particular and rare combination made him a pleasure to edit.

- Paul's first book was not only an important landmark in my life but in the annals of Yale University Press as well. We were enormously excited about adding Paul's book to the Yale list, although in another case we might have thought of it as "an orphan," a publisher's term for a book with no companion list. Instead we knew a book by Paul Rand would be a strong enough entry on its own to give us distinction in the field of graphic design. And indeed it did. *A Designer's Art* received a front-page review in the *New York Times Book Review,* Yale's first in more than a decade, and sold out of its first printing in record time. Moreover, it spawned other design books – by Bradbury Thompson, Herman Zapf, and others – and ushered in a list that reflected the formidable tradition of graphic design at the Yale School of Art.

- Paul Rand knew instinctively about the relevance of design not only to other forms of communication but to ordinary life, and he of course wrote about this. The rules and tools he took to work every day – line, harmony, color, composition, artful tension, asymmetry, humor, balance, tone, juxtaposition – all have their analog in language, and when I worked with Paul, I felt we were working from the same toolbox toward the same goal. This strikes me now as very generous on Paul's part, especially when I think of the many who consider editing a service one employs simply to avoid embarrassment. It wasn't until I came across the following passage in *Design, Form, and Chaos* that I fully understood why a line, skillfully drawn or uttered, had equal weight for Paul Rand.

- "Ideas are the lifeblood of any form of meaningful communication. But good ideas are obstinate and have a way of materializing only when and where they choose – in the shower or subway, in the morning or middle of the night. As if this weren't enough, an infinite number of people…must scrutinize and pass on the designer's ideas. Most of these people, in management or otherwise, have no design background. They are not professionals who have the credentials to approve or disapprove the work of the professional designer, yet of course they do. There are the rare exceptions – lay people who have an instinctive sense for design. Interestingly, these same people leave design to the experts."[2]

- I realized that Paul himself was in the category of the very few designers with an instinctive sense for language, and that his willingness to trust his editors, to leave his language in our hands, was his way of practicing what he preached. So while I set out to edit Paul Rand with trepidation, I wound up editing Paul Rand with Paul.

Editing Paul Rand: Metro

1. Here family historians would remind me that the pleasure was mitigated by Paul's impatience in other areas. It was well known that Paul suffered no fools, nor waited patiently for return calls. I can still picture my pie-eyed young children running into the room to tell me that I had another "loud message" on the machine from Paul Rand. What courage they thought I possessed when I called him back instead of quitting my job. I'm sure Paul Rand deserves some of the credit for instilling in my daughters – one a firefighter and the other a political activist – the notion that every worthwhile job includes some hazardous duty.
2. *Design, Form, and Chaos* (New Haven and London, 1993), p. 19.

...It was the achievement of one individual which brought the Glass Bead Game almost in one leap to an awareness of its potentialities...

...Above all, however, the Magister had to keep strict watch over the further elaboration of the Game...

The Glass Bead Game (Magister Ludi) by Hermann Hesse

Nathan Garland
Homage to
Paul Rand:
Peeks Behind a
Wizard's Curtain

- Paul Rand's stature as a designer, teacher, and original thinker speaks for itself. It was my good fortune to have him as a mentor and friend, which exposed me to his thinking and persona. These recollections are meant to add further dimension to what is known about him. He urged me to write. Finally, I am. Paul was tough, uncompromising, and outspokenly honest. He also had great charm, a wonderful sense of humor, and was very generous. His bigger-than-life personality and charisma were both captivating and intimidating as he stuck to his authoritative commitment to principle. He was also surprisingly available. I came to Yale as a graduate student primarily to study with Paul, but was surprised to find he was on leave. He visited once, the last day of Armin Hofmann's class. Soon after, I called him, introduced myself, and saw him for several crits. While I had a rich experience at Yale, I always felt cheated at not having experienced Paul's class. Years later, at John Hill's suggestion, I called Paul again. He remembered me and invited me to visit and show him some recent work. I did, and was devastated. He tore the work to hell. I listened, asked questions, and learned. I respectfully absorbed the verbal zaps, and just when I thought I was about to be vaporized, Paul began to reveal what he liked in my work. We talked for several more hours, and before I left, he said I could return whenever I wanted. I came back frequently, and we often joked that my visits more than made up for his being on leave.
- We met for lunch two to four times a month for many years until he died. During those several-hour-long visits we would show each other work in progress and talk. Being curious generalists and avid readers reinforced our common bond. We always had a lot to talk about – including art history and theory as well as design. We frequently referred to Arnheim, Dewey, Gombrich, Panofsky, and Wohringer, among others. Paul's insights about our work frequently dealt with formal concerns such as proportion, scale, placement, and the grid – but above all, germinating the key idea. He generously urged me to call or send him a fax if I ever got stuck on a project. Since I ultimately had to

decide what final form my work would take, however, sparks could fly. During one visit he criticized the jacket that I designed for *In the Camps,* a book by our photographer friend Erich Hartmann, as being inappropriately bold. I defended it and explained that I had also done a modest, restrained version. Erich, Jim Mairs, the editor, and I all preferred the bold one. He called me two days later to say that he was still upset at my defense and said it reminded him of a dissenting reply he made to Amedée Ozenfant, the modernist pioneer, once when they were riding in a New York taxi with Sigfried Giedion, the architectural historian. Ozenfant, whom Paul admired, was so incensed that he tried to turn around and punch Paul from the front seat.

- He asked me to read the latest chapter in progress of each of his last three books and comment on the draft at hand. I was glad to be a sounding board or devil's advocate and bear witness to the workings of a brilliant mind. His writing developed like his work through a process of rigorous, meticulous revision. He wanted to get it right and was honored that William Zinsser, in his book *Writing to Learn,* included an excerpt on the use of stripes in the IBM logo from *Paul Rand: A Designer's Art.*

- I relished the visits. One-on-one with Paul was intimate, intense, and endlessly challenging. I often left feeling exhilarated by what I had learned, but also exhausted by the pace and depth of the penetrating discourse. Responsibility was key. Everything was on the record. I was held responsible for everything I showed and said.

- The conversations were wide-ranging and idea-driven. My comments were scrutinized like my work. If I did not reply quickly enough to a question, Paul would slowly say, "You're awfully quiet." If Paul questioned my word choice and subsequent definition of a word, he would pop up from his chair and grab a dictionary to check it out. Words fascinated him. His favorites included "apodictic" (clearly proven or demonstrated; incontestable) and "facture" (the manner in which something, such as an artistic work, is made: execution). Paul's work ethic was defined by intense curiosity, concentration and passion together with a childlike sense of wonder and play. He would constantly switch from the intuitive to the analytical. He wholeheartedly believed Louis Pasteur's dictum that chance favored the prepared mind.

Paul's design of a logo for the Connecticut Art Directors Club was an appropriate homage to both letterforms and symbols. The familiar acronym CADC was varied by substituting the playing card "club" sign as a rebus in place of the last letter. In order to avoid reading CAD, the misleading word made by the remaining three letters, he arranged the four elements in two rows of two each, which also made a simple square. This was reinforced by diagonally alternating two colors—solid black for the C and the club sign and red (or grey screen of black) for the A and the D. Finally, it was approved by the Board and used.

- Paul read widely to learn what others knew and wrote to crystallize his own thinking. He wanted to be aware of what others were doing, and he worked obsessively to meet his own high standards.
- One fascinating ritual that occurred at many of my visits was the "logo challenge." This was when Paul would use a kind of Socratic case-study method to teach me. If he had just designed a new logo, he would tell me the client's name, briefly describe what the organization did, and then expect me to draw his solution on any paper napkin or placemat that might be handy. I had to think fast. I learned a great deal, but I could never "win," i.e., please Paul. It seemed that if I came close to his design, he would be disappointed that his idea was not more elusive, while if I did not come close to his solution, he would be critical of me. As the pattern of his responses became clear, I would try to come close, but not too close. This demanding, time-sensitive, and complex game of graphic chess was similar to what Paul would often challenge himself to do. When called and first asked to design a logo, he would attempt to come up with the basic idea for the design *before the phone conversation was over.* He relished the degree of difficulty that this added to the problem. It sharpened his wits and his skill and reinforced his sense of play and competition with himself.
- Paul's interest in solving design challenges included many pro bono projects. One occurred in 1986, when I was on the board of the Connecticut Art Directors Club (CADC) and it was unable to select a logo from the designs submitted by members in an open competition. Several submissions had interesting aspects, but none attracted wide support. I suggested that Paul might solve the club's problem and offered to ask him to design a logo for the club. The board authorized me to go ahead. So I asked Paul, who agreed on condition that I oversee the application of his design. He was engaged, in part, by the fact that others had tried and failed. He enjoyed the role of relief pitcher throughout his career. Several weeks later he called to say that he had it. Without having seen the earlier attempts, Paul had remarkably expressed several of the best ideas and combined them in one resolved configuration. If considered to do a logo, but not retained, he would solve it anyway and save it … just for the practice. He urged me to do the same and also to follow his example of presenting every new logo or identity program in a document that included a written text

that explained the evolutionary thinking behind the design. Paul published many of his in a reduced format as chapters in his books.

- Paul often suggested that one way to solve graphic problems was to "defamiliarize the ordinary." He also put it this way: since a cliché has power by its universality, if used in a fresh and appropriate manner it can lead to a provocative and meaningful result. Much of his work juxtaposes relevant yet disparate elements in a new way that generates surprise, interest, and clarity at a glance.

- While Paul's opinions were clear, some have been misunderstood and misrepresented. One glaring myth that persists is his thinking about computers. He was not anti-computer. He was pro-design. Paul valued the computer as a glorious tool mostly for its precision, speed, and memory, but felt students often used it too soon – before they learned certain fundamentals of design and typography. He was concerned that it distracted students, teachers – and sometimes practitioners – from focusing on ideas, problem-solving and "quality," his all-encompassing obsession. As Paul wrote, "The tangibles of computer technology are obviously easier to cope with than the intangibles of design."[1]

- I am one of many younger designers Paul helped. He was constantly in demand, yet still found time for us. Requests for his opinions, examples of his work, and lectures were ongoing. But he answered his own phone and, time permitting, every serious inquiry was considered. Work came first and he would not suffer fools. He demanded respect for the wisdom and experience of an elder, as well as a basic understanding of the issues at hand. If those unspoken requirements were met, he would often honor the request. For the first few years of our long lunch visits, I felt the need to pose questions and issues that would engage Paul and sustain our relationship. Then, one day, Paul said to call him sometime when I didn't need anything. I was startled at first, but realized that we had become friends.

1. *Design, Form, and Chaos* (New Haven and London, 1993), p. 179 – 87.

Postscript

None of us could presume to speak for Paul. His work and his writing represent him best. However, his legacy has been generously memorialized and preserved by his widow, Marion Swannie Rand, in several major gifts to Yale University, where he taught for so many years. His correspondence, job bags, miscellaneous files, printed samples, and a traveling exhibition of his work, among other items, are held in Manuscripts and Archives at Sterling Memorial Library. Several hundred books that represent his primary areas of interest were carefully selected from the thousands in his personal library to form the Paul Rand Collection in The Arts of the Book Room, also in Sterling. Many of his books on color were given to Yale's Art and Architecture Library. In addition, Marion made a substantial contribution to fund part of the renovation of the building that now contains Yale's School of Art. The plaque in that area identifies it as The Paul Rand Center for Graphic Design.

John Maeda
Paul Rand
Mentor

- As a youth I was known by my teachers to be gifted at drawing and mathematics. Aware of a potential future conflict, my parents made a conscious effort to sway my interests away from the arts. "How will you support your future family?" they would continually ask me, from elementary school all the way through high school. Naturally I responded to their cries, being the responsible person that I have always tried to be, and I went to Massachusetts Institute of Technology to study computer technologies. There would have been a sad ending if it weren't for a simple fact. In 1984, the year I was admitted to Massachusetts Institute of Technology, the computer was heralded as no longer a text-driven machine, but an inherently graphical one. A new canvas suddenly awaited manipulation by a new generation.

- The launch of the icon-laden Macintosh computer fueled a hunger for graphical attention to type, symbols, and eventually color on the Massachusetts Institute of Technology campus. I was fortunately at the right time with the right skills to be able to address an endless need for visual custodial work on the computer screen. All of my skills were acquired informally, carpentry through my carpenter grandfather, Japanese food preparation with my chef father, and calligraphy and origami as hobbies. I believe I was in my third year when somebody told me to study design. "Design? What's that?" I thought. I began to look for books in this area, starting with technique books and annuals, a nice book on Herb Lubalin, but nothing that I could really identify with. It was in my senior year, when I was taking an architecture course, that I stumbled upon a small book lying on a counter in the library, *Thoughts on Design* by Paul Rand. I was immediately humbled by the masterful manipulation of space and meaning, coupled with simple prose, that carried a consistent sense of honesty and truth. I immediately found my direction. Eight years later, I was at Mr. Rand's house around lunchtime. "Do you want mustard on your sandwich?" He paused and looked at me for a bit, then looked away and said in a gruff tone, "You know, I don't make sandwiches for just anybody, so you better like it." Through the introduction of a mutual friend, I had arrived in the morning from Japan en route to an interview at Massachusetts Institute of Technology. From the moment I stepped through the door, I was immediately thrust into the position of finishing some of the mechanicals for his last book, *From Lascaux to Brooklyn.* I was concerned with one of the rags and remembered making a point, "Uh, maybe you want to adjust this." To which he quickly retorted, "If I say it is right, then it is right! Don't touch it. It is perfect. Do you understand me?" What else could one reply but, "Yes." I dutifully labored away and after all the additions were in place, he said to me in a very solemn voice, "Do you know the secret to creating work you can be proud of?" I of course awaited his answer with great anticipation. "Money." I raised my eyebrows. He raised his eyebrows. "Money?" I asked in pure disillusionment. At this point my disillusionment had peaked. I thought to myself, "Have I spent the last eight years in the graphic arts in tribute to this grumpy tyrannical man in error?" "Yes, money." Rand asserted. My immediate instinct was that it was time to pack up and leave, but then Rand added, "Without investing my own money, I cannot make this book at the level of quality that I desire. The publisher does not provide a worthwhile budget to create a great book. Therefore I used over a hundred thousand dollars of my own money in the production of this book. All projects require that you have some level of financial freedom, otherwise the creative choices cannot be your own." I was more than satisfied with this most primitive piece of advice that I see at the heart of all that Rand espoused as a clear sense of morality, pragmatism, and underlying everything – idealism.

- I then began to notice other things. Marion Rand constantly coming over to stand in mutual embrace with Rand. His offer of one his posters, which he volunteered to sign and said, "It's worth five hundred dollars signed." (And the humor in noticing that he had already signed it for someone else in lighter ink.) Finally when it was time to go home, I asked to borrow their phone to call a taxi, to which he replied, "You gave me something today, now I will give you something back – a ride to the train station."

- Approximately a half-year later I accepted a position at Massachusetts Institute of Technology, and the first thing I did was invite Rand to speak at the Media Lab. He spoke to an overflowing auditorium about his various escapades, inspirations, and philosophies. After the lecture we got into the car, and he said in a gruff tone, "Step on it!" All the way to Connecticut I could see Mr. and Mrs. Rand lovingly holding hands. A few weeks later, Paul Rand passed away. The shock was amplified by the fact that I was in the midst of finishing the paperwork for Rand to join the faculty at the Massachusetts Institute of Technology Media Lab. I lost all my bearings until, a few months later, like all of us influenced by Rand, I dusted myself off and resolved to take on the world to do something that would make him proud.

Mentor: Maeda

Diane Gromala
The
Trouble
with Rand

You can only start out by being straightforward and honest.[1]

- At the end of what seemed my two-year internment in the graduate program in graphic design at Yale, the last thing I wanted to do was to study with (or "under," presumably) Paul Rand.
- The waning years of the 1980s also marked the end of an era in the program, convulsing as it was in the death throes of its rigid modernist orientation, or so it seemed to me. But I went to Yale anyway, precisely because of the other classes I could take, a back door in. While other units on campus scintillated with deliberations of postmodernism and poststructuralism, the design department remained disengaged with those ideas, and failed to tolerate what became my rather ungenerous and impatient quest for new ways to understand design beyond the strictly formalist enterprise and the cult of personality. I looked forward to having Rand as an instructor as I looked forward to a root canal.
- Paul Rand did not go gently into the night. Near the end of his life, Rand seemed to fear he had become irrelevant and forgotten. Visits to his home by those interested in his work became less frequent, a new generation of designers seemed to reject his ideas in the name of postmodern theory, and he was embroiled in a dispute about the new leadership in the design program at Yale. Yet, I would argue, this is evidence not of his loss of relevance, but a clear indication of his significance. It also reveals the extent to which we in the field of graphic design have not scrutinized the recondite ways in which we are (and postmodernism is) enmeshed in modernity, and the multitudinous ways in which our field and our work operates.

Thank God for people who do awful things.
It gives me something to say.
Every time you put something down, something happens.[2]

- **The trouble with canonization**
In order to survive one more semester, I focussed my attentions on the dark, soft underbelly of the program, its faculty and its attendant cultural regime. I intended to bear witness to the person who inspired a climate of fear and veneration among students. Rumor had it Rand was irascible, notorious for rigor, impatient with anything less than perfection in form, and exhibited behavior that was decidedly not politically correct. The unspoken pedagogical approach was mentoring in the old, patriarchal, European sense, but without the attendant noblesse oblige.

- To maintain a sense of perspective, I created a votive candle, replacing the face of Jesus with Rand's. Rand's image, I discovered, was carefully calculated and supervised – it was a challenge to find any frontal views of him.
- Paul Rand's eminence in the field of graphic design is indisputable. Canonized as the father of postwar corporate graphic design in America, his work is highly visible in design books and journals. But unlike so much design that exists more in design journals than "out there," Rand's work still functions on an everyday level of the American – and now global – landscape. Through these vehicles and numerous hagiographies, girded by his own cantankerous reactions, Rand reassured those who prefer the comfort of orthodox ideas, and posed the perfect foil for postmodern discussion and debate. He had become an icon of modernist ideas of design.
- In a positive sense, Paul Rand became a lighting rod for generating discussion and discourse in a field badly in need of it. Rand's modernist notions of timeless and universal design, his idea that design intensifies a coherent meaning that can and should be self-evident, and his insistence that design was intentionality, for instance, were called into question. Likewise, his formal innovations had become, to some, official design culture, and thus what some designers react against. Through these exchanges, Rand and his "opponents" were linking critical energies to chart future directions of discipline. In a negative sense, however, these discussions polarized into uncomplicated, black-and-white disputes. The nuance of Rand's thinking, the man as a complex figure, and the possibility that a reexamination of his ideas might be useful for discourses of contemporary design became lost.

There are no rules about these things. Rules are dangerous things.

If you have to question something, why did you do this, it's always suspect.[3]

The trouble with theory

- On the day of my final critique, I went up the stairs as if to the gallows. Sitting at the table, Rand seemed impatient, bored, looking for all the world like a garage mechanic, a figure for black-and-white television. He responded to my work with an inscrutable gaze, assessing me, it seemed, as much as my work. My design experiments and "critical interventions," to this point, were dismal failures. But Rand listened with respectful, if grudging, silence to explanations of

Unless otherwise specified, all quotes from Paul Rand are from a recording taken during class on April 6, 1990, at Yale University.

1. Alvin Eisenman, quoting Paul Rand from his first class teaching at Yale University. Founder of the graduate program in graphic design, Eisenman retired in 1990 after forty years. His retirement signalled a change of leadership and direction of the program.
2. Ibid.
3. Among numerous books: Philip B. Meggs, *A History of Graphic Design*, third edition, New York: John Wiley & Sons, Inc., 1998, pp.337-39.
4. Amadee Ozenfant and Charles Edouard Jeanneret (Le Corbusier), *On the Plastic in Art: An Examination of the Primordial Conditions*, Paris: L'Esprit Nouveau, 1920.
5. Unlike other fields and practices, such as architecture, graphic design lacks a rigorous engagement with theoretical concerns that extend beyond formalist discussions. As an object of study, works of graphic design are all too often absent, falling between the cracks of art history, media studies, and visual culture. This is, most probably, the result of analysts in these fields, but also the result of graphic designers themselves who often fail to engage with and insert themselves into larger discursive realms. There are however, notable and sustained exceptions.

why I used images from Mapplethorpe and prehistoric peoples as a counterpoint to the modernist manifesto he assigned us to design.[4] Using jargon or referring to theory had long been beaten out of me in the design program, so I never admitted that, indeed, that was what we were actually discussing. Yet it was clear he knew what was unfolding and embraced it. It became impossible not to respect this man who displayed such a stunning knowledge of literature and art history and who, with an open mind, relished an intellectual challenge.

- The trouble with theory is that it is necessary.[5] In the best case, theory is a body of organized thought that allows us to question our assumptions, to critically analyze what we do, to legitimize our field, and to engage with other disciplines. In the worst case though, it becomes a limp, generative means for form-giving, a wobbly crutch used to justify remaining on the formalist treadmill, no matter how new the imagery. Rather, theories should be understood as lenses through which we can attain a greater level of understanding of design in its multiple uses, roles, contexts, and consequences. While the postmodern reactions to Rand were a useful and welcome point of departure for the field, it was a version of postmodernism that was singular: the result, denial, and rejection of modernism. In more complex terms, though, a careful reexamination of Rand's work and ideas could also posit another strand of postmodernism as the development of modernism, an extreme continuation of countertraditional experimentation, the continual afterbirth of modernism in the way we see, think, create, and analyze.

- After what seemed a lifetime of discussion condensed into an hour, after trying to make sense of why Rand seemed so energized by discussion, it occurred to me that what Rand was missing was engagement and challenge. When I asked him if it was a pain to be just worshiped, if that didn't cause a certain sense of loneliness, he proffered a knowing smile. What I received from Paul Rand was an unexpected gift – a crucible where my work and understanding took a new direction. At the end of our session, I couldn't help asking him, "What do you think about the idea that designers are complicit tools of the postindustrial, military, media complex?" Rand replied, unflinchingly, "The only reason we need designers is to make stupid things interesting."

98:   99:

Armin Hofmann
Paul Rand:
Teacher
Colleague
and Friend

- Perhaps it was the similarity of our philosophy on design that united us and established a fruitful and long-standing friendship. The autumn of 1956, when the opportunity arose for me to teach at the Department of Art and Architecture at Yale University alongside Paul Rand, was also the beginning of a close pedagogical association. The exchange of ideas subsequently led to new insights into the establishment and implementation of educational and training projects.
- It must be described as a stroke of luck that other internationally acknowledged designers with prominent educational backgrounds collaborated on the teaching program alongside Paul Rand. This meant that all areas of visual design could be incorporated into the curriculum. The course was actually concerned with encountering visual phenomena from several angles, in depth, analytically, and with a view to research. I mention this type of interdisciplinary integration in order to point out the undeniable existence of a distinct team spirit amongst all of the teaching staff involved. This is where Paul Rand played a pivotal role. Although he followed his own mind, being a renowned designer and teacher, he was concerned that his contributions should be considered as a "part of the whole thing." Also, as far as questions of artistic and didactic direction were concerned, there were no clashes of ideology during the year-long collaboration.
- In 1972, the opportunity arose to develop the pedagogical experience gained from the Yale program by organizing a summer school. Paul Rand was extremely committed to the project. In Brissago, on the southern slopes of the Swiss Alps, and far away from his home, he found a scholarly environment that allowed him to devote himself entirely to his students and to concentrate his efforts on completing his projects. In particular, he lent his support to the summer school with lectures, discussions, practical research, and demonstrations. This southern panorama, which was conducive to the cultural domain of art history, created a working environment that came close to the pedagogical aims of Paul Rand, particularly as far as "holistic education" was concerned.
- It is an interesting fact that Paul Rand's activity in education increased in his later years. His work as a writer, reflected in reference books that are actually textbooks, shows that he was seriously committed to passing on his professional, artistic, and social wisdom to a younger generation. A further characteristic of

100: 101: Friend: Hofmann

his later work in the teaching profession is his critical view of unstoppable mechanization within designer training. He was the one who spent half his life associated with the highly developed technology industry, and he also appreciated the high quality of tools made in the traditional way. The fact that the meaning of "slowness" is increasingly fading into obscurity has something to do with this. Here was the crux of the Brissago design ideology: to work together to oppose the threat of dehumanization in the teaching of creative subjects. To put it more precisely, it was a question of finding an alternative to the current educational techniques, which are oriented toward using instruments and are dependent upon practice.
Paul Rand's extensive knowledge of art history, his broad education, his artistic nature, and his tendency to investigate that which is pictorial in our world made him more than one of the most influential designers of our time. As a personality in the teaching profession, he was able to equip the students with an outlook on life, which was more like a meticulously crafted plan, reaching beyond the limitations of career-oriented thinking.

Translation from the German by Hans Dieter Reichert

Derek Birdsall
A Master

- I still remember the impact of *Thoughts on Design* when I first saw it in the Central School Library in London in 1952. I was an eighteen-year-old student in Anthony Froshaug's typography class; under his tutelage we were producing our own synthesis of the traditional and the "new" typography.
- What Paul Rand had done was to synthesize the new typography and modern art into a new and wickedly witty graphic language. The text vividly articulated his thoughts (the title still reverberates); our task was to transform the arbitrary to the purposeful, and the mundane to the magical. A Master.
- His influence on younger American designers had a knock-on effect on my generation. In the sixties, along with the arrival in London of Robert Brownjohn and Bob Gill, we developed a further synthesis of the American and Swiss Schools. Paul developed close friendships abroad, particularly with his European contemporaries. Among these were Hans Schleger, Armin Hoffman, and also Tom Eckersley, Abram Games, FHK Henrion, Müller-Brockmann, and Emil Ruder, like Paul all born in 1914 – a vintage year for designers. His work became more and more direct – appropriate to the corporate clients he was now attracting, especially IBM.
- I first met Paul Rand in 1963, at a party at Fletcher Forbes Gill in London. Bob Gill introduced me by saying, "Paul, you should take this guy on – and get him outta here – we don't want him in competition." Paul did not take the bait, but in the seventies, through my own work for IBM, he and I became friends. Thereafter my wife Shirley and I met many times with Paul and Marion, eating, drinking, and swapping stories. My most treasured possession is a copy of *A Designer's Art* inscribed "For Derek Birdsall, with admiration, Paul Rand 6.11.86." On his eightieth birthday I sent him a greeting card showing seventy-nine stencil cap Ps and one stencil cap R (the tail of the R was in green) with the message "to the evergreen Paul Rand" (parodying a job he had done for a Yale Prospectus). Parodying a job of mine, he immediately faxed me back "Thanks a 1,000,000 love Paul."
- To emulate Paul Rand is as honorable and fruitless a task as Woody Allen describes trying to play like Sidney Bechet: "You can get the same instrument, you can get the same reed, you can copy the breathing and the blowing. And nothing happens."

Georgette Ballance
A
Paul Rand
Retrospective

- Paul Rand was one of the most influential designers of the 20th century, and I admit that I was in awe of him. I felt fortunate to study with him at Yale University, and I remember the moment at graduation when Mr. Rand, as we all addressed him then, told me I could now call him Paul. He invited me to telephone him anytime or to come see him and his wife, Marion, in Weston after I got settled in New York City. I have been a frequent visitor at the Rand home ever since.
- Those visits often included "pop quizzes" about design, because Paul was an extraordinary teacher, both in and out of the classroom. He always had ideas, books, articles, designs, and opinions to discuss. I kept a pencil and paper handy to take notes. There might be "homework," too – something for me to read that we would discuss on my next visit.
- Paul was pleased when I started teaching design history, which he felt was an important responsibility. He was convinced that a knowledge of the history of art and design was an indispensable part of a designer's education: "If he doesn't know history, boy, he's in bad shape." He introduced me to designers who weren't well known in America and rarely mentioned in readily available design books. Thanks to Paul, I spent many hours at the New York Public Library going through back issues of European magazines, reading about designers who had influenced him, such as O.H.W. Hadank or Anton Mahlau.
- During one of my visits, I asked Paul if he would consider allowing a comprehensive exhibition of his work that would stand as an historical survey. I had just been appointed interim director of the Lubalin Center at Cooper Union and offered to host the exhibit there. He agreed to do it only if I would be the curator.
- Working with Paul on the exhibition was the beginning of a very special partnership. We spent even more time together during the year before *A Paul Rand Retrospective* opened in October 1996. While I made selections for the show, Paul continued working on new projects. We often took breaks to talk about his work, both old and new. Paul enjoyed telling stories and sharing anecdotes about his jobs and clients.
- The last logo Paul designed was for Enron, the now infamous Texas pipeline company, and it would be the most recent piece in the exhibition. Paul got the idea for the logo while discussing the project on the phone with his then-prospective client. He even did a drawing before he had the job, because he was eager to see

how "this great idea would look." Once he took the job, he spent time refining the design, "tweaking and turning it." The most difficult part of designing a logo, he claimed, was "making something that looks OK look even better." Few logos incorporate the name and symbol in one unified system, and Paul felt that this logo, in terms of solving a problem, was practically perfect. When it was completed, many people interpreted the large letter E as three pipelines, but, he insisted, "it's just an E." Paul often commented that no matter how good a design is, "if a company is second rate, the logo will eventually be perceived as second rate." He would have been dismayed that Enron is now mired in scandal.

- Sorting through work that had been tucked away and forgotten for years was like going on a treasure hunt. It was exciting to find sketches, mechanicals, and student work that Paul was surprised he'd saved – and I was thrilled he had. He agreed to let me exhibit early pieces that had never been seen before, as well as fragile mechanicals and delicate sketches. When I asked him about an early maquette that was meticulously hand-lettered, he smiled and said, "Hey, I was just a kid when I did that!" Remarkable student work done in 1929, when Paul was just 15, were the earliest pieces in the exhibition.

- We decided not to produce a catalogue, because Paul's book, *From Lascaux to Brooklyn,* had just been published. I suggested that we develop a chronology of his life's work and publish a timeline for gallery visitors. I began to research in earnest, finding many articles about Paul in magazines and books. Whenever I found contradictory information, Paul and I would discuss it. For one piece in particular, several references cited different dates, and I asked him which one to use. "That was over 50 years ago," he answered. "I can't remember everything – you decide." I decided to dig a little deeper to confirm which date was correct.

- We often turned to Marion for information, especially about Paul's years with IBM. His IBM logo evolved over time, and he finally stopped making changes because, he said, "the cost of reprinting stationery was getting out of hand." One of Paul's best known posters featured the IBM rebus. He was initially told to stop "fiddling around" with the logo, and the poster was pulled from distribution. Years later, when it was finally released, Paul recalled "it went like hot cakes and now that logo is on everything: pens, stickers, mugs, sweatshirts..."

- For many of his clients, Paul produced presentation booklets describing the process of designing their logos. For IBM, the booklet was produced many years after the logo had been in use, "to document the origin and development of the IBM logo, to illustrate its use, and to point to some of the design problems involved in its implementation." Most presentation booklets "walked" the client through Paul's analysis of the project, leading to a final – single – solution. He put a great deal of thought and effort into writing these booklets, and I wanted to include as many as possible in the exhibition. Paul produced elegant presentation booklets for clients such as NeXT, The Limited, The Bureau of Indian Affairs, Ford, EF, Okasan, and American Express. While not all the logos were realized, these booklets remain important documents of his design process.
- Marion also made sure we took lunch breaks (usually with sandwiches of corned beef on rye), and we would discuss a variety of topics. When Paul was engaged in reading a lengthy book about the Spanish Inquisition, he discussed it. If religion was on his mind, he'd talk about his morning prayers. If he disagreed with a recent article on design, Marion and I would be peppered with questions, usually starting with, "Can you believe this guy?" Paul was very outspoken about "the state of design today."
- When it was time to choose an image for the exhibition's invitation, Paul showed me a photocopy he had made of a leaf he found especially interesting. It looked like a drawing of small leaves inside a larger one. He thought that using it on his invitation would be a good opportunity for other people to see it – perhaps even someone could tell him what kind of leaf it was. The image would be easy to remember, a good mnemonic device, and, he pointed out, we wouldn't have the problem of singling out one image from the exhibition.
- For the first time in the school's history, all three galleries at Cooper Union were devoted to the same exhibition. Paul's carefully rendered student work, mechanicals for children's books crafted with wit and humor, magazines, book jackets, annual reports and posters were installed in the Lubalin Center. His books, *From Lascaux to Brooklyn, Thoughts on Design, A Designer's Art,* and *Design, Form, and Chaos,* were available for reading in the entrance hallway beneath fourteen large panels of the timeline of Paul's life and work.

- In the Houghton Gallery, there were examples of advertising design from the thirties, forties, and fifties; package design from the fifties and sixties; identity design; and more posters, including the wonderful 24-sheet billboard for the 1950s movie, *No Way Out,* which we found on the top shelf of the Rands' hall closet. In addition, corporate manuals and presentation booklets were displayed in the Humanities Gallery.
- The Great Hall was literally overflowing with friends, colleagues, and students who gave Paul a standing ovation after he spoke at the opening reception. His observations that evening were insightful, witty, and heartfelt. Because of the overwhelming response to the retrospective, I lobbied to extend the exhibition beyond the scheduled closing on November 8, 1996. I was able to keep his work in two of the galleries until December, and attendance remained high throughout the duration of the show.
- Sadly, Paul died on November 26, 1996. Even those of us who knew that he had been battling cancer were shocked. I was asked to organize a memorial service, and again his admirers crowded into Cooper Union's Great Hall, this time to pay tribute to an extraordinary man.
- Since his death, Marion tells me that I seem to be on a mission to make Paul's work available for future generations of students and designers. With her encouragement, I organized a small version of Paul's retrospective which we've already loaned to several university galleries, and I'm still working with Bob Burns, another former student of Paul's, to sort through his archive. Both the traveling exhibit and most of the archive have now been donated to Yale University's Sterling Memorial Library. Nathan Garland has also been involved in this process, and with his help a selection of books from Paul's own extensive library has been given to Yale as well.
Our work isn't finished yet, but we're getting close. My visits will continue, however, because when Marion greets me at the door, it feels like coming home.

Bob Burns
Ex Libris
Paul Rand

- "The hardest thing to see is what is in front of your eyes." This quote from Goethe, which appears in the beginning of Paul Rand's second book, *A Designer's Art*, was one of his favorite mantras. During the eleven years that Paul was my teacher, mentor, critic, and friend, I was fortunate to get to know his interests and his genius for design.
- I met Paul Rand in the fall of 1985. As a first-year graduate student at Yale, I had made up my mind that I was there to study with Paul Rand. When I was told that he only taught second-year students, I was not deterred. I asked the advice of my first mentor, Lou Danziger, with whom I had studied at the California Institute for the Arts (CalArts). Lou said, "Bob, call him up and tell him I told you to call." When Mr. Rand answered, I told him that I had come to Yale to study with him. He replied sharply, "I'm the reason everyone comes to Yale. What makes you any different?" I asked him if I could come to his studio and show him my work. He replied, "It's a free country," and then proceeded to give me directions to his house. That was the beginning of my relationship with Paul Rand. There were only a few select people that Paul would spend time with, and I consider it an honor to have been included in that group. "You know I have to see a person's work to see what he sees," Rand would say, "then I can tell if he or she is worth talking to."
- Paul Rand was a self-taught designer. Most of his early education took place in Room 313 at the New York Public Library. He spent endless hours looking at art books, early design magazines such as *Commercial Art and Industry* or *Gebrauchsgrafik* and various journals on printing and typography. It's there that Paul became passionate about books and learning. "You know I grew up very poor, we never had money for books when I was young," he often said.
- Paul began buying artbooks early in his career when he was with Metro Associated Services. As his income level grew, so did his acquisitions. He bought books on European artists such as Klee, Miro, and Picasso, and others on drawing, painting, lettering, and color. It wasn't until later in the 1940s, after being asked by Moholy-Nagy if he ever read any art criticism, that Rand started reading leading philosophers, art criticism, and art education.
- When he lived in New York and worked at the Wientraub Agency, he often went to the Wittenborn bookstore on Madison Avenue. "Wittenborn had the best stuff, books and journals from Europe. It was

about the only place you could find good stuff at the time." His book buying was not limited to New York. When Rand traveled to Europe each summer, he always brought along a separate suitcase to ship books home. He knew all the best bookshops in London, Paris, and Zürich.

- My first insight into the depth and breadth of Paul's knowledge and interests came when I saw his library. It was extensive, in everything. "Any good designer has to have a great library," he would say. "Design is a tough business, brother. You have to know a hell of a lot to do a decent job."

- When I visited, he always challenged me with many questions about art, design, history, philosophy, or mathematics. Then he would sit and wait for an answer. Often, like a deer caught in the headlights, I would search for an appropriate answer. If you didn't know the subject sufficiently, you experienced the wrath of Paul Rand. Rand did not suffer fools. He would retrieve a book from his library on the specific topic and ask me to read it while he sat there working, and then he would ask the question again.

- Books permeated his house. The central library is located in what was his first studio in his house. It is made up of fifteen to twenty thousand volumes of books. There are roughly twenty-three different library stacks, in three floor-to-ceiling aisles. The library could easily match a small town library. The topics range from typography, design, printing, symbols, art, book arts, Japanese design, games, photography, film, Spanish art, Asian, Indian and Islamic Art, Judaica, Early Chinese art, architecture, iconography, animals, history, art appreciation, theory and criticism, aesthetics, mathematics, travel, popular culture, philosophy, psychology, education, economics, illusion, form, medicine, anatomy, opera, and sculpture. There are volumes of art books and artist monographs: one hundred twenty volumes on Le Corbusier, and two hundred fifty volumes on Picasso. In addition, there are shelves of encyclopedias and Oxford dictionaries, as well as volumes of books on Cubism, the Bauhaus, and artists such as Braque, Klee, Miro, Léger, and Schwitters. Books on the Italian Renaissance, Impressionism, and de Stijl take up one aisle. Subjects ranging from folk art to Chinese calligraphy to African art are in another. Paul had a great interest in philosophy and literature. There are several dozen volumes on Roger Fry, many on John Dewey, John Ruskin, and Henry James, as well as Shakespeare, Kafka, and George Orwell.

- His library also included several original booklets and rare volumes. If we were talking about Futurism or the typography of Marinetti, Paul would show me an original copy of *Les Mots en Liberté Futuritsts* from 1919, or original books designed by Depero. He was an avid collector of design books and publications. He had all of the original Bauhaus books and the Bauhaus magazines. He owned many limited and rare editions on typography given to him by Jan Tschichold. He also collected early Russian Contructivist publications, artwork, and portfolios by El Lissitzky.
- This led to many great discussions about design in Europe and early designers whose work he admired. He introduced me to the work of early German designers such as O.H.W. Hadank, Wilhlem Deffke, Max Koerner, and Anton Mahlau. These publications were limited and hard to find and always in German. If there wasn't a book to collect, Paul would keep printed ephemera. At Rand's house, I got to see the actual pieces and touch the paper they were printed on.
- One weekend last year, I was looking at a bookshelf containing oversized editions and saw a large volume in a slip case. It simply said *Jazz* on the spine. I took it off the shelf and brought it to the table where Marion Rand was sitting. I asked her if she would mind if I looked at it. "Sure. Where'd you find that? I haven't seen it in years." As I opened it I could not believe my eyes, it was an original copy of Matisse's book *Jazz*. The color exploded off the pages. The only other time I had seen this book was under glass at the Museum of Modern Art. It was in pristine condition and was probably only opened once or twice. It was beautiful. It was number fifteen out of the edition. "Oh, Paul bought two of those when he was in New York. He gave the other one away as a gift to a client. I think Paul paid $1,500 for each copy in the late forties," Marion said. Paul's generosity was enormous, and on many occasions he presented clients and friends with gifts of books or paintings.
- Paul Rand's library was as diverse and interesting as he was. It is the yardstick by which his interests and passions, so well reflected in his work and writings, can be measured. Paul used his library as a resource. His books were a working entity from which he built his knowledge and visual vocabulary. He was uncompromising when it came to producing quality work. And through example, he would teach about the importance of ideas in design, the elegance in simplicity, and the economy of means. His appreciation for

fine paper and printing came out of the books and materials he collected.
- He believed that books were meant to be used and not passively sit on the self. While looking through a book or very rare art journal such as *Verve*, I would find a page or a cover with a shape cut out of the corner or a square cut out of the background. When I asked Paul about the missing shape, he would say, "Oh, I did that. Brother, look at that beautiful color. I wanted to remember that color for a job, so I cut it out." His cutting and saving didn't stop with fine art journals. He tore or cut edges from books, posters, and even menus – wherever he would see a color that caught his attention, a small piece would end up in his pocket.
- Paul read extensively. He took notes compulsively, writing in the margins of books, on any scrap paper, the backs of envelopes, or napkins. When Rand wrote his essays, he kept a copy of *The Complete Plain Words* by Sir Ernest Gowers on his table to use as a reference to simplify his writing. Paul wrote constantly, not only to educate, but to clarify his own thoughts and convictions.
- When interested in a topic, he studied it voraciously. While looking through his library, I came across several hardcover books that were bound by hand. Inside were photocopied pages of complete texts translated from French or German. "If I find a book that's important and can't find it in English, I'll have it translated and copied, because I should know it."
- Once you got past the gruff exterior, Paul was a warm and caring person with a great sense of humor. He was direct and honest, and you had to have a thick skin when he challenged you. He held everyone and everything to his high standards. Even entering a restaurant with Paul was amusing: I could count the seconds before I heard him say, "Boy, look at the color of this interior. This is some real crap." or "Look at that type. Man, this place is for the birds."
- Paul Rand was always teaching, always studying visual relationships. He bristled with the curiosity of a seven year old and the savvy of an accomplished master. For him design was total devotion. It consumed him twenty-four hours a day. During the time I spent with him, whether it was in his studio, doing yard work, or going to the hardware store, he was constantly observing what was before him and analyzing it. Even walking down the street with Paul Rand was a visual exploration. Suddenly he would stop, transfixed on

something he saw, studying the relationship, proportion, color, or its place in the environment. At these times, I would ask him a thousand questions on what he was seeing and thinking. These were invaluable lessons that taught me how to see, think, and stay curious. I miss him.

Kyle Cooper
Goodwill
on
Goodhill

- I heard Paul Rand's voice approximately eighteen months before I met him. That is to say, I heard Hugh Dubberly doing an impersonation of Peter Levine doing an impersonation of Paul Rand. "Looks like a girl did it," Hugh said in the now familiar nasal tone, referring to one of my experiments. I hear the nasal tone lovingly admonishing me toward good work to this day. "You are doing that raised pinky design," Peter added, in what I now know to be a slightly more accurate Rand dialect. Peter, Hugh, and all the other designers at Wang Laboratories Corporate Communications Department in North Chelmsford, Massachusetts, were all well familiar with "Mr. Rand," as they called him. They each had received at least one master's degree from either Yale or the Rhode Island School of Design, some two. The two who had not yet been indoctrinated were myself and the other University of Massachusetts non-paid intern, Jim "Stickman" Waldron.

- The Wang design department quite often shared Mr. Rand's legend and mythology with the "Stickman" and myself. "Wait until you meet Mr. Rand," they would say, as if our admission into the graduate graphic design program at Yale was a lock. Jim was a gifted orator, and I could understand how he talked his way out of a security guard position and into his postgraduate internship in the design department at Wang. I, however, wondered what they saw in me. I understood that when Jim interviewed me (after I had stolen his credit documentation from the University of Massachusetts internship office to prevent other candidates from pursuing the position I coveted) that Hugh's only criterion was to discern whether or not I was an ass. Apparently I convinced Jim that I was not. Still, I wondered what a working class, failed interior designer could be doing in such dignified company. Why was I being groomed for a Rand discipleship? My portfolio consisted of monster drawings, and as Mr. Rand would later say, horrible typography. "Why would anyone use a typeface like this?" I remember Hugh remarking during my initial interview. Nonetheless, I assumed that my Boston accent amused them, and I put my head down and did whatever they told me to do. In doing so, I vicariously developed a familiarity with Mr. Rand's work and his teaching. I began to believe that I too could sit at his feet. I had always loved the UPS, Westinghouse, and Colorforms logos even before I understood that people actually designed these things. As a child, these marks made me happy.

- I liked the little Colorforms man as he reminded me of my toys, and it was obvious to me that UPS was at once a present and an acorn. Obviously, the Westinghouse logo was a face. Logos, I was told later by Mr. Rand, should provoke some kind of familiar association, whether it be a literal interpretation of what the company does or not. The associations these logos provoke in me today are quite different. They still make me happy, but now when I see them I recall the man who created them and who encouraged me to play, be intuitive, and trust the opinion of a child. Surprisingly, Stickman and I both got into Yale. At our orientation, we met Bob Burns who had studied at California Institute for the Arts, where Lou Danzinger fully immersed him in the Rand mythology. Bob, who was originally from Boston, talked like me. We agreed that we were at Yale with the primary purpose to study with Mr. Rand. Our enthusiasm was quelled, however, when we were firmly told that first-year students were not allowed to take Paul Rand's master class as it was reserved for the second-year students. We would have to wait another year.

- On the day of Mr. Rand's class, obligatory powdered doughnuts were provided, his table and lamp were set, and the second-year students gathered. Unwilling to be confined by Yale's customs, Bob and I arrived. We were scowled at and told to leave, but Mr. Rand said we could stay. Bob and I were from Boston; Mr. Rand was from Brooklyn; he was our idol, yet he was one of us. People like us tell you the truth and give you a hard time if we like you. The people who Mr. Rand made cry did not realize that, where we come from, this is the way people talk to one another. Also, those who cried did not realize that his words were for their own good. There were also the unfortunate ones who sought to glorify themselves by stumping the master. Regarding our design efforts, Bob and I would ask Mr. Rand, "You'd tell us if it sucked?" He would, and he did. Mr. Rand gave us framed posters; we shoveled his driveway. He gave us books; we cleaned his garage. The Stickman chided us for doing work for Mr. Rand, but going to his house for tutorials was the highlight of my Yale experience and perhaps my life.

- I would have cleaned his toilet, but it never came to that. The "Randisms" flowed freely. "Helvetica is a display face. It looks like dog excrement in text."

"Making something bold and making it all caps is like wearing a belt with suspenders." "Too much color is no color at all." And most important, "That's not contrast!"

- I actually did not graduate with my class and stayed a third year at Yale, my primary justification being another year of study with Mr. Rand. Although at first observation some of the Randisms seemed doggerel, as time passed, I tried to unpack them. "Looks like a girl did it" was really not intended to be chauvinistic, (although he was). He seemed to be referring to excessive decoration. "If you came here for a pat on the back, you came to the wrong place." If the work was good, gender was not an issue. After seeing a presentation of April Grieman's work, he told us, "Hey, you gotta give the devil her due." "Raised Pinky" design seemed to refer to work that was just too fussy, not expressive, clean, but not emotional.

- Obviously, Mr. Rand encouraged the refinement of one's craft. Considering the notion of creative direction or collaboration, he offered, "You need to keep your hand in it or you will get rusty." We wondered aloud if he had ever collaborated with another designer. "I would, but Jan Tschichold is dead," he told us. We quickly familiarized ourselves with Jan Tschichold's work, which was refined, and found a picture of him where his pinky was, in fact, raised. So it seemed that it was okay to be decorative, and it was okay to be rigid; you just needed to do it brilliantly. It was clear to me that Rand was right in saying, "An idea is only as good as its execution" and "Form is an idea." Bad form then, is a bad idea.

- Mr. Rand encouraged me to read Gestalt psychology, and I came across the notion that an idea, riddle, or design work that communicates is apparently more memorable than something where the interpretation is subjective. For something that relies purely on form to be memorable, the form would need to be sublime. I gravitated toward storytelling, jokes, metaphors, and visual puns. In retrospect, I imagine my mentors at Wang saw this propensity in me as did Mr. Rand. After repeatedly hearing, "This stinks," and "What the hell am I looking at?" when we made the biweekly trek to Mr. Rand's house on Goodhill Road in Weston, Connecticut, he decided that it was time for me to be tested.

- "Kyle, I am making a logo for a Japanese company called Okasan. What is my idea?" he asked. My nerves cooled. Could I finally say something that would make him realize that I was a worthy student and not just entertainment? "How about a Japanese character?" I asked, what about using just the "OK." He smiled his little smile, raised his glasses off his eyes, and showed me the logo he had just finished. It was an OK rotated ninety degrees clockwise; it was a little man; and it was also a Japanese character. I had solved his riddle, which pleased him. He had made another logo that made me happy. He had told me another joke, and I got it.

- Perhaps I have not yet realized all that I have learned from Mr. Rand and from studying his work. My favorite pieces of his involve an expressive moment in time – a freeze frame, a single event in an implied sequence. "Cast your bread on the water," for example, shows a beautiful asymmetric configuration of several pieces of bread tossed up in the air, or at least arranged on the page to look as if they were tossed in the air. The static layout is meant to suggest a moment captured before the slices fall into the water. In a film title sequence, if I freeze on any single frame, the same formal measurements applied by Mr. Rand to his composition on the page, will apply to the still frame of the film sequence.

- Rand made moments. I try to start with a moment that lives up to his standard and fill in the rest. Are the elements in each still frame asymmetrically laid out in an interesting way? Is there any contrast in the frame? Is there a story? A riddle? Is there too much color? Is the font well drawn? I read a design essay, which talked about the state of motion graphics and my own work and suggested that handmade expressive typography was nothing new and that Mr. Rand had done it long ago. "You gotta disguise your sources, brother," I remembered him saying. He was mine and I have no interest in disguising it. I told him that I was excited about film titles, and I wanted him to be my thesis adviser. We talked about Saul Bass. "That guy will talk your ear off," he said, and then suggested that if I was interested in film I should forget about titles, because there was nothing interesting happening in that area. "Go read 'Film Form' and 'Film Sense' by Sergei Eisenstein, and then come talk to me." I did, and he was right. My thesis was called "Sergei Eisenstein/Collateral Stimuli" and explored the work of the graphic designer complementing the visual sense of the filmmaker. Fortunately, Mr. Rand lost the only copy of my final thesis. "I think some guy from IBM that came to my house took it by mistake," he explained.

- The last time we spoke, Saul Bass's name came up again. I told Mr. Rand that I did a title sequence for a film called *Seven*. He had seen it and said, "Oh you're making that trash art." I asked if he heard that Saul Bass had died. "Yeah, I just talked to him last week. One minute you are here, and the next minute that's it, that's it," he repeated. I think Mr. Rand knew that it would be only a short time before that was "it" for him, and perhaps he was letting me know. But, that was not it. He is in my work and in my thoughts daily. He was a devout man, and his life demonstrated to me that creativity was a way to identify with, and to thankfully acknowledge your creator. Or as he would say, "I did not decide to be a designer, God did."

Richard Sapper
Artist
Designer
Poet
and Scholar

- On the anniversary of my twentieth year as a design consultant for IBM, the company gave me a poster by Paul that is, for me, a symbol of his work and philosophy, and of the man himself. Apart from its being a precious treasure in and of itself, that poster makes me think of Paul Rand every day. It shows a little yellow butterfly flying toward a huge black sunflower, and under it is written a quotation of Vincent van Gogh: "What would life be if we had no courage to attempt anything?"
- Paul was my colleague at IBM for twenty years – as a matter of fact he was influential in hiring me, though I had never met him before. We worked together, and I know many of his wonderful designs – but I do not know of any other that expresses so clearly what Paul Rand was: an artist, designer, poet, and scholar of equally unsurpassed, extraordinary levels. He was one of those people who have excellence in their blood, who could translate important philosophical messages into powerful, elementary graphic expressions like nobody else. He was really the perfect illustration of his own definition of a designer:
- A designer
  makes poetry
  out of prose.

Shigeo Fukuda
Paul Rand

- In 1955, a group of Japanese designers put together an exhibit in Tokyo, titled *Graphic'55*. Featured in the show was work by the renowned American graphic designer Paul Rand, who had been invited to the exhibit.
- At the time, I was a design student at Tokyo Geijitsu University. I remember how impressed I was by each piece of Paul Rand's work. While the exhibition only lasted one week, I visited the show ten times in those seven days. I remember being deeply moved by his perceptive work, refined use of color, sensitive forms, human touch, wit…. As a creator, Paul Rand proudly believed that one communicates through design. He conveyed that philosophy to Japan's design world. I believe his exhibition was an historic design moment in Japan.
- In 1967, I designed toys and other playthings for my daughter, Miran. Paul Rand chose to show those items in an exhibition *Toys & Things Japanese: The Work of Shigeo Fukuda*. Mr. Rand produced the entire exhibition of my designs, to be shown at IBM's gallery in New York. For three days I worked with this great master, observing and learning from his expertise. It was my highest experience.
- On Paul Rand's recommendation, I had the opportunity to teach the graduate class in graphic design at Yale University in 1982, and again in 1985. I arrived for work on a cold, snowy morning. Despite the weather, Mr. Rand took the time to personally show me around the campus. Along the way a number of students recognized him and they approached to greet and chat with him. He introduced me to each of them and with smiling eyes he took the time to speak with them. He was unconcerned about the snow accumulating all over him. I remember the event like it was yesterday. Again I would express my belief that Paul Rand was a great design teacher, and a design pioneer.
- Of the body of work of which I am knowledgeable, I would recognize his distinctive achievements as follows: communication and play as important elements in the design of the logotype; corporate graphics and poster series for IBM Corporation (1956 and beyond); *Direction* (1938 and beyond); cover designs for the *American Institute of Graphic Art* (1968 and beyond); a wonderfully artistic book design series; an ideal example of graphic picture books, *I Know A Lot Of Things* (1956), *Sparkle & Spin* (1957), *Little 1* (1962), *Listen! Listen!* (1970); and *A Designer's Art*

(1985), the bible for graphic designers worldwide. America's Paul Rand influenced and stimulated graphic designers everywhere. With his creative talent and strong convictions, Paul Rand enlightened the field of graphic design in the twentieth century.

Translation from the Japanese by Hiroko Oba Insinger

Paul Rand: Fukuda

Philip Burton
Rand in Brissago

- On the southern side of Italian-speaking Switzerland, the Alps gradually descend to a region where large, ice-cold lakes are fed by melting snow. The peculiar geographic configuration of mountains and lakes captures semitropical air from the south that stimulates the growth of exotic flowers and palm, bamboo, and banana trees, making this one of the most desirable destinations in central Europe.
- Armin and Dorothea Hofmann have been coming to this part of the country for years. As far as Armin was concerned, the situation was ideal: a quiet place in the middle of a beautiful landscape and climate, with none of the usual art school paraphernalia for students to use — no typesetters, darkrooms, stat cameras, not even a photocopy machine. Whatever the students created would be a result of their own ingenuity and imagination. At first the majority of the students came from Kent State, and the teachers from the Kunstgewerbeschule in Basel, where Armin directed the graphic design program. As the program grew, students from other schools in America and Europe started attending, and Armin expanded the faculty. In 1976 Ivan Chermayeff and Wolfgang Weingart were invited to teach, and in 1977, Herbert Matter and Paul Rand.
- Paul made his skepticism known the minute he arrived in Brissago. He couldn't imagine that the students would achieve anything of value in such a short time, and he wasn't so sure that he wanted to teach all day, every day, for a full week. But in spite of the reservations, he came armed with a project statement describing "Visual Semantics," an exercise he had developed just for the occasion.
- In typical Rand fashion, it was a very carefully structured project arranged in categories of process, theme, color, format, materials, and bibliography. The students were to use letters as compositional elements and manipulate them to illustrate the spirit of a given word. The use of simple letterforms was encouraged because they were "unencumbered by individual eccentricities and sentimental associations." Students were told to bring paper in four specified colors. A first composition was done using black and white only, the second black and white and one color, the third using all four colors. Format specifications were 24 x 24 centimeters mounted on 26 x 26.6 centimeter bristol board with a one centimeter border at the top and on both sides. The first year four words were given: maison, H_2O, China, and 1776. When the allotted

Rand in Brissago: Burton

time proved insufficient to complete four compositions, Paul reduced the required number the next year to three. Eventually only one word was described in three compositions: Banjo, then Miró, and finally Paul settled on Léger. "Many of the working procedures and design processes, formal and otherwise, which concern all artists, are especially discernable in Léger's work. Important is to discover the fundamental ideas and design principles governing the work and not mimic the technique or style." Paul usually couldn't wait until class began to get the students started on his project. He would make some very brief introductory remarks after dinner and hand out the project statements, telling them he had no idea what to expect for results. Some students would sit back down at the dinner table and start to ponder the outline, others disappeared into their rooms to sketch ideas.

- Classes were held in the new elementary school, the pride and joy of the village. Paul would officially start the first day of class with an informal lecture. From his vast collection of slides he would choose to show examples of paintings and sculpture that would explain universal composition strategies and design principles. Eventually he accumulated slides of student work from previous years and would show them to help the students with their task.

- Once the students got down to work, Paul would carry a chair or garden stool with him from desk to desk, sitting with each student for as long as it took him to help them formulate their ideas. When he thought it appropriate he would recall instances from his own career to make an especially significant point. He would show them the proper way to draw well-proportioned geometric letters using a straight-edge, triangle, and compass, and then carefully cut them out with scissors or a small blade and if necessary sand the curves smooth with sandpaper. Every day was the same.

- The room was completely silent as long as Paul was there; everyone profited from what he had to say. If the students to whom he was speaking were often so nervous that they would miss the pearls that were being dropped at their feet, they would have a classmate nearby take notes of the encounter.

- The students couldn't get enough. After dinner, almost all of them would return to the classroom and work through the night. Around three in the morning the smell of fresh baked goods would fill the air, and in the early years of the program, it was possible to visit the bakery where all the bread for the village was being prepared. Caesar Conti-Rossini, the baker, was also the mayor. His family had been baking bread for Brissago for five hundred years, and he was very proud to show off his bakery and offer piping hot samples to students who unexpectedly appeared in the middle of the night.

- Each morning Paul would be astonished at the progress the students had made since the day before. This buoyed his spirits, and theirs. It was understood that the compositions had to be finished by the end of the week, but an anticipated final critique never happened. "What more is there to say?" Paul would ask. He preferred the more personal one-on-one exchanges with the students to public extravaganzas. Some students found Paul unsympathetic, but for Paul that wasn't an issue. He just wanted them to "do it," and to get the meaning of his exercise. Occasionally all the work would be lined up along the wall so that everybody could see what had been done and appreciate just how much had been accomplished.

- It took only one teaching session in Brissago for Paul to be converted. He became convinced that the conditions that existed in the summer program in Brissago provided the best way to teach graphic design. Paul was instrumental in convincing the School of Art at Yale University to assume sponsorship of the program. He even tried to introduce the same structure to the curriculum, but found it practically impossible given the convoluted schedules of the graduate students.

- Nineteen ninety-six was the last year the summer program was held. That year health problems prevented Paul from spending his usual full week in Brissago. He gave the students an abbreviated project to design a logo commemorating the centennial of Pratt Institute in New York. Mornings were devoted to showing slides of pages from his new book, *From Lascaux to Brooklyn,* and explaining some of the issues he raised in it. Almost without exception, studying design for five weeks in Brissago proved to be a life-changing experience for the students. What the students never saw was that it meant as much to Paul as it did to them.

- A small group that had been particularly inspired by their time in Brissago tried for two years to contact the four hundred who had studied there to invite them to return for a weekend reunion in July of 2000. Those who learned of the reunion fell into one of three camps. The first would return at any cost, using the occasion to bring along spouses, loved ones, and children to show them what they had been talking about for so many years. A second group wished to return, but "someday," and alone. And a third group wanted to hold on to the memories, but never go back. Armin once remarked that there were two summer programs, one with Paul and one without. Paul was totally devoted to design; he never stopped talking about it or showing others something he thought was especially beautiful or poignant. It obviously gave him great joy, a joy that he desperately wanted to pass on to his students.

Julie Klugman
Five Days
with
Mr. Rand

- Just over ten years ago, I had the opportunity to attend Yale University's summer program in graphic design in Brissago, Switzerland. A small envelope of literature promised courses with Phillip Burton, Armin and Dorothea Hoffman, Pierre Mendel, Richard Sapper, and Paul Rand, in an intimate setting in southeast Switzerland. I was particularly eager to meet and study with Paul Rand, the designer who had so inspired me while I was in school.
- As for so many students, Paul Rand was one of the reasons I had decided to study design. *A Designer's Art* had been published just prior to when I began art school, and I can vividly recall poring open-jawed over its illustrations of Mr. Rand's work with my classmates. The work was deceptively simple. It was smart. It inspired me.
- On the boat ride to Brissago, I was filled with emotion: anticipation, excitement, and, mostly, nerves. While I had studied Mr. Rand's work, to me he was just that: his work. What was the personification of a *Direction* cover? The IBM rebus? The Westinghouse logo?
- Mr. Rand arrived in Brissago just two days into the program in mid-June. My first exposure to my teacher was a lecture held in the small, lakeside classroom where our classes would be held. He didn't disappoint: He shared with us simple yet profound words, peppered with the wit and honesty so apparent in his design and writing:
  Whatever you design has to communicate.
  Everything else is for the birds.
  As designers, what we do is intuitive,
  but you must know how to talk about design.
  Continue the process of learning by reading.
  All you can do is try to be a good designer.
  Learn how to be a good designer,
  and understand what you're doing.
- After the lecture, Mr. Rand introduced the problem: using the letters in the name Léger, we were charged with creating three compositions evocative (but not derivative) of the artist's work and ideas. We listened, then sketched as Mr. Rand navigated the room, stopping to meet and talk to each student. He offered strong opinions: sometimes critical, but always honest. He listened to us, questioning our ideas or nurturing them as he saw appropriate. Mr. Rand challenged us. We worked through lunch, and returned to the studio after dinner, often staying late into the evening. The next day, Mr. Rand would return with his unique

blend of sharp humor, brutal honesty, and above all, caring.

- At times it was difficult to communicate my ideas to my teacher, and I would struggle to put my ideas on paper. Mr. Rand was intuitive. "Relax," he would tell me as he pulled a chair to my table. The five short days I spent in class with Mr. Rand were not enough time to relax. I can't say I was entirely satisfied with my work in the end, but I certainly learned in the process. In his lecture, Mr. Rand compared the design process to peeling back the layers of an onion: the more it is peeled, the more is revealed. For me, working through the process wasn't always easy, but it was certainly educational and beneficial.
- When I reflect on those five days with Mr. Rand, I learned lessons that still apply and will continue to apply. Communicate, learn, and relax.
It's really quite simple: all you can try to do is try to be a good designer.

Guenet Abraham
The Lessons
in Clarity
and Sharing

- In 1986, when I worked in Random House Publishing's design department, Paul Rand was to me a distant figure. Seven years later, when I entered Yale School of Art, I still did not know anyone who had studied or worked with him. I knew his work and its impact on graphic design. I did not know his personality and reputation as a teacher. I did not know what he looked like.
- I finally met Paul Rand in the summer of 1994 after Inga Druckery, one of my professors, suggested that I attend the Yale Summer Program in Graphic Design in Brissago, Switzerland. I applied immediately. That summer, after the six-week program had ended, I began to understand Paul Rand's intensity and genius though, it took years to appreciate the gift he gave me. On a quiet Sunday evening in the second week of the program, I stood outside our hotel by Lake Ticino as Paul Rand arrived with Armin Hofmann and Philip Burton. I could not believe my eyes. Was Rand the diminutive figure climbing up the hill so slowly between them? His first words to me were also surprising. "What do you want to be when you get out of school?" We stared at each other until I replied I was already a graphic designer, and hoped to become a better one. Thinking back to that moment, I often wonder if I would have stared back as I did if I had known then of his reputation as a teacher who, as legend has it, reduced students to tears.
- After dinner, we assembled for what we thought would be a short introductory lecture. No one expected a three-hour ride through Rand's creative history from the age of twenty-one spelled out in vivid detail. He spoke about his clients, the concepts he used to create their designs, the creative process, and how different ideas were presented before a final product was completed. All through the lecture, he stood in the hot classroom, while we sat mesmerized, listening, watching, and trying to absorb it all. It was clear he loved all aspects of his work. He trusted and believed in design as an art for communication.
- Rand's one-week seminar centered on how to use and manipulate letterforms and words to illustrate an action or an idea, to evoke a pictorial image. Prior to meeting him, excited anticipation had swept through our group. His sessions during the week had the same intensity. Our assignment was to discover the fundamental ideas and design principles governing the work of Fernand Léger. For materials, we used matte sheets of PMS 186 (red), PMS 646 (brown), PMS 549 (blue),

and PMS 405 (dark grey), and matching markers.
- Each day, he taught from 8:30 in the morning until 5:00 in the evening. At eighty-one years old, and in spite of the obvious physical toll it took on him, he pushed us to do our best work, moving from student to student, probing, encouraging, teasing, and gently correcting work after pointed and intense critiques. He would stare into my eyes, as if reading my thoughts, then suddenly grab my pencil and rapidly sketch a simple, yet direct and elegant direction toward a possible solution.
- In preparing for this essay, I sorted through a box containing material from that summer, and found several pages of Rand's sketches and drawings. I saw for the first time that he had signed them. I look upon these sketches as memory, and as tokens of his generosity. He helped shape my philosophy as a teacher and design consultant.
- Decades after designing the UPS trademark, Rand revisited it because the bow still bothered him. The layperson might miss the point because it is subtle, but he could see it. To his displeasure, the UPS executives refused to change it. That story, he said, should remind us that while clients engage us to communicate ideas effectively and artfully, it is important to provide solutions that meet our expectations as graphic designers first. Ours is a unique discipline that straddles art and commerce. Like Rand, I ask my students, "What do you want to be when you get out of school?" I share with them what Rand shared with me – that graphic design is the art of ideas and communication. It is not art for art's sake.

Naoko Matsuzono
Learning to
Observe
Hear
Feel
and See
from Mr. Rand

- I first encountered Paul Rand's works when I studied graphic design at the University of Maryland Baltimore County. His books *Thoughts on Design; A Designer's Art; Design Form and Chaos;* and *From Lascaux to Brooklyn* were requirements for my classes. I found *A Designer's Art* at the university library, opened it, and was instantly captivated and brought into his world. "This is it! This is visual communication!" I do not remember how long, but I sat on the floor for hours, thoroughly engulfed in his work. I felt heartwarmed by his powerful and lyrical work, and even thought at times about how to see through his particular point of view. I remember wondering how he learned how to observe, hear, feel, and see. I also wondered what design meant to Paul Rand.

- I had the opportunity to work on this book, *Paul Rand: Modernist Design,* with Professor Franc Nunoo-Quarcoo. I was very pleased and honored to be a part of this project. In preparation, I was assigned readings about Paul Rand's work and life, followed by discussions. Through this process, I found that the essence of Rand's design came out of natural sensations we feel in everyday life. Especially important were his deep attachment to nature, his observation of daily life, the details of changing seasons, and the deep reflections on miscellaneous aspects of life. It seems to me that design to Rand meant more than anything else – the small discoveries of daily life, the subtle sensations evoked by seasonal changes, and design as an endless stream of ideas.

- I feel close to the essence of his designs because I see the similarities between his aesthetic and the Japanese aesthetic. His illustrations, drawings, and handwritten typography, with their delicate, sensitive pen strokes are similar in spirit and character to Japanese calligraphy. One of the finest Japanese expressions, *zuihitsu*, exemplifies the simplicity, brevity, and curiosity that Rand's work evokes. *Zuihitsu* also means "to follow the brush," or "to leave oneself to the brush."

- I find parallel characteristics of *zuihitsu* in Rand's designs – quality, subtle sensibilities, simplicity, and creativity. His skillful use of form, shapes, space, typography, and materials translate fleeting momentary impressions and sensations of our existence.

- I am naturally able to communicate with his works as if we are communicating with each other. The simplicity of his works takes me directly to a design atmosphere in which one mainly follows an inner voice. In the presence of his work, I feel the atmosphere, the feeling of a moment; in short, the emotional momentum creates a feeling that directly affects the viewer. In this respect, his designs have been described as an exercise in observation, hearing, feeling, and seeing.

- Although I did not have the opportunity to meet and study with Paul Rand, he left many treasures to learn from. I learn from his works every day. Working on *Paul Rand: Modernist Design* has brought me close to understanding and appreciating how to observe

    hear

    feel and

    see!

130: 131:

Dialogues:

132: Kent Kleinman and
     Leslie Van Duzer
144: Virginia Smith
161: Mario Rampone
165: Bez Ocko
175: Franc Nunoo-Quarcoo

Kent Kleinman
Leslie Van Duzer, eds.
Paul Rand
and
Rudolf Arnheim

Paul Rand: What do you call yourself?

Rudolf Arnheim: When I was at Harvard they called me a professor of the psychology of art. But this title had not existed before, as far as I know. How much it is used, I don't know either, because it is a special field. It is the application of psychology, mostly that means psychology of perception, to art.

pr: Gestalt psychology?

ra: Gestalt psychology as applied to the senses: vision, hearing, touch. That is what my work was on in Berlin when I was studying psychology. I then got interested in the arts, and I wanted to apply psychology to the arts. For quite some time I did just that. In *Art and Visual Perception,* for example, I applied the psychology of perception, and then I looked for examples to illustrate it. In the last few years I have sort of done the opposite. I have looked for the psychology to apply to whatever I could.

pr: Is the origin of Gestalt psychology medicine or is it art?

ra: It's not either. There was a method in science that went back for centuries that maintained that if you wanted to deal scientifically with something, you had to cut it into its parts, describe it piece by piece, and then put the descriptions of all the pieces together to get a scientific statement. The Gestalt people found out what the artists had known for thousands of years: if you cut something into pieces you don't get a whole. If you deal with something piece by piece, it won't sing, it won't cohere. All that Gestalt psychology is saying is: in whatever science, whether it is medicine or biology or psychology or aesthetics, you have to deal with the structure of the whole. That's really all it is. I've been thinking that it was so nice to be able to meet you because I believe we have many views and attitudes in common and then again, it would be nice to see if maybe we find some things that we disagree on.

pr: I have an advantage over you because I read your books when I was young, but you didn't read my books when you were young, because there were no books. I learned a great deal from you.

ra: I just noticed that you have recently written about chaos, and I have done that too. I have written a paper on chaos, which is not published yet.

pr: Is that the new discipline: chaos? There is a chaos that isn't chaotic, the chaos of order.

ra: I think we both have the same attitude: we don't like chaos.

pr: Mandelbrot comes to mind.

ra: He is not really dealing with chaos. Mandelbrot is actually dealing with fractals. If you do a mathematical statement about fractals as he does – he takes a mathematical formula and then puts it into a visual application – as long as you stay in mathematics, it's perfectly structured. If you look at the fractals, they don't look chaotic. They look very pretty.

pr: Oh, I think they look weird. I remember visiting his studio at Yale, and there was an assistant trying to reinvent the Swiss Alps with these fractals. There was something extremely depressing about it. It was almost like an embalmed mountain.

ra: You are absolutely right, and there is an additional factor. When you apply the Mandelbrot theory to an actual situation, you have a combination of a mathematical formula and a certain degree of accident and randomness. And that combination begins to look like the Alps, even if it isn't like the Alps. That seems to me to be a sort of deviation for people today who have no creativity. But, maybe we shouldn't bother with that. Maybe we should deal with things that are of interest to us. For many years I have thought that the applied arts – typography and architecture and industrial design – all had a curious way of distinguishing the purely practical functional object from the aesthetic. In other words, normally when someone is making a house or making a table, he first thinks about the function of it. What does the customer want, and what does the object want, and how do you make it less expensive? That is the functional part. Then you do the beauty and attach the beauty to it; the aesthetics are additional, a kind of icing on the cake. I have always fought against that distinction. It has always seemed to me that what we call the aesthetic is really a part of the function of an object. What do you think?

pr: The origin of my new book is based on just that idea. I asked myself: why do I like Lascaux, the Parthenon, and the Tower of Pisa, Cézanne, Brugel, and Picasso, Mies van der Rohe, and Le Corbusier? What is it that they all have in common? That is how the book started. I wrote a short essay on each of these subjects that deals primarily with form problems. But of course you can't deal with form without dealing with content, because if you ignore content you have pure formalism, which isn't about anything.

ra: Exactly.

pr: So automatically the function, even though it isn't mentioned explicitly, is implied. You must have content in order to have form. I never could find a definition of aesthetics. In a footnote in my book I quote Nelson Goodman, who said that he wouldn't have the nerve to offer a definition of aesthetics. But I, not knowing anything, decided that I would try. I started off by saying that aesthetics is the standard by which all works of art are judged. Aesthetics has to do with the fusion of form and content. It is the fusion that is so important; that is what makes the work of art. Most problems in art come from the fact that the fusion isn't there, or is only partially there. There is either too much form or too much content. In the book, I explain the difference between the artist and the spectator, and the Hegelian idea of synthesis and antithesis and thesis, and all the various problems that we run into: form and behavior, form and idea,...a long, long list. Although the method isn't very sophisticated, I think the reader will get the idea. It took me two years to write.

ra: Oh, I can believe it. I've been trying to do the same thing in a way. I've just been looking at what Kant says about beauty. He uses such qualities as perfection, harmony, balance, and simplicity. I have asked myself, What are these things for? It occurred to me that anything that you want to say clearly and to the point has to have coherence, symmetry, and simplicity. If we look at your books, we see that you do that all the time. You have a particular subject, let's say for example the announcement for the summer session at UCLA. When you look at that, what does it have? It has simplicity and austerity. And at the same time it has a great clarity. It has all the alphabet, and all the letters have a clarity and a lack of nonsense, a lack of the superfluous. So what is this? These are functional statements about the object to which you are giving a significant form.

pr: Yes, they are functional statements, but they are revealed by formal means, aesthetically.

ra: In other words, the function is the overarching concept. Within that, you have practical function and you have the function of making the meaning of the object or institution apparent. If you make a logo for a bank, you want to say the bank is solid, it is not given to temporary changes, it is open to its customers, and so on. That is all part of the so-called aesthetics. And this so-called aesthetics is nothing but part of the function of what you are saying about the bank.

pr: It is the fusion of form and function, or content; they are the same.

ra: I wanted to get beyond just the statement of fusion. I wanted to know what the fusion is. In other words, what is the particular function contributed by the aesthetic? The particular function contributed by the aesthetic is that is makes the nature of the object visual and expressive.

pr: You don't see the function, you see the object and the form. We are going to have a hell of a discussion because we don't disagree on anything.

ra: Well, maybe we do.

pr: Oh, sorry I brought it up.

ra: It seems to me, and this is also interesting, that the notion of the aesthetic is not very old.

pr: Baumgarten.

ra: Yes, Baumgarten is eighteenth century.

pr: The materialization of the idea isn't old, but aesthetics began in Genesis when God created the world. There it was. When the drawings were made in the caves of Lascaux, there were aesthetics. It had nothing to do with what the artist was thinking; it had to do with what he was doing. The artist worked intuitively. If you could ask him why he did it, he wouldn't know; it didn't matter.

ra: The subject of the aesthetics has always existed, but not its theory.

pr: People don't understand this. To me, aesthetics don't change.

ra: I agree

pr: Style changes. I remember I was asked to write an essay about Jan Tschichold, the typographer from Berlin who had been selected as one of the ten greatest designers in the world. He had just changed from modern typography back to traditional. He said the modern typographers were very opinionated and they didn't have any leeway. I wrote the essay, but it just occurred to me that it would have been much easier to write it if I had talked about aesthetics, because what happened with Tschichold was not that he changed his aesthetics, but rather his style. His modern work was of the highest quality, and so it was with his traditional work as well. I loved both; it didn't make any difference to me which style he used. I wrote an essay about the big argument between Tschichold and Max Bill.

ra: What was the argument about?

pr: Max Bill accused Tschichold of being reactionary, and being against the modern movement, which is nonsense. One can explain it aesthetically. It is easy to explain how one can change his preferences and still basically not change. One just changes ones lifestyle; instead of wearing this jacket, one wears another.

ra: If you look at the differences between Tschichold's works done in the traditional way and those done in the modern way, you find that in each case there is a clarity, a great beauty, but each talks to a different sensibility. It sings another melody. By that I mean it refers to another way of life. For instance, his later works have a kind of softness and roundness and quietness which the earlier works did not have. The earlier works had a kind of austerity. But both are legitimate parts of representing life, aren't they?

pr: They both represent the highest quality. You know, Harold Bloom said if literature or poetry are not aesthetic, they are something else. I thought that was a wonderful statement because it made the whole concept of aestheticism clear to me.

ra: There are certain qualities that we call the qualities of works of art. And what I am trying to insist on is that that quality is at the service of the statement the artist wants to make about the object. It seems to me that you are doing that all the time. You ask: What is the image my client wants? How does he want his project to be seen? And then you are asking yourself, How can I give this a material form, a visual form? One problem that I find quite interesting is, what are the ethics of this? I'm sure this is something you are very familiar with. Let me take an extreme case. Somebody comes to you and says: Mr. Rand, I need good publicity for a tobacco company. I want to introduce smoking to teenage children. If he is that blunt (and most likely he isn't), you would probably have ethical problems, and you would say: I don't want to get involved with that. Suppose you have an objection to banks. Suppose you say: I am a designer, but I am also a Marxist, and I believe that the banks are capitalist enterprises that exist to exploit the proletariat. Then you would say: I'm not going to do that work. It seems to me that there is a point to which you identify yourself with the client. This is what he wants to do, this is the image he wants you to create of him. You agree with that, but there may be other things you don't agree with. Is that at all acceptable?

pr: In my work I have experienced the fact that the client never knows what he wants. For example, six months ago I did a logo for American Express. They told me they were going to have other studios also do the logo and that they would then survey focus groups to see if the public likes or dislikes them. I don't believe this method works. It's impossible.

ra: Can you explain what was on your mind when you thought about what kind of image to create for American Express?

pr: Well, I am very practical. I don't believe that work should be put in a drawer to rot; I believe that work should be used. I knew that since the American Express people had shown this image of theirs for so many years, that I couldn't just throw it away. There had to be some connection between the old and the new.

ra: What image is that?

pr: That Roman legionnaire with the bad lettering you can't read. It is very bad because it tries to look like money or a stock certificate, which it isn't. Already that idea can't possibly produce anything that's decent. They liked my logo better than anybody else's, but once they tested it, they didn't think it was sufficiently different to warrant the expense of redoing it. It would have cost billions of dollars to change everything. So it died, but I think that was wrong.

ra: That's just the problem. Imagine if there had been a popular judgment as to whether Cézanne was a good painter or not. It's amazing. People will run to Chicago for a big Monet exhibit because it's very pretty and very popular; they go there essentially to have been there. They only have five minutes per painting, so there is no way of really looking at anything. I think there is not really much opportunity for appreciating art left in this civilization of ours.

pr: It is very sad.

ra: All you can do is your best and say: here it is, take it or leave it.

pr: Yes, but of course you need a lot of luck if you don't want to starve to death. I've had a lot of luck in my life.

ra: I don't think so. Quality shows.

pr: But one must have the audience. Look what happened with American Express. They just dismissed the work out of hand.

ra: But those are a few people who happen to be in charge.

pr: Yes, but the problem is that you and I are people who try to be logical, reasonable, but the world is not reasonable. Now you spoke earlier about the logic of logos. Logos are not logical; logos are emotional. Few people understand that a logo is essentially an identifier but rarely an illustration of a corporate enterprise. In the long run a well-designed logo will not necessarily rescue a downtrodden business, nor will a logo that is badly designed necessarily bankrupt a flourishing business. There is ample evidence of successful companies with lackluster designs. A logo is like a signature on a check. One doesn't object when the signature is ugly, as long as it represents a large sum of money. Who cares? A beautifully designed logo, however, is infinitely more useful, practical, valuable, economical, and memorable than one that is poorly designed.

ra: I think we are talking about different things, because I am not talking about how people react or anything like that. I am talking about the aesthetic quality of the object. In other words, I am looking at a logo which you have made, and I say this is a beautiful thing. I don't mean that it is going to go over, that it is going to be successful and all that. I don't know that and I don't care. That's not my business. You see, what I care about, what I want to go after, is what you called aesthetics. I want to go after the quality of it. I confess that I have very little tolerance and very little interest in, let me say, ninety-five percent of the popular civilization in which we live. I'm not interested in sports; I'm not interested in television. I never look at it.

pr: We are brothers.

ra: One pays a price for that, but I am concerned with certain things, which I would agree with you are the lasting and eternal things. That's good enough for me.

pr: I would be very curious to know what you think is going to happen today with the computer and art?

ra: Well, I'll tell you. It seems to me that a tool is a tool. Whether it is a hammer or a toothbrush or a computer. The one thing about any tool is that although it may be extremely useful, it depends on what you do with it; it should never be in charge. What they are doing now with computer art or electronic art looks dreadful to me. It is pathetic. And that is because they think that by letting the tool do what the tool can do, it will create something beautiful.

pr: You haven't said anything I don't agree with. I know all this, and I have written about it; it as a problem. For example, art students today can't get a job unless they know how to work on the computer, but once they develop the skill, they will never get off the computer. So there won't be any designers left. That is a serious problem.

ra: It seems to me that a computer is exceedingly

helpful for mechanical things, for making models and for many other purposes. Architects today are doing things that they never dreamed of doing before.
I think that cannot be appreciated enough. So I think it is important that every student of design and architecture learn how to work on the computer.
I never learned it, but they should. If you didn't have a ruler and a compass, you would have some practical problems, but the ruler and the compass can never create a good design. Tools can help you, and that is true for an architect, for a dentist, for a surgeon, or for anybody else.

pr: The problem still exists that teachers and students see this instrument as a creative tool. Not that the person is going to create, but that the tool is going to create. That's not possible. A tool has never determined the appearance of things. A tool may help establish a certain style because of its possibilities, but it has nothing to do with aesthetics. Nothing.

ra: This is interesting. What kind of a style do you think the computer could create?

pr: So far the style that it has created is just awful.

ra: It is awful alright, but every tool has its preferences. For instance, if you did everything just with a ruler you would get a certain style; you wouldn't get any curves. Do you want to hazard a guess as to what would be a style congenial to the computer?

pr: I know a little about computers. I use the computer a bit for practical reasons. But I have no idea what kind of style it could create. I know what it has created, what I've seen, and that is terrible. But I don't think styles work that way. When Robert Fulton invented the steamboat, they didn't change the style of art. Styles of art have only changed by the impetus of the artist. Nothing else changes them.

editors: What about the invention of photography?

ra: That was a very important change. Photography is a very interesting medium, because it is a completely new cooperation between nature and man-made form. Before photography, the cooperation was by people looking at nature and saying, I am going to make a picture. But with photography, nature itself became part of the medium. The photographic cooperation between nature as a medium and man as a medium seems to me to be a novel thing that has been very productive.

pr: Nevertheless, at the beginning, the object of photography was to imitate painting.

ra: But what happened in photography was that

photography had to find its own style. It is now unusual that something starts first with a medium of the past.

pr: Cartier-Bresson proved just the opposite. He went back to drawing and painting and abandoned photography.

ra: I know, but that was a late personal decision of his. In the meantime, he created the very essence of photography. Cartier-Bresson had a sense of what nature would do for him, what the accident, the momentary thing, would do for him as an artist. That was his greatness. Don't you think?

pr: Yes, but it was also what he would do with nature...the exposure, the cropping, the editing, the lighting, etc. All of these things have to do with aesthetics. It always comes back to aesthetics. When Clive Bell published *Art* and wrote about significant form, none of the philosophers agreed with that, that is, none of the philosophers except me. I absolutely agree with him.

ra: I do too.

pr: I remember seeing a copy of da Vinci's *Last Supper*, a very bad copy, but it was hung proudly in the house of a person who was very religious. To him, that painting was no different from da Vinci's original in Milan. But the difference aesthetically was one thousand percent.

ra: That is a very interesting problem. It is true that a cheap print of the *Last Supper* is of course miles away from the original, but it is also true, it seems to me, that even the worst reproduction of a Leonardo painting still has some of that quality.

pr: You must know that book by a famous art historian that shows Goya's *Maja* in focus and then shows the same picture out of focus. It demonstrated that you still recognize the out-of-focus image as the Maja.

ra: Yes, it still has some of the proportion and some of the qualities.

pr: The values, the composition,...really in a certain sense, it showed the essence of the picture. I showed the ABC logo out of focus in one of my books. And you should still recognize it. The things that always prevail are the formal qualities. But at what point does the recognition stop?

ra: That is interesting. What conditions do you need for recognizing things? Does it have to do with size or distance or what? I remember once walking into a museum and I saw a painting from a distance. I said that must be a Delacroix. I couldn't recognize it at all, but I could see it.

pr: That is very important with logos, for example, on signs viewed from a distance. Simplicity is so important. There must be an image that is easy to remember and that doesn't require literal reading. For example, a logo I just did for TV is in the form of a five-pointed star. Five letters make up the star. That in itself is easy to recognize; you don't have to read it. When you can do something like that, it is a great help. You said earlier that the trademark for the bank should represent the bank. Good design is not necessarily related to subject matter. You don't want to do anything that is misleading, but what you do often has nothing to do with the subject. For example, the octagon of Chase Manhattan Bank, what does that have to do with the bank? Nothing. If it is a good bank and if you make a lot of money, then it is a wonderful logo. If the bank goes out of business, it is a terrible logo. A logo is affected by the company or object it represents. If a logo represents George Washington, people have a good impression because they think Washington was a wonderful man. If it represents Aaron Burr, they can't think it is a great logo, because he was a bad boy.

ra: Years ago in my book on "visual thinking" I happened to do a brief analysis of Chermayeff and Geismar's logo for the Chase Manhattan Bank to show how its geometric and dynamic properties pointed precisely to characteristics desirable for a good bank. Aren't you now disavowing your own trade? Aren't you saying what you are presenting as a logo doesn't mater because all that matters are the condition of its acceptance?

pr: No, it does matter, because to me art represents a quality of life that is very important. Aesthetics, logic, and ethics are the three sciences. It is very important that things be done well, just for the sake of being done well, just to improve the quality of life. It has nothing to do with making money. That has to do with merchandising and advertising and promotion, but what the logo represents is how well these other factors operate. If they are bad, then the logo is bad. If they are good, then the logo is good. From that standpoint, it doesn't matter. But what does matter is that the logo be simple, that it be memorable, that it be easy to understand. And that takes an artist.

ra: I agree with that.

pr: An artist can do it intuitively; he doesn't have to do research. I never do research. I know the logo should be good and it shouldn't mislead, but it cannot lead in the sense that if you look at it you'll know it is a great bank. That's not possible. Not even desirable. If it is a great bank, eventually the logo will represent this great bank.

ra: Let me ask you now another thing. I was quite interested to see that in some examples of your work you deliberately turn a word sideways so it is not easy to read. The mystery of that, the fact that one has to figure out what it is, seems to be part of what you are doing.

pr: Absolutely. It engages the reader. It becomes a puzzle that they have to solve. Take, for example, a rebus. The IBM rebus with the eye and the bee intrigues people because they have to figure it out. Even in Germany it is very popular, and there "eye" is *auge,* not "I." I just did a poster for some conservationists. It is a picture of the juxtaposition of a rose and a skull. CH precedes the picture of the rose and the death head, and that is followed by SE. That's the poster. People look at the rose and the skull and say: oh yes, those must be two OOs. That is one way of making design interesting.

ra: This shows that clarity and legibility are not the only criteria.

pr: Not at all. Sometimes it is so clear that you just pass right over it. A design must stop somebody. Of course you don't want to stop them to the point where it is impossible to read, but you must stop them somehow.

ra: Can you think of anything else we should have talked about?

pr: I feel so humble in front of you. I am afraid to even open my mouth. I have read all of your books.

ra: For me it is most productive to have live contact with artists. It nourishes my mind when I sit at my desk, dealing with concepts. I talk to artists and to architects and my feeling is, and I wonder if you feel the same way too, that nowadays the applied arts are really the only ones that work. When I look at what is happening in the fine arts, I think that much of it looks empty. It has no objective, it has no statement to make. I think we agree that in the visual arts something is the matter, and it would be interesting to say with more precision what exactly is wrong with them. My feeling is that they have no image, no conviction, and no purpose they want to give shape. In other words, they have no function. The visual arts need a function.

pr: Function in a special sense. Absolutely. There is no way that I could disagree with you. No way. I have to thank you for all the wonderful books you have written. I have them all. *Alle*.

ra: Well, I'm about talked out. That was a great treat for me.

pr: I can always outdo you. Mine was more of a treat.

ra: Okay.

Virginia Smith
Roslyn Bernstein, eds.
Paul Rand
Artograph 6

Artograph invited Paul Rand to present his work (from his then-recently published seminal book *Paul Rand: A Designer's Art*) and to be interviewed by students in the graphic design program at Baruch College in New York City. The following is a transcript of that interview in 1987.

Artograph: Tell us, do you think of yourself primarily as a corporate designer, a book designer, or an advertising designer?

Paul Rand: I don't think of myself as primarily anything. The only way you can not specialize is to be a permanent amateur. I'm not an expert on anything. Of course that makes me an expert in everything. I'm not like some people who specialize in one area exclusively – say, calligraphy – which I hate.

a: You hate calligraphy? Why?

pr: I hate the idea of calligraphy. I don't hate beautiful, natural typography, like that of my friend Herman Zapf. I just received a letter from him, and I sat and admired the way he writes, perfectly, naturally. However, most calligraphy is not natural at all. It always reminds me of ancient or medieval scribes, of people who are completely out of our time, and therefore, are, in a sense, our enemies.

a: You made the point in your recent book *A Designer's Art*[1] that an artist works very much in his time.

pr: The artist has to be a product of his time, otherwise he is a hypocrite.

a: We are intrigued by your expression "a permanent amateur."

pr: I just made it up.

a: Maybe we could get behind it. What does an expert-amateur bring to design? What are the things you bring to it, if you don't bring expertise?

pr: Well, there is an aspect of design that is all-embracing. The same things that are true of architecture and dance and, in a sense, music are also true of design. Graphic design is one aspect of painting. It has the same requirements. Instinct or intuition has to operate, as well as reason, in both disciplines. There's no difference at all. I can say so because I have painted, and I have felt just as miserable doing painting as doing graphic design (when misery was part of the picture). Or, when elation was part of it. No difference. The difference that some artists like to believe exists between fine art and commercial art is pure snobbism. Saying, "I am better than you." They are not better. They may be better than me, but they're not better graphic designers who are better than me. Cassandre, for example, was a marvelous painter, as good as the best painters. But he left painting to do what he called "pure painting." That consisted of nude women and chickens running around farmyards. Or little houses and clouds. I saw them in his studio – tons of pictures stacked up against the wall.

Paintings that were beautiful in a technical sense but they were, you know...

a: It's interesting that you say that you're in the emotional state of whatever is required at the time, misery or excitement. Do you have to work yourself up into that?

pr: I'm afraid you just get worked up without wanting to. You know, parenthetically, why I don't like being interviewed? Because people look at you as if you are an expert, and I don't consider myself an expert. It's a little bit like asking a horse how he wins a race. He can't answer. It's just natural for him. He just wins the race. He has talent, he's a horse, he has four legs and he wins. It's the same thing with an artist. I'll give you an example of how it works. Somebody calls me and asks me if I am interested in a design job. If I'm not interested, if I have no time, or if I don't like the subject, I turn it down; nevertheless, when I hang up, I sit down and figure out a design solution. I do it anyway; I always do it.

a: Is it discipline?

pr: No. I hate discipline. It's a natural urge. It's animal instinct, like a cat going after a mouse. I go after solutions; it's a challenge. You know, sometimes you get very difficult problems. People call me to ask if I will design something, and I sometimes do it for the sole reason that I am curious to see if I can. And I often try to solve the problem before I even meet with the client.

a: You have said that you hate discipline. But in your writings you recommend a disciplined approach.

pr: Oh, yes, you have to be disciplined, but that doesn't mean you have to like it. I remember saying to Herbert Matter once, "I hate doing maps." He said, "Well, you don't have to love it to be able to do it." There are people who love doing things, but they do terrible things.

a: Were you taught in a disciplined manner?

pr: Not the kind you get in, let's say, the Kunstgewerbeschule in Basel. No. When I went to school, the instruction was lackadaisical. There was no system. When I studied with George Grösz in the 1930s [2], he had just come over from Europe, and he did not speak a word of English. You can imagine what his classes were like. He walked around and looked at your work and made a few marks, and you wondered what he was driving at. I'm still wondering. I am not an expert in teaching, although I have been teaching for forty years. I learned a lot from magazines in the field. The old *Gebrauchsgraphik*[3] was a marvelous source. There has never been anything like those prewar issues of the magazine. A man by the name of Franzel was the editor. He had wonderful articles, and understood, really understood, and talked above the commercial viewpoint. But also he stressed the need to be practical. If it wasn't practical, it was nothing, neither art nor commerce. Another magazine of the time was *Advertising Art*. Ruth Fleischer was the editor. I was dying to get my stuff in that magazine. I managed to get one thing in I did that I think today is just terrible.

a: What was it like?

pr: It's kind of abstract, very simple. In those days you were ashamed to do anything if it wasn't done by hand. You didn't use rub-on type, or photostats. I never used a photostat, everything was drawn. If your students don't do it, you should. Drawing letters. To make you sensitive to curves. Like [Josef] Albers used to say, "Come on, fellows, get out of your steel suits and work." Relax and be able to move your hand around.

a: Solutions don't come from application or concentration or discipline, then. Where do they come from?

pr: Well, they come from experience, in part. Some problems are more difficult than others because they don't lend themselves to visual interpretation, and maybe they shouldn't even be interpreted. People want you to design their product, and they may expect you to come up with flying angels and Bach cantatas, but that's not appropriate. I try to keep things pretty earthy. For example, I did the UPS trademark, and I had only a week to work on it (because they had already tried everybody else). I showed it to my daughter, who was about ten years old at the time. I showed her a sketch and I said; "Catherine, what's that?" She said, "That's a present, Daddy." I said, "Perfect." Ten years old. And I often show things I do to people who have no preconceived notions about design. I just say, "Can you read this?" I think that things should be read. I am not particularly interested in these fancy solutions to trademarks, this tendency to be as circuitous as possible to attain the most "elegant" kind of solution. Real elegance doesn't scream. It's very modest.

a: Does everyone respond to certain basic symbols? The cross, the mask, others?

pr: Yes. There is a misconception about symbols and about trademarks. It isn't the designer who makes the trademark, it's the corporation who uses it. For example, the Nazis made the swastika, which was an ancient symbol, into one of the most terrible signs in history. A company could make a trademark done by Michelangelo look terrible, merely by association. I remember when the Chase Manhattan trademark was done. When it first came out, I was in London, and I stopped at the Chase Manhattan Bank there and asked the teller what he thought of it. He thought it was terrible. Now everybody thinks it's great, because it has become associated with a rich Rockefeller bank. So it has become meaningful, but in itself it is merely a nut (nut and bolt).

a: Let's discuss the humor in your work. It seems, sometimes, there is a certain humor born of anticipating spectators' reaction to things.

pr: There is an aspect of humor in my work, but it's not the same kind of humor, for example, as the little Dubonnet man. That's funny, I mean that's humorous – the little nose and the little derby. Or, in this piece [pointing to page showing Tipton Lakes logo]. I remember when I did this. This is not a ha-ha humorous, but its humorous. It is serious business; it is a real-estate business, selling tracts of land that are very expensive. I remember when I did this thing my liaison said to me, "You know, everybody likes the design, but...," and I knew something was coming, and was ready for him. I didn't know what he was going to say, but whatever he was going to say, it was going to be "no." And he said, "Some of the people thought it looked too much like a toy." And I said, "They are going to have to live with it, or if they don't like it, too bad, then don't use it."

a: Why did you use the ducks?

pr: Because they have several duck ponds in the place. In fact three of them. Oh, yes, it is definitely illustrative, and very rarely can you do that. But we are talking about humor. [Looking through the book and pointing to various designs] This is sort of humorous, the man with three eyes. This is humorous, you should have heard the comment by the board of directors when I did this. Ah, this is sort of funny....

a: The Chopin advertisement for Westinghouse?

pr: Yes. Often when I have a logo to do, I'll zip through a type book.

a: And look at forms?

pr: No, I look at ideas, not at forms. I look at things that associate with the problem, and make connections. Take this AIGA cover design. The "eye" stands for the letter "I." That ancient practice of using an image for this purpose is called a "rebus." The whole idea of a rebus is humorous. Visual puns: those are also funny. I have written about these concepts. But the important thing to remember is that you try to do them because they are mnemonic devices. They lend themselves to being remembered.

a: In your recent book you wrote that one shouldn't use an oriental typeface when designing an oriental product.

pr: Don't take that too literally. There is always someone who can show you up. You never say "never" in design or art.

a: What about the UPS logo?

pr: The UPS logo is humorous, too. I mean it's not too serious: you wouldn't use it for an undertaker.

a: The top part is easily identifiable as a gift. Is the bottom part a shield?

pr: Yes. That was a given. Previous designers had developed a shieldlike element. The company had used about fifty designers, including the best. It can be a problem when you see what another designer has done. You either build on it or you avoid it. In this case they insisted on it. So, it was something to work with. Another problem was that the UPS employees – the men and women who deliver your packages – were to vote on the design. They are stockholders in a small way. There is one part of the logo I wanted to do differently, but I didn't, because I knew that it would become a problem. Specifically, I don't like the points; I prefer the half circle. But I anticipated that they would read it not as a shield, but as a pocket. So I avoided it, but I think it would have been better with the half circles.

a: Did you use brown and beige because they are colors associated with paper and packages?

pr: I used brown because that was their color, and I never change the color if I think it's good. Why change it?

a: In the IBM Product Centers you used colors as a unifying force.

pr: Yes, everything is red – furniture, signs, everything.

a: How much is it the color, the beauty of the red, and how much is it just keeping it the one color that makes it successful?

pr: That's a very good question. Obviously it has to be a color that you can use. I mean not pea green. But it might even be pea green under certain conditions. But all things being equal, the idea is less the attribute of red than it is the idea of having only one color. So that the concept "the red store," "the yellow store," or "the blue store" is simple and easy to remember. Take Benetton. One thinks of green in connection with Benetton, right? You don't have blue and red and yellow, even though they might sprinkle it through the store. But one also thinks of green at Benetton. Green also happens to be one of my favorite colors. But red, whether you like it or not, is an extremely potent color. Ask any bull. I did one of the first IBM Product Centers in Silicon Valley. I remember the first morning the people working at IBM walked in. A woman said, "What a wonderful feeling it is to be in this store!" You know, the sun was shining, the red was reflecting in her face, and she like she had just come from Palm Beach; she looked so healthy with the reflection of the sun on her face. But there's nothing new about using red. It's as old as the hills. In medieval days red was one of the most common colors. It's greatly used in the Roman Catholic Church – look at the red robes, the mitered hats, the carpets.

a: You wrote an essay titled "Black Black Black" about the power of black. What is the psychological advantage of black?

pr: Now you are asking me to be a psychologist. I don't know. I happen to like black. Black is the absence of all colors, but it is also the implication of all colors, too. Today most TV monitors are black. Compare them to the crummy things they had not too long ago, the walnut trimmed with chromium. I had a Sony TV that was walnut, and when I saw another monitor I got rid of the Sony and bought the nicer one. For me things that look good are preferable to things that don't look good. Even if it costs a lot of money, I buy the better-looking object. I don't know how other people feel about it. Some people won't even spend a cent even if the world were coming to an end. They're either insensitive or indelicate, I don't know. I have bought every electric razor that Braun ever made, because they're absolutely beautiful, but they're not very good razors compared to Remington. I have a lot of Braun products that I buy just for their beauty and then put in a drawer.

a: You are talking about reputations. What is associated with a company, or product?

pr: You can't avoid this whole problem of association. I get jobs, big jobs sometimes, because I have a reputation. That's annoying. People don't understand that I can do some things better than somebody else, but there are some people who can do some jobs better than I can. I remember when I did the "7," and they said, "Well, we'd like to see if you can do something." I tried, and then I got back to them and I said, "No, what you have is better than I can do." I think you have to be honest about it. A lot of people change things just because they are given the opportunity. For example, I could have changed the UPS truck to several other beautiful colors, but that would have been a waste. There is an ethical problem. Ethics is a very important part of design. Its almost by definition the nature of design. Design means organizing, and organizing means something positive, putting things together so they become presentable, become interesting, become amusing, become fascinating. All of these things are part of the organizational problem, which is an ethical problem. And just to change things for more money or more business or to show how clever you are is, I think, unethical.

a: How can an ethical sense be instilled in designers?

pr: I don't know. It seems to me to be innate in some people and not in others. Just like people who are religious or aesthetic, or people who are amusing. They just are.

a: Why is it unethical to change a design if it will bring more business to the company? Isn't that what business is all about?

pr: You ask such leading questions. From the point of view of business, it's certainly not unethical. My credo, and I don't mean to sound fancy, because I am a very simple guy, but my credo really is that when you design something it must have a certain standard of quality. It makes no difference what it is, it must have quality. So, if somebody changes something that is already good, he has to change it to something that's equally good or better. But if he changes something that is already good to something that's bad, for business reasons, then I think that's unethical.

a: Suppose a designer does a job to the best of his abilities, but his ability is not as good as what went before?

pr: Well, now we are getting into a different kind of problem. Now you are talking about individual talents. I've really said all I can say about ethics. You've had my Sunday sermon.

a: Do you think that the IBM logo had any influence on the style of the corporation?

pr: I have no idea. All I can tell you is that, before I did that logo I never saw a logo with stripes, and afterwards stripes were taken up by the whole industry.

The stripes had nothing to do with speed or electronics. I'll tell you the reason why I did it that way. There was a problem to be solved, because of the nature of the three letters I, B, M. The letters are in a sequence of little, bigger, biggest. That's uncomfortable because you expect the sequence to keep going; it could go on forever. It has a rhythm – like do-re-mi. Also, I wanted to introduce the idea of authority. Have you seen in old documents lines where you are to sign your name? Those lines are put there to prevent counterfeiting, to prevent people from erasing or copying the name. I thought, "Why not just take the letters and make those lines?" That's how it happened. But, again, it is the company that has made the mark. It's a very good company, and by association, the stripes have become symbols of quality.

People have some sort of superstition about a trademark, a belief that you cannot touch it. I was asked to do the Ford Motor Company mark some years ago, and I did it. We printed a big book and there was a big production and everybody liked it except Mr. Ford. He looked at it and he said, "I don't think what we have is old-fashioned." And that was the end of it.

a: If you change an existing logo, don't you risk losing the recognition it has with the public? Isn't it dangerous?

pr: I don't think it is dangerous. I think it is expensive. Look at Nissan. Look at what they did. You don't even remember the name they replaced. Visually, they obliterated the old mark. What was it? Datsun? Right. They put a lot of money into changing it, and did it. But these are things that have nothing to do with design. Don't get things mixed up.

There is another matter when you're dealing with visual things (or even with verbal things). Opinions are so personal, so subjective. When someone says to you "I think that's a great design," and you agree with him, it means you agree for the same reason. We may be talking different languages. Even in discussions like this interview, I wonder how well you understand me, and how well I understand you. We are talking about things that are in a sense, ineffable, ineluctable. The real thing, the real art, the thing that makes something art, one can talk about. And as for opinion, whether somebody likes something or doesn't like something doesn't have to do with design. I recently read an essay by Henry James called "The Art of Fiction." In it he refers to the very difficult problem of liking or not liking. Liking or not liking is unavoidable, but also, the reasons are unprovable. I like it, and if somebody else doesn't, like Ford, that's the end of it. You can't do anything about it unless you have some special skill and can talk people into, or out of anything.

a: When you present a new logo to executives of a corporation, do they ever say, "I'm not really sure… I have to think about it a while."

pr: Big business people are usually pretty definite. They don't shilly-shally around. And I am very direct. But you never work with the chief executive of a large corporation in these design matters. The decision comes down through three other executives. There's no way you can do anything about it, unless you want to go over their heads.

a: To what extent does presentation affect the design decision?

pr: Well, the art of presentation is part of our business, the art of deception. Much bad design can be sold through a great presentation. When you look around at bad design, you can say, "It must have been a terrific presentation!" I never make a presentation, personally. I usually send it in the mail.

a: Why?

pr: Maybe because if it's going to be rejected, I don't want to be there. But more importantly, I think that the thing has to stand on its own merits. I've seen skillful presentations made by people doing terrible work and selling it. People spend money making presentations with three-dimensional things and lights and theatrical effects, dancing girls, and music – true! I mean, if you get a million dollars or two, you have to do something, you can't just do a mark. That's one of my big problems. If I charge a client a million dollars and give him only a mark, I've got to make it worth his while. You may think that I'm kidding, but this is an aspect of the serious side of the business: the problem of selling.

a: To what extent were you involved in the presentation to Ford?

pr: I didn't go to the presentation. I just sent it in. I might have succeeded in selling it, but I might have also been thrown out. You know, they set you up in a hotel for VIPs, a very uncomfortable place. They send a limousine for you, and you go to lunch and sit in a Mies van der Rohe chair. The whole thing is very ritualistic.

a: Let's talk about some designers and type designers

and how you have related to them.

pr: It would be wonderful if you could deal with people who have the same sense of values you have yourself. That's one of our big problems. You know, W.A. Dwiggins,[4] who was a designer in the twenties, referred to me as one of those "Bauhaus boys." He was being perfectly honest, but his values weren't mine. He was a medieval scribe and I'm just a guy who just went to the moon. We don't speak the same language. This is true of so many of those early moderns: Stanley Morison,[5] Frederick Goudy,[6] and others. Stanley Morison referred to modern designers as "gigolos." That's what he called them. Not me. I wasn't illustrious enough to be mentioned by him.

a: Did you know Morison?

pr: I once had the pleasure of meeting him at the Garrick Club in London. He was sort of like the Pope. He sat there in a black suit with a little white collar, just like a priest. I decided, this is too much. I started to drink, and haven't the faintest idea of what he was talking about for about two hours. Fortunately, I was with a friend who was talking to him while I was supposedly listening. However, after a while I got up and I walked to the dining room. It was a beautiful room, and the tables were set with silver flatware, flowers and candles, the chandeliers were lit. In the midst of all this, in the midst of this empty room, stood T.S. Eliot. He was standing there, and this was no vision. That sums up my experience with Stanley Morison in London. {At this point in the interview slides of modern painters and slides of Rand's designs were projected.}

a: When you use photographs, as in this cover of *Direction* magazine, you often alter them in some way – here you fragmented the picture. Why? What does it accomplish?

pr: What it accomplishes, if it accomplishes anything, is to dramatize parts of the body that make dance, and it does it in a way that's unusual, unexpected, and memorable. A photograph of a dancer is a million dancers, not memorable. But this one you won't forget.

a: So defamiliarize the ordinary?

pr: Yes. Right, but I don't do it with any such specific purpose, except that I like to do it. If I happen to be lucky enough to get an idea, I do it. Also, in case you haven't noticed, I also happen to be a big fan of Hans Arp.

a: Yes, we are just about to show some slides of his work. Let's talk about Arp.

pr: I think he was one of the great men, original men of our time. One of the very few originals. Amazing the way he could abstract forms. This is extremely rare.

a: Your *Direction* cover takes from Arp the practice of making the parts become a whole.

pr: Well it is the nexus of the design, you know, the coming together of the elements.

a: You were influenced by Arp?

pr: No, if you want to go into something like how people are influenced, I can show you people who've more than influenced each other; they have stolen from one another. Like Lissitsky and Malevich. I'm speaking of *The Story of Two Squares,* where there is no difference at all between Malevich's painting and Lissitsky's design. The application of work from one discipline to another is the genius of Lissitsky, not that he was such an original. Art has to do with doing the right thing at the right time. Not necessarily first, but at the right time. It is a question of giving a right answer at the time the question is asked, and getting the right idea at the right moment. One of the big problems a designer has is that ideas are very open-ended. You can go on forever getting ideas from something but you don't have time for that. So, the big problem is to pick the right one and do it quickly. And how often have you done a design and then found out you had a much better idea later? I've done it. I did a cover recently for a Japanese magazine about thirty-five of the world's greatest designers. I don't know how they picked them, either the designers or the number. But I did a cover with a lot of different color dots, representing thirty-five eyes. After it was printed, I had a much better idea. So, timing itself is part of the process. If a guy is on his feet, you know, fast.

a: Let's look at graphic design in the context of the modern movement. We have slides of some early, influential modern artists. [Slides are projected]

pr: This is Suprematism, Russian Futurism, if you like. The designers were working in the style of the period, in the style of the painters. This was Malevich's application of graphics to painting.

a: Do you see the suprematists as having some kind of influence on graphic designers of the twentieth century? Where would you put Malevich as an influence in graphic design?

pr: Well, Lissitsky as I said before, adapted Malevich's paintings and used the same ideas. Exactly. He took two squares and made a book called *The Story of Two Squares.*

a: Cassandre, of whom we spoke earlier, was both a painter and a commercial artist.

pr: He was a painter. His work was painterly.

a: You refer to Léger often. The painterly quality is important to you? Could you speak about that? And painters in particular?

pr: I use painters more for content than for the quality of the paint. I never use the word "painterly" in my book. I'm not talking about that, I am talking about the design aspect, the way Vasari talked about it. It is in the very first sentence of the book. What Vasari said was absolutely what I was talking about, too.

a: Here's Klee's painting *Around the Fish*. In much of your work there is something central. What elements keep recurring in your design?

pr: I cannot answer that question. No. I just do a job, you know, whatever it calls for.

a: Picasso and Braque turned to collage.

pr: Collage is the direct consequence of Cubism in the sense that it destroyed the traditional concept of space. By traditional space I mean the space of Rembrandt. They consciously destroyed that idea of Euclidian perspective, of Renaissance perspective, and they went to the extreme of not only destroying it, but of actually painting and gluing things that cast their own shadows on the canvas. It was getting away from the old style of painting that imitated reality. They did not try to give the illusion of reality through painting shadows, they glued things on that would cast their own, real shadows. They used newspapers rather than painting letters. There is a great misconception about Cézanne. He didn't say anything about Cubism; he only talked about perspective. Other painters misunderstood what he said, and did great paintings not because they understood, but because they misunderstood.

a: If a product is shown in a collage, what is the relation between that product and the other elements in the design? Does it have to be in the foreground? Does it have to be larger?

pr: No, it must be part of the composition. You know, this whole business of art in advertising has been completely misunderstood. People think if they use a painter like – oh, Boticelli – it associates their product with great artwork. It is a form of selling, and a kind of art that is for the birds. To take a Cubist painting of Braque to sell paper cartons is ridiculous. It's not art. Part of the definition of art has to do with usefulness. Real art is always useful, in one way or the other. Real art comes in doing the work, custom-made, for each product. If you are a real artist, it may be art, and if you are not, it won't be. Art is a question of quality, not classification.

a: What do you think of corporations collecting art? Do you think it is right for corporations to buy these paintings and make them inaccessible to the public?

pr: Well, what about private individuals who have collected? Look at Morgan, and Berenson, and Guiness. With corporate collections, you can go and see the works. You can go to Chase Bank (they even have tours), you can go to IBM. They are actually supporting art, so it's hardly negative. But perhaps a more important issue is whether the companies should be employing good design, instead of buying art. They buy art and produce bad graphic design. But IBM has always been exceptionally supportive of good art. Look at their beautiful new gallery at 590 Madison Avenue. It's open to the public – go and see it. The Container Corporation did a series of ads that were beautiful, but they had nothing to do with the Container Corporation. They used de Kooning, Ben Shahn, and other artists in the series (I did six of them), but when I visited their studio in Chicago and saw the actual work that was being done for the company's needs, it was extremely commercial stuff.

a: Do you still paint?

pr: Well, not at the moment, but I haven't thrown my easel away. You know, the difference, essentially, between painting and advertising is one of metier. It's like different kinds of birds, but they are still birds, the genre is the same, it's just the species that's different.

a: Certain techniques were used by the modernists, like fragmentation. That's why I showed that cover of *Direction*. Were you aware of such techniques in painting?

pr: I never claimed to be an original, never.

a: There's nothing new under the sun. But was there anything in modern painting, in fragmentation and abstraction, that you can cite specifically as appealing to you?

pr: Well, this is the vocabulary of art, the vocabulary of form. In the Léger problem I give to students, I went to the trouble of examining the things that I thought Léger contributed, and I actually broke it down. It's in my book. The assignment has been done by Harvard and a couple of other schools. That's the idea, it's the way one learns. Léger was another original. He was an architect. He liked a compass and ruler and straight edge. But he also had a terrific sense of humor. Most of these things are also very funny. Look at that kid, [Looking at slide] and the face and the hair, the impossible fingers and hands!

a: Was Léger influential on graphic designers?

pr: There is a big book on the subject that shows his influence in everything – in painting an in graphics. I think Cassandre was influenced; I certainly was influenced. But you know, when I give this Léger problem to students, I don't expect them to do a Léger. I expect them to learn the principles. Many try and succeed. Most people don't. I have hundreds of slides of student solutions to the Léger assignment and the results are amazing, both in range and in quality. But when you talk about influence, there is a kind of old-fashioned conception that is different from what I am talking about. The old-fashioned way, which was characteristic of those who are sometimes referred to as "serif-benders" – Dwiggins, Goudy, and others – was to use references like historical ornaments. You actually lift them and use them. You extrapolate and you interpret. When I talk of Picasso and Léger and Ernst and Klee, I'm not talking about doing things like them. People try. But they fail miserably when they try to imitate Klee. What I try to do is learn what they did. To understand what they did and understand the principles of design, contrast, color.

a: What about the "serif benders"? What did they do?

pr: They had a different sort of perception. They were perpetuating the past. Literally, not just spiritually. Morison wanted to revive Gutenberg and Caslon and Baskerville, and he did, for Monotype Corporation. They're marvelous things. But when you think of the ornament of Dwiggins, for example, although it's very skillful, and in a way original, it gives me the creeps. For want of a better word call it old-fashioned, although that's pejorative, and I don't really mean to be pejorative.

a: You use your own handwriting often rather than use typefaces.

pr: I do it as long as I can get away with it. It's very fast. I used it on many books for Bollingen as a means of contrast until one day they stopped me. This very nice guy said, "Paul, why don't you try something else?"

a: Well, if you had a gun put to your head like that, what typefaces do you use? Some of those Stanley

Morison faces? Perpetua? Times Roman?

pr: No. I think Times Roman is ugly. It's very practical, very readable, and in the old *London Times* it was quite beautiful. It was small and the paper was delicate. But when you use Times Roman big, it is horsy. My real typographical mentor was Jan Tschichold, and before that a man I worked with, a man of whom nobody has heard. He's nobody, poor guy, and he was famous, too, in the 1930s. George Switzer, You know, sometime I'm going to come up here and give you a talk on these designers of the twenties and thirties that everyone has forgotten. There are plenty of them, really. Has anybody heard of Gustav Jensen? Nobody. And Jensen was a designer's designer. Jensen was marvelous. He was a Dane, and he had a decorative touch that was not unlike that of the Wiener Werkstatte. He was a former opera singer, and he had a big voice. As soon as he opened his mouth, you would fall backward, you know, "Hoooow Doooo Yooouuu Doooo?" I remember walking up to his studio. I was a little kid about seventeen years old with a portfolio that was too big for me. I almost got the job with him that I wanted so badly. But his business manager decided that I would just be in the way. In a way it was a good thing, because he had such an individual style that I was already copying him. He had a beautiful script signature, GBJ, Gustav Borge Jensen. I used to sit and look at it all night long. I tried to make my own initials look like his, but it was impossible. He had three letters that lent themselves to that sort of rhythm, but mine didn't.

a: I don't think he's well known.

pr: Another one is Joseph Sinel. You don't know him? This is a tragedy...You people are living in the dark, the dark of the New Wave. There were so many wonderful European designers in the early part of this century.

a: Give us names.

pr: You want me to give you names? I'll start with A. Arpke, Otto Arpke. B is for Binder, C is for A.M. Cassandre, D is for William Deffke, E is for Ernst. I could give you the whole alphabet.

a: Go ahead. Give us the names and we'll find examples of their work.

pr: G is for Gerog Goedecker. H is for O.H.W. Hadank...M is for Alfred Mahlau. You must know his work because he designed all the packaging for the German marzipan company of the twenties. I once traveled to where he lived in northern Germany, near

Hamburg. I believe he designed the building for the Niederegger Company, as well as the cups and carpets, and I think even the shapes of the cakes and cookies. Then there is S...Paul Scheurich, who did beautiful drawings, the most elegant fashion drawings, in a style not typical of German artists. He also did beautiful figurines in Dresden china. He did posters, too. Go to Z...Valentin Zietara. Another Z would be zero, my old friend Hans Schleger...Back to B...there is someone everyone should know, Lucien Bernhard. He lived here most of his life, after he left Germany in the twenties. He had a beautiful studio on 86th Street. The very first poster he did was beautiful. It was a picture of a match, just one match, and the name of the company, Priester. There was a brown background. The match was yellow and the tip was cerise, and blue, and the name was in white. Beautiful. It was around 1917, a long time ago. But I remember it. I know all these people's work, because that is where I learned how to design.

1. Paul Rand, *A Designer's Art*, New Haven: Yale University Press, 1985.
2. George Grösz, a Berliner who practiced art in Paris and Berlin, joined the Dada movement shortly after it started in 1916. He became well known for his satirical drawings, which appeared in German magazines. He came to the United States in 1932 and became an American citizen in 1938. He died in Germany in 1959.
3. *Gebrauchsgraphik* was founded in 1924 by H.K. Frenzel, who was its first editor. This German magazine, originating in Berlin, covered all aspects of graphic and advertising design, including poster, package, and book design. Because so many small-scale examples of artists' work were reproduced, and because the text was in English as well as German, the publication was widely influential. Since 1972 it has been known as *Novum Gebrauschsgraphik*.
4. William Addison Dwiggins was a designer of books, ads, and the typefaces Electra, Metro, and others. He lived until 1956.
5. Stanley Morison was the typographical advisor to the University Press at Cambridge (England) and was responsible for launching, in 1922, a program of designing new metal typefaces based on the originals of early printers such as Jensen and Aldus. Out of this program came Centaur, Arrighi italic, Bembo, Poliphilus, Granjon, Fournier, Bell, Perpetua, Felicity, Times New Roman, and others.
6. Frederic W. Goudy started to design typefaces in 1895 and continued to do so for a half-century. He holds the record for having designed more typefaces than any other person. Among them are Goudy Old Style, Kennerly, and Deepdene.

160: 161:

Mario Rampone
Type Talks

Mario Rampone: How do you feel about the "new" typefaces that are inundating the marketplace today?
Paul Rand: The announcement of anything new is bound to call attention to itself. When one considers the wonderful old faces that have passed through the sieve of time, one wonders, why new faces? Unless they're really new, there seems to be no reason to add to an already overloaded stockpile. A new typeface is ideal for the neophyte who is intent on one-upmanship, and who equates the latest with the greatest. "There are as many different varieties of letters as there are different kinds of tools," commented Eric Gill, a long time ago.
mr: How do you regard "freedom of expression" – about the person inspired to design a new typeface?
pr: One must accept the good with the bad, the fanciful with the freakish. Out of a hundred designs, there may be one that's really new. Who knows?
mr: IBM has recently adopted Berthold Bodoni as its house style, without altering its design. Does that make more sense than creating a new typeface?
pr: Yes, unless it can be improved. Increasing the x-height and shortening ascenders and descenders might be useful. Berthold Bodoni is based on the original design. Incidentally, it is similar to Didot or Walbaum. They are the same modern type family that the old typographic fraternity frowned upon.
mr: Why?
pr: Because the contrast between thicks and thins was enormously exaggerated. The serifs were square and uninteresting. They were, apparently, too mechanical, some would say too cold or too geometric. "Swelteringly hideous" is how William Morris is said to have described it. A speech by Talbot Baines Reed in 1890 in *Ars Typographica,* edited by Goudy in 1920, dealt with these very same problems. The need for anything to be designed has nothing to do merely with wanting to do it.
mr: Some people are going to love that comment.
pr: But it's true. It's an ego trip or a ploy to attract new business.
Once Univers was done, for example, there was no apparent reason to have a new sans-serif typeface.
mr: Univers is a beautiful typeface and it made as big a splash as Helvetica did. And it is still the most popular sans serif.
pr: Well, Univers is better in some respects; it fits better. In my view, the very bold is far superior to Helvetica. In some instances, one can't use the very

bold; the counters are much too small.

mr: That can be rectified.

pr: In typography things get revived. Now there is a revival of Futura, a typeface that was designed in 1925.

mr: But it's one of the classics.

pr: Yes, but it's not exactly the most legible face; it has certain characteristics lacking in other sans-serif faces. Compass and ruler are quite in evidence. It is, nevertheless, unique. Still, one must understand how to use it. Appropriateness, not timeless, is the guiding principle.

mr: It seems that designers often go out of their way to attract attention.

pr: That's an understatement. There are essentially two kinds of typography: The familiar kind for reading, and the other, simply for viewing, like a painting. Some say that readability is most important. There are really two important things about typography: readability and beauty; both are equally important. However, many readable typefaces are visually offensive. The design of a typeface, ugly or not, is only one aspect of the problem of readability. How a typeface is used is equally, if not more, important. The trick is to choose a readable and beautiful face like Baskerville, or Caslon, or Garamond. Tschichold's favorite typeface, incidentally, was Janson, which is similar to Caslon.

mr: Does a typeface have to be new to attract attention?

pr: Although newness has its place, good design is not merely a question of novelty. The typographer is more important than the type he uses. You can't blame the type if the typography is poor. It's like putting the burden on the music when the musician is at fault.

mr: Do you believe that the proliferation of computers in design schools is a good thing?

pr: It depends on how the computer is built into the curriculum. To the extent that the machine replaces the hand and prevents the student from practicing the manual skills, it is wrong. To the extent that computer theory replaces and is confused with design theory, it is equally wrong. Of course, there's a time and place for everything. Once a student feels at home with design – and this takes a very long time – he is free to choose his tools. A student once said, "I came here to learn how to design, not how to use a computer." Design schools take heed. After all, for every competent designer, there are at least a thousand competent computer operators – and we haven't even begun to deal with the products of computer-generated design, nor with the competence of those who teach design. The computer is surely one of the most astonishing machines of our time. However, the language of the computer is not the language of art/design. It is the language of machine – of production. It enters the world of creativity only as an adjunct, as a tool – a time-saving device, as a mean of investigating, retrieving, and executing tedious jobs – but not as the principal player. In education this art/production relationship is inescapable. The moment the balance is disturbed, it becomes a hindrance to invention and a barrier to the link between hand and tool. Of course, the computer is capable of producing visual effects not possible by other means. In the hands of a thoughtful designer, this may be useful. It may even help in the creative process – the realm of ideas – by suggesting visual possibilities undreamed of with other techniques, or by helping to solve problems specifically designed for the computer's capabilities. But these very means may also be the source of exploitation, merely for the sake of effects but not of essence. The expression "garbage in, garbage out" is more than a quip. Unless the computer is used properly, it will only encourage the kind of trendiness so profuse today – worse, in a way, than that stemming from more conventional means. The abundance of visual possibilities the computer makes available is its virtue: at the same time, it may be a source of confusion and baffling complexity. When to use it is certainly more important than how to use it. In the school environment it should be only a part of the curriculum but not the curriculum. I sometimes wonder if the fuss about computers in design schools isn't simply a decoy to show that the school is au courant. Or does it indicate some other problem? The tangibles of computer technology are obviously easier to cope with than the intangibles of design.

mr: Do you believe design by computer will be as enduring as more conventional systems?

pr: Enduringness has little to do with technique.

mr: The computer is not the ideal tool to learn design fundamentals, is this what you're saying?

pr: As a production tool for a seasoned designer the computer is ideal. As a tool for the beginning student it is a distraction. It produces more than the student needs, or is capable of absorbing. I don't use a computer myself. My supplier is better equipped to satisfy all my typographic needs, as he was in the Linotype days. I have never set type. I just look and "feel" if it's right or wrong. I don't think one has to set type in order to be aware of its intricacies. It's a bit like expecting a doctor to experience the same illness as his patient, in order to validate his prescriptions.

mr: Do you feel this technology can satisfy the requirements for good typography?

pr: Computer-generated typesetting lacks the built-in discipline so essential to proper spacing. The limitations of metal typesetting provided the restrains for finer word spacing. On the other hand, the unlimited, variable spacing possibilities of the computer are the source of endless problems, unless the designer is a pro.

mr: Metal typesetting required greater skill because type was set "wrong reading." Today, the computer operator sees his "proof" on the screen as he is keyboarding.

pr: Computer composition, nevertheless, presents its own peculiar problems, especially for students, who are only potential specialists.

mr: With the arrival of desktop publishing, a typographer's skills are being put to test. Companies are installing Macs, memos are beginning to look like ransom notes. This prompted a large corporation to rid most of the typefaces from its laser printers. How do you think this will affect the quality of typography?

pr: That kind of publishing is bad for the art of typography. It may sound fascinating to produce your own printed piece, but it will probably result in the accumulation of a Matterhorn of rubbish. Wishful thinking never took the place of experience or talent. Here's an example why one must be discriminating in choosing the right typeface: Some students send me letters set in type so impersonal as to be indistinguishable from direct mail advertising. The old Egyptian square-serif typewriter face has a certain charm about it, and it looks like a letter, not like a printed piece.

mr: Alphabets for computer programs are unitized the same as metal type was. The programs provide kern tables to cut the sidewalls off in order to bring the characters closer together. Today, unitizing provided with each font is not accurate enough for critical spacing. To correct this problem, custom kern tables are necessary. PostScript devices have exacerbated the problem. Do you believe that good typography is possible with this technology?

pr: Yes, of course. The principal problem is spacing. It depends on people who are sensitive to the kind of typography that was possible when metal setting was available.

Bez Ocko
On
"The
Rand
Book"

I conducted this interview with Paul Rand in 1987 over the course of several meetings at his home in Connecticut. At that time I was a student in the M.F.A. design program at Yale University. In the fall of that year Rand had given an eight-week project to my class, which the students called "The Rand Book." The project called for a total book design, from grid to typography and image selection, for the 1920 essay "Sur la Plastique," by Amédée Ozenfant and Charles-Edouard Jeanneret (Le Corbusier). This article was published in the first issue of their journal *L'Esprit Nouveau,* in Paris, and the title has been translated to "On the Plastic" or "On Form." The interview's points of origin and departure are this particular essay, the nature of this particular design project, and the education of a graphic designer.

Bez Ocko: Why did you select this essay by Le Corbusier and Ozenfont as the text for an educational design project? How does this relate to your teaching philosophy?

Paul Rand: In the past I've chosen several other essays, but I always come back to this one. It is the best one. Well, you are assuming that I have a philosophy. I mean, if I do, I am not aware of it. I gave this project because I read the essay myself and I learned a great deal from it. It was very clear to me what Le Corbusier was saying, even though I don't agree with all of it. I don't agree with a lot of what he says, but generally I think he's terrific. Now practically, this kind of educational design problem is all embracing because you have to do everything. You have to do the mechanics; you have to understand a little bit about typography, not too much because it's basically simple. It is not an annual report, which can get very complicated. And it's also a way of introducing students to the grid system. The essay also teaches something about the history of architecture and painting.
I've given several essays by Eisenstein, William Strunk and E.B. White's *The Elements of Style,* but I always come back to this one. It is the best one, the simplest one. It is not loaded with jargon. It says, "This is a cylinder," and describes all the different configurations of cylinders.
It is very clear. Le Corbusier talks about the golden section and how he thinks compositions were done in reference to works by Michelangelo and Cézanne.
bo: What about the discrepancies, the mistakes in the theories in this article?
pr: The authors universalize too much. They say everybody thinks this way and reacts the same way. That is not true. But I think you can dismiss that, pretend it is not there. Or disagree with it. But basically, I don't disagree with it.
Also Cézanne's quote "Everything is spheres and cylinders" is taken out of context in the essay. The paragraph is unfinished. Cézanne continued, and what he was speaking about was perspective. I was always aware that there was something wrong with this statement and the way people quoted it. Other things Cézanne said were also misread. Ironically, the statements that were misread were things that helped to generate very good things, for example Cubism. They certainly influenced Léger, who literally painted cylinders, spheres, and cones. And Malevich, too, who was

a real bug on Cézanne. He wrote a great deal about it.
bo: How did you choose the format for this project, 7.75 x 11 inches?
pr: It is a Root 2 rectangle. It is arbitrary. It could have been anything. I didn't choose a square because I think a square is not a practical shape for a book, unless it is small. When you open a square book up, it is no longer a square. Big books are very awkward in squares. Le Corbusier did his *Modular* books in squares. It is based on nothing reasonable. It's like Malevich's squares. Speaking of the *Modular,* do you think this was the inspiration for the use of the grid by Swiss designers? No, nothing to do with it. The grid system happened before the *Modular*. It has been attributed to people like Anton Stankowski, who was German and lived in Switzerland, I believe, in the thirties. But I don't think you can attribute the invention of the grid to anyone. The grid was here from the year one. The grid was used by the Egyptians. It was a proportional grid. It was not used the same as we use it. There were two systems of eighteen and twenty-one human heads. The Egyptians were a very systematic people.
bo: Are some grids better than others?
pr: That's like asking, "Are some shoes better than others?" It depends on what fits. I don't think there is such a thing as a better or worse grid. I think a grid, by definition, has a certain complexity. It can't be too simple; then it is useless. I remember the first time I was teaching the grid system at Yale. One of the students decided to make a grid of four squares. Four boxes. It has to be at least four squares. That is the simplest grid you can make. Well what can you do with four squares? Nothing. It doesn't give you any nodal points; it doesn't locate anything. You have no elements of repetition. You have none of these things.
bo: Why do you encourage the use of squares?
pr: The most common grid is a nine-square grid. There is no such a thing as an ideal grid. The orthodox way of doing grids is to do it with perfect squares. That is practically impossible to do all the time. Ken Hiebert manages somehow to do it. I don't know how he does it, but he does. He is a very good grid-nik.
The square is a very practical, economical form. It is also easier to remember two by two inches, than two by two and fifteen-sixteenths inches. Also the divisions of a square are equal. If you are using half squares, it is easy to remember. If you have a two-inch square the half square is one inch, if it is a quarter, it's a half inch. So it's a very good dimensional device. It is also

easy when you are calling on the phone, especially if you have work like annual reports, because a lot of this is done on the telephone. In order to tell the printer or the typesetter where to locate something, you make yourself a guide – A, B, C, 1, 2, 3, and 4. When you say "column A, row three," he knows exactly where it is. If it's a square, it's easier to measure it. If it's two and fractions, he has to start writing.

Also squares look right. But there is one problem with squares, the problem of optical illusions. A square does not look square if it's a square with nothing in it or a solid. A square looks higher than wide. The ancient Chinese had a system for reducing the height of a square by one-tenth and that looks square. I have the book in Chinese. If I look at the pictures I can figure it out.

bo: Do you think any good work in page layout has been done or can be done without a grid? Do you ever work without a grid?

pr: Absolutely, plenty. Alexei Brodovitch's work, Gutenberg's Bible.

Not very often. I usually have some reference to a grid. I certainly did in my last book, *A Designer's Art*. When we first became aware of the grid system we used to ridicule it and say, "Who needs this?" I think chauvinism had something to do with it then. Also, there was something about the grid that seemed stiff, very restricting. If you really are a good designer you can do anything, with a grid or without a grid.

Or you can do conventional typography. Like Jan Tschichold. Whatever he did was good. Whatever style he used, it was always good. So the problem was not just the grid. The problem is sensitivity to typography, sensitivity to space, orientation and sequencing of images, and, especially, an awareness of contrast and dialectics. If you do something, something else happens. Always. You change it, something else happens. Always.

bo: Can you tell me something about the evolution of your own ideas about page design and typography?

pr: The design of my first book, *Thoughts on Design*, which was published in 1946, was not based on the grid system. At that time we didn't have decent typefaces, not the good sans-serif typefaces. The only one we had was Futura. Plus some of the very old ones like Franklin Gothic, which is ok. In the first book, the title page was designed with Baskerville and Futura Bold, because there was no good bold Baskerville, and there still isn't. Bold faces in classical families just didn't exist, except for Bodoni. Also, in those days type was always set with miles of leading, but that had nothing to do with typography – a mere affectation. Put a lot of leading in, he's doing it, I'll do it, the other guy will do it. Actually type wants to be set compactly, not so compact that you can't read it, but enough so that lines and letters and words don't fall apart. For a while the Swiss advocated setting type as a uniform gray area. Some of the books designed this way are simply impossible to read, even when the type is big. Because it is boring.

One thing about typography – you have to make it interesting in some way, but not to the detriment of readability. If one's objective is to use type as a picture, the sky is the limit: upside down, inside out, negative, positive. This is what Wolfgang Weingart does very often, and he says so. He is a very talented guy. But if you try to imitate that kind of stuff for straight typography, you're as dead as a doornail. It becomes an affectation and a trend and it is bad, bad stuff. I also don't like raised-pinky typography. Fussy typography. Little bitsy things thrown in. It's weak, as opposed to delicate – flourishes, script, little initial letters that are bold, lots of leading. Which was very common in the early thirties. Gustave Jensen used to do beautiful pages. The kind of page that you have no desire to read. None. It could tell you that "if you read this you'd get a million dollars," you won't read it. It's pure decoration, in the pejorative sense.

bo: How did you choose the grid and typeface for your book *A Designer's Art*? What process did you go through?

pr: It is always trial and error. You try whatever comes into your mind. It could be anything. Someone could walk in and talk about Bodoni. You try Bodoni. Someone talks about Futura. You try Futura. I'm not stuck on any particular thing.

The reason I used Univers 65 in my book is because I could use a very small type that was extremely legible. It has a presence. I don't like wispy looking type that sits on top of the paper. One of the things that's a problem with Futura is that the medium is too heavy and the book is too light. I'm using it anyway on a poster I'm designing for the Art Director's Club International Show – as a challenge, to see if I can do it. Very often problems like this can be solved. But it is a type, Futura, to stay away from.

I thought I would use Futura for this poster, only because it was the first type that we could get that was so-called "modern" in this country. This was about 1930. We had sans-serif types. We had Franklin Gothic and Modern Number Seven. They were all kind of condensed. I'm not wild about condensed typefaces. I like things that are round, sort of cute. I don't like squeezed-in stuff. Futura is difficult to use for text for many reasons. The capitals are much too big. If you have a lot of caps or figures, as in an annual report, it is an impossible type. However, in display, Futura Demibold is beautiful. It looks much nicer than Helvetica or Univers.

I tried the display text for the poster in Bodoni, Univers 65, and Futura — which was the nicest. But the reason I used Futura is more historical than aesthetic. The poster was done for the Art Director's Club of New York. They are traditionally more business-oriented. An art director at an average agency is not necessarily interested in art, per sé. What he does is use artwork in ads, like Cellini's cup or a Stradivarius violin. That is supposed to be artistic. This has nothing to do with art. This is merely using art as an endorsement. The total effect has nothing to do with design. I purposely used Futura because that is about as far back as the Art Director's Club went in modernism. Back to 1930.

bo: Didn't you also try different grids? Did you start with sketches?

pr: No. I tried different layouts. Grids come later. Never. I start with the stuff, the things, the pictures, the type. If I don't have the type, I cut it out of a magazine. A sketch doesn't mean anything. Just a few lines, what does that have to do with typography? This business about learning how to use a chisel-pointed pencil is for the birds. You learn how to use the chisel, but you still don't know anything about typography.

bo: But when you have an idea, you start sketching?

pr: I almost never make sketches for anything. That could be misleading. I don't sit and fiddle unless I have an idea. Because it takes you away from the subject. Oh, I could make a million drawings, literally millions. I do finished artwork many times over. That is nothing to brag about. It is a hell of a way to work, but that is how I do it. I have to see what I am doing. The funny thing about that, I think, is that almost everything I do is intuitive anyway — even drawings. I'll sit and do a drawing, and it looks great, or it's lousy. But I don't think about it; I just do it. If I start thinking about it, I'm finished. If you do things intuitively, by definition, you are not thinking about it. It doesn't mean you are not thinking. Because you have to make a judgment after a thing is done. If you do a lousy drawing and use it, your judgment is wrong, you see. Really, any creative work is more a matter of judgment than execution. That is why a guy like Duchamp can just take a shovel and hang it up. That is the idea; you don't need any sketches for that. That is an extreme example.

bo: So you tried a number of things for the book based on what you had and your intuition...

pr: It's always intuition. I looked at most of the things I tried and I thought they were lousy. It takes me a long time to do anything good. I think that most of the things most people do are lousy.

bo: Certainly you don't think the design of your book is lousy?

pr: No, I don't think it is lousy. I don't show lousy work. It never gets out. I don't think it is sublime, but I don't think it is lousy. But, you can always do better.

bo: Then what do you think is sublime?

pr: There are not many things that are sublime. Masaccio is sublime. Michelangelo, da Vinci, Picasso. Picasso is the sublimest of anybody, including Michelangelo, for me. Unbelievable. Can you imagine Michelangelo taking a bunch of boards and putting nails in and getting a terrific piece of sculpture out of it? He had to do the real thing. But Picasso could do it with a couple of boards. You know that series of figures outside at the Rockefeller estate. Things crossing, with arms sticking out, all sort of nailed crudely together, not carefully. It would be terrible if they were carefully made like a cabinet. He just nailed together things that he picked up; he bent the nails here, put a hole there. This is the whole idea. They are absolutely marvelous. I'd love to have it somewhere. My bedroom. But it is true. If that isn't intuitive, what is?

bo: You often speak about good and great. How do you define the difference?

pr: It's always very little. It is that ineffable something. It can't be described. Right?

It's the difference between good and sublime. The sublime would be the equivalent of great. I think that Armin Hoffman, for example, very often does things that are great. Weingart does things that are great. I think that he is a very talented guy, and I think that what I consider terrible, he considers a joke and tongue-in-cheek.

Good is something that works, but it isn't particularly terrific visually. It's something that does the job.

I was once questioning Le Corbusier. We were spending a weekend not far from here. And I asked him all kinds of questions. He was dying to jump in the water, but he answered my questions. He was in shorts; we were out on a beach. He said, "Young man, you're much too serious." And he jumped into the water.
He was a great guy. This was a great man. But he also did work that was just good, and sometimes he did lousy work. His very early buildings were really unbelievable. We went on a tour, Müller-Brockmann, the four of us, to see his old buildings that he did as a kid. They were the worst buildings in the neighborhood. But then he did these marvelous buildings. The Jaoul House. We spent an entire day, looking, taking pictures, and talking to Madame Jaoul. Absolutely terrific houses. Interesting, never empty-looking, dull, or dreary. Always busy and funny, colors everywhere. Just marvelous. Surprising windows. There was a window down here, one up there. For example, in the dining room the window was near the floor, so it was dark. The idea behind having a window at the bottom is that it usually is in the bedroom. So you can find your shoes when you get up in the morning.
I also like the way he draws. His drawings are very earthy. They aren't namby-pamby. They can be very brutal but also very delicate. The orientation of the drawing is always in terms of design. For example, how it sits on the page and his use of exaggeration. The same is true of his architecture. His architecture is always interesting. It isn't just a box, or these terrible things being done today in the name of architecture. Postmodern. Which I compare to the New Wave design in graphics. Both depend on fads and shock, but have no real content, basically bad and very untalented work. Fatuous clichéd color combinations, which may be harmless, but nevertheless the fact that they are clichés makes them bad.
You know, I believe that all jobs can't be done the same way. Function has to be satisfied first. So you can't do New Wave everything or Postmodern.
You have to do what the job calls for. The reason why these trends are popular is more nefarious. It's an attempt to be original without being original. Going to sources that are dead requires lively interpretation, for example Picasso.
bo: What influenced you as a young designer?
That is a really big question. Everything influences you. Your background, where you live, whether you are rich or poor.

pr: We were quite poor. First of all, I think you have to be born with an interest in the subject. I used to draw all the time. When I was a little kid, I was absolutely avid about drawing, and I used to do it all the time. In fact, I'll tell you how little I was. I used to use a chair as a desk, sitting on a little stool. When I went to school, instead of listening to the teacher, I used to sit and draw. They kicked me out of class several times, complaining to my mother. It is something you are born with. I don't think it is something you learn. Picasso always said he "never looks for anything; he finds." For example, he sees a handlebar and says, "Oh yeah, that's a bull." He didn't think of the bull first; then find the handlebar. He had to see the handlebar. That's what sparked the bull. I think that's a very good example of finding rather than research. Because after somebody tells you, everybody is running around looking for old handlebars. It's easy.

bo: Picasso also seems to be a tremendous model for you...

pr: Discovery is confrontation with something, out of the blue. That's how ideas come. I think Picasso is the best source for learning about ideas. Look at his drawings, at the relationship between objects. He draws a fish in a birdcage. A bird in an aquarium. Always the dialectics of vision, different things that don't belong. That's what makes things interesting.

bo: I've spoken to some of your former students, and they have told me that they learned so much from their time with you. They say that at the time they didn't even know exactly what they learned, but later they find they are using it in their professional work.

pr: I don't have any teaching method. It's too complicated. There are too many things involved. I mean to sit down and write an organized, systematized book on design. I could never do it. I've never seen a good one. Usually they are awful. Boring, full of clichés. I think you learn by being curious. If I used to admire somebody, I would write the guy and ask him to give me some advice. I would ask, "What kind of books do you read?" I always did it when I was a kid. I wrote Gus Jensen once and he was nice enough to reply. I must say his bibliography was very short. One book. It was *The Beautiful Necessity* by Claude Brangdon. He was a contemporary of Sullivan and Wright. He was a theosophist, sort of a mystic. Kandinsky was also a theosophist, a lot of people were. Then I found out about contrast, the yin and yang, the yo and the in. Chinese and Japanese contrast. And other things too.

It's mysticism. But it is good, because it gives you something. I remember I was working on a bottle for maraschino cherries at the time when I found out about this idea of contrast. Brangdon's examples were mostly based on classical material, frets and borders, egg and dart. The egg is the female; the dart is the male. So I did a round thing and it had little berries going around the stem like a little necklace. These were the maraschino cherries. So there is a direct interpretation of contrast, and yo and in. Thanks to Gus Jensen. Anything like that can be useful, even if it is kind of silly. The best example of a misunderstanding of something is Cézanne's statement about the sphere and cylinders, which was misunderstood by Leger and all the modern artists.

bo: What can students learn from you about dealing with clients?

pr: The only thing that I have in common with a client is acceptance or rejection. But acceptance and rejection in the classroom is not the same thing. In a job situation, the client rejects because he doesn't think the work is going to do the job. In the classroom, work is rejected because it is poor design. But the average client doesn't usually care what the design is, as long as it makes money. Good design to the businessman may have nothing to do with good design the way a designer thinks about it. You may be talking about the subject of good design, and you both seem to be agreeing about good design, and still you are not agreeing about the same thing. That's why talking about design and art is difficult and often pointless. What is art? Not only is design art, but also art is design. Without design there is no art. There isn't any because that's what art is. Art is design. Design is the animating principle behind all art. Vasari said that in the sixteenth century. This is also true of literature. It's how it's done, the spirit, the form, the structure, and the sequence, all these things. In the Renaissance they were able to do everything well, painting, architecture, furniture, all the arts. Da Vinci was the paragon. He was also an engineer. Things worked and they were beautiful. What else do you want?

bo: Could you tell me what you think your function is when you meet with students?

pr: My function is to keep the student on the straight and narrow and get him or her out of a rut. In other words, to keep him or her from doing bad work, pretentious or trendy work. That's about all a teacher can do. He can show you models. He can keep you from doing bad work by not letting you proceed. In other words, you do it by saying, "This is bad, don't do it." And he'll try to explain, if it's possible; much of the time it's not. It's funny; a former student of mine who teaches at a university in upstate New York comes to see me with her students' work. She was showing the class some of my stuff, including the logo I designed for NeXT Computers. Some of the students said, "But that is so simple." It's an interesting problem. I don't know how she explained this to the students. She could have made something good out of a sort of stupid remark. She said to me, "What can I do when they say this?" Anything is simple. How to get an egg to stand. You crack it and then it'll stand. That is simple.

bo: How do you feel about students who don't take your advice? Who continue to do "bad" things?

pr: They shouldn't be doing design. The case is clear. There are not many good designers in the world. I'm not just talking about the USA.

bo: I'd like to ask you why you teach?

I like young people. I always have fun. Also I can save them a lot of time. Tell them things that would take them years to find out, and they might never even find out because they wouldn't be aware.

bo: You are very demanding of your students and of yourself. Why?

pr: I ask for the best from my students because it's my job to get the best out of you.

Things can always be done better. If Michelangelo had the chance to work on the Sistine Chapel today, I'm sure he could make it better. It's just not possible to say anything is perfect. Many things get changed because they can be made better. And many things need to be improved. On the other hand, some things get changed because of money.

My assistant used to ask, "Why are you doing this job over so many times? The client isn't paying you for all this work." I never work for money. That's not my object. The job is what matters. Fear seems to motivate most people. But there are some people who are not like this; they are compelled to express themselves. Every time I took a chance I won.

bo: What advice can you give to students going out into the world? Quit?

pr: My advice to a student who is first going out is: It's only the beginning. And this is true. I learn all the time. But as much as one would like, it's just not possible to learn everything. It's just not possible.

Franc Nunoo-Quarcoo
Charles Hillman
on
Working
with
Paul Rand

Franc Nunoo-Quarcoo: How did your association with Paul Rand begin?

Charles Hillman: My first association with Paul Rand was as a result of a print quality competition conducted by the Cummins Engine Company to determine which printer would be the printer of their annual report. It was to be judged by Cummins Engine and Paul Rand. There were four printers involved, two from the Midwest and two from the New York area. Each printer was asked to submit three samples of their work, plus a print of the previous year's Cummins annual report cover, which was designed by Paul Rand. Before printing the cover, I called Paul Rand and asked him if we could dirty up the yellow by adding a touch of red, so the reverse type would be more legible. Mr. Rand's immediate answer was, "Let's get something straight. I'm the designer and you are the printer. Don't confuse the two, understand?" But then he added, "That's not a bad idea; let me see it both ways." Mossberg & Company won the competition and printed the 1975 Cummins Engine Company Annual Report. This was the beginning of a great relationship with Cummins and a wonderful friendship with Paul Rand that lasted right up to his death.

fn-q: What was the first project you and Paul Rand collaborated on?

ch: The 1975 Cummins Engine Company Annual Report. The most difficult part of doing the annual report was talking Paul into travelling to South Bend, Indiana, to approve the report on-press. Fortunately there were direct flights out of New York to South Bend, and Paul had such a good first year that future trips were not a problem.

fn-q: What was the working relationship like in the beginning and in subsequent years? Did it progress to collaboration?

ch: Getting to know Paul Rand and his work habits and his requests took time and patience. However, as time passed, we got to know one another better, and a friendship developed that grew stronger over the years. At first his demands for instant turnaround on jobs were difficult to understand and accomplish. In fact, we couldn't do it most of the time. But by delivering him excellent proofs along with a few searching questions that really made him think, the tension disappeared and a really fine working relationship developed.

fn-q: What was his process from the beginning of a project – preliminary meeting to discuss the project, etc.? When meeting with Paul to discuss a project, he would have either a rather complete dummy or just an idea, which, as we talked, he would sketch out on a piece of paper. In any case, he would emphasize the purpose of the piece, the anticipated audience, how the piece flowed from page to page, from spread to spread. We would review every piece of art and/or transparency as to size, line weight in drawings, color in transparencies. We would talk about important pages and skip over "filler" pages. We would discuss fifth and sixth colors, especially solid color pages and what color should underlay the last color down. In most cases, it was up to me to determine the percentage of blow up or reduction, based on the dummy. Paper was an important part of any project. Usually it was on a dull enamel, natural finish, or a high quality off white offset paper. Strathmore was a favorite as well as Mohawk.

fn-q: Was the collaboration unique? Was this collaboration different than those you experienced with other designers you worked with? How and why?

ch: Paul was in many ways quite different from other designers. I don't mean to take away from other designers, because many that I worked with in my printing career were very good. Paul Rand was different in that he was very sure of himself and truly believed that he was one of the very best graphic designers in the world, if not the best. He was very knowledgeable about the great artists and authors of the past and present – Picasso, Fernand Léger, George Bernard Shaw, John Dewey, Shakespeare, van Gogh and others. Paul read a lot, and he was an excellent writer, as witnessed by his many seminal books on design. He designed for visual effect and at times would ask me what came to my mind when I looked at a newly designed logo or a page from an annual report. He would explain what he was attempting to illustrate, and if it was too abstract, he at times would add an additional piece of art to help a novice such as myself understand what he had in mind.

fn-q: What was a typical press check with Paul Rand like?

ch: Paul loved to work on the press when approving press sheets for one of his jobs. He enjoyed working with the press crews and they enjoyed him. He would often praise the head pressman when jobs came up to good color quickly. Even though proofs had been submitted and approved prior to going on press, Paul didn't use them very much to approve press sheets; rather he remembered what each subject should look like and approved things from memory. However, if during the make-ready process he saw a picture or page that he liked better, he would approve that. An extreme of this was when he would see a make-ready sheet that had been run through the press two or more times and had colors on it from colors over color that he liked, particulary when choosing solid colors, he would stop the job, have new film and plates made incorporating the new color and then proceed with the job. Paul would do a lot of color designing on press and in some cases page design. Approving a press sheet sometimes took quite a while, but most of the time press approvals went quickly. On many jobs, he would approve the first good sheet off the press. Working on press with Paul was a learning experience and everyone learned something new each time.

fn-q: Were there difficult projects that pushed your knowledge and know-how to limits? Did his way of working—organic and structured—affect a project?

ch: The most difficult projects with Paul were those involving solid colors, especially blacks. He would choose a high quality offset sheet for a job and then want large solids of dense high gloss black that would not fingerprint, or the reverse: on a glossy enamel sheet such as Kromekote, he would use dense dull black with five point reverse type that would not fingerprint. Remember that at that time presses had not been developed with extended deliveries with coating towers and special drying units like we have today. Back then sheets would have to be run through the press, let dry, and then run through the press one or more times. Expense was never a deterrent to achieving the desired result.

fn-q: Was his process much more like that of an artist than that of a designer? What was working with Paul Rand like?

ch: As I stated above, Paul was both an artist and a designer. In truth, he was a genius. He would sit at his table or desk, thinking about a project, draw things that came to his mind, and continue until he arrived at the final design. There might be a hundred different drawings to achieve what he wanted. During or after this process he would, for some projects, draw beautiful pictures of men, women, animals, or other objects that the particular piece required. These could be line drawings or full-color renditions. Paul's artistic and design abilities were unlimited.

fn-q: What were his views of the technical and artistic aspects of printing?

ch: Paul was always interested in new developments in the science of lithography. If new technology gave an improved visual image over older technology, then he would want to use the latest technology. A good example of this is when Sci-Tex color correcting capability was developed. Paul spent an entire day with our people learning the capabilities of this new technology. The fact that you could add or subtract images from a transparency or a piece of artwork was a revelation, and he used this capability frequently.

fn-q: Is there a particular project that exemplifies Paul Rand and Mossberg's career-long collaboration?

ch: The various books that Paul wrote and designed about his thoughts and ideas on design, *A Designer's Art, Design, Form, and Chaos,* and *From Lascaux to Brooklyn* to mention a few, are good examples of the Paul Rand – Mossberg career-long collaboration. These were difficult projects to print, and Paul trusted us because of our longstanding relationship. Another could be the "eye-bee-M" poster. I believe we printed about twelve variations of this poster, and it became a worldwide example of Paul Rand's design. Another could be the corporate image for NeXT. While on-press printing the original corporate image-users brochure, my son James, who is now president of Mossberg & Company, suggested that rather than have a simple square for the logo, why not tip it on its point to make it more unique. Paul immediately liked the idea, so the printing was stopped. It was submitted to Steve Jobs and approved, and that is what the logo looks like today.

fn-q: How did the analog and digital changes in technology affect your collaboration?

ch: As I mentioned earlier, Paul was very interested in new technology. As new technology came along, he quickly adopted it. Designing on the computer was a different story. Paul insisted to his dying day that real, original design cannot be done on a computer, but must come from the head of an accomplished designer. Once he or she has thought out the design, it can be put on the computer and be enhanced or modified. Paul liked computers for design in that he could think of variations and quickly see them on the computer screen. Actually Paul never became very good on the computer; rather, he worked with computer people in Weston, Connecticut, or the surrounding area to get material onto discs so we could use them rather than keylines.

fn-q: What inspired your collaborations over what essentially was a working lifetime?

ch: Paul himself was an inspiration. He always had new ideas, his artwork was exciting and always stimulating, it affected everyone in our plant in a positive way. His mind never stopped working, so he always had new projects for us to do. The two of us worked well together.

fn-q: Was Paul Rand a pragmatist and/or a perfectionist?

ch: Actually Paul was both a pragmatist and a perfectionist. He was a pragmatist in that his artwork treated historical phenomena with special reference to their causes and results – he was practical, his designs were understandable, and he made sense. Anything Paul did had to be as perfect as he could or we could make it. But again he was practical. If his request was impossible, then we would modify it to where it was possible, sometimes after a great deal of discussion.

fn-q: Could you talk about what both you and PR looked for in a successful job?

ch: It's easier to talk about what I looked for in a successful job. Certainly all the mechanical things had to be as near perfect as possible – correct paper, very well printed, excellent registration, folded and trimmed precisely, bound to Paul's exacting requirements. For Paul, a successful job must always be visually appealing, clean, sharp, legible type, plus all of the above. Ultimately both of us should be pleased with the job.

fn-q: Did you feel an affinity with Rand's sensibilities as a designer?

ch: Paul was an excellent designer, and the longer I worked with him and saw the many different items that he designed, the greater my admiration for Paul and his art and design. When you see the various logos that Paul designed, you know what company they represent. Today, many companies have logos that are meaningless, that give no clue as to what type of business the company is in. Not everyone likes a Paul Rand design, but I like it more today than I did yesterday. It continues to have a modern feel and appearance. It is easy to understand.

fn-q: Did you see your work process change in the course of working with him?

ch: The more one worked with Paul, the more exacting you became and that applied to everyone at Mossberg & Company. With each job you began to expect greater perfection. He was a great teacher and had a certain charisma that drew you to him and his work ethic.

fn-q: What do you think is important to know about Paul Rand as a designer and as a person?

ch: Over the years, I got to know Paul and Marion quite well, and to a lesser extent his daughter in Cincinnati. I wish I could have taken his design course at Yale, but having read all his books, I know that good design was the number one thing in his life and that he constantly strived to improve his skills as a designer, and as a teacher of his beliefs.

180: 181:

Franc Nunoo-Quarcoo
Mario Rampone
on
Working
with
Paul Rand

Franc Nunoo-Quarcoo: How did your association with Paul Rand begin?

Mario Rampone: I began my career in the graphics arts in 1944, and my association with Paul Rand started in 1970, when I was in management and customer service. It began as it ended, that is, involved, sustained, informative, and professional. I attended the New York School of Printing, which had journeymen teachers whose experience in the trade was excellent. While my college preparation had nothing to do with the printing trade, it later helped me understand better the emerging field of graphic design.

fn-q: What was the first project you and PR collaborated on?

mr: I worked with Paul on the IBM Design Guide, a document conceived to formalize standards for a global entity. This was an ongoing project, and he updated pages as needed. This guide was composed on a grid, an organizational device for which Paul was famous. The grid made for ease in organizing very complex information. The key to his method was accessibility and ease of use.

fn-q: What was the working relationship like in the beginning and in subsequent years? Did it progress to collaboration?

mr: Paul valued my experience in dealing with and resolving complex issues concerning typography, and he asked for me often. Our collaboration is something that took years to develop, and it lasted a lifetime once it was established. I believe we took to each other almost immediately. It was a lot of give and take, and sometimes I would question certain things, at times suggest things, and he reconsidered before going ahead with a project. Often, he had it resolved before seeking my thoughts. What is important to know is that he worked tirelessly to achieve flawless typography. Every job, small or large, received the same attention to detail. I respected that in his ethic and in our working relationship.

fn-q: What was his process from the beginning of a project – preliminary meeting to discuss the project, etc.?

mr: Paul did not have meetings. All his work was handled over the phone, and he was ingenious in describing what he wanted. He would fax a design, and give you detailed specifications over the phone. Occasionally, because of a large project such as cartons and packaging for IBM products, we would meet in his office with his clients. Alongside detailed verbal descriptions and instructions, I would bring back some large prototypes. We would review it and make necessary changes along the way. Paul was so experienced that he knew what would work right away. Sometimes the process had more to do with new ways of looking at things. In the case of the IBM packaging, you can see the fresh use of graphic elements that enhance the already successful existing graphic identity.

fn-q: Was the collaboration unique? Was this collaboration different than those you experienced with other designers you worked with? How and why?

mr: It was a unique relationship because it was a long, respectful, and sustained one. With Paul, it was like making art, in that there was no formula. Each job was treated with special attention and care. Sometimes decisions were definite, sometimes we would send proofs back and forth for what seemed like an eternity. This was always augmented by numerous phone calls to me. We always worked with a grid, looked at proportion, text column widths, word breaks, rags, the color of composed type, the relative depth of ascenders and descenders, type size, leading, legibility, the structure of the typography in relation to photography, illustration, a graphic element, a field of color, or a blank page. In the end, it was always right and beautiful. It was especially this way with the three books he wrote and designed, *A Designer's Art, Design, Form, and Chaos,* and *From Brooklyn to Lascau*x. Of course how can I forget those beautiful booklets he made for his corporate identity presentations? Paul rarely had meetings, and even more rarely made presentations, so the booklets were his presentations, and that is why they had to be clear, informative, and above all communicative. They worked well all the time. What I have just described is not the norm with other designers. In my long career, I have learned that every designer works differently, and I responded to each according to their specific needs. Many designers took to my manner of working.

fn-q: What was a typical typography job with PR like?

mr: Paul called himself the "typographer" and us the "typesetters." Therefore, you would have to let him lead, unless you wanted to tangle with him. Typically, after he had thought out his plan of action, he might send you thumbnails of rough layouts. I seldom received tight comps from Paul. He knew in his mind what he wanted, and you had better be able to understand him. I learned to understand his way of working, and I could sometimes anticipate certain things. For example, I knew his preferences for letter and word spacing for certain favored typefaces, word breaks, leading, and rags for certain column widths, all relative to certain proportions and page sizes. This was just the beginning. It was done when he said it was done, and done well with no flaws.

fn-q: Were there difficult projects that pushed your knowledge and know-how to limits? Did his way of working – organic and structured – affect a project?

mr: I felt very comfortable with Paul. I was not afraid to challenge him, and that made it sometimes testy. His manner of working was professional, and my preparation and understanding of his process made it possible to follow his process. It wasn't smooth all the time. Sometimes, because of deadlines, and very little time, I had to work with limited instructions and hope for the best. We knew each other's working process well, but there was no predictability. Our feelings through the process never affected the eventual outcome. He would say, "Pretty good, Mario, but let's do something to make it better." One time he said, "What are you getting upset about? You can't get everything right. It's your batting average that counts, and, I have to say, yours is pretty good." That's about the best compliment you can expect from Paul.

fn-q: Was his process much more like that of an artist than that of a designer? What was working with Paul Rand like?

mr: I would say he was very organized like a designer, but at times, his artistic sense could take over. Working with him, you did not have to know what it was. He led the way. Often, he tried things because he needed to see the real thing in order to make the right decisions. He was astonishingly brilliant about making the right decisions. He made the complex look so simple. That is a gift few designers have.

fn-q: What were his views of the technical and artistic aspects of typesetting?

mr: Rand would always want to use the best method to produce the best work, meaning, using true-cut italics on the linotype, and not the duplex matrix with accompanying italics. He, at times, might use Monotype italics because they made a better letter fit. One thing he did not like was tight letterspacing. He referred to it as "intercourse spacing." He also disliked excessive leading. He did not follow a trend or a style. He always managed to marry the practical with the beautiful. He was considerate that way.

fn-q: Is there a particular project that exemplifies Paul Rand and your career-long collaboration?

mr: I think that would have to be the time he developed the corporate image for NeXT Computer with Steve Jobs. This undertaking had to be done in secrecy because he could not let the design out of the bag.

It was an exciting and exacting project. Paul worked very hard and long on this project. It was important because Steve Jobs wanted Paul to design his company's logo and had to clear hiring Paul through IBM. Paul was the design consultant for IBM, and as you can imagine, there could have been a conflict of interest, contractually. I worked with Paul as usual. It was a complex and involved project that took a while to complete, and all the processes I have described earlier were in effect. In the end was a unique mark that exemplified what Steve Jobs was looking for. Paul and Steve were a good match. They both respected each other's art and that is why it worked well.

fn-q: How did the analog and digital changes in technology affect your collaboration?

mr: It all has to do with how you think about it and how you use it. For me, it was not a problem. For Paul it was a problem because of how the new technology was used, and not because of the technology itself. He wrote about this. The misuse of the computer infuriated Paul because he felt that many, many designers made bad typography and design decisions because of simplistic impressions and a misunderstanding of the role of the computer in the process of designing. Most of the experienced designers of that day felt the same. As a matter of fact, most of them refused to do anything on the computer, and many still don't. Unfortunately, the misuse of the potential of new technology resonated throughout design schools, and eager and inexperienced professors showed little thought in properly integrating it into their curricula. I have visited many design schools in past years, and I have to agree with Paul that the students are not learning design the right way. They are not learning how to see and think. They are not learning the *art* of design.

fn-q: What inspired your collaborations over what essentially was a working lifetime?

mr: Respect, and a mutual desire to work together. We liked, respected, and understood each other's desire for quality and good work.

fn-q: Was Paul Rand a pragmatist and/or a perfectionist?

mr: Probably both, but mostly a perfectionist. Fortunately, Paul had the confidence of top corporate executives who actually gave him a blank check when he worked. This permitted him to reconsider anything that did not quite measure up to his approval. He revised as many times as needed. He was respected, and he used his access quite skillfully.

fn-q: Could you talk about what both you and Paul Rand looked for in a successful job?

mr: It was whatever we wanted. It was based on the simple criteria that it would have to be practical, legible, and pleasing to the eye. The process was always what it was – professional, involved, and sustained because that was the only way to satisfy the criteria.

fn-q: Did you feel an affinity with Rand's sensibilities as a designer?

mr: Absolutely so. From the beginning to the last job we worked on, I found most of his work extremely beautiful. There were some odd jobs I was not too crazy about, but this was not the norm, as almost anyone would think of his designs. This is best illustrated through the many corporate logos he designed. His logos were memorable and recognizable. You knew that UPS represented UPS, that IBM represented IBM, and that the W represented Westinghouse. The IBM logo booklet and all the others we worked on say it all. In contrast, compare the Verizon company mark. In no way do I find that representative of a telephone and communications giant. Of course, Paul did not design that. It would have been interesting to see what he would have come up with.

fn-q: Did you see your work process change in the course of working with him?

mr: I can't say that it changed. The important thing is that I recognized Paul for what he was – the epitome of a great artist, and a designer who did great work, redefined the standards for all in his profession, and made it understandable to the public.

fn-q: What do you think is important to know about Paul Rand as a designer and as a person?

mr: He mastered the *art* of design, and taught those who wanted to learn through his work. The books he wrote are the ultimate textbooks. They clearly are the best books about design, because they relate the process, the message, and the importance of good design and its many benefits to society. As a person, Paul was different to many people. Our relationship was unique because we were business associates and then friends for a very long time.

Paul would seldom not allow a visit to his studio from anyone with interest in design. Many designers and non-designers made "pilgrimages" to his studio in his beautiful house in Weston, Connecticut, where he worked until the end.

He was a generous man. The many posters he designed without fee are symbols of his desire to continue to produce good design at all costs. He was not a complicated man, he was a complex man, and you either liked him very much as I did, or you did not like him very much, as some did. Perhaps those who may have disliked him were afraid of not being able to come close to the master and his works.

His influence and legacy is immense. He cast a large shadow, and does even now.

186: 187: Rampone: Nunoo-Quarcoo

Franc Nunoo-Quarcoo
Marion Rand
on
Paul Rand

This interview with Marion Swannie Rand was conducted on December 2, 2002, in her Weston, Connecticut residence.

Franc Nunoo-Quarcoo: Could you start by telling me about yourself, where you're from, your education, your introduction to IBM, your various responsibilities there?
Marion Rand: My life is fairly conventional. I grew up in Buffalo, New York, and earned a scholarship to Chatam College for Women in Pittsburgh, from which I graduated in 1945, a long time ago. During my senior year I was interviewed by representatives from the IBM Corporation. They were looking for young women who they hoped could take the place of the young salesmen, the lifeblood of the company, men who were all off at war. So they decided to try a few girls and see if they could do the same job as the men. So I was accepted in that program. At that time, they visited several women's colleges for the same reason. Many of my friends from schools like Smith and Wellesley were also interviewed. All this was the idea of Thomas J. Watson, Sr., the president and founder of IBM.

The orientation to IBM was unique. It was held at an outdoor open camp called Tent City in Endicott, New York, and that was how the men in the sales training classes were also introduced to the company. So that in itself was an experience. During this time we obviously learned a lot about IBM, including the company songs. It was that kind of a company, and everybody knew songs dedicated to Mr. Watson. It was an interesting experience, which of course companies do not do today – that I know of. But at that time, in order to get young people interested in the company, its goals and aspirations, they were interested in trying girls in the role of what they called system service representatives. They weren't called "saleswomen" but "systems service representatives." The role of the systems service representative was to learn about the punchcard equipment and machines and how to set them up. The punches, sorters, counting machines all ran on the punchcard system.

So we all learned about all that stuff. Some girls I think were better at it than others. I wasn't terribly interested, having gone through the course, which cost IBM a fair amount of money. So at the time they were giving people assignments to various cities and locations. They asked me if I'd like to go to Buffalo or Pittsburgh, because I knew those two cities very well. I declined because I really didn't want to do that and didn't think I'd be a terrific systems service woman.

So they asked what I would be interested in. In college I majored in English, so I chose advertising, even though I knew very little about it. They took that into

Marion Rand: Nunoo-Quarcoo

consideration, and said, "Well, advertising is a New York City operation, and IBM hadn't done any of it during the war." The Second World War was just ending, and the men were coming back, some in sales, some in advertising, and some probably as department heads in other areas. My interest was in advertising and New York City.

So I was placed in the New York City Office of IBM at 57th and Madison. At that time there was really no one there to give any guidance or programs for advertising for the company. Shortly after I arrived, I met people, three or four whom had came back from the war, and we organized ourselves into a network of people writing sales literature. So that began my IBM career.

fn-q: So after you started, how did you rise through the ranks to the executive level?

mr: Well, there was no structure within IBM for any job like advertising. In other words, no hierarchy. There was no way you could go from level one to level two. However, there were a lot of openings in IBM at that time because the men were just returning from the war. Advertising at IBM had to be built up. For several years in the beginning, I helped build it mainly by writing sales literature and then buying the printing to get it produced. Also, on the fringes, I was learning some things about advertising in general in New York City. In about 1955, ten years after I started working in the advertising department, IBM decided to have a formal corporate design program. They decided to use well-known consultants in graphic design, product design, and architecture; Elliot Noyes in architecture and product design, Charles Eames in filmmaking, and Paul Rand in graphic design, the best-known graphic designer in America at that time.

To help Paul Rand, I was asked to be the liaison to graphic design. I agreed to do that, and that was how I met Paul, and also how we developed a whole design program for IBM. We started the program by visiting with various national and international offices around the world to spread the word about what we were trying to do. We showed examples of good work as measures of the quality standards we were trying to maintain in any printed material or graphic design. The basic problem in having a good design program is one of education. How do you show people what you want to do? What is good design? That became Paul's and my and all the consultants' major problem. It involved the education of currently employed designers, not only in the United States but all over the world. It took a lot of time and money and communication, a lot of travel to visit every plant and laboratory location in this country, Europe, and the rest of the world. That took a lot of figuring out within a network of communications with all these people. We succeeded in instituting the program in cities like Stuttgart, London, and Paris, all of which were producing literature and other materials that IBM needed and wanted. We also delivered lectures. Paul and I conducted seminars and meetings in virtually every foreign city in which IBM had a big operation, in order to make sure the design program was adhered to properly. That was a major undertaking all by itself.

It turned into a very interesting job, especially meeting a lot of people, doing good work in foreign countries, and having teaching sessions with them. We created a true and very successful corporate design program. Nobody else had one in our field except Olivetti. They had developed a comprehensive and successful program that they used for years. Olivetti's program was very well known and quite exemplary. The products and graphics they designed were unusually good.

fn-q: Had you been aware of Paul Rand before meeting and working with him?

mr: Oh yes! I'd been aware of him, as were most people who read the *New York Times* and magazines, and who lived in New York City. He had very important clients like Ohrbach's, which was located in Manhattan, and every Sunday there would be an Ohrbach's ad designed and signed by Paul Rand. Everyone would talk about them on Monday morning: "Did you see the Ohrbach's ad?" Many of his ads were wonderful surprises. When you'd see a new copy of a magazine and there would be a new Paul Rand in it, it was quite the thing people talked about. We were all aware of his brilliant work.

I then became aware of who was doing good work in other companies. For example, Olivetti was also doing good work. Giovanni Pintori was the master graphic designer at Olivetti, but there were other very well-known people, especially in product design like Gio Ponti, Vico Magistretti, Etore Sotass, Achille Castiglioni, and Mario Bellini. Olivetti produced outstanding products including typewriters and adding machines. They were pretty much in the same field that IBM was in. Although most of their clients were in Europe, they were beginning to be known in New York because of their fine products and innovative advertising. In front of their building on Fifth Avenue, they affixed an Olivetti typewriter on a pedestal mounted in the cement. It was a dramatic installation, and a person walking along the street could stop and type on the Olivetti typewriter. That was a very good idea. We were all aware that the world of design was beginning to be felt and to influence popular culture. IBM and Olivetti were good examples.

fn-q: I believe Paul Rand had done some advertising for Olivetti before he started working for IBM?

mr: Yes, he'd done full-color page ads primarily. Paul had worked initially at an advertising agency called the Weintraub Agency. He did outstanding work there, most signed by him, like prominent artists did. He was the lead art director and was very well known in the art and design community in New York City and beyond. Everybody knew Paul Rand was a top designer.

fn-q: Was he the only one who signed his work?

mr: Yes. That's true. At one point a client asked that he not sign his name on their work, so Paul indicated to this client that he wasn't interested in doing their work since it was his custom to sign everything. The client relented and he did sign it. It was very unusual and very few have done it since. I think many young designers have fantasized about it. Many clients came to expect and want it because the signature had value. I don't know what caused Paul to start signing things. He signed virtually all of his advertisements during that time.

fn-q: Did he seek other assignments during his time with the Weintraub Agency and after?

mr: Yes, he designed book covers and jackets, posters, books, packaging, and other advertising accounts on his own. That was additional work other people asked him to undertake. In IBM's typewriter division he did carbon paper and ribbons, and they were all in packaging designed by Paul.

fn-q: Could you talk about his family and his beginnings?

mr: I knew his family. The main thing to know about Paul is that he was an identical twin, and that in itself is a very significant life experience for anyone who is born an identical twin. You obviously develop a great relationship with that person and great interdependency. Paul's brother, Philip, died at the young age of twenty-seven. Paul realized he was by himself, a single person like everybody else is in the world. Twinship is an unusual kind of life, a very different experience than any single person ever experiences. That bond was the essence of Paul's life until he found himself alone. That he was brought up in a conservative Jewish religion, that his family was quite orthodox, were other important factors that shaped his life. Paul, like many young Orthodox Jewish kids attended religious schools called Yeshivas, where young rabbinical students were the teachers. There, everybody learned Hebrew and took other subjects. Perhaps, in the morning they learned nothing but religion and in the afternoon they learned other standard material. Paul hated it, and so did his brother. They didn't like it at all! They pleaded with their mother not to be at the Yeshiva and eventually convinced her to let them both go to public schools, out there, in the wide unknown world. Many, many years later she confessed to me many times that "the biggest mistake I ever made was letting those boys get out of the Yeshiva school system." The Yeshiva system was akin to the Catholic church's parochial school system. It's taught by priests, and most people that have Catholic children send them to Catholic schools. It's the same idea.

fn-q: Where did his parents come from and what did they do?

mr: His mother was one of about ten children and her family were all Orthodox Jews, born in the United States. His father, also was an Orthodox Jew, was born in Vienna and emigrated to this country. They met and married. They had one daughter and then there were the twin boys. I don't know what ever happened to her. That was the family. They lived in Crown Heights in Brooklyn, the most conservative Orthodox community of American Jewry.

fn-q: What did his parents do?

mr: His father had a grocery store in Brooklyn, and the family lived behind the store.

fn-q: Later in their lives, did his parents emigrate to Israel?

mr: Yes, they did. They moved to Miami at one point, but eventually they took a boat trip to visit Palestine (a life-long dream), as it was called then, to see the growth of Israel as a country. They knew they were going to stay when they got there. A lot of Jewish people were moving to Jerusalem and Tel Aviv. His parents did that.

fn-q: This was a new country then.

mr: Yes. Look what's happened since. Very definitely a new country. Paul knew they were going there to settle, so he bought them anything they might need. They liked Israel. They had a very nice apartment in the town of Netanya, north of Tel Aviv. They lived in Israel until his father died. His mother came back to the United States briefly after that, but eventually she was buried in Netanya beside her husband.

fn-q: What sort of person was Paul? There are many

impressions of him.

mr: Yes. He was a straight arrow, yes. He had great integrity and great intelligence, a very intelligent guy. He was also generous to many people and institutions. I'd say he was exemplary as a person.

fn-q: It's interesting to also hear he was religious and private, but chose to work in a very public profession.

mr: He was very private and religious man. He didn't impose his views of orthodoxy on anyone, at all. He was very private about his personal life, as many who shared his strong faith were, I think. He just lived a simple and decent life. His brother was a musician. Paul was a designer rather than a musician, but both very public professions.

fn-q: What were his passions aside from his work? I've heard gardening.

mr: He didn't do a lot of gardening himself. He liked the land and that's why we are here in Weston, Connecticut, where we live. Paul grew up in a tight Jewish community without any grass and trees, and wanted to have a piece of land in the country someday. So he did. He moved to Weston and built this house, which he designed with Ann Rand, who was then his wife. She had architectural training, and they designed a very nice house, this modernist house.

fn-q: This wasn't the first modern house he built and lived in?

mr: No. He had one designed by the Hungarian émigré architect Marcel Breuer. It was designed in the modernist idiom, and is still standing in Harrison, New York, just outside New York City.

fn-q: What else did he enjoy doing?

mr: He enjoyed being in the sun and getting tanned. It wasn't a vanity thing for him, but he liked being outdoors and he got a naturally terrific tan. He was not interested in sports or athletic things at all. He once said he got out of doing most of the sports things when he was a school boy by volunteering and making posters for the sport or activity. He made a lot of things for his school and that kept him away from having to play sports. He never joined in any of the activities kids engage in, like playing kick the can, or any of these street games kids play; Paul was never interested in any of that. He just loved art work. That was his main interest and he was good at it. He always sat on the sidelines with a pad and drawing pencil, crayon. The Wanamaker Company had big awards for big competitions they sponsored citywide and Paul won several of the awards. He spent weekends at the big Wanamaker department store in downtown Manhattan because they had contests for kids. That's what he enjoyed doing, drawing things and copying things. That's what he spent most of his free time doing, nothing else, just concentrating on art. According to his family, his aunts and uncles, from the time he was a little kid he would use the seat of a chair as a table and draw, putting the paper on the seat to use as a desk to draw. Everybody remembered that about him – that he was always drawing. That's how strong an interest he had in art.

fn-q: For some time after his advertising days, it seems he worked mainly from home in his studio.

mr: His life went on when he was out at the advertising agency. He always had freelance accounts during his advertising days, and most of them were done at home. The third phase of his career as a corporate design consultant, which started with IBM in 1956, was conducted from his studio here at home in Weston.

fn-q: What was his work process?

mr: Paul could work on any schedule. This is the terrific training he got as the key graphic designer at agencies where he worked. Often, clients would want to see ten new ideas at ten in the morning, and Paul fulfilled those requests as needed. He really could produce on time. He was able to work quickly and on a second's notice and meet any deadline. He was challenged by the work, if he was interested in it.

fn-q: I have heard of his voracious appetite for reading because of his singular passion for information, learning, and discovery. Did he do it also for relaxation?

mr: Reading. We have an enormous library here. He loved to go to bookstores, always, and bought a lot of books. Through reading and the supplemental learning that comes with it, he quickly became a very good teacher, and many schools were always asking him to teach night school, that kind of thing. He did some of it. Most of it he didn't like particularly, until he eventually got to Yale. He was asked by Josef Albers and Alvin Eisenman to teach there, and he did for the rest of his life. He made a real career in teaching, and everybody who came to Yale usually came because Paul was teaching and they wanted to study with him. Later on, he extended his teaching through the Yale Summer Program in Graphic Design at Brissago, Switzerland.

fn-q: There was such a beautiful relationship between the two of you that was special to watch. Did you do many things together?

mr: We traveled every year to Brissago because Paul was always asked to do that. We also traveled to other places, anything that intrigued Paul. Many things have interested him because of the art in the area. For instance, he wanted to go to Egypt, I remember. That was one of the many places we went. We'd do most of that in the summer, and Brissago was only a week. They had a different teacher every week. Paul usually took the first week. We tacked on a trip to another place we wanted to see. He loved Switzerland. Paul liked certain architects like Le Corbusier. He was very enamored of him. I think he had every book that's been published about Le Corbusier. And he wanted to see all the buildings he ever did, and we visited all of those, many in Paris. We concentrated on that.

Paul saw what he wanted. The only thing I don't recall him being interested in was India. I do not know why. He didn't feel comfortable about India, and I don't know why. I would like to have seen it, but it's the only place in the world we didn't go. He was invited to Tokyo, and he went in 1958 for the first time. We went together on three other trips in probably the late seventies or late eighties. But Paul had a terrific eye for things. He could see anything that was well designed, and those are the things he bought. He sought out things that were interesting to see, whether a building by Le Corbusier or something done in Japan. He just was interested in seeing things. He educated himself on every subject you can imagine.

fn-q: Seems Japan held a special interest for him.

mr: Yes, it did. That's true. There was a book that was published, a square format in a brown cover.

fn-q: It was edited by Yusaku Kamekura.

mr: Yes, well, he wrote an introduction to it; one of the chapters was written by Hans Schleger, a close friend and very good designer in England. Bernard Rudofsky, the writer, and Giovanni Pintori, both good friends, also wrote chapters. Paul designed the cover and the book. It had animals with dots on them. That was Paul's work. He had a very good friend, a Japanese friend called Hideo Kobayashi, and every time Hideo came to this country he wanted to see Paul, wanted to come up here, and we always had him here through the weekend. He was a cute guy. He got cancer from smoking so much. He was a good friend, and when Paul was in Tokyo on his first trip in 1958, Hideo took him around to various places and to people and designers like Kamekura. Every designer who was well known in Japan wanted to meet Paul. That was a very important trip for him.

fn-q: Did Kamekura become a friend?

mr: Yes. They became great friends for so long. Kamekura

died shortly after Paul, in 1997. He and Paul were also a year apart in age.

Paul also liked and respected Ikko Tanaka. Ikko was terrific. He died recently. He was a wonderful person. He came here and brought Paul a whole collection of posters, and he was one of the best of the Japanese designers. He was second after Kamekura, who was the number one designer in Japan, a very hierarchical situation there, but after Kamakura died, Ikko then became the leading designer.

fn-q: It's amazing how you feel when you walk into this house – the scale, colors, textures, transitions, and connection between the inside and outside.

mr: Yes. Everyone is comfortable in this house. Many people have made a point of talking about that. "I love your house. I always feel good here." Or, "What's that?" They'd ask you certain things about what Paul had, sometimes a lot of questions about decorations or furniture. Everyone was aware of his excellent tastes and interests.

fn-q: Nothing seems forced. It seems quite natural from the exterior and interior architectural materials and the complemetary furnishings and accessories.

mr: Everything is natural about the house. That's very true. He collected works of art, and unlike most people who collect, it's not because of vanity, but out of sheer interest and enjoyment. Paul was interested in all kinds of art. Many people gave him paintings and art objects. Sometimes, when Paul did a job for someone or something like that, they'd give him a work of art. Those times were unexpected and very nice.

fn-q: Did he collect with some sense that he might need to use them in his work?

mr: No. He collected because he liked to, including furniture and objects for the house. A Japanese artisan made that wooden object over there. The Persian jug on the end is from a very early century. This handmade marching band set is from Portugal. We gave it to a lot of friends for Christmas one year. This little tiny town here is a reminder of Brissago. Paul was interested in antiques as well. He didn't trade in antiques, but he bought certain things for the house that he liked to look at. One was the coal stove beside the chair out there, that's the sort of thing that would catch his eye. He bought the rooster from a man who had Early American things. He collected because he enjoyed to and not because he thought they were valuable.

fn-q: I'm well aware that you've been doing a great amount of work, along with Nathan Garland, Georgette

Ballance, and Bob Burns to preserve Paul's work and legacy.

mr: He had a lot of stuff here at the house. What do you do with it when somebody dies? But fortunately Yale was happy to take anything Paul had, and they have a Paul Rand Archive at the Sterling Memorial Library at Yale. So if you want to know anything about his work, his posters, Yale has copies of all that. They do that for certain people only, for some some of their most famous professors, to have examples of their work.

Nathan Garland, Bob Burns, and Georgette Ballance have helped a lot in sorting out the things in the house. Here is a complete set of all the paints he used for his work, cabinets specially made with just the right size for paint tubes to fit in, one after another.

fn-q: Have national and international museums requested his work for their archives?

mr: Yes. A lot of them have. We have sent work to those who have requested it. The Victoria & Albert Museum in London has a lot of his work.

fn-q: Did any American museums request things?

mr: Yes. The Smithsonian Institution's Cooper Hewitt National Design Museum has a lot of his posters. The Museum of Modern Art also requested and has a lot of his work. All the prominent national and international museums have collections of Paul's work.

fn-q: Could you talk a bit about your own philanthropic work and contributions to the Paul Rand Design Center at Yale University?

mr: There's a new art building for all the art disciplines, and they started working on this right after Paul died. So I asked if I could make a memorial in Paul's name in this new building named Green Hall. The memorial is in the form of spaces students can work in. There's a plaque on the wall that identifies it as the Paul Rand Design Center. Nathan Garland designed the plaque, and I think he also wrote an article about it. He has been a terrific friend to us over the years. I like Nathan a lot.

fn-q: As you walk through the house, you see Paul's terrific use of color, a clear link to his work. You often talk about his terrific sense of color.

mr: Yes, there is a link, isn't there? Well, I only know that many people asked him his advice on color. He just had that kind of an eye, and he could see the difference between various shades of color. He read and observed a lot about color and was always able to tell people what color(s) to use, whether it was something they were painting or designing. Many people asked his advice on color, always. He was happy to give it and discuss color as it related to form and content.

fn-q: There's a terrific picture of him visiting a garden somewhere in Europe. He was standing there looking at the colors quite intensely.

mr: Did they have flowers? It must have been the one that we used to pass by everyday when we were walking to the school in Brissago, and it had beautiful gardens. The town had beautiful floral patches hither and yon. Yes, he used to do colorgraphs a lot too. They'd change all the time. He took a lot of pictures of the flowers. That is a wonderful town.

fn-q: Paul often said that for a clear understanding of color, all he had to do was "look at nature, it's all out there."

mr: That's right. It is. He had a terrific eye. He saw maybe what we all don't see. He was always combining unusual colors, and yet it worked. Did you know his favorite colors were red and green?

fn-q: When I look at photographs of him over time, I notice that he did not subscribe to fads, trends, and fashion. He didn't change his appearance, what he wore, his haircut. Once, he told me he cut his own hair for years and years.

mr: He had hair that was difficult to manage. He had it trimmed, obviously, by other people early in his life, but he didn't like the results. He was very concerned about his hair, so he decided the only way to make it look decent was to cut it very close, and that's what he did, and that's the look we all know that is Paul. He developed it himself. His glasses and everything else was not an affectation. It was really just him. From the time his brother died, he started wearing black knit neckties. He never wore any ties except black knit neckties for the rest of his life. He had many of them. For Paul, wearing black knit ties was a sign of love and friendship to his twin brother, Philip, and he wore nothing else but black knit neckties. It was his tribute to his brother, which I think was born out of true love.

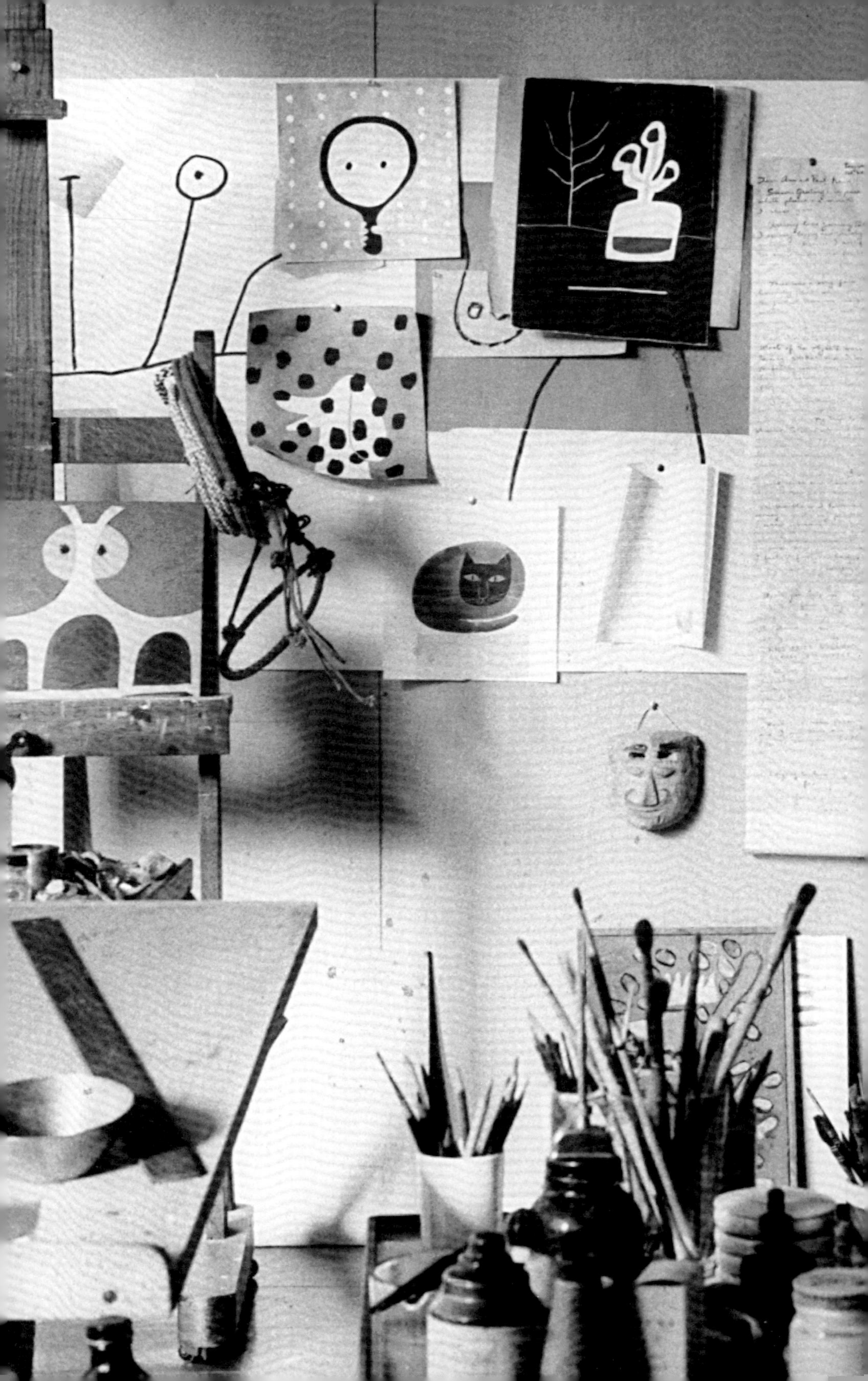

Plates:

200: 201

The Graphic Art of Paul Rand

Thoughts on Design

Paul Rand

Exhibition
IBM Gallery
New York NY
1970
Curated by
Paul Rand

Seamarks
St.-John Perse
Translated by Wallace Fowlie
Bollingen Series LXVII
Pantheon
Jacques Maritain
Creative Intuition in Art and Poetry

Christian Iconography
A Study
of Its Origins
André Grabar
Asklepios
Archetypal Image of
the Physician's Existence
by C. Kerényi
The Gothic Cathedral by Otto

Complex / Archetype / Symbol
in the Psychology of C. G. Jung
Jolande Jacobi
The I and the Not-I
Miguel de Unamuno
Our Lord Don Quixote
Archetypal World
of
Henry Moore
Erich Neumann
Pantheon

Hindu Polytheism
by Alain Daniélou

Bollingen Series LXXIII
Pantheon

Mircea Eliade
Shamanism
Archaic Techniques of Ecstasy

Bollingen Series LXXVI
Pantheon

the Living Sy

Love against Hate
Karl A. Menninger

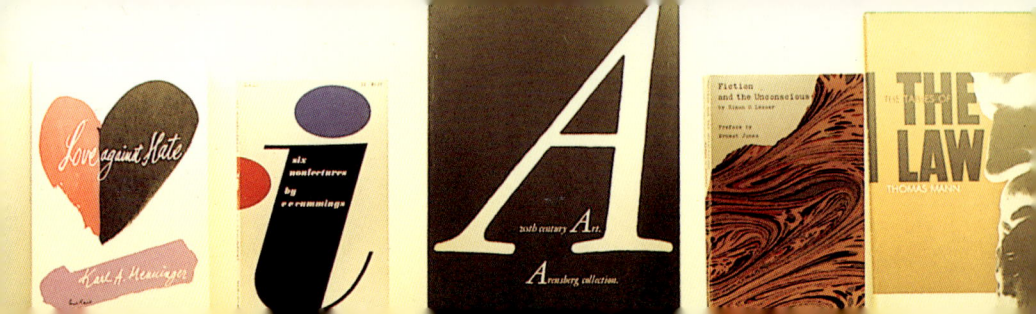

six nonlectures
by e e cummings

A
20th century Art.
Arensberg collection.

Fiction and the Unconscious
by Simon O. Lesser
Preface by Ernest Jones

THE LAW
THOMAS MANN

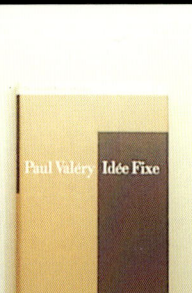

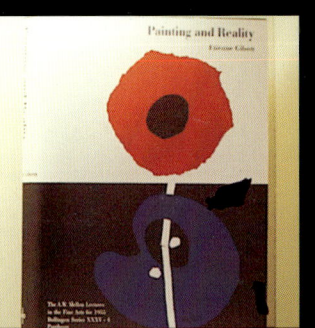

The Origins
and History of Consciousness
by Erich Neumann

Art and Illusion
E. H. Gombrich

Paul Valéry | Idée Fixe

Painting and Reality
Étienne Gilson

The A.W. Mellon Lectures
in the Fine Arts для 1955
Bollingen Series XXXV · 4

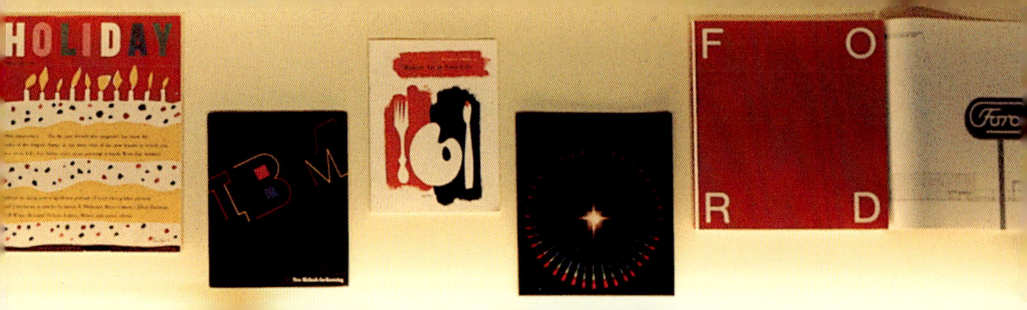
HOLIDAY
IBM
F O
R D

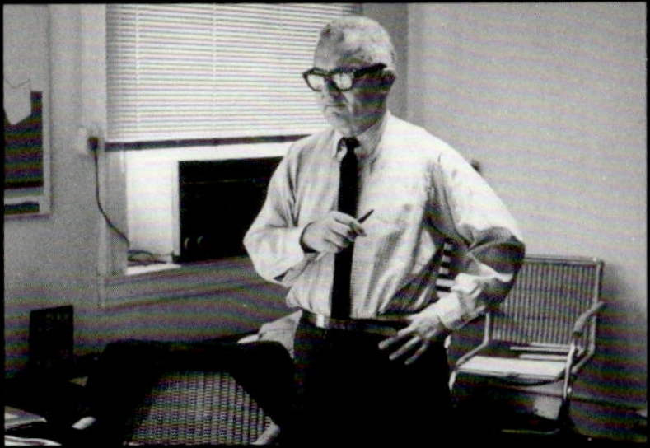

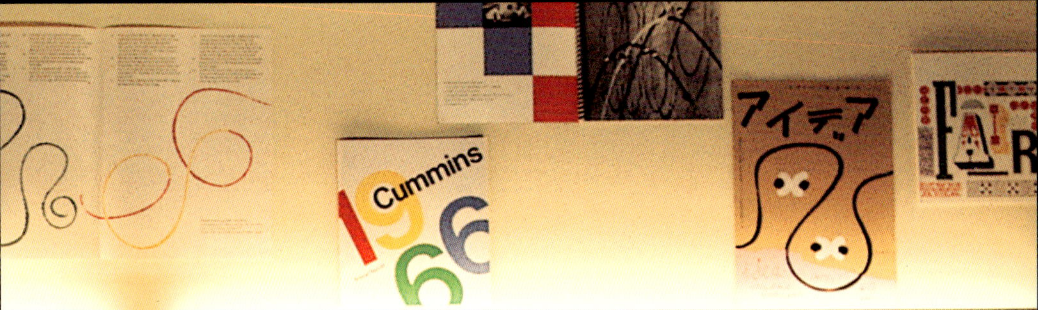
Cummins
1966
アイデア

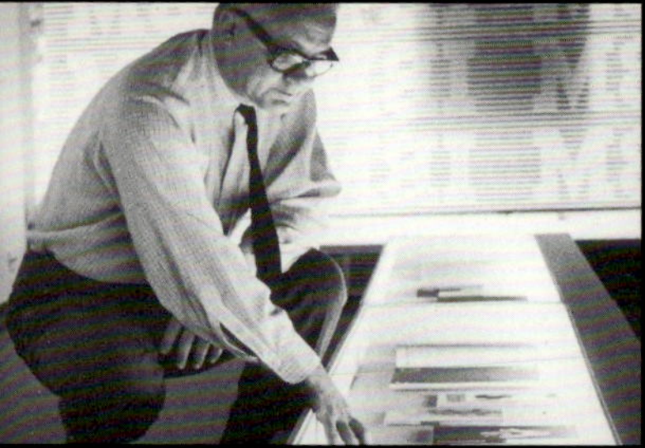

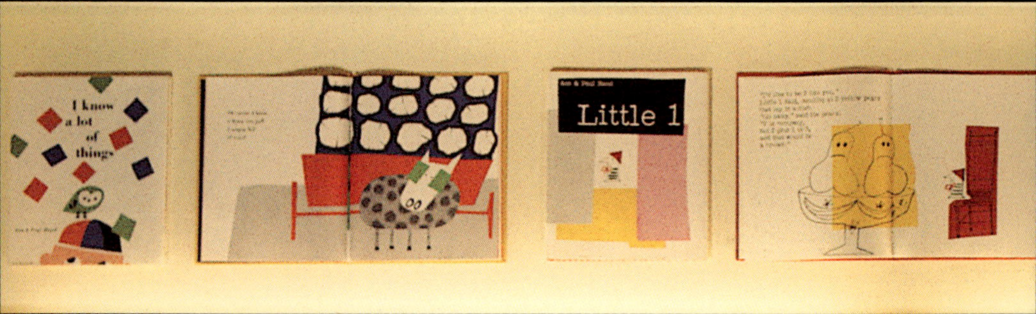
I know a lot of things
Little 1

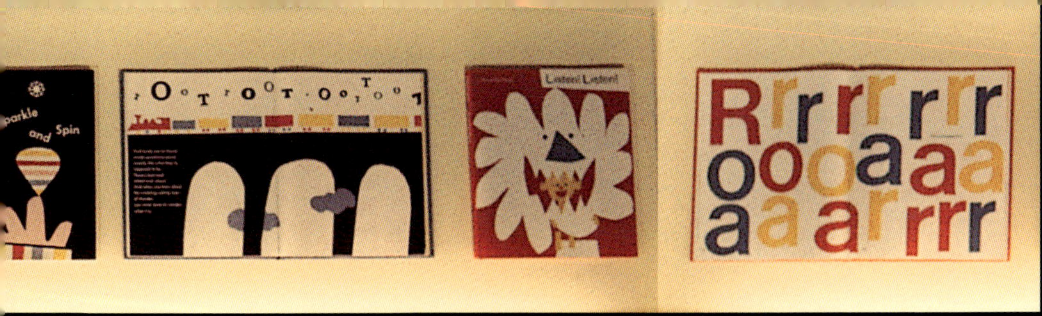
parkle
and Spin
Listen! Listen!

250 cards Type T 2
IBM
Micro-Processing Cards
250 cards Type T-1
IBM
Micro-Processing Cards
250 cards Type B-1

IBM
Carbon paper
"Selectric" Ribbon Cartridges
IBMIBM
IBMIBM

extra life light bulbs
100
watt
extra life light bulbs
75
watt
extra life light bulbs
60
watt
color-tone light bulb
EL PRODUCTO
Cigar Album
Bab-O
Fleetguar
Oil Filter LF 552

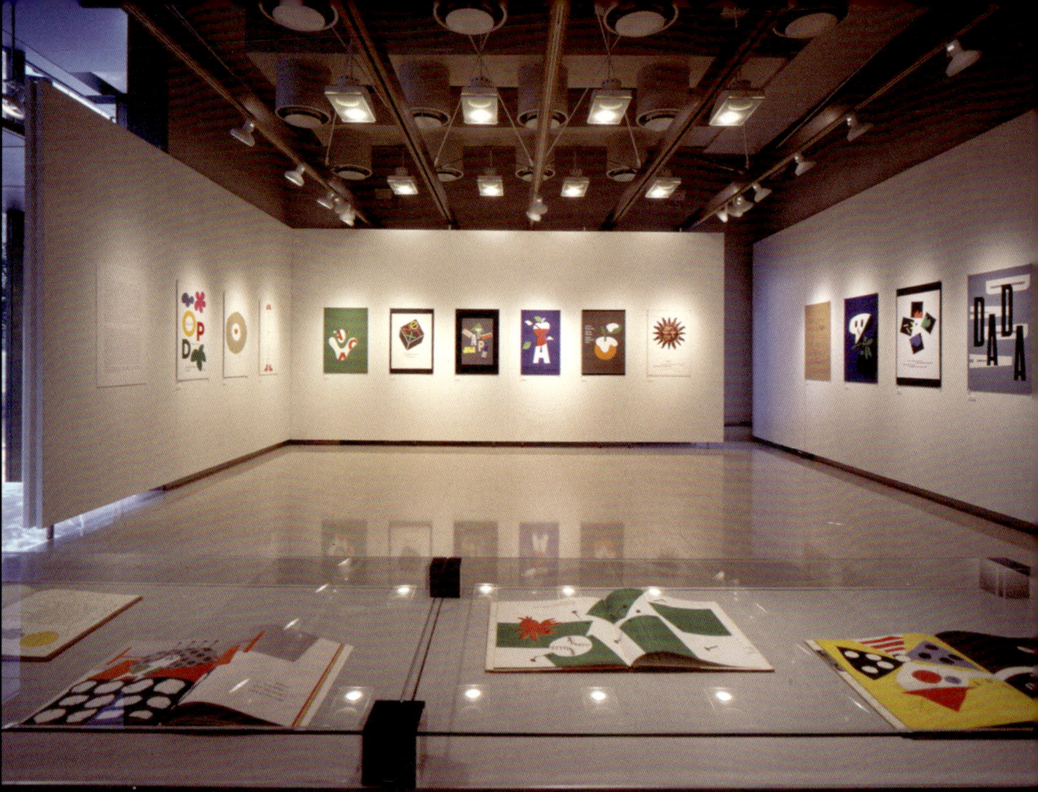
DADA

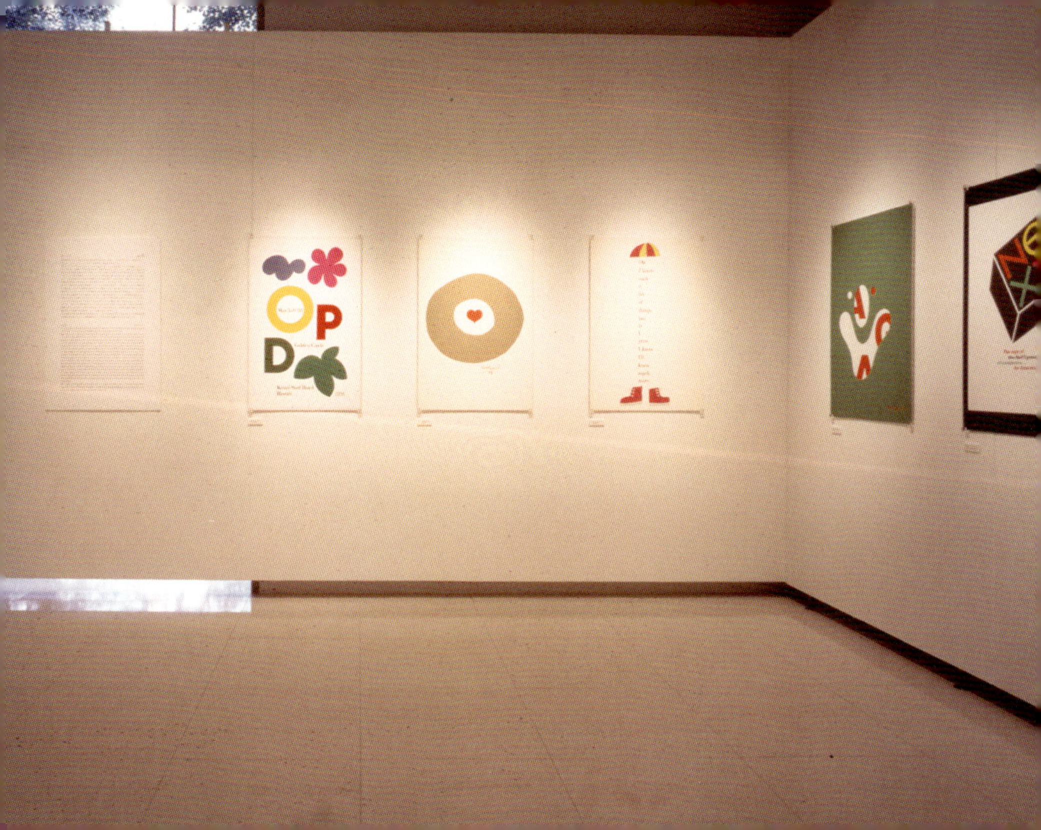

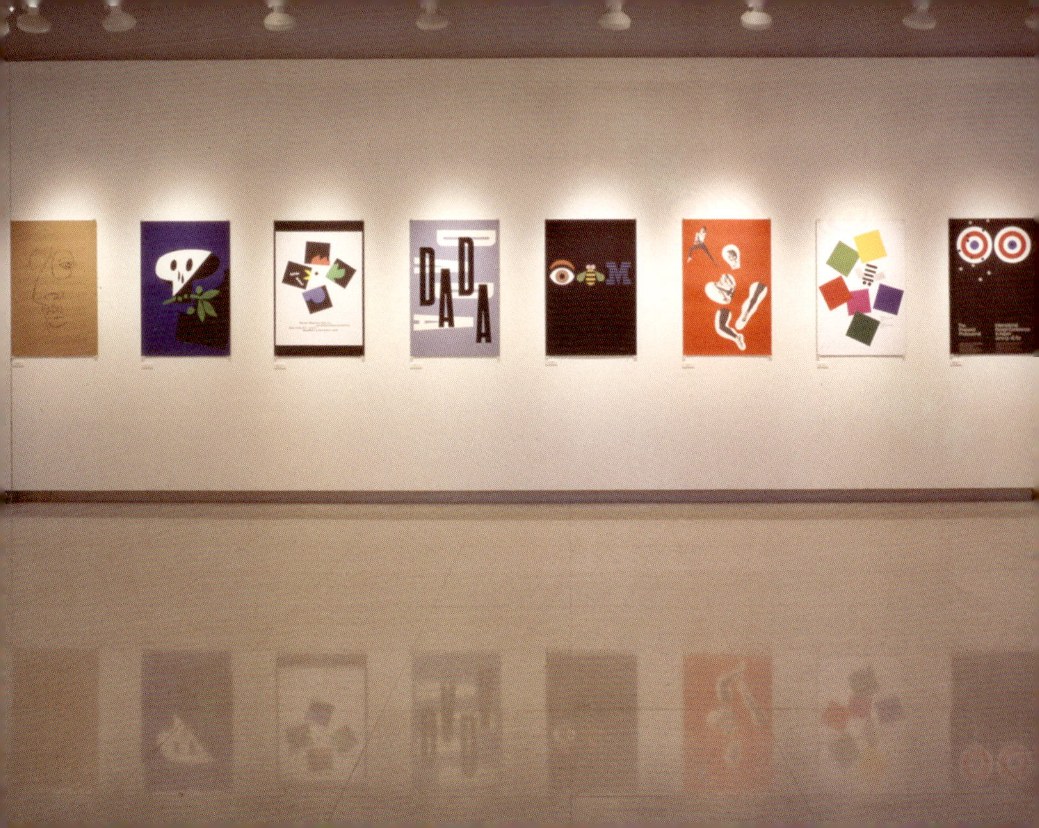
DADA

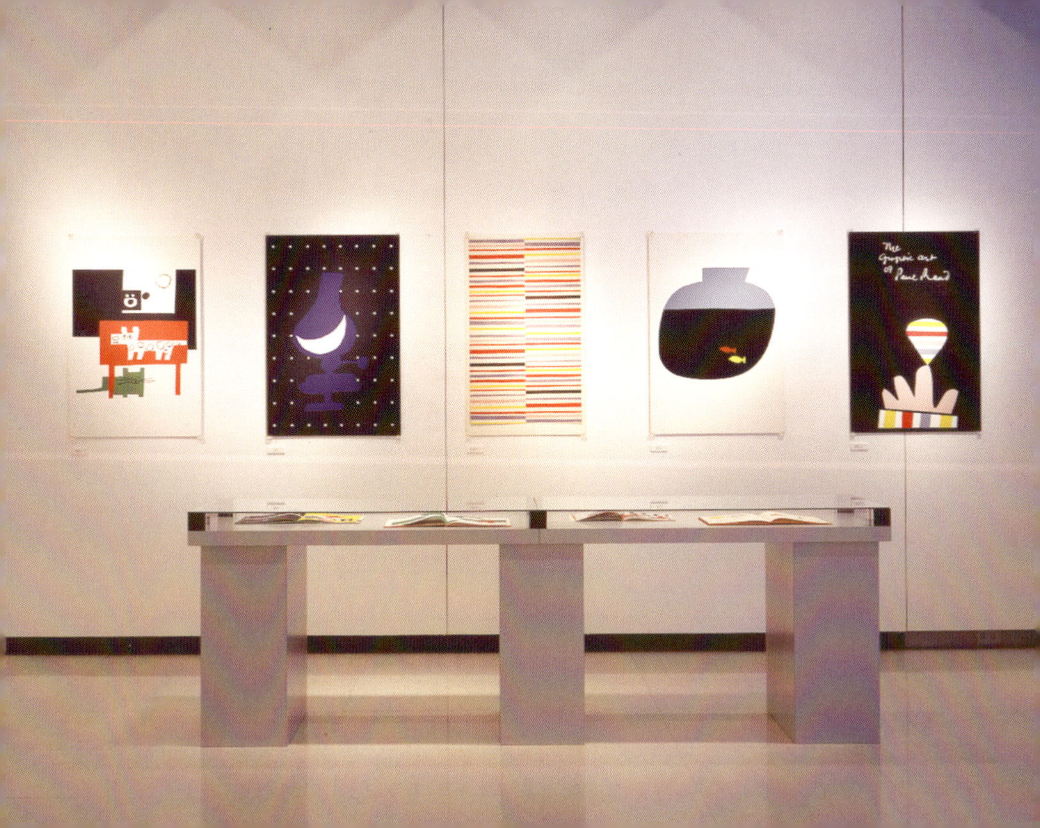
The Graphic art of Paul Rand

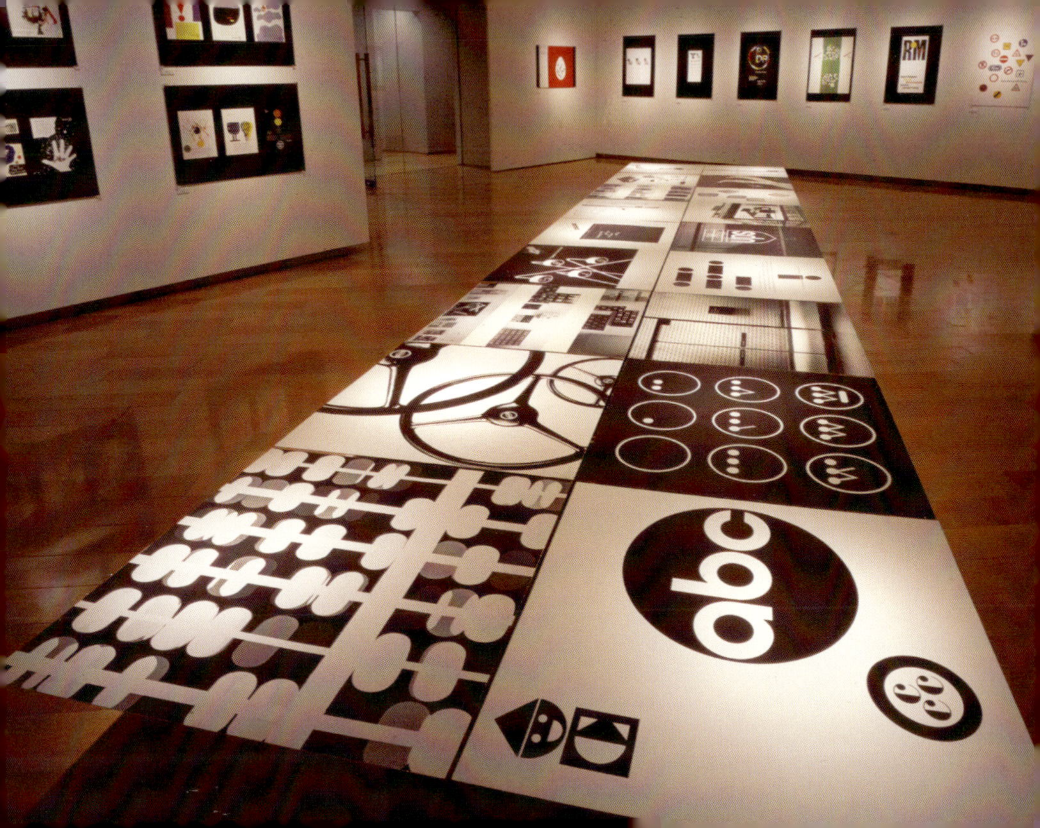
RM
abc

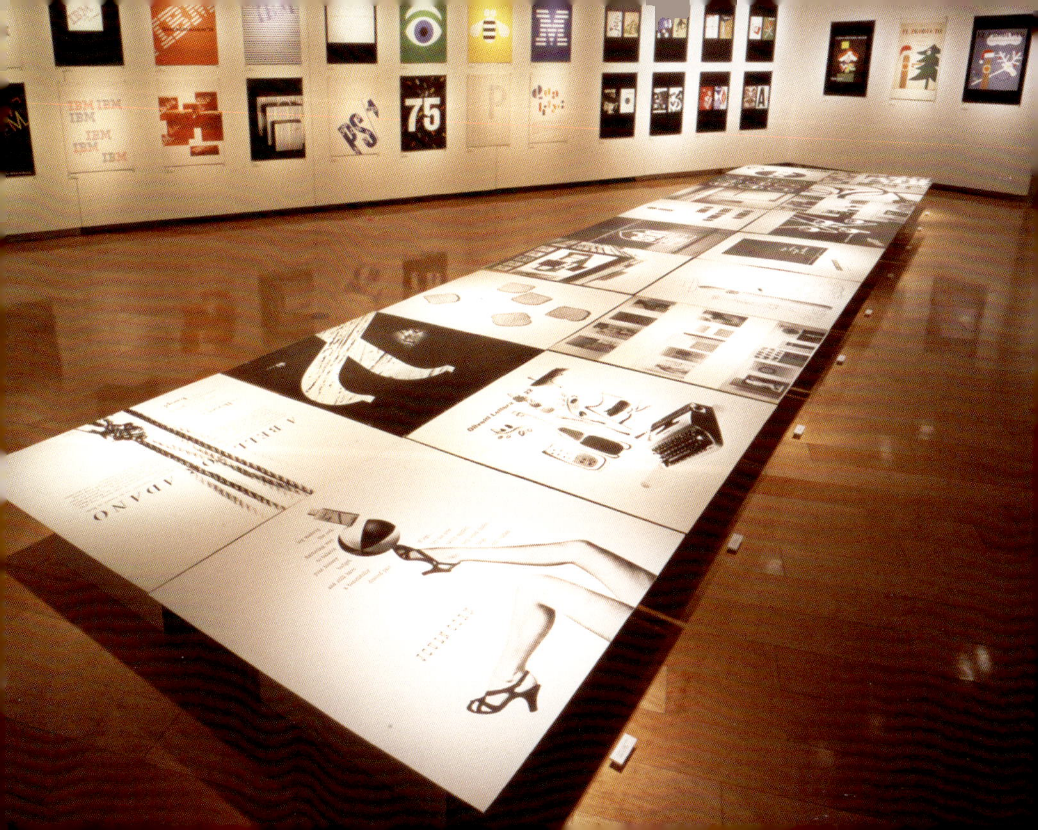
IBM IBM
IBM
IBM
IBM
IBM
75

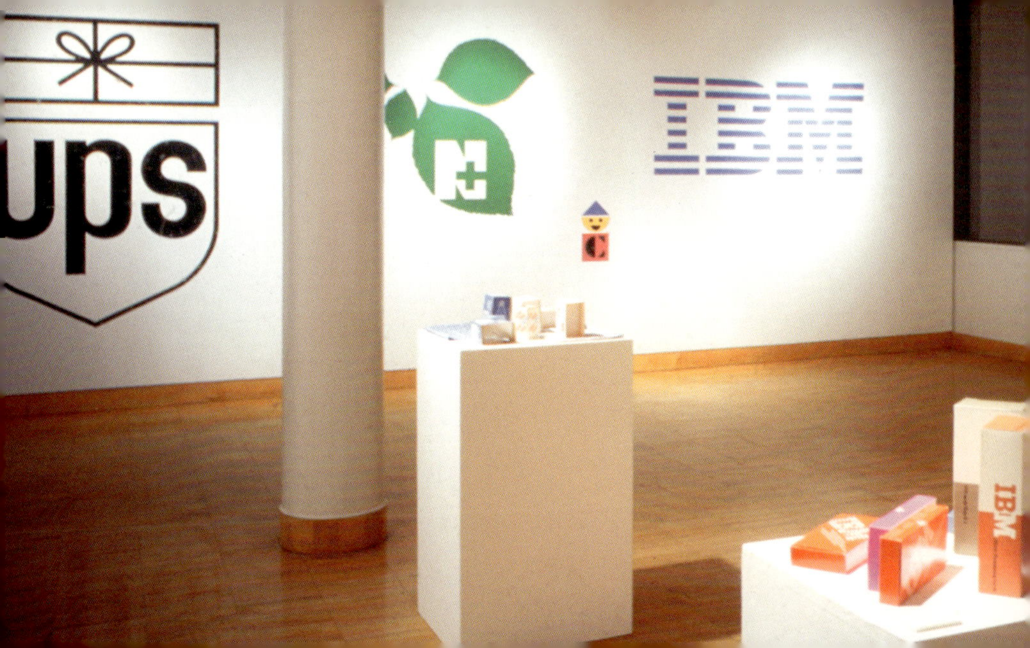
ups
IBM
IBM

presents Richard Widmark
Linda Darnell
Stephen McNally
no way
out

Drawing the Dirt

age spread
Graphic Arts
Production yearbook
1950

Logo
    Enron Corporation
    1996
Computerized
    outdoor sign
    Westinghouse
    Corporation
    1960s
    Programmed to
    generate an infinite
    number of patterns
    and lighting
    sequences

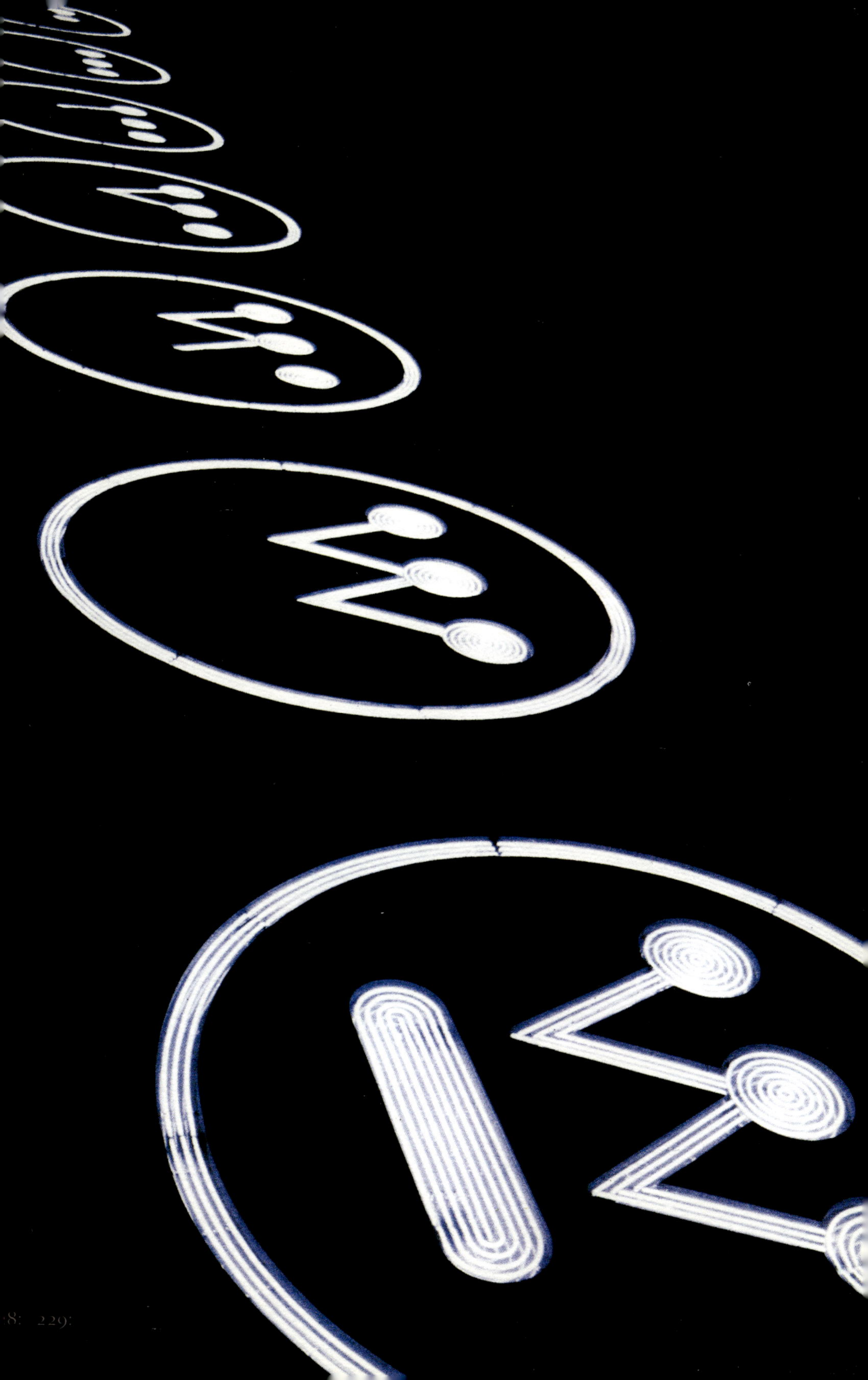

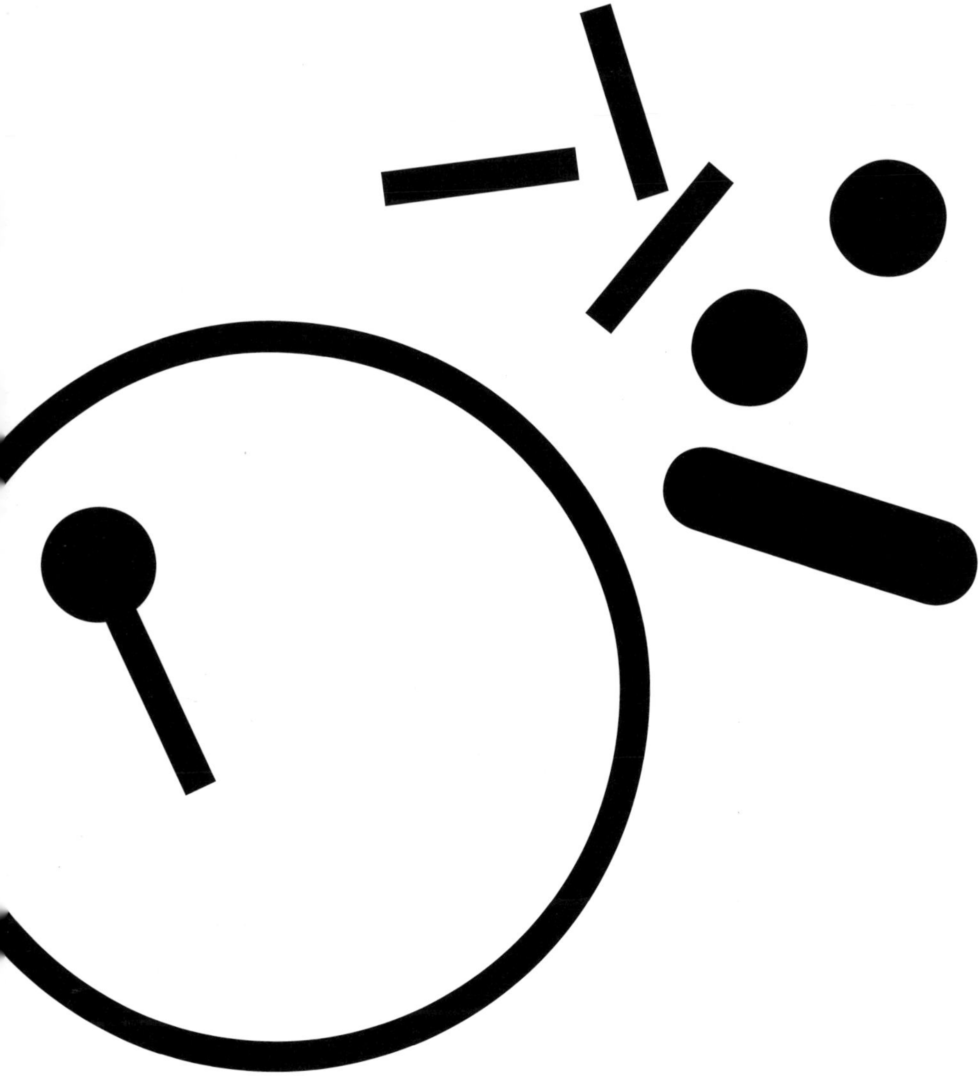

Magazine advertisement (detail)
  Westinghouse Corporation
  1968
Type design
  Westinghouse Corporation
  1961

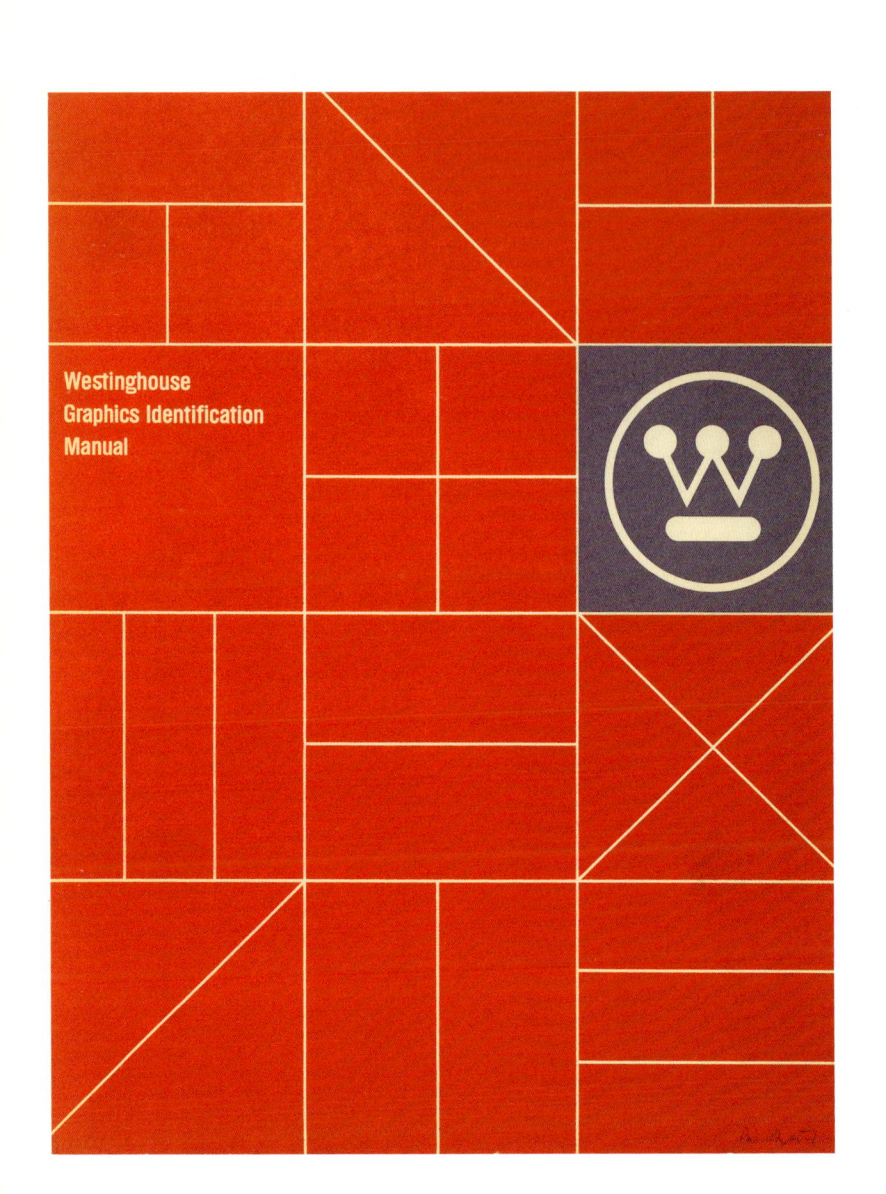

**Westinghouse
Graphics Identification
Manual**

graphics
identification
manual
Westinghouse Corporation
1961

Westinghouse Graphics Identification Manual

Page	
3	The Look of Excellence
4	Use of the Manual
5	The Trademark
7	The circle W
9	The Logotype
10	The Selling Statement
11	Westinghouse Blue
12	Westinghouse Gothic Typeface
14	Product Packaging
16	Identification Labels
19	Standard Carton Imprinting
20	Shipping Banners
21	Vehicle Identification
24	Nameplates
26	Binders, Calling Cards
28	Matchbooks, Window Decals
29	Postmark Advertising
30	Property Identification

Westinghouse Gothic Typeface

An exclusive typeface, designed especially for Westinghouse, is available. Some
its distinguishing features are:

1: Smaller capital letters, (in comparison to the lower case) than are found in ot
   typefaces, as well as short ascenders and descenders.
2: The forms of the lower case f, g, r, t, $, ¢.
3: The ligature "st." (Note: this "st" may not be used for any word but "Westinghouse
4: Short ascenders and descenders permit large size type in small areas.

Use of Westinghouse Gothic in advertising, TV, packaging, and other printed m
ter has demonstrated its practicability. It is one more factor which helps to dis
guish Westinghouse graphics from hordes of other printed material. Primarily,
typeface should be used in display, rather than text matter.

Westinghouse Gothic comes in two weights: heavy and light. Type sizes ra
from 8 point to 72 point, and it may be obtained from Westinghouse Electric C
poration, Printing and Nameplate Department, Trafford, Pa., from your local s
plier of Protype, or from Photo Lettering, 216 E. 45 St., New York (MU 2-2346)

abcdefghijklmnopqrstu
vwxyz st ABCDEFGHJKL
MNOPQRSTUVWXYZ&( )
234567890$¢!?.,:;-"""'
abcdefghijklmnopqrstu
vwxyz st ABCDEFGHIJKL
MNOPQRSTUVWXYZ&( )
234567890$¢!?.,:;-"""'

Two distinguishing features of the Westinghouse logotype...the ligature "st" and g.

Westinghouse

Westinghouse

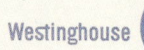

Westing

Light bulb package showing use of logotype, circle W and Westinghouse Got®

9

The Logotype

The logotype was specially designed for Westinghouse. It has two distinguishing characteristics: the "st" ligature and the lower case "g". These letters and the relative proportions of the capital "W" to the lower case are the basis for the Westinghouse Gothic, which will be discussed later. To insure continuity and recognition of the corporate name, the logotype (in other than text) must be used in no other style.

There are both light and heavy versions of the logotype and, like the circle W, it may be used in positive or reverse, in black and white, or in color.

Use of the Circle W with the Logotype: The circle W and the logotype will become Westinghouse standard bearers through consistent use in advertisements and other printed material, on products, packaging, motor vehicles, and property identification. Listed here are some basic principles by which this can be accomplished:

1: The circle W and the logotype must appear in every advertisement, on products, shipping cartons, labels, and all other printed material.

2: Wherever possible, these devices should be used as companion pieces, as shown by some of the variations in this manual. However, the overall design is ultimately the determining factor.

3: The circle W should be used emphatically, generally larger than the logotype.

4: The circle W and logotype should be kept clean and distinctive by avoiding the use of additional border decorations, divisional symbols, or insignia, tune-in plugs, industry slogans, etc. If it is necessary to consider the use of extra elements, such use must be cleared through the office of the Director of Advertising.

Reproduction proofs and/or electrotypes of both the circle W and the logotype are available from Westinghouse, Printing and Nameplate Department, Trafford, Pa.

(Sizes in inches:)					
Positive circle W:	2 to ¼	B-7975	Heavy logotype: 7½ to 5	B-7971
Reverse circle W narrow border:	2 to ½	B-7976	Heavy logotype: 4½ to ½	B-7972
Reverse circle W square:	2 to ¼	B-7977	Light logotype: 7½ to 5	B-7973
Reverse circle W wide border:	2 to ½	B-7978	Light logotype: 4½ to ½	B-7974

WOMEN

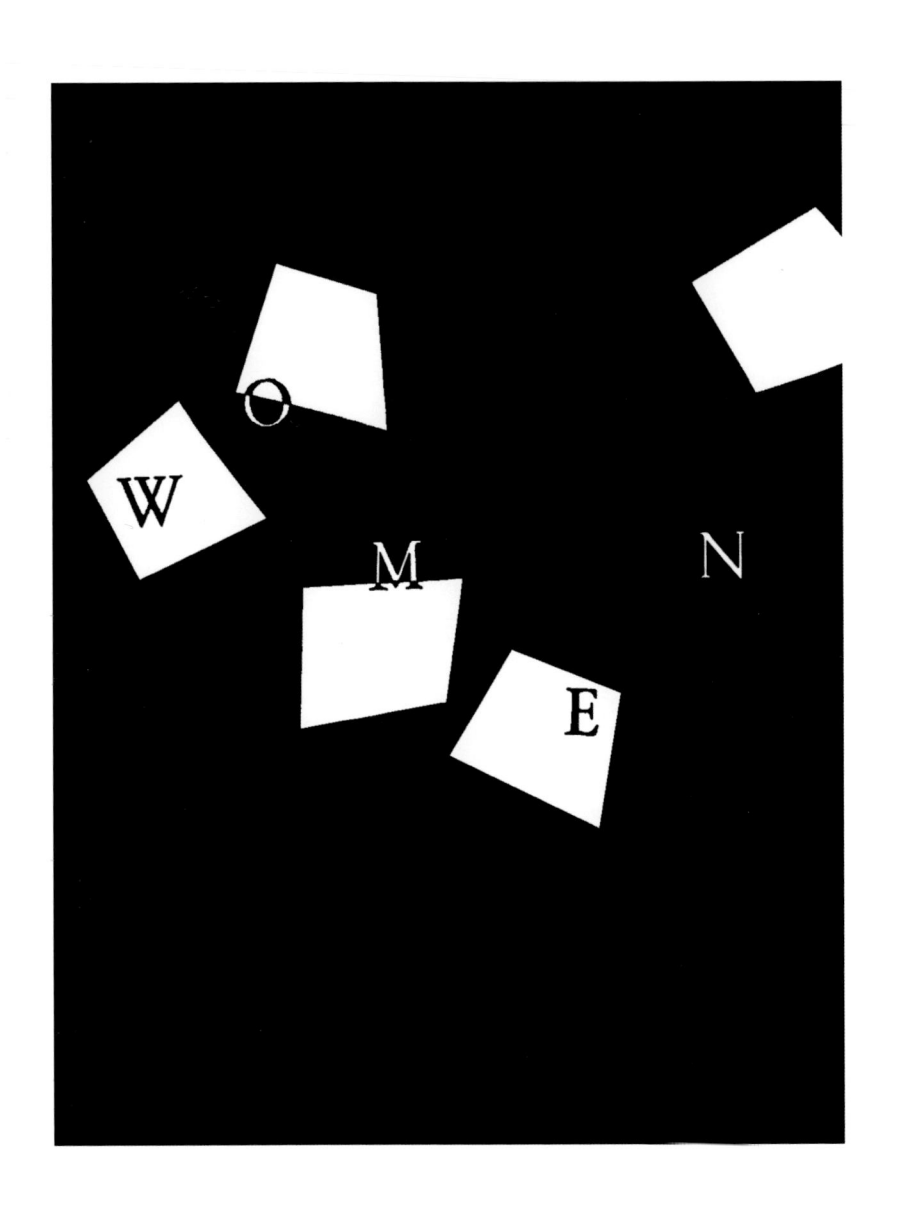

portfolio of broadsides
Museum of Modern Art
Samuel M. Kootz Editions NY
1948

WOMEN

*A collaboration
of Artists and Writers*

Samuel M Kootz *Editions*
New York

Copyright 1948 by Samuel M. Kootz   *15 East 57th Street, New York 22, N.Y.*   *Printed in the United States of America*

Designed by Paul Rand

The paintings came first. Before the writing.

Preface: *The idea for an exhibition of paintings of "Women" came into being in February, 1947, with my acquisition from Picasso of his savage "Woman in Green Costume" (which aroused such violent controversy in the great London show in 1945). I began to compare this picture with the painting of women done in the French tradition, which reached its sensuous culmination in the work of Renoir and Bonnard. And I thought of all the modern artists who have painted women: how different their points-of-view from the Renoir tradition, yet how inevitable their return to and concern with this same subject-matter.*

So, with the Picasso to start with, I consulted the other artists associated with the gallery about a special show to be devoted to "Women". Their response was immediate, enthusiastic. And, when in September the show was finally on the walls, came the additional thought: to preserve this exhibit in book-form, and to ask modern poets and writers to collaborate. No restrictions were imposed on the writers. A few, Greenberg and Sartre and Ulanov and Tennessee Williams, wrote in general appreciation of the artist they admired; others, Galantière and Goodman, were inspired by the artist's specific picture. The balance chose to write: a poem, a story, an article, that could stand beside the picture, having its own life but sharing the mood of the artist.

The writing came after the paintings. This has been so during much of our time. As Apollinaire and Baudelaire quickened the spectator's understanding of modern art decades ago. Here too, I believe, is a particularly happy collaboration.

Samuel M. Kootz

Collaborators:

Artists: Pablo Picasso
Georges Braque
Fernand Léger
William Baziotes
Romare Bearden
Byron Browne
Adolph Gottlieb
David Hare
Hans Hofmann
Carl Holty
Robert Motherwell

Authors: Lewis Galantière
Paul Goodman
Clement Greenberg
Weldon Kees
Benjamin Péret
Harold Rosenberg
Jean-Paul Sartre
Barry Ulanov
Tennessee Williams
William Carlos Williams
Victor Wolfson

The Painter: Fernand Léger   *The Author:* Clement Greenberg

The Painter's Conflict

Of all the great painters in the last one hundred years who worked, as if possessed by a will not their own, to flatten out that deep pictorial space which was a unique achievement of Western painting between Giotto and Delacroix, none has done so more reluctantly than Léger. Yet this same artist has done more than any other in our time, save Matisse and Picasso, to restore the picture plane to its pristine flatness. It is this conflict between his reluctance, on the one hand, to surrender volume, mass, and sculptural form, and his energy, on the other, in forcing this surrender upon his art that makes Léger's painting a continuing drama.

• Why Western painting has become increasingly flat since Courbet is a question that cannot be answered here. Suffice it to say for the moment that this flatness corresponds, apparently, to late scientific man's distrust of the unverifiable, a distrust that makes itself felt in the arts by requiring each to adhere as closely as possible to the limitations of its respective medium and to function only in its own area of competence, the sole area in which the art in question can produce statements incapable of being examined—or "verified"—in terms other than those proper to itself. We should not, for instance, ask that painting correspond or refer to the content of three-dimensional visual experience; for painting takes place on a two-dimensional surface and cannot attempt the illusion of three-dimensionality without leaving its own absolutely safe area of competence and risking "unverifiability."

• Léger, like every 20th-century artist truly in touch with his times, feels urgent necessity of protecting his art from demands it cannot meet exclusively on its own terms. But this necessity cannot suppress completely a deep instinct, a craving for sculptured volumes, filled-out mass contoured surfaces. He is willing enough to surrender the spatial recessions of pre-Cubist painting, b he cannot altogether give up relief. And he attempts to compromise by formalizing and simplifying into decoration the means—modelling, shading—by which the illusion of re is contrived. Modelling becomes conventionalized and is handled li the element of a decorative pattern the shading that brings into relief those cylindrical forms of which Léger is so fond is applied in relati regular strips and bands to compose surface pattern that tends to suppre the illusion of mass and depth. Th procedure does not, however, eliminate a chronic contradiction between sculptural form and picto flatness, between decoration and drama, in Léger's art. Where, as i "Le Grand Dejeuner" at the Museu of Modern Art or the much more recent "Three Bicyclists," the press of the plane surface wins the uppe hand, the result is a masterpiece o equilibrium—equilibrium dramati itself. But where the sculptural gair the ascendency—where, for exampl Léger places his forms in free space instead of articulating every inch o the surface in what I would call "plastic detail"—there results a disequilibrium, and the artist's last-minute effort to prevent the bas-relief effect from breaking up the picture plane produces, paradoxically, an emblem, a piece of decoration, rather than a picture. For here Léger will tend to use his bands of shading too evenly, too monotonously, and he will strain for too absolute a balance in his design.

- This conflict between the sculptural and the flat still persists, and we have a prime instance of it in the picture at hand—which also documents Léger's fascination with tubular forms, here organized with typically ponderous facility in that whirling, heraldic knot or garland which has become such a characteristic scheme of composition with this painter since the late thirties. Whether Léger has resolved the conflict successfully in this picture I hesitate to say. But what I like about the canvas is its Romanesque quality, which is an abiding quality of the artist himself—the slow, heavy curves, the rough abbreviation in the drawing of details, the compactness. And superimposed, so to speak, upon this picture is another emblem of Léger's achievement: his disenchantment of the human form.

- Léger has contributed in a major way to the conversion in modern pictorial art of the human being from a subject into an object (these are his own words). The human form has been deprived of its special role in the course of a process, beginning with Manet, in which the difference in general between the animate and the inanimate as portrayed in painting has been obliterated. Léger's immunity to sentimentality—an immunity that aligns him with Matisse and separates him from Picasso—has helped him no little in the part he played in this process. But perhaps contemporary man inclines too much to treat man, as such, as an object. The liabilities of this attitude have become most painfully clear of late. Nevertheless, in the period in which Léger grew up its advantages seemed more operative than its liabilities. To approach man as an object can also mean to learn more about him. And in any case Léger, as an artist, can only report the truth about feeling, he cannot correct feeling itself; and the "objectivization," or reification, of man has become one of the most fundamental truths involved in any description of contemporary feeling.

- If Léger withdraws his human sympathies from his subject, it is only to put them into his painting. He does not paint humanity, sex, animation, personality—he paints *with* them. If all humanity seems drained from the four women represented in this picture, it is because they are only representation, *fictions*, and the humanity has been put into the paint, which is *real*. And equally real is the rippling of the darks and lights of the modelling, the heavy contour lines, the sausage shapes, all of which is the content and form, simultaneously, of the picture, and evidence that raw matter has been made more human.

Clement Greenberg

A

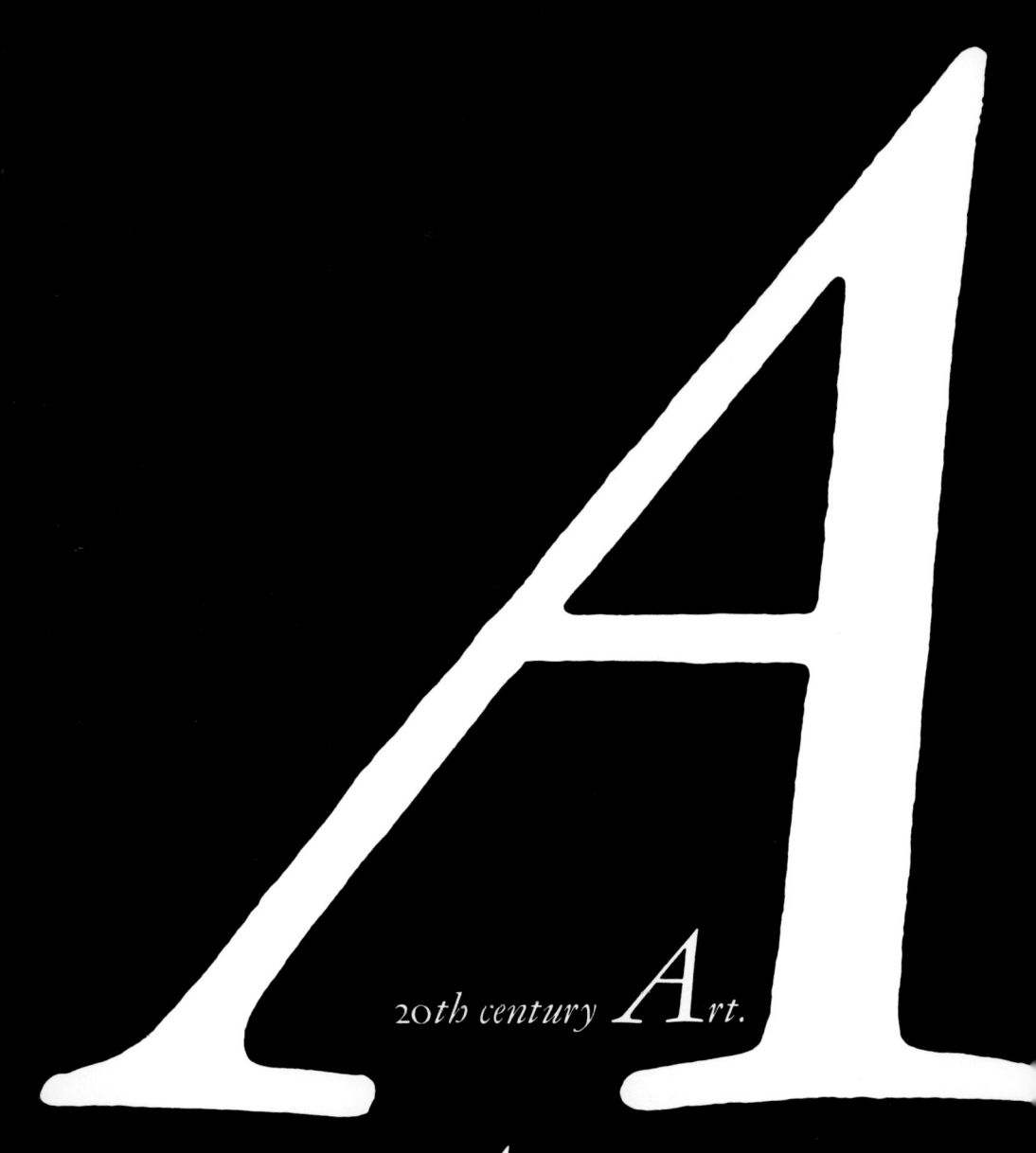

20th century Art.

*A*rensberg collection.

Catalog cover
 Arensberg Collection
 The Art Institute of Chicago
 1949
Course catalog
 UCLA Extension
 1997
Cover design
 AD magazine
 1941

a
paul rand
miscellany

nq1z3

cover design
Design Quarterly
1984

type design (booklet)
New York World's Fair
1939

Portrait of Picasso

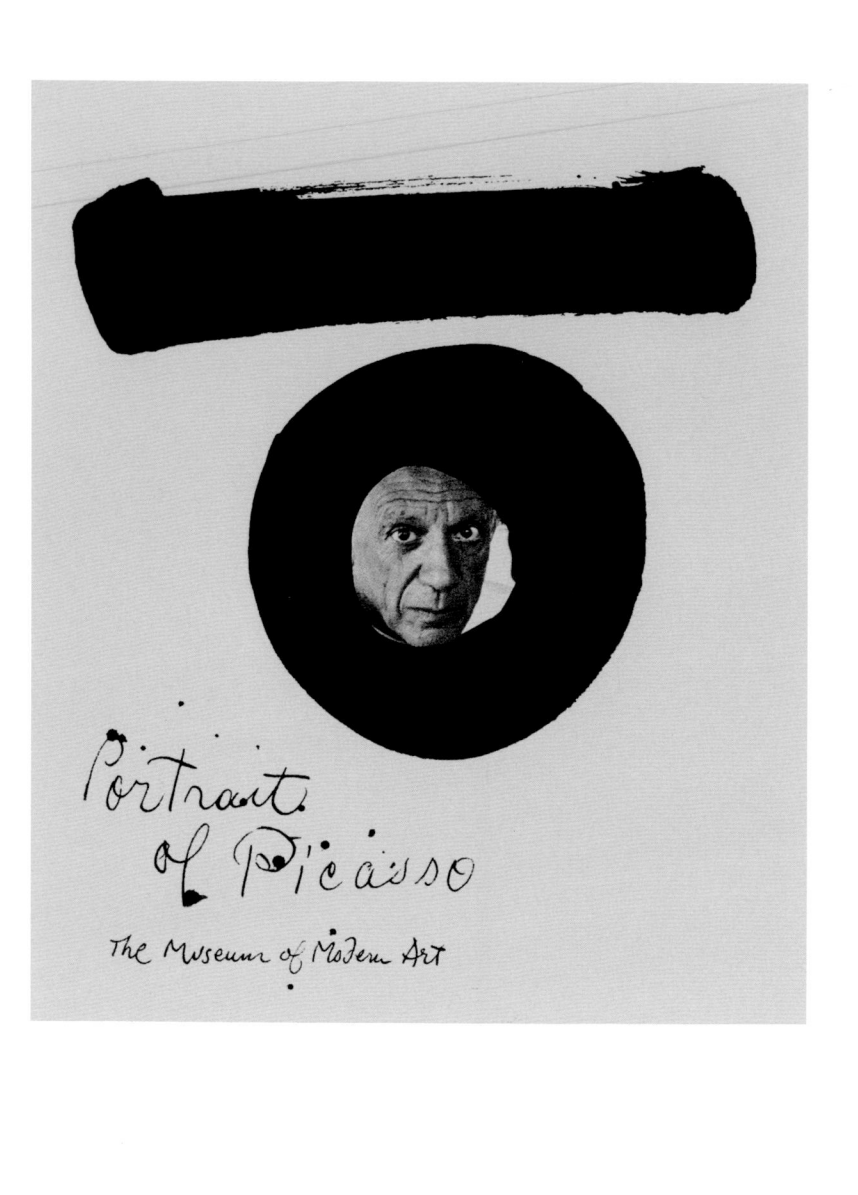

The Museum of Modern Art

Catalog cover
Museum of
Modern Art
1957
Book jacket
Alfred A. Knopf
1956

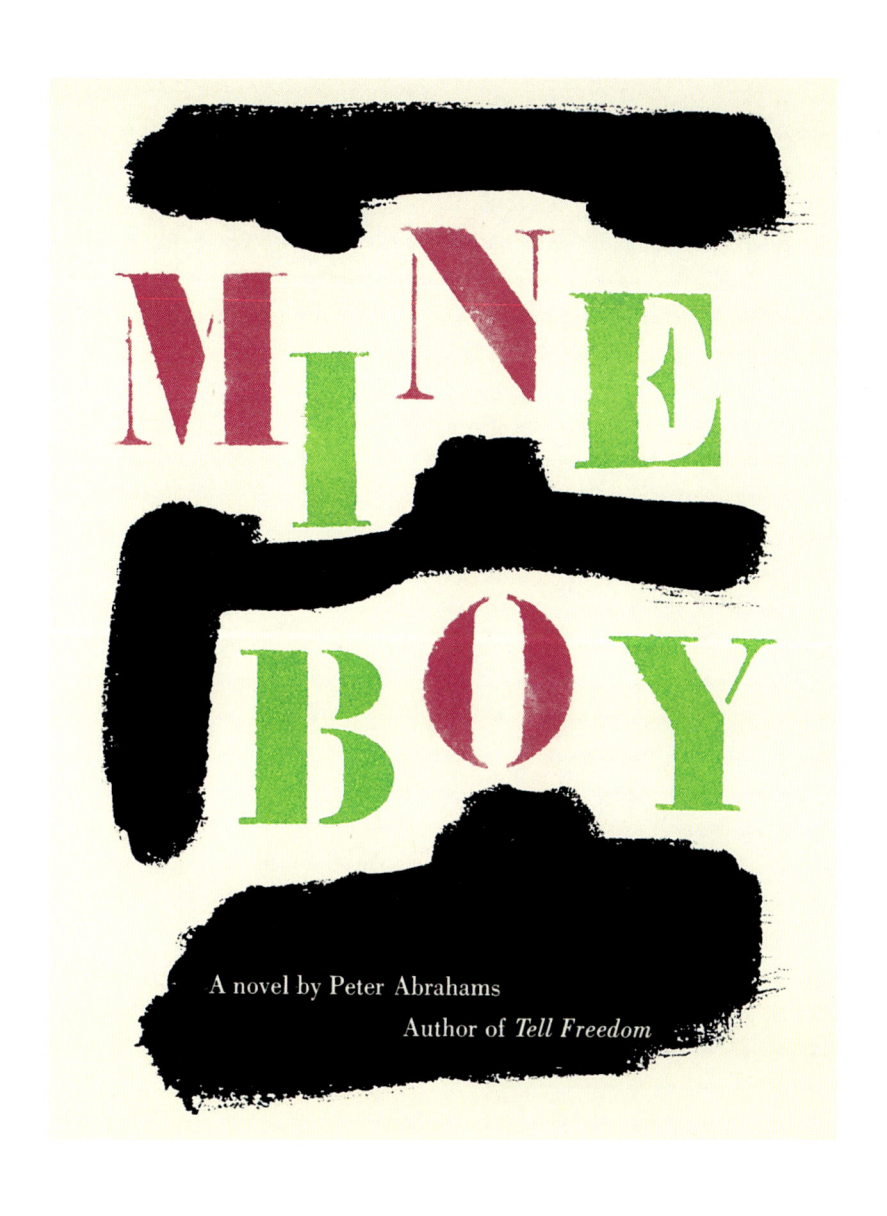

MINE BOY

A novel by Peter Abrahams
Author of *Tell Freedom*

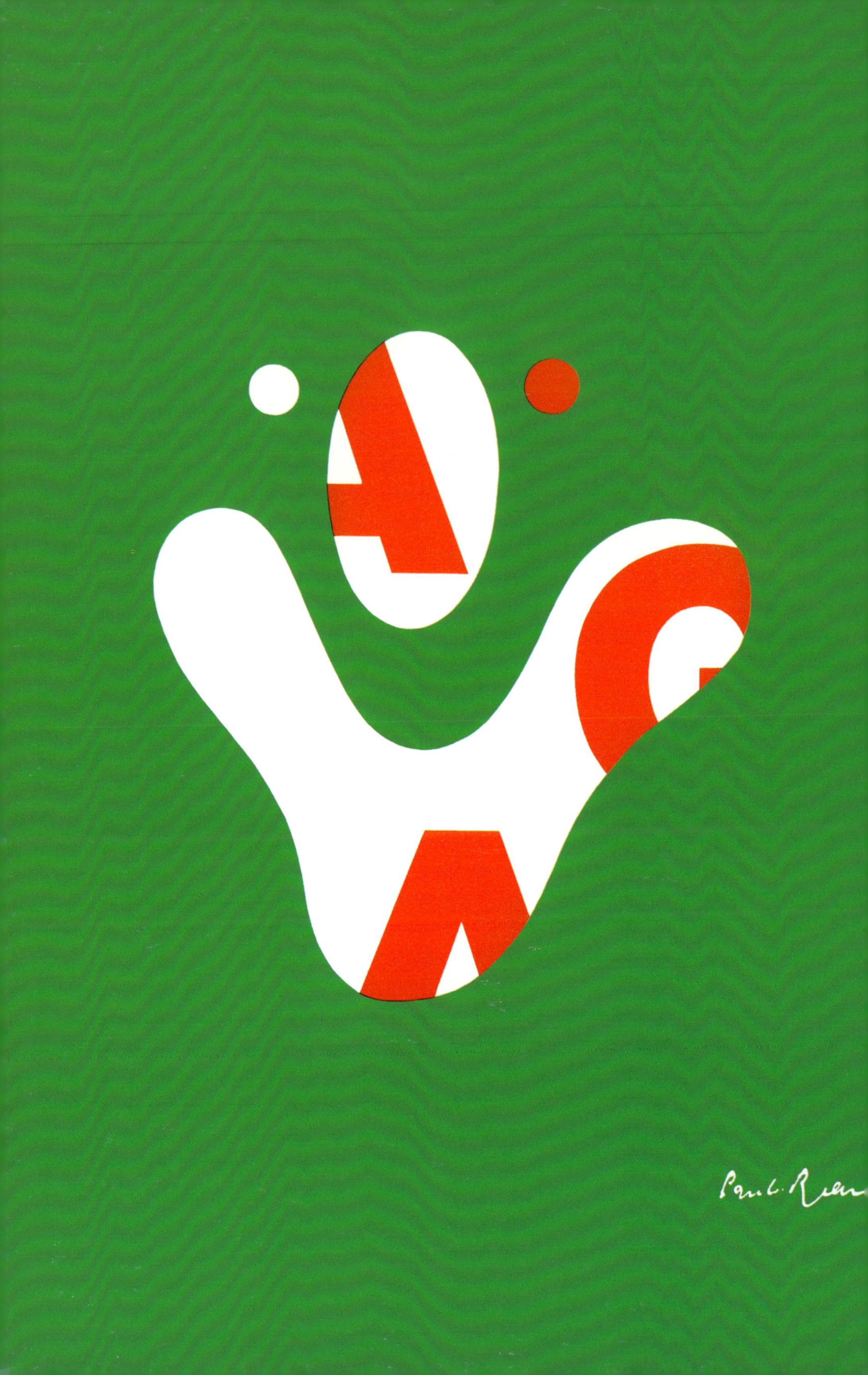

Cover design
American Institute
of Graphic Arts
(AIGA)
1968

Cover design
Vintage Books
1958

Cover design
*AIGA Graphic Design
USA 3*
1982

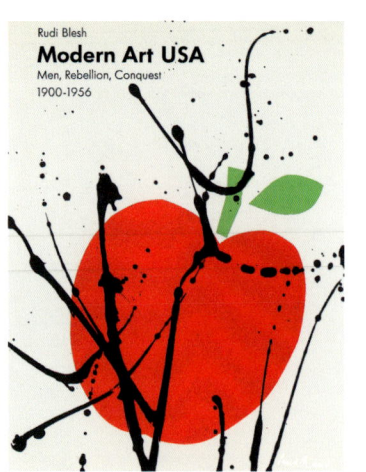

the documents of modern art
wittenborn & co., new york

guillaume **apollinaire** **the cubist painters**

Rudi Blesh
Modern Art USA
Men, Rebellion, Conquest
1900-1956

cover design
The Cubist Painters
Wittenborn & Company
1944

jacket design
Modern Art USA
Alfred A. Knopf
1956

jacket design
*Modern Art
in Advertising*
1946

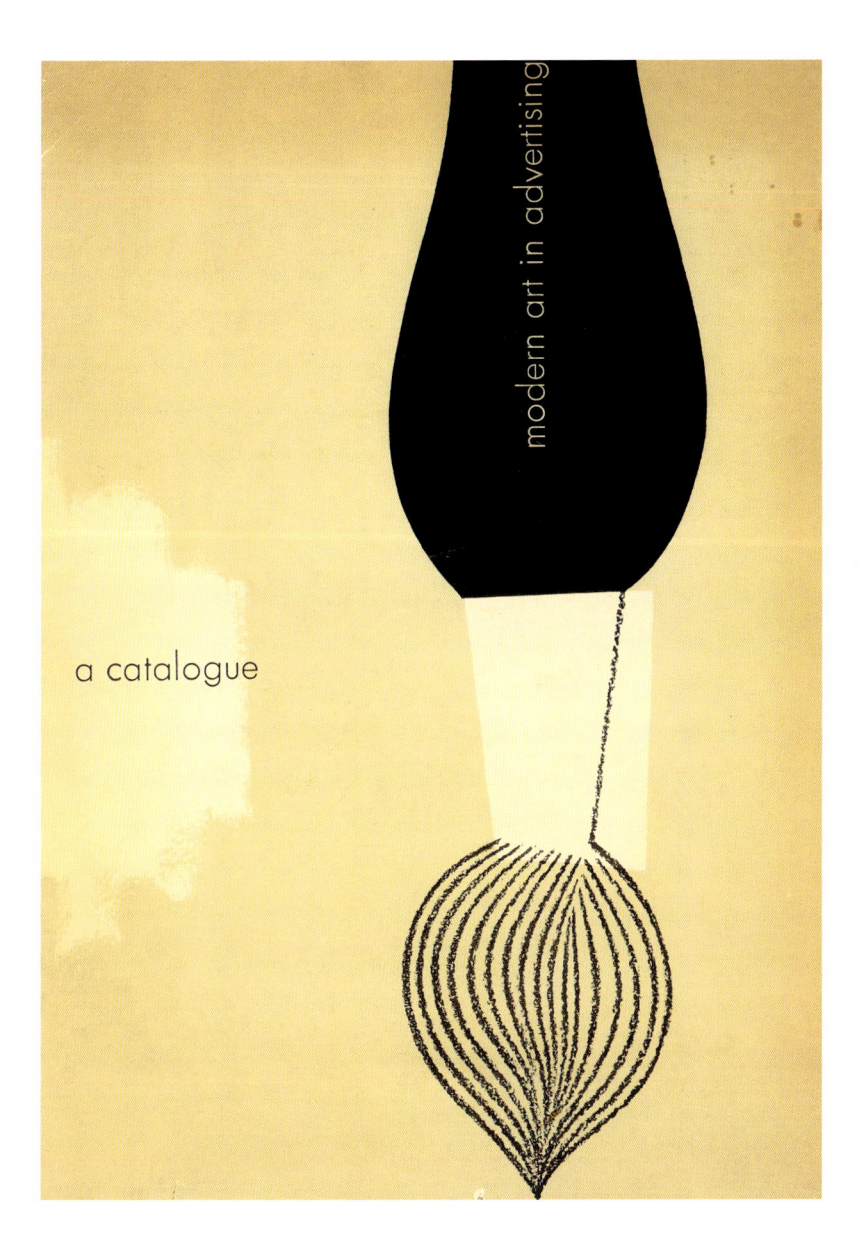

"if

it's out

of

this world...

it's

here!"

Kaufmann's
Pittsburgh, Pa.

Encore, the shirtwaist
frock. And bravo
for such charming gestures
as the three bows ...
the graceful flare.
It's starring at Kaufmann's,
that endless fair
of all that's good
and all that's fine
in all the world;
"the city of shopping"
that has everything
in prodigious
variety ...
that does everything
with overwhelming verve.

dress by McMullen

Magazine advertisement
Kaufmann's
Department Store
1944

Magazine advertisements
Stafford Fabrics
1944

spring time is stafford time

keep in the swing with a stafford robe

Comes the desire to luxuriate...and you'll
keep in the swing with a Stafford Robe®. Superbly styled...
flawlessly tailored in cheerfully patterned foulards
of lustrous Celanese®® rayon yarn...
woven in the Pennsylvania hills and printed with integrity
in the little New England town to whose name
they've brought fame. At better men's wear
and department stores everywhere...
STAFFORDWEAR, INC., 3 East 40th St., New York 16, N.Y.,
or 608 South Hill St., Los Angeles, Calif.

Olivetti Lettera 22

Magazine advertisements
   Olivetti Corporation
    1953
Drawing
   La Cascade Gardens
   Paris
    1951

Portfolio *Portfolio*

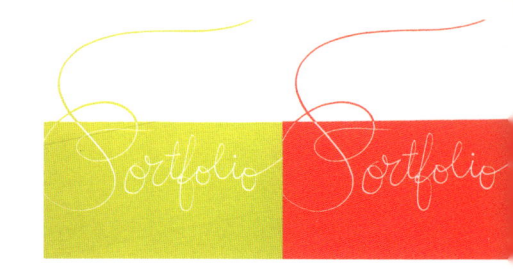

Genesis: 3

The Bible, since the days of Gutenberg,
has been an inspiration to typographers of many lands.
The text of this interpretation is from
the translation issued by the Jewish Publication
Society of America in 1917.

1. Now the serpent was more subtle than any beast of the field which the Lord God had made. And he said unto the woman: 'Yea, hath God said: Ye shall not eat of any tree of the garden?'
2. And the woman said unto the serpent: 'Of the fruit of the trees of the garden we may eat;
3. but of the fruit of the tree which is in the midst of the garden, God hath said: Ye shall not eat of it, neither shall ye touch it, lest ye die.'
4. And the serpent said unto the woman: 'Ye shall not surely die;
5. for God doth know that in the day ye eat thereof, then your eyes shall be opened, and ye shall be as God, knowing good and evil.'
6. And when the woman saw that the tree wa[s] for food, and that it was a delight to the ey[es] and that the tree was to be desired to mak[e] wise, she took of the fruit thereof, and did and she gave also unto her husband with h[er] he did eat it.
7. And the eyes of them both were opened, a[nd] they knew that they were naked; and they figleaves together, and made themselves g[irdles]
8. And they heard the voice of the Lord God walking in the garden toward the cool of t[he] and the man and his wife hid themselves f[rom] the presence of the Lord God amongst the[trees] of the garden.

Logotypes
Portfolio magazine
1940s
Broadside
Westvaco Corporation
1968

22 E. 12th St., Cincinnati 10, Ohio

nd the Lord God called unto the man, and said nto him: 'Where art thou?'
he said: 'I heard Thy voice in the garden, I was afraid, because I was naked; and I hid yself.'
e said: 'Who told thee that thou wast ked? Hast thou eaten of the tree, whereof ommanded thee that thou shouldest not eat?' d the man said: 'The woman whom Thou vest to be with me, she gave me of the tree, d I did eat.'
d the Lord God said unto the woman: 'What this thou hast done?' And the woman said: e serpent beguiled me, and I did eat.'

14. And the Lord God said unto the serpent: 'Because thou hast done this, cursed art thou from among all cattle, and from among all beasts of the field; upon thy belly shalt thou go, and dust shalt thou eat all the days of thy life.
15. And I will put enmity between thee and the woman, and between thy seed and her seed; they shall bruise thy head, and thou shalt bruise their heel.'
16. Unto the woman He said: 'I will greatly multiply thy pain and thy travail; in pain thou shalt bring forth children; and thy desire shall be to thy husband, and he shall rule over thee.'

17. And unto Adam He said: 'Because thou hast hearkened unto the voice of thy wife, and hast eaten of the tree, of which I commanded thee, saying: Thou shalt not eat of it; cursed is the ground for thy sake; in toil shalt thou eat of it all the days of thy life.
18. Thorns also and thistles shall it bring forth to thee; and thou shalt eat the herb of the field.
19. In the sweat of thy face shalt thou eat bread, till thou return unto the ground; for out of it wast thou taken; for dust thou art, and unto dust shalt thou return.'
20. And the man called his wife's name Eve; because she was the mother of all living.

21. And the Lord God made for Adam and for his wife garments of skins, and clothed them.
22. And the Lord God said: 'Behold, the man is become as one of us, to know good and evil; and now, lest he put forth his hand, and take also of the tree of life, and eat, and live for ever.'
23. Therefore the Lord God sent him forth from the garden of Eden, to till the ground from whence he was taken.
24. So He drove out the man; and He placed at the east of the garden of Eden the cherubim, and the flaming sword which turned every way, to keep the way to the tree of life.

Design and typography: Paul Rand
Composition and offset printing: Tri-Arts Press
Text: 14 Linotype Garamond #3
Paper: Clear Spring Book, antique offset natural

XXIV

Logotype
1980s
Trademark
Cabbages & Kings
Catering
1980s

Cabbages & Kings **Catering** 203 226 0531

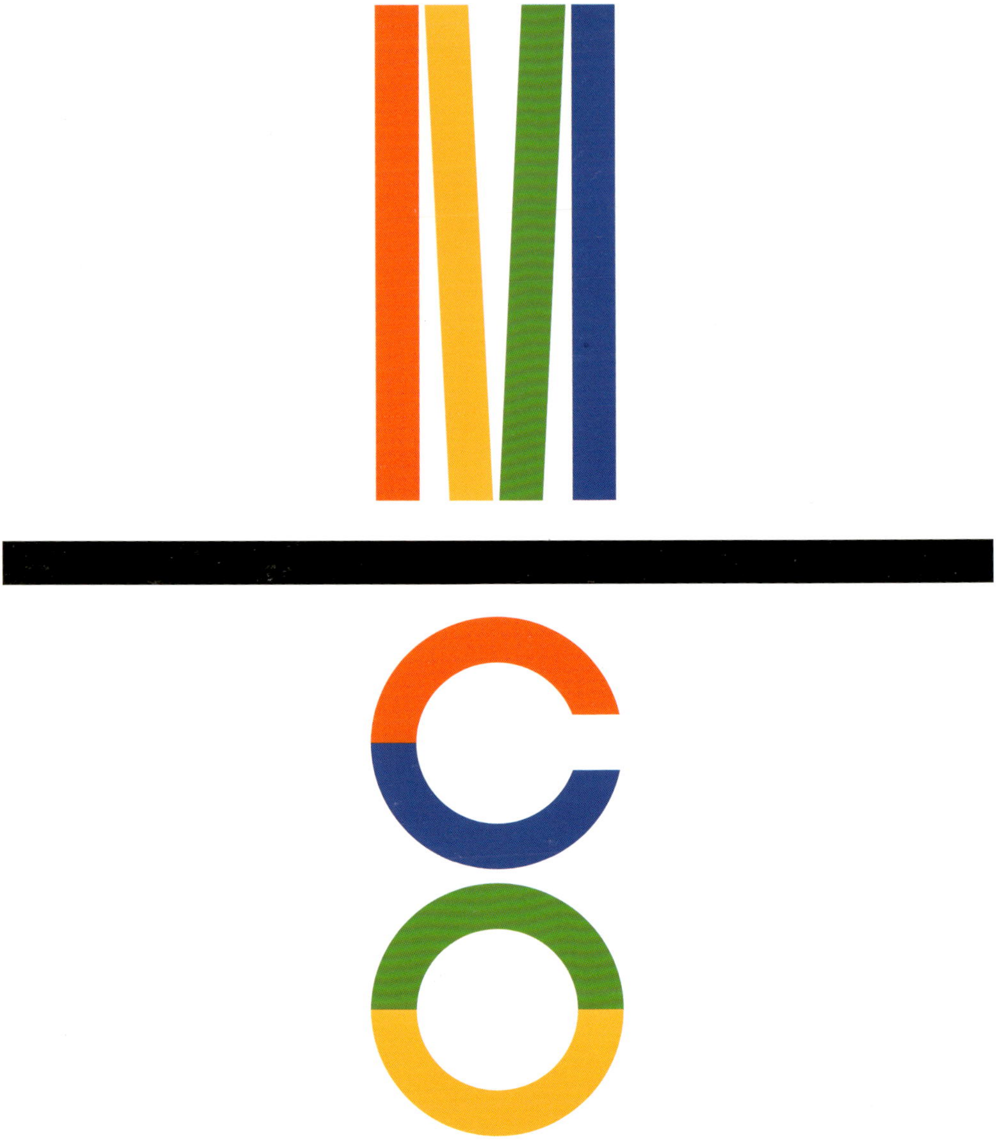

Logo
  Mossberg & Company Inc.
  Printers of corporate,
  institutional, and cultural
  publications
  1987

Logo
  Pastore DePamphilis Rampone
  Typesetters and printers
  1987

Poster (detail)
The Art Director's Club
Call for entries
1988

266: 267:

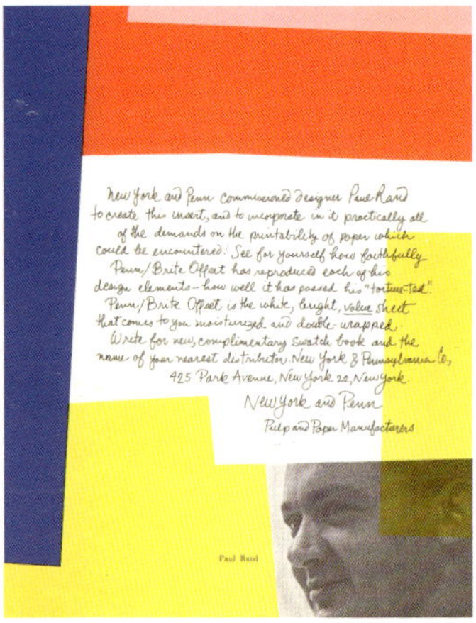
New York and Penn commissioned designer Paul Rand to create this insert, and to incorporate in it practically all of the demands on the printability of paper which could be encountered. See for yourself how faithfully Penn/Brite Offset has reproduced each of his design elements—how well it has passed his "torture-test".
Penn/Brite Offset is the white, bright, value sheet that comes to you moisturized and double-wrapped.
Write for new, complimentary swatch book and the name of your nearest distributor. New York & Pennsylvania Co., 425 Park Avenue, New York 22, New York.
New York and Penn
Pulp and Paper Manufacturers
Paul Rand

Paul Rand
this is Penn/Brite Offset—the value sheet

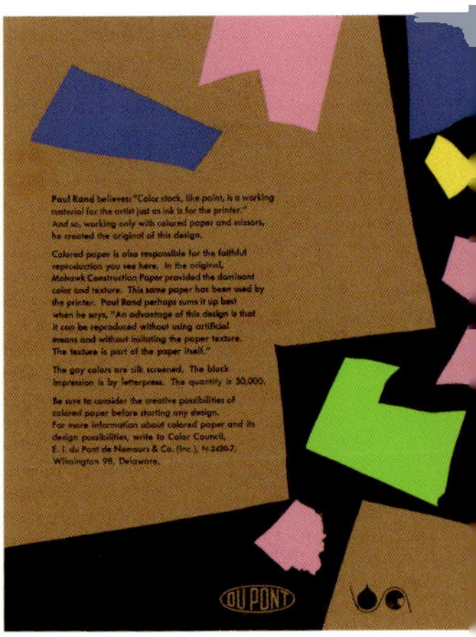
Paul Rand believes: "Color stock, like paint, is a working material for the artist just as ink is for the printer." And so, working only with colored paper and scissors, he created the original of this design.
Colored paper is also responsible for the faithful reproduction you see here. In the original, Mohawk Construction Paper provided the dominant color and texture. This same paper has been used by the printer. Paul Rand perhaps sums it up best when he says, "An advantage of this design is that it can be reproduced without using artificial means and without imitating the paper texture. The texture is part of the paper itself."
The gay colors are silk screened. The black impression is by letterpress. The quantity is 50,000.
Be sure to consider the creative possibilities of colored paper before starting any design. For more information about colored paper and its design possibilities, write to Color Council, E. I. du Pont de Nemours & Co. (Inc.), N-2420-7, Wilmington 98, Delaware.
DU PONT

Advertisement
 Penn/Brite Papers
 New York &
 Pennsylvania
 Company
 1964
Advertisement
 Dupont Corporation
 1966

Magazine advertisements
and goblet
Casa Blanca Wine Company
1945–46

CORONET v.s.q. BRANDY

delicious with soda
or ginger ale

if only you could be seen in lingerie* from Ohrbach's!

Ohrbach's
14th Street facing Union Square
Newark store: Market and Halsey Streets
"A business in millions... a profit in pennies"

newspaper advertisement
Ohrbach's Department Store
1946
visual pun
U symbol
1970s
Magazine Advertisement
Dunhill
1946

Newspaper advertisement
Frank H. Lee Company
1947
Newspaper advertisement
William H. Weintraub
Advertising Company
1954

Bread

Over

The

Waters

People of America: The food you piled on the Friendship Train
has been delivered in Europe...a practical symbol of American good-will.

It said: Here is food for the hungry, hope for the hopeless,
help that gives without question, that expects no reward.

But there is a reward. It is the still small voice of gratitude,
the whisper that goes around the world blessing the name of America
for help in a dark hour.

And over there, they praise the name of Drew Pearson, the man
whose energetic compassion forged your instrument to turn aside the cruel
blade of biting hunger...your Friendship Train.

To Drew Pearson, we say, well done! You are a faithful messenger
of the American spirit.

It has been an honor and a privilege to have Drew Pearson initiate and
foster the idea of your Friendship Train on his weekly broadcasts for Lee Hats.

Tune in Drew Pearson and his "Predictions of Things to Come"
every Sunday, 6 p.m., coast-to-coast over the American Broadcasting Company network.

To the executives and management of the Radio Corporation of America:

Messrs. Alexander, Anderson, Baker, Buck, Cahill, Cannon, Carter, Coe, Coffin, Dunlap, Elliott, Engstrom, Folsom, Gorin, Jolliffe, Kayes, Marek, Mills, Odorizzi, Orth, Sacks, Brig. Gen. Sarnoff, R. Sarnoff, Saxon, Seidel, Teegarden, Tuft, Watts, Weaver, Werner, Williams

Gentlemen: An important message intended expressly for your eyes is now on its way to each one of you by special messenger.

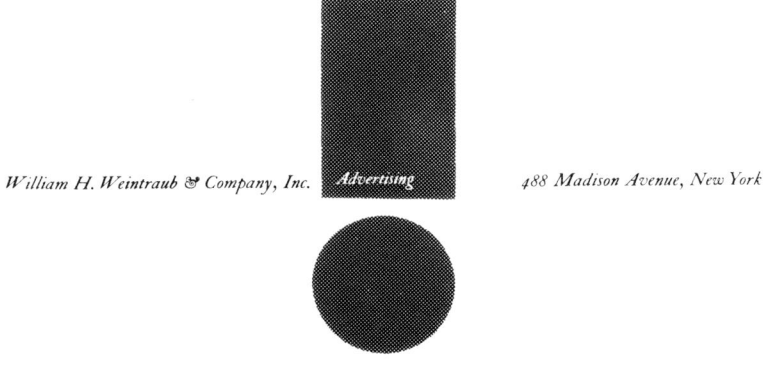

William H. Weintraub & Company, Inc.   **Advertising**   *488 Madison Avenue, New York*

The House in the Museum Garden
Marcel Breuer, Architect

Museum of Modern Art, New York
Entrance: 4 West 54 Street

Admission: 35 cents   Daily 12 to 7, Sunday 1 to 7

oster
Museum of
Modern Art
1949
oster
Interfaith Day
Movement, Inc.
1954
ne sheet poster
New York Subways
Advertising Company
1947
oster
Advertising Typography
Association of America
1965

with the sense of sight,
the idea communicates the emotion...
Alfred North Whitehead

276: 277:

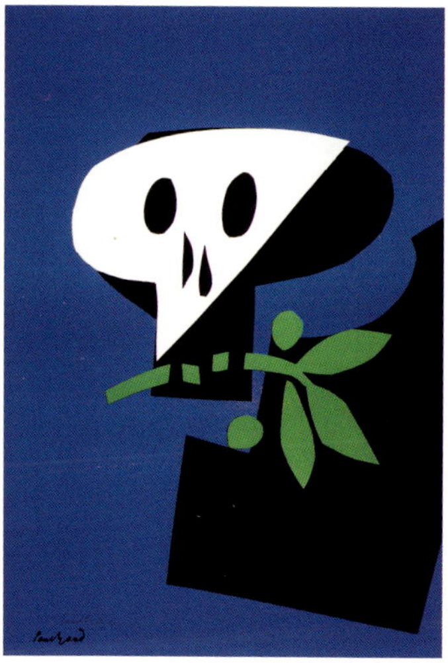

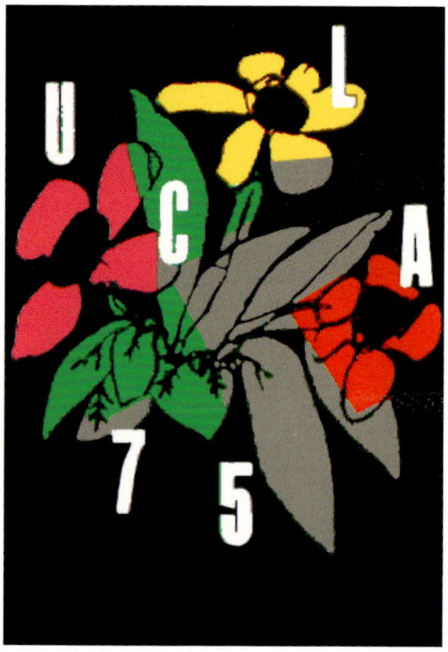
U
C
L
A
7
5

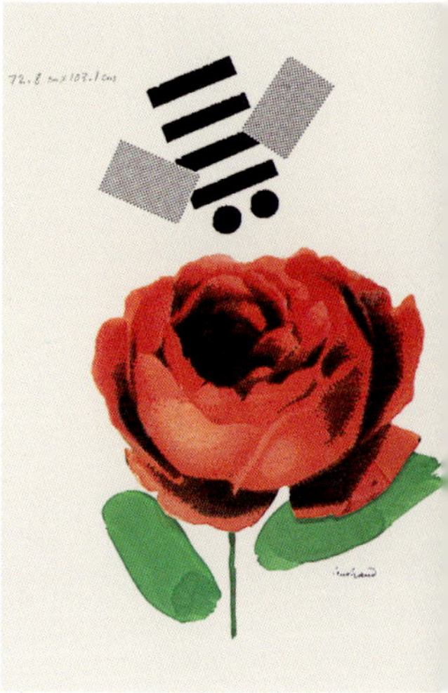

poster
Death Mask
1968
poster
University of California
Los Angeles
1994
poster
Sketch for a poster
1991
poster
Pastore DePamphilis
Rampone
1985

"What   would life be
            if we had   no courage
    to attempt   anything?"

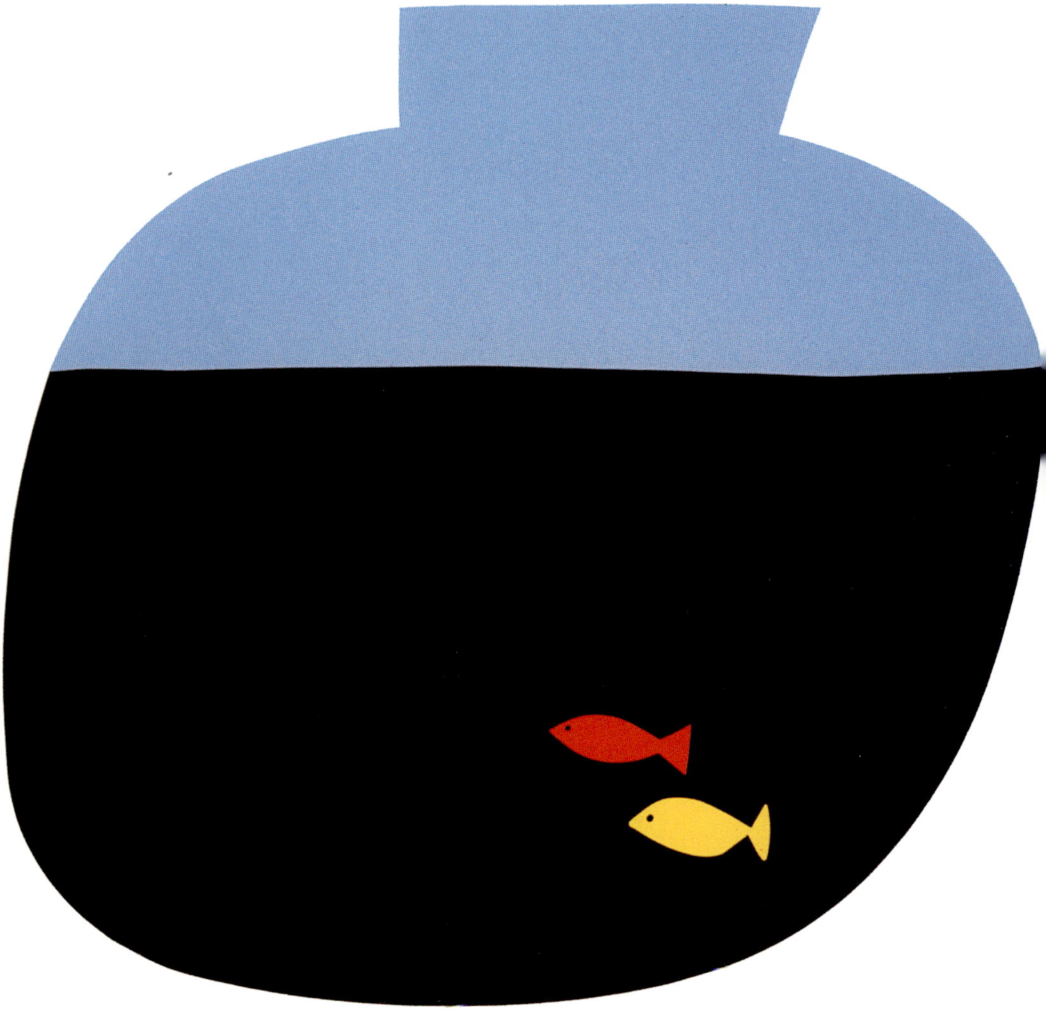

Magazine advertisement (detail)
  Westinghouse Corporation
  1962
Magazine advertisement
  Westinghouse Corporation
  1961

Earth Day... '95

Poster
Earth Day
1995

Poster
Aspen Design Conference
1966

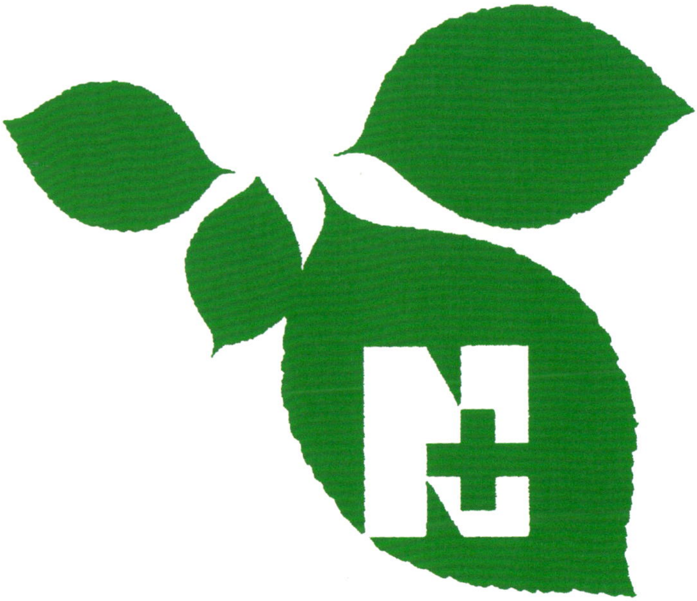

Campaign contribution
A Big Apple
for the Big Apple
1993

Poster
UCLA Extension
1990

Logo
Norwalk Cancer Center
Norwalk Hospital
Connecticut
1996

UCLA Extension

Winter Quarter

begins January 6 1990

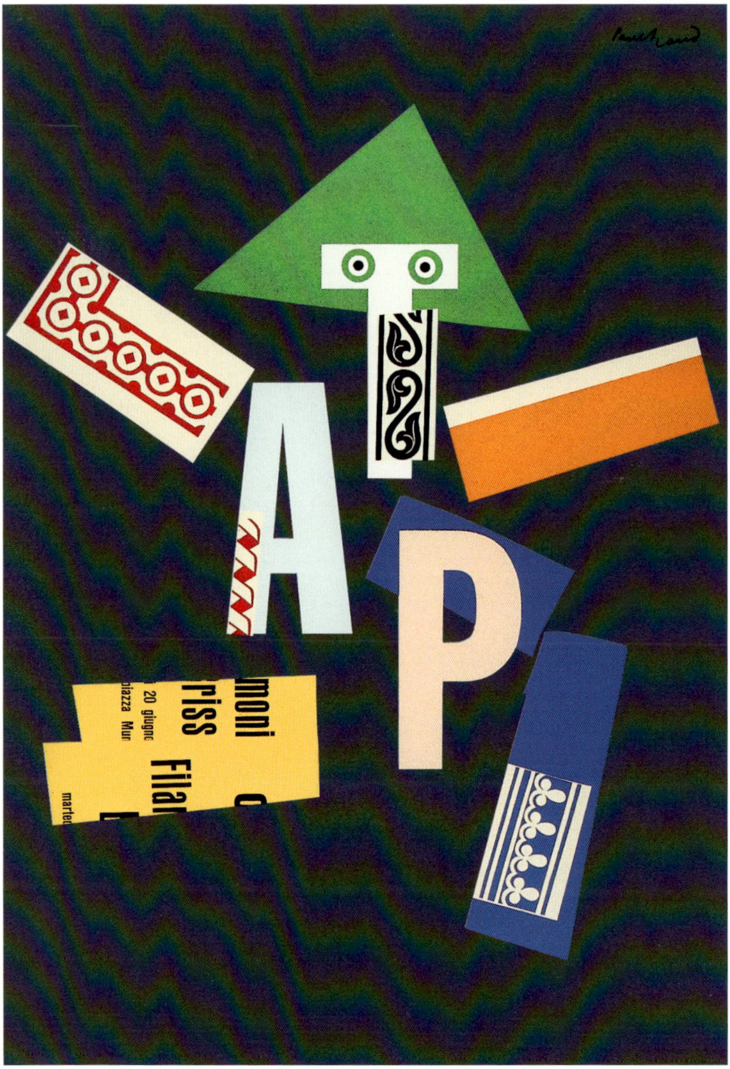

oster
 Tri Arts Press
 1980
oster
 U.S. Department
 of the Interior
 1974
acket design
 Wittenborn Schultz, Inc.
 1951
acket design
 Intercultural Publications
 1951

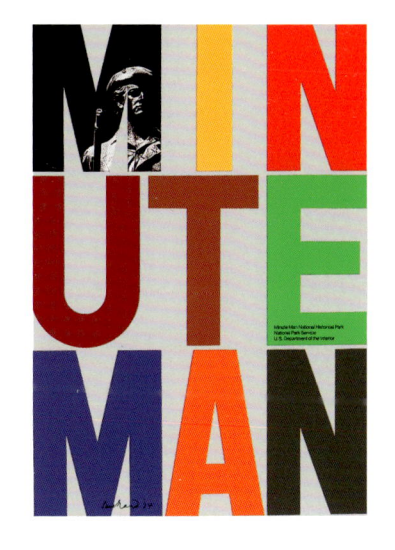

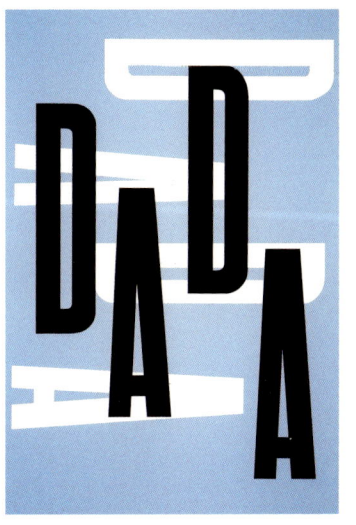

Richard Sapper Design

7. Mai – 27. Juni 1993
Di – So 10-18 Uhr, Do 10-21 Uhr

Museum für Kunst
und Gewerbe Hamburg

Raymond Loewy Stiftung
zur Förderung von zeitgemässem
Industriedesign

Quality:

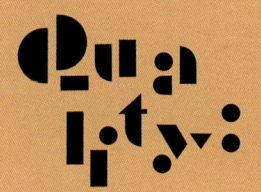

The concept of quality is difficult to define, for it is not merely seen, but somehow intuited in the presence of the work in which it is embodied. Quality has little to do with popular notions of beauty, taste, or style; and nothing to do with status, respectability, or luxury. It is revealed, rather, in an atmosphere of receptivity, propriety, and restraint.

Quality is concerned with the weighing of relationships; the discovery of analogies and contrasts; with proportion and harmony; the juxtaposition of formal and functional elements – with their transformation and enrichment.

Quality is concerned with truth, not deception; with ideas, not techniques; with the enduring, not the ephemeral; with precision, not fussiness; with simplicity, not vacuity; with subtlety, not blatancy; with sensitivity, not sentimentality.

    Paul Rand

DIRECTION
october 1939, vol. 2 no. 6
art, fiction, documentary material

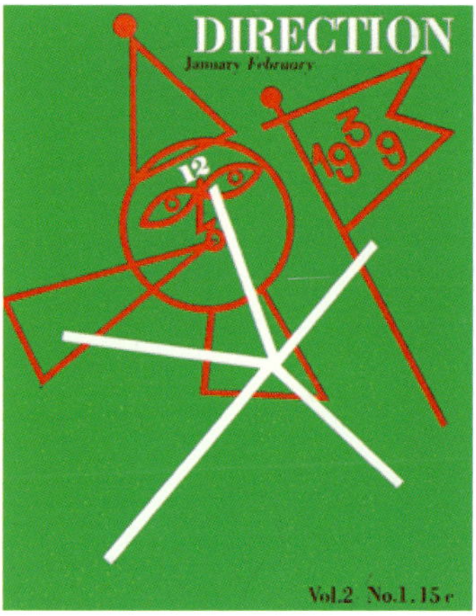
DIRECTION
January February
12
1939
Vol.2 No.1. 15 c

DIRECTION

rection magazine covers
Published by
Marguerite Tjader Harris
1938–45

DIRECTION

25¢

Vol 6 #1

Spring 1943

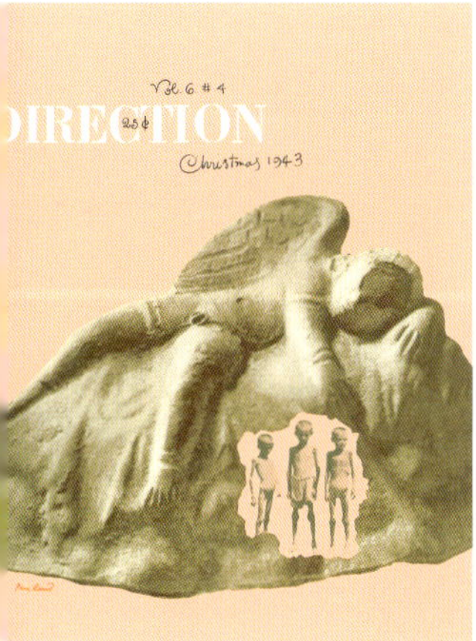
Vol. 6 #4
DIRECTION
25¢
Christmas 1943

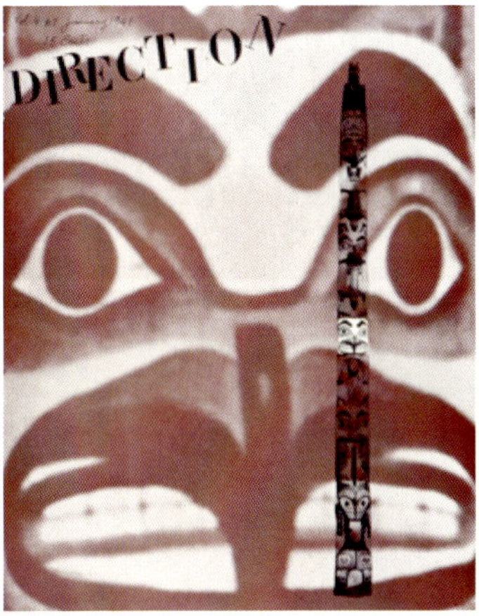
DIRECTION

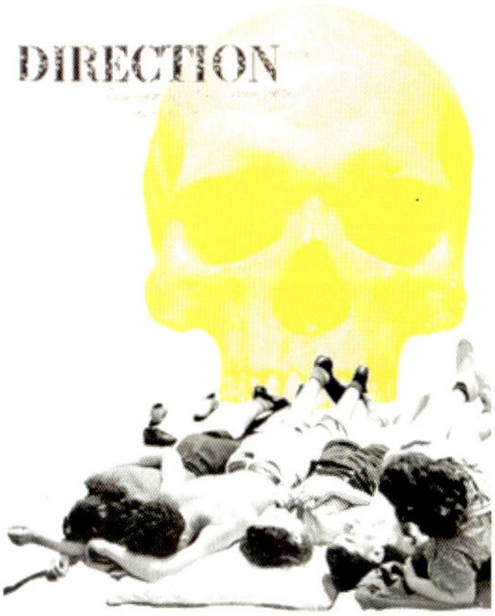
DIRECTION

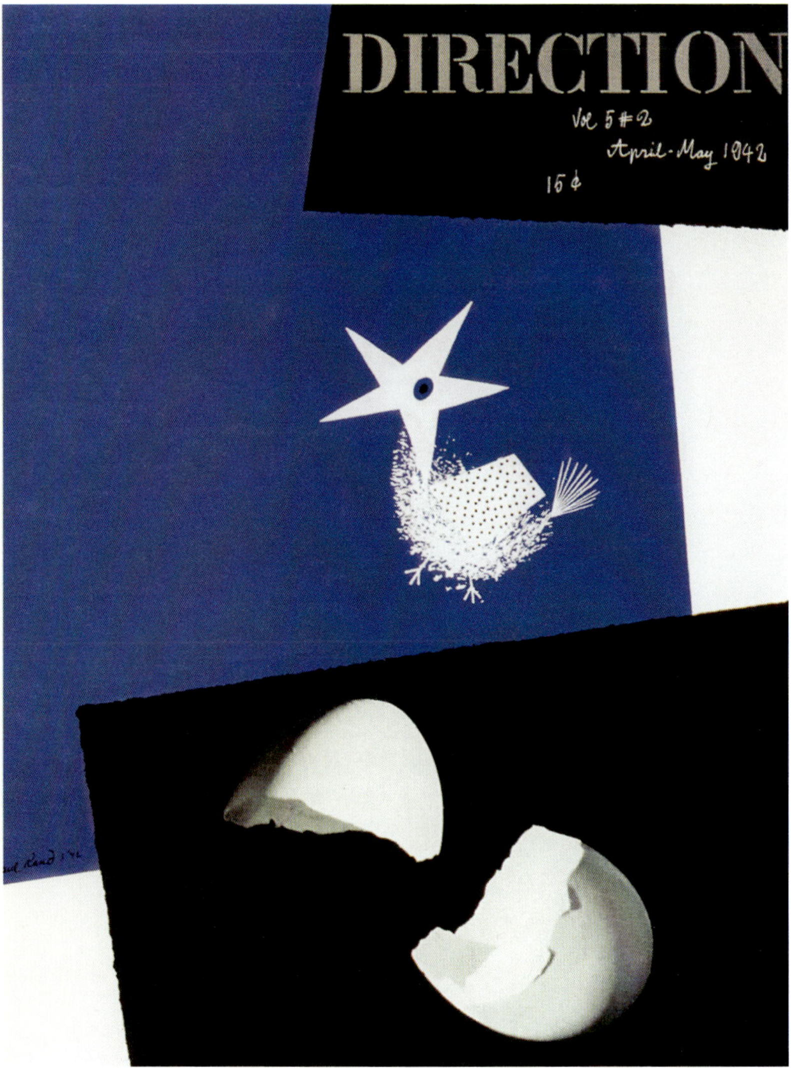
DIRECTION
Vol 5 #2
April-May 1942
15¢

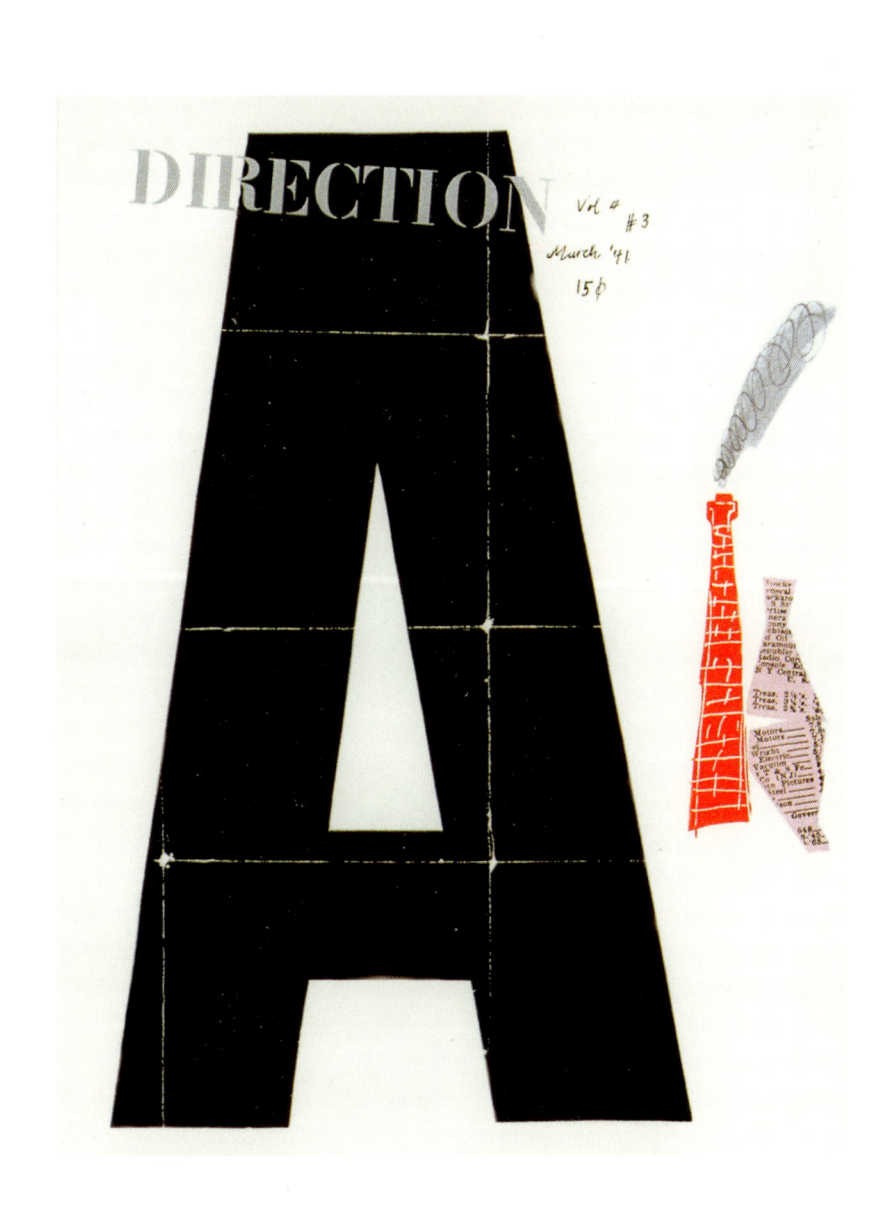

DIRECTION Vol 4 #3 March '41 15¢

DIRECTION

Vol. 1 / Number 9

November, December, 1938

15 cents per copy

DIRECTION
SUMMER FICTION NUMBER
VOL 3, NO. 6
SUMMER, 1940

DIRECTION

DIRECTION

25¢

Fall 1945
Vol. 8 #1

One Race

Paul Rand

Vol 4 #6
DIRECTION
December 1941
15¢
V

DIRECTION
Vol 6 #3 November 1943 25¢
French culture
lives on!

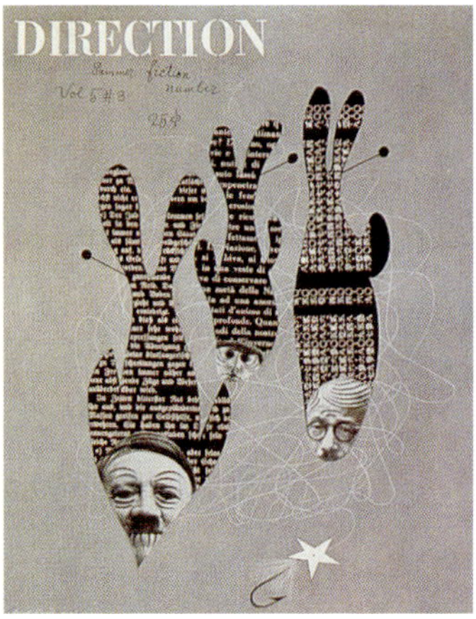
DIRECTION

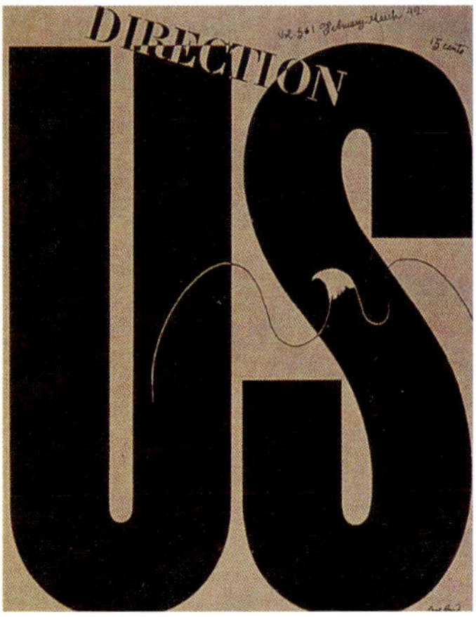
DIRECTION
US

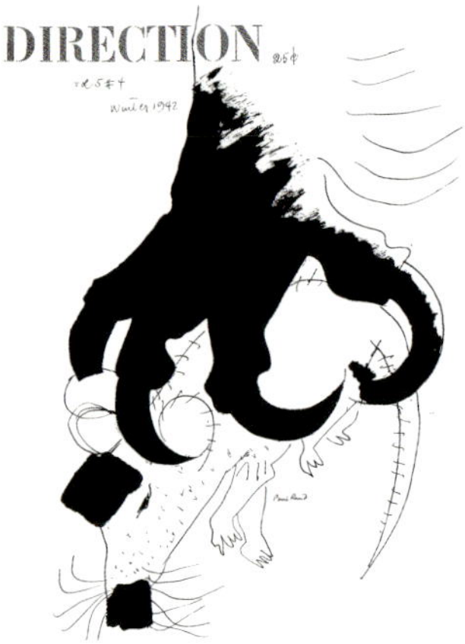
DIRECTION

Summer
fiction number **DIRECTION**
Vol 7 # 3
25 ¢

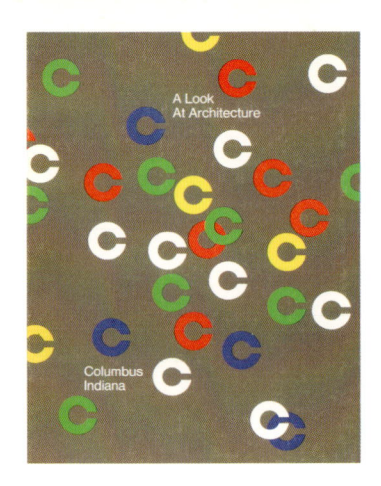

Book, architectural
   tour map
   (cover and detail)
   Columbus Area
   Chamber of Comme
   1974

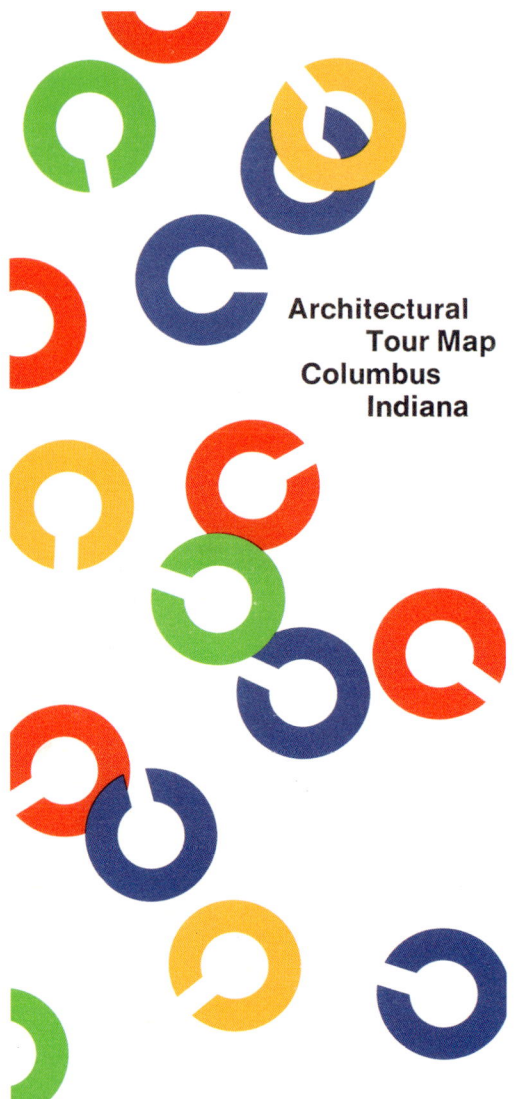

**Architectural
   Tour Map
   Columbus
   Indiana**

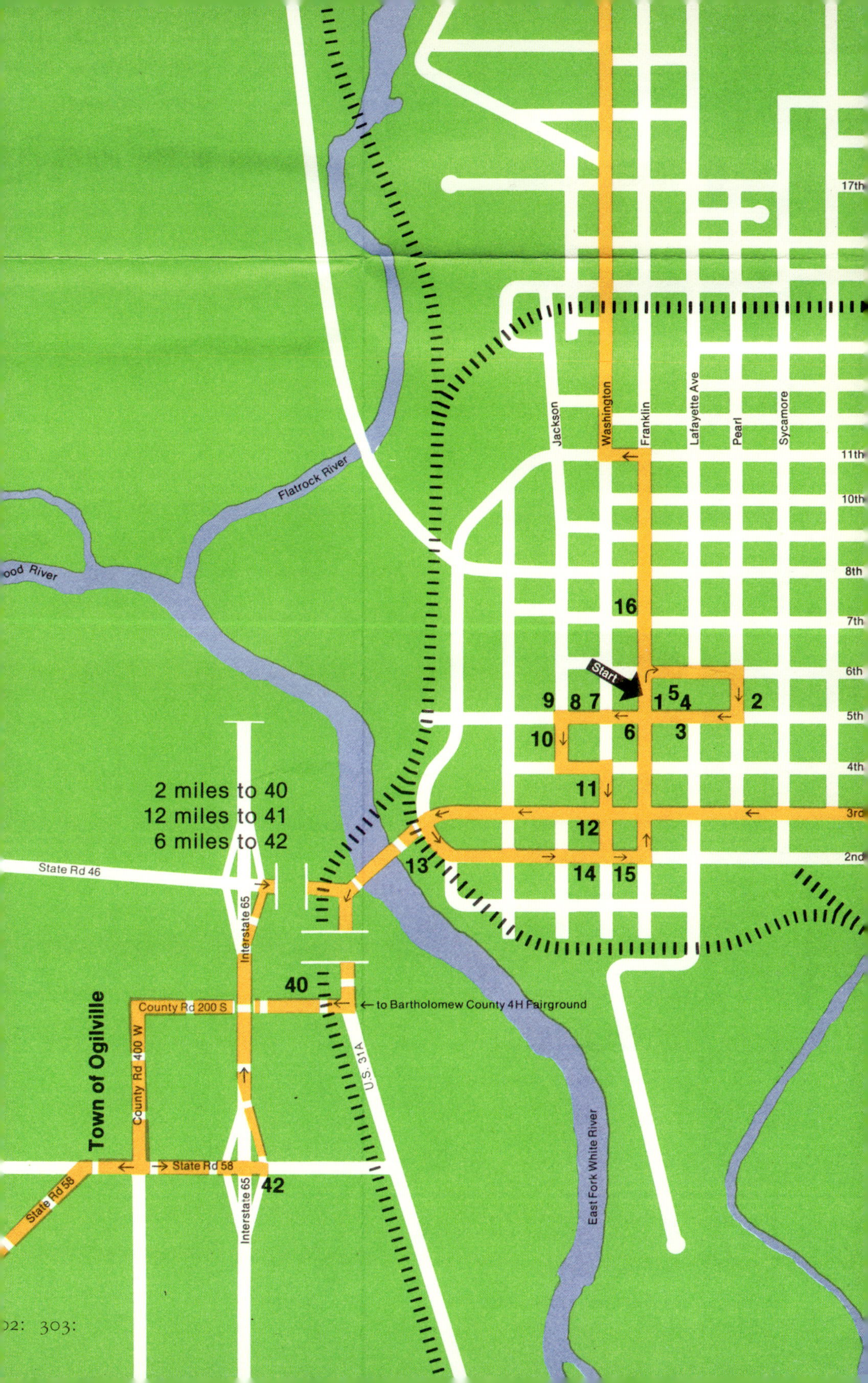
17th
Jackson
Washington
Franklin
Lafayette Ave
Pearl
Sycamore
11th
10th
8th
7th
6th
5th
4th
3rd
2nd
Flatrock River
ood River
16
Start
9 8 7
1 5 4
2
10
6
3
11
12
13
14
15
2 miles to 40
12 miles to 41
6 miles to 42
State Rd 46
Interstate 65
40
County Rd 200 S
to Bartholomew County 4H Fairground
U.S. 31A
Town of Ogilville
County Rd 400 W
State Rd 58
State Rd 58
42
Interstate 65
East Fork White River

02: 303:

タイポグラフィ

ogo
Cummins Engine
1973
ogo presentation booklet
Education First
Stockholm, Sweden
1993

Poster (next page spread)
IBM Corporation
1981
Package designs
IBM Supply Kit
1979

A B C D *E F*
G H I J K L M
N O P Q R S
T U V W X Y
Z A B C D E
F G H I J K L
M N O P Q R

English
First

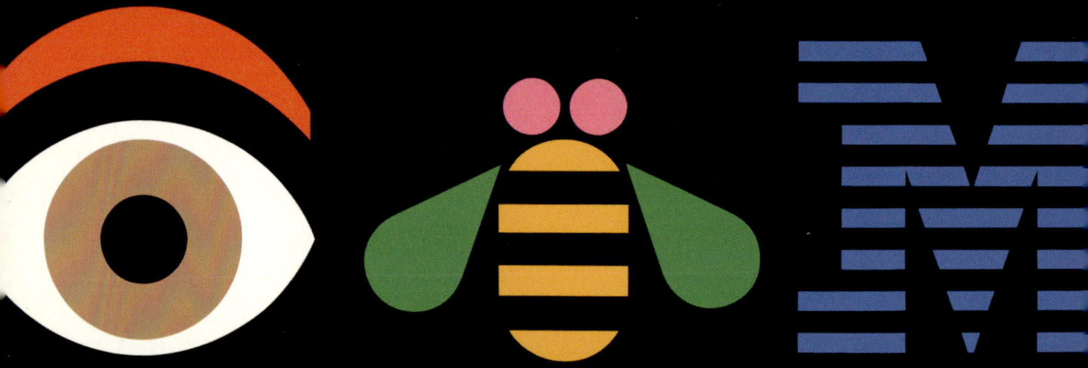

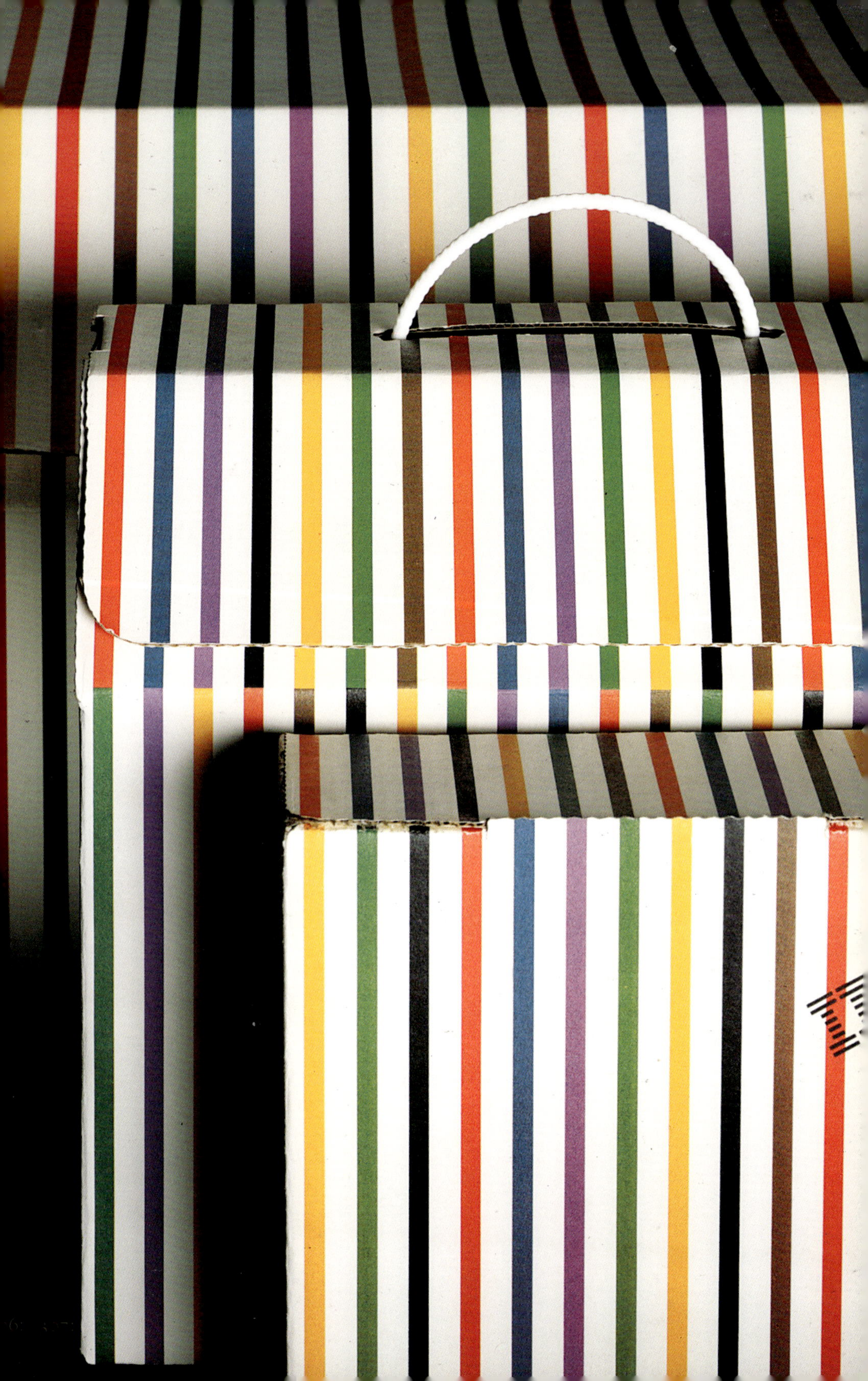

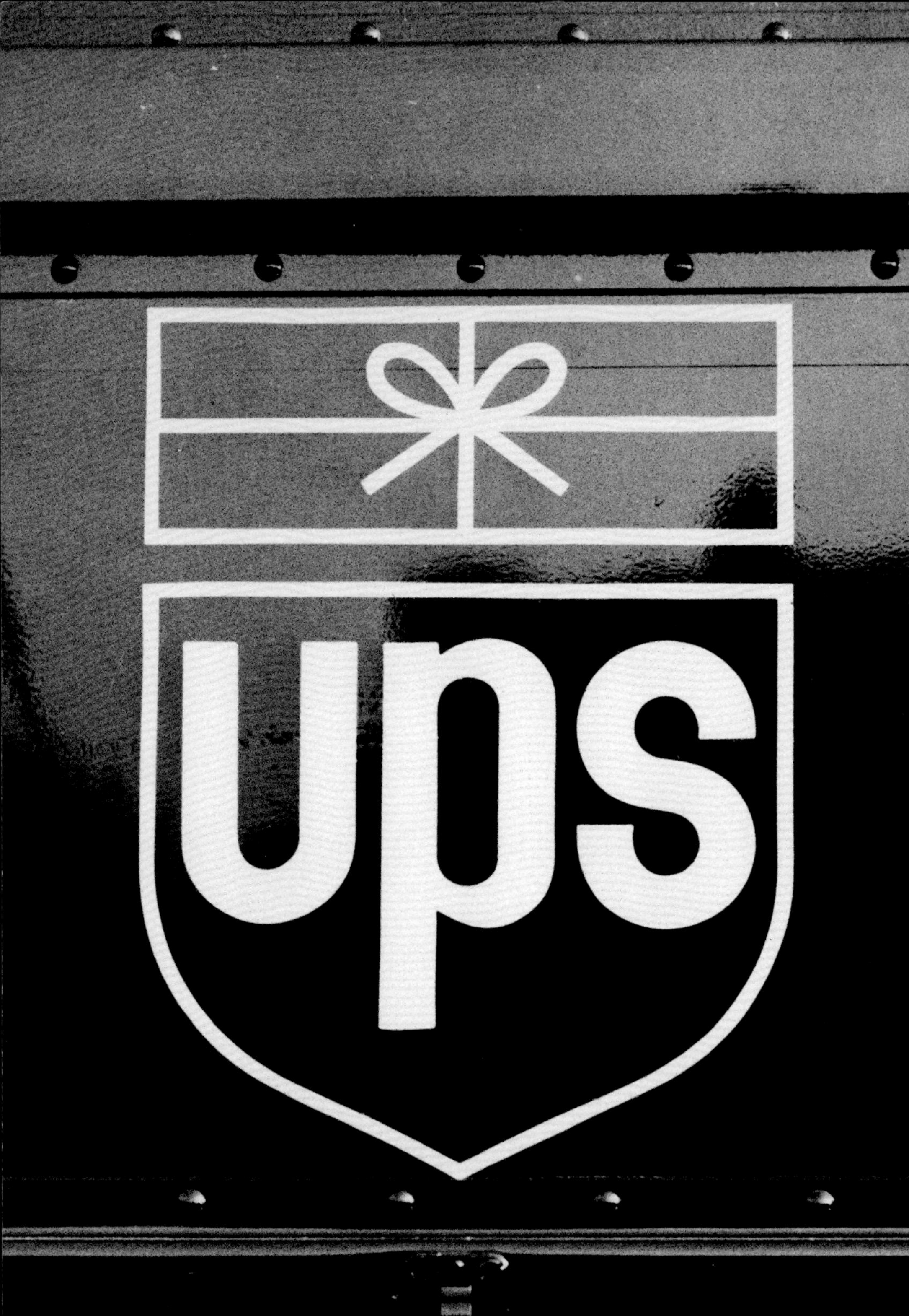
ups

Trademark
   United Parcel Service
   1961
Trademark
   Colorforms
   1959

25
EL PRODUCTO
santa's favorite cigar
25
El Producto Queens
EL PRODUCTO
every cigar says "merry christmas"
EL PRODUCTO
Cigar Album
EL PRODUCTO
Cigar Album

Packaging
El Producto
Cigar Company
1952

Trademark
American
Broadcasting Company
1962

MOR

logo
Morningstar
Investment Advisers
1991

logo
Okasan Securities
Company
1991

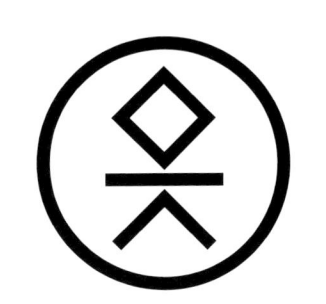

Signs that say   Safe Drivi

resentation book
(Logo not used)
Ford Motor Company
1966

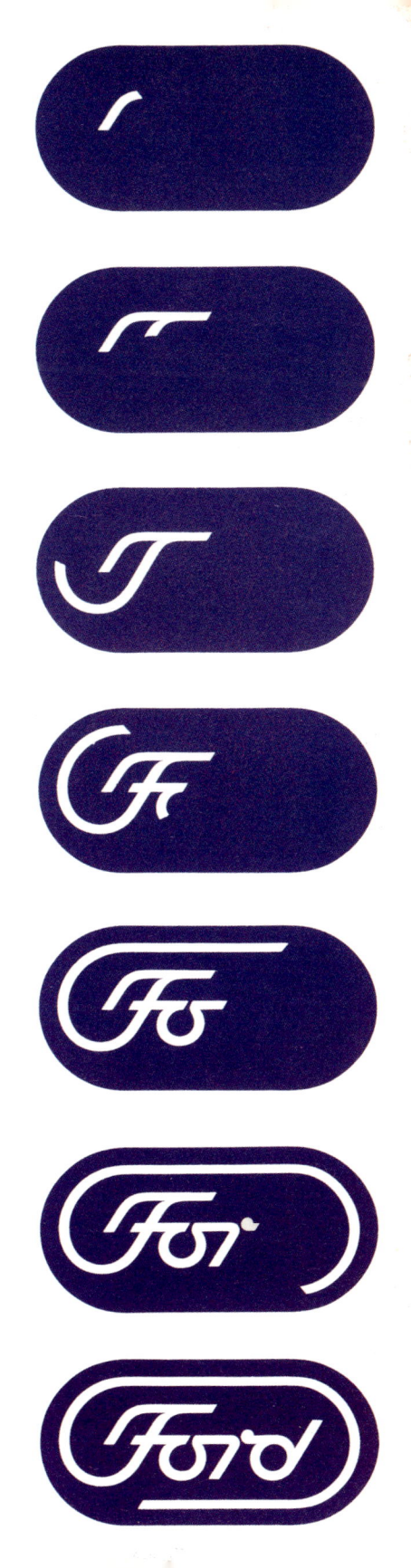

Irwin Financial
Corporation
1992 Annual Report

nnual report
Irwin Financial
Corporation
1992

resentation book
American Express
Corporation
1994

Don't leave home without it...

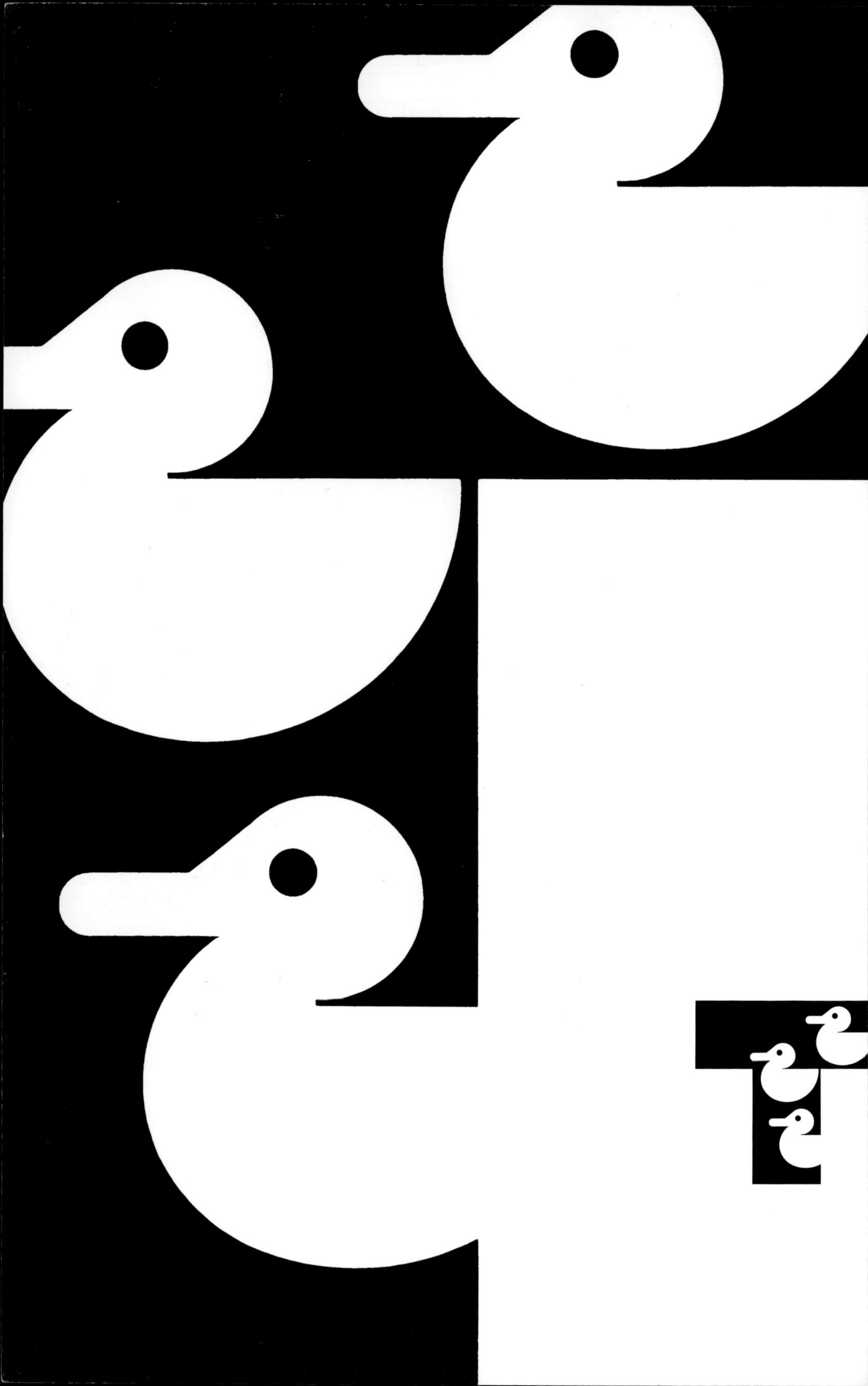

go
 Tipton Lakes
 Corporation
 Real estate
 1980

 go
 U.S. Department
 of the Interior
 Bureau of Indian
 Affairs
 1968

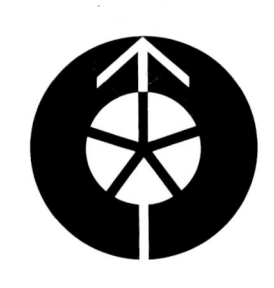

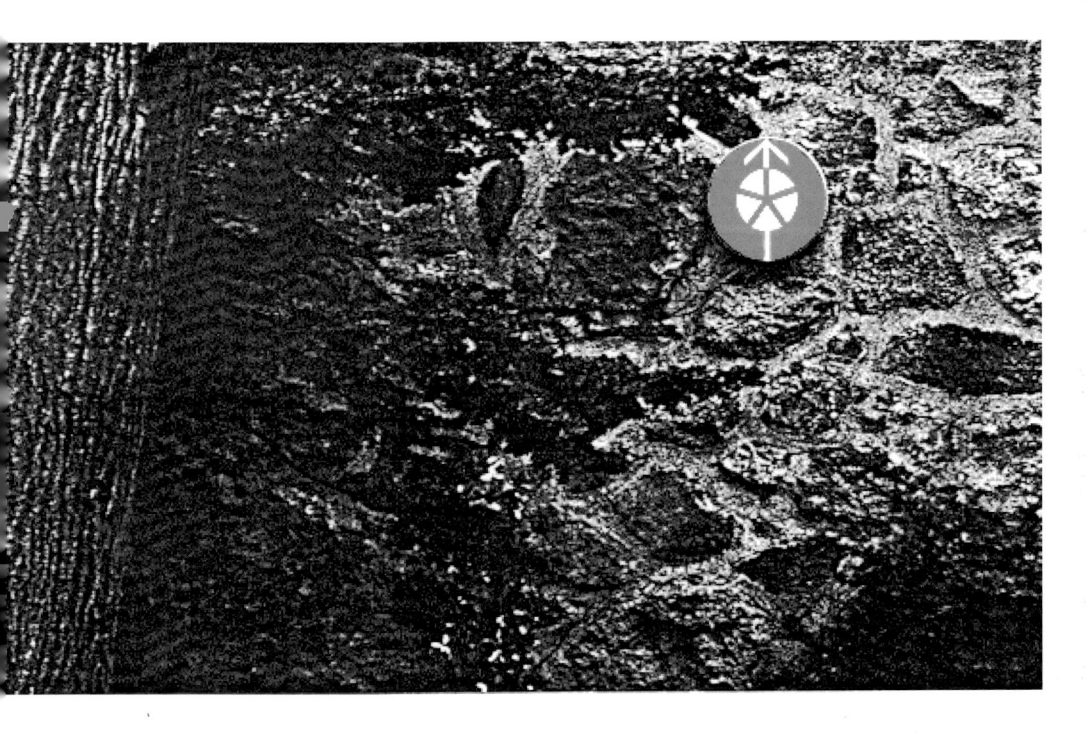

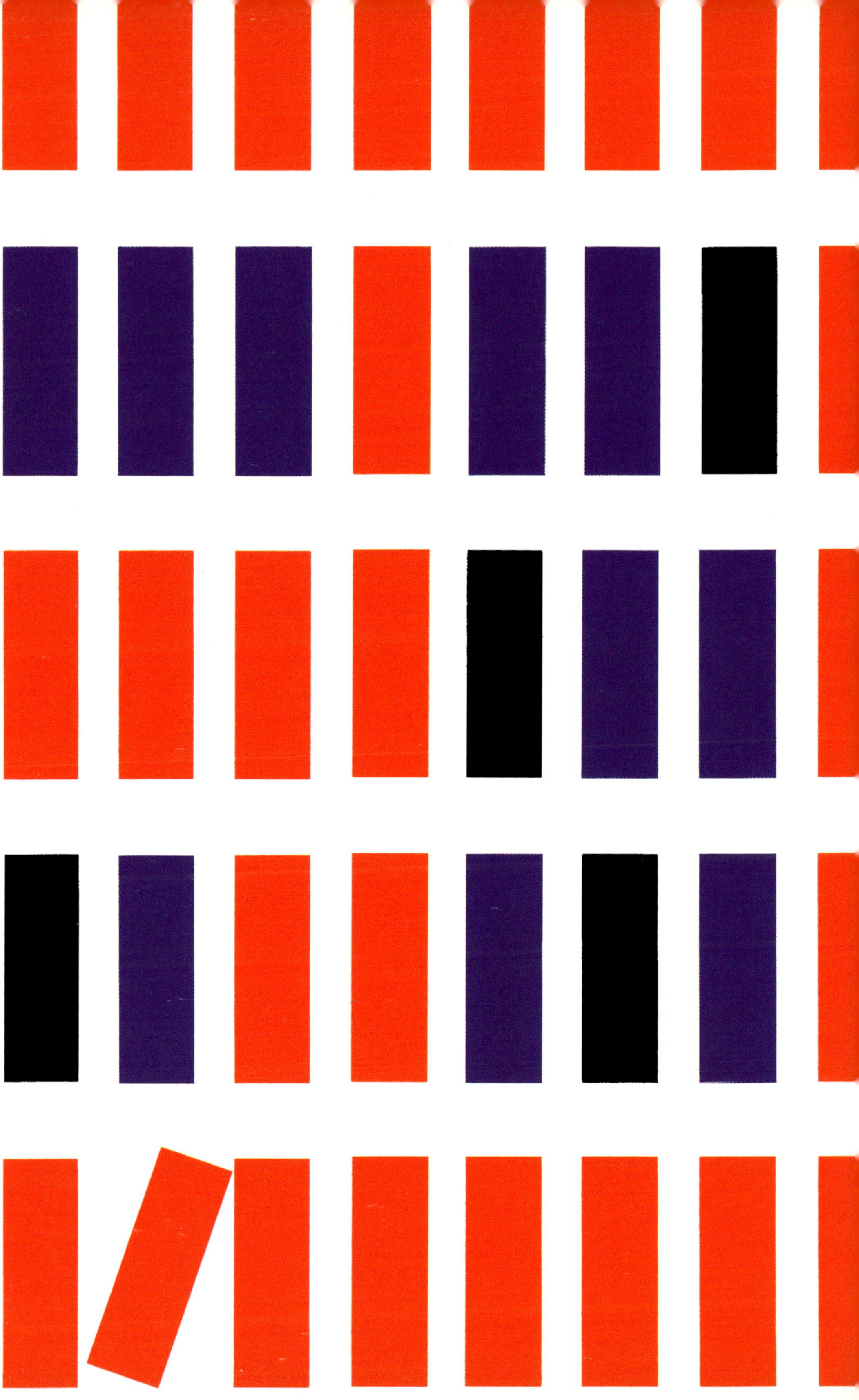

Brochure cover, interior
*AIGA 50 Books 50
Covers competition*
1972

Journal series
Advertising
Typographer's
Association
1989

アン＆ポール・ランド
ぼくは
いろいろ しってるよ
青山南 訳

ぼくは
いろいろ
しってるよ

アン＆ポール・ランド

青山南 訳

福音館書店

キャサリンに

ぼくは
いろいろ
しってるよ

アン＆ポール・ランド 作

青山南 訳

福音館書店

book pages
I Know A Lot of Things
Ann and Paul Rand
Harcourt Brace & World
1956

Japanese edition
Fukuinkan Shoten Publishers
1999

ぼくは いろいろ しってるよ……
かがみに
うつってるのは
のぞいてる ぼく さ

ねこは にゃおと ないて

いぬは わんと ほえて
そうやって
はなしを してるのさ

木を いっぱい つんだ ワゴンも
うまならば
へいきで
ひっぱれる

ありも
その気に なれば
いちご みたいに おおきな ものが
へいきで しょえる

木のは は
かたつむりの フェリーでしょ

ぼくは しってるよ
ほらあなは
とっても
きもちの いい
かくればしょで

うみの あおい なみは　　　　　　　　　　　のりもの なのさ

ぼくは しってるよ

おおきな あなでも
ほるのは かんたん

そらぐらい たかい 木でも
のぼるのは かんたん
ぼくの よこを とりが とんで
ぼくの したで どんぐりが
こつんと おちる

ぼくは　　　　　てを　ふるんだ　　　　　ちっちゃいくせに　おおきな　かさを　もった　きのこにさ

ぼくは　しってるよ
ものの　しくみもね
いえは　ガラスと　レンガと
たくさんの　木で　できてる
ましかくの　はこは
うえと　よこが
おなじ　おおきさだ

ほんは かみを
とじた ものでしょ
ケーキは
じっくり
やいた ものでしょ

ぼくは しってるよ
せかいは ひろい
おほしさまは とおい
おつきさまは よるの
ランプで
おひさまは
とっても まぶしい
まるい パン

うん
ぼく
は
こんなに
いろ
いろ
しってるんだ
でも
おおきく
なると
もっと
もっと
いろ
いろ
しってるんだ
よね

Paintings (a and b)
 Oil on canvas
 1952
Photograph of cat
 1952
 Estate of Paul Rand

Ceramic ash tray
 From *I Know
 A Lot of Things*
 Collection of
 Gerald Gross

Rand's paintings and
photographs influenced
his children's books, as
well as other projects.

a

b

c

d

Collage
Colored paper
1960s
Collection of
Adam Gross
Photography by
Dan Meyers

332: 333:

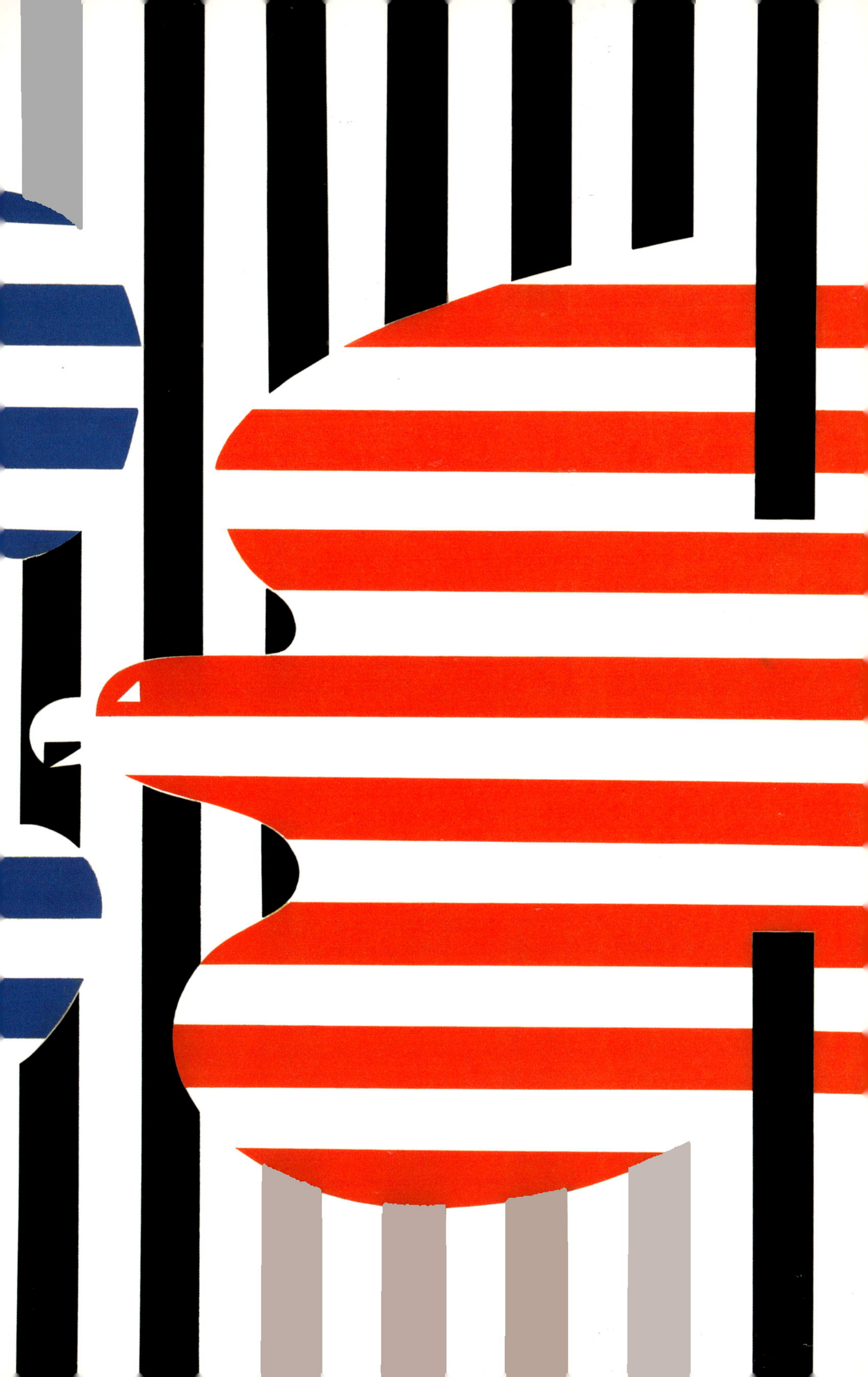

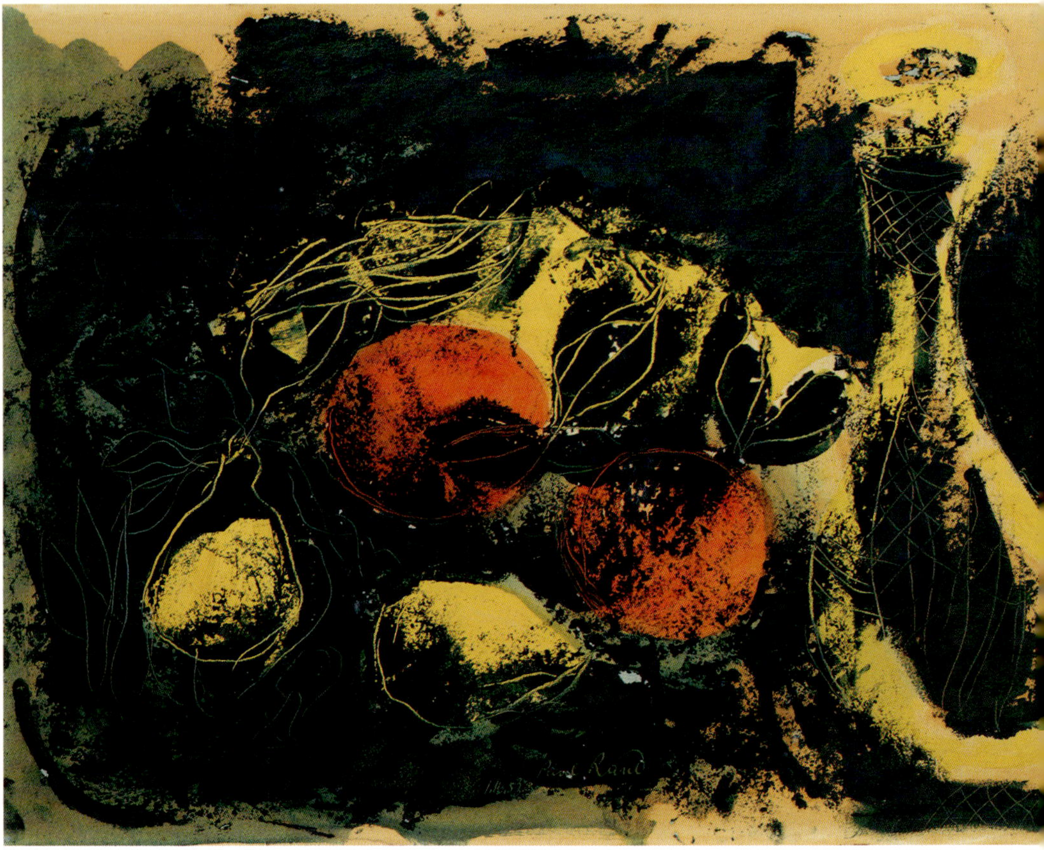

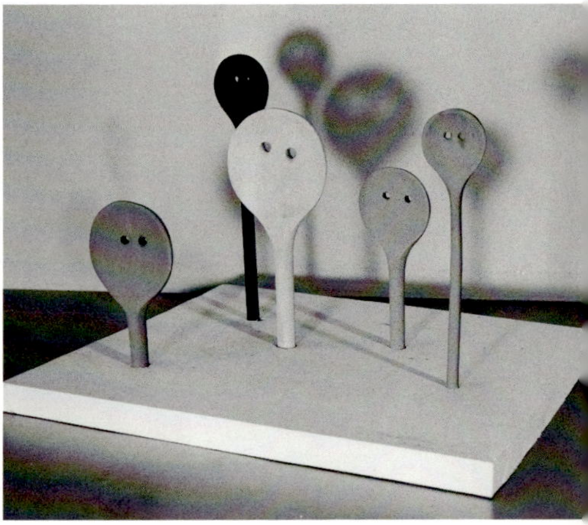

ainting
  Gouache on board
  1953
  Private collection
  Photography by
  Dan Meyers
culpture installation
  Wood
  1954
ainting
  Oil on canvas
  1954
ainting
  Watercolor
  1952
  Estate of Paul Rand

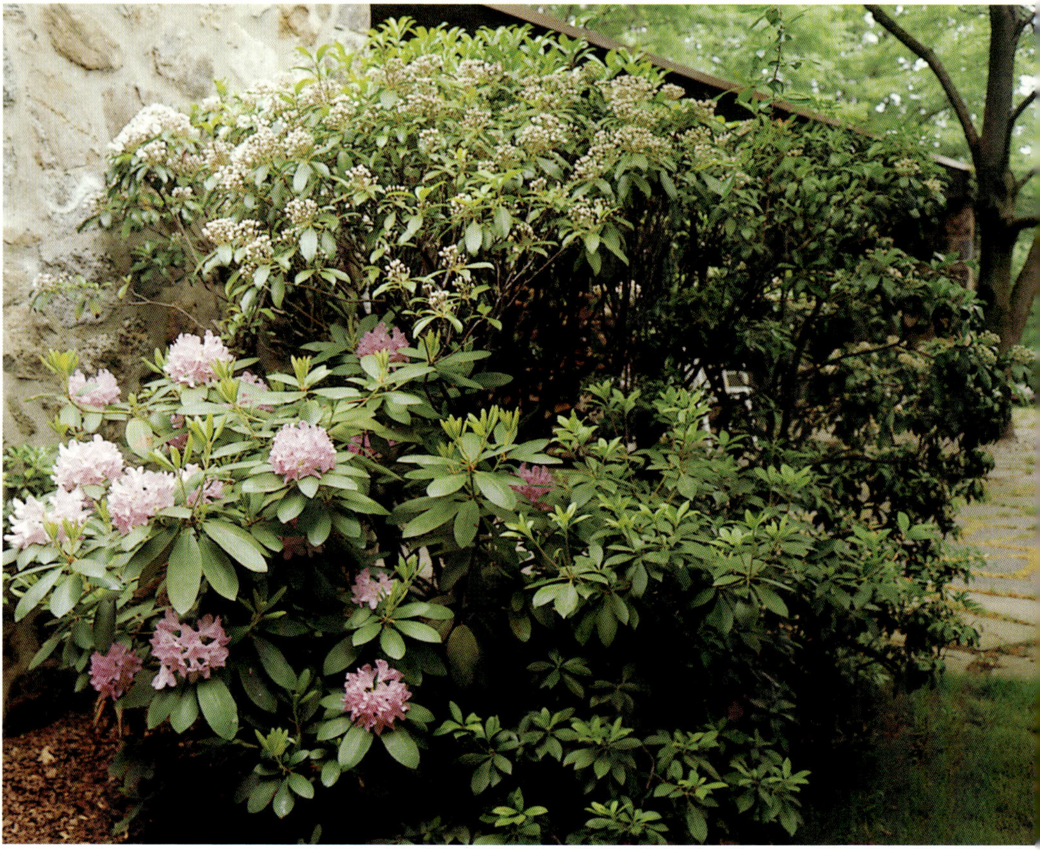

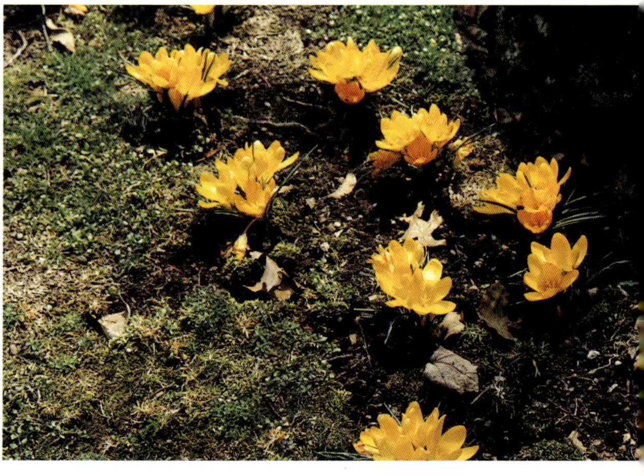

The Rand House
The seasons
Estate of Paul Rand

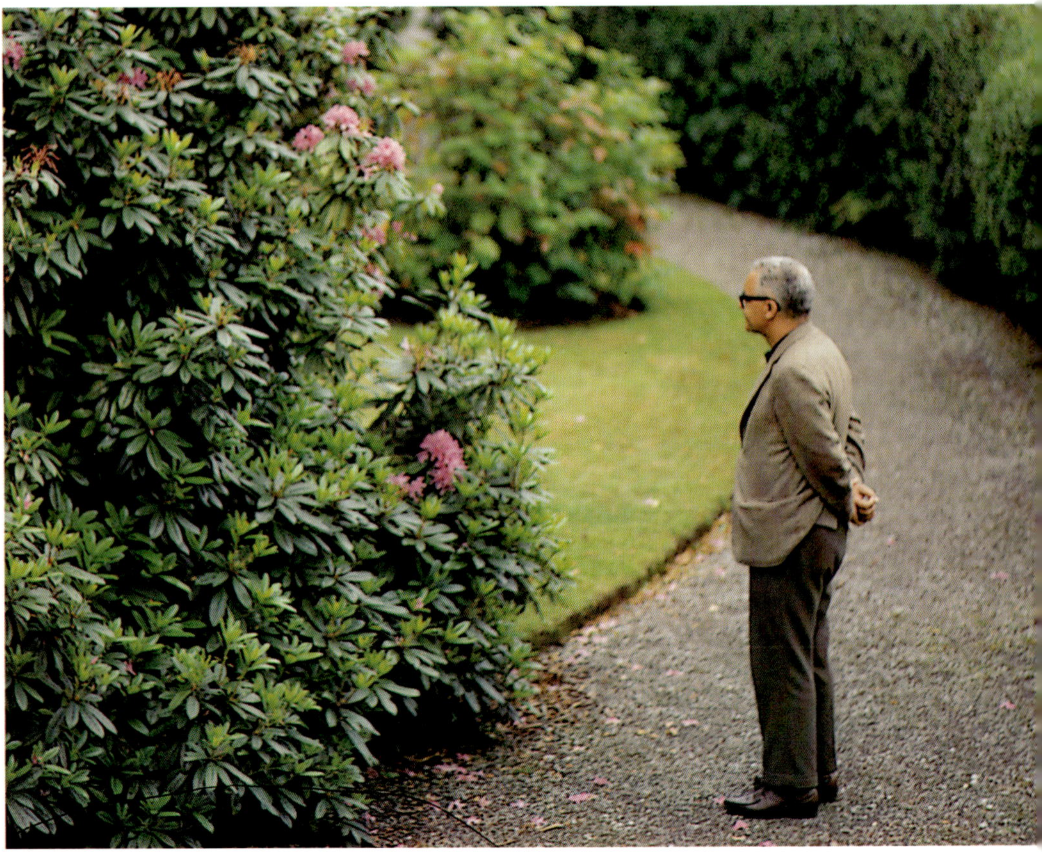

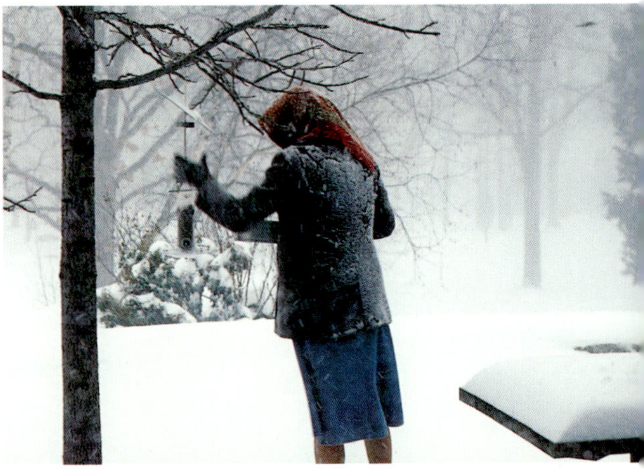

Paul Rand observing nature and color.
Marion Rand feeding the birds.

North Elevation

South Elevation

West Elevation

East Elevation

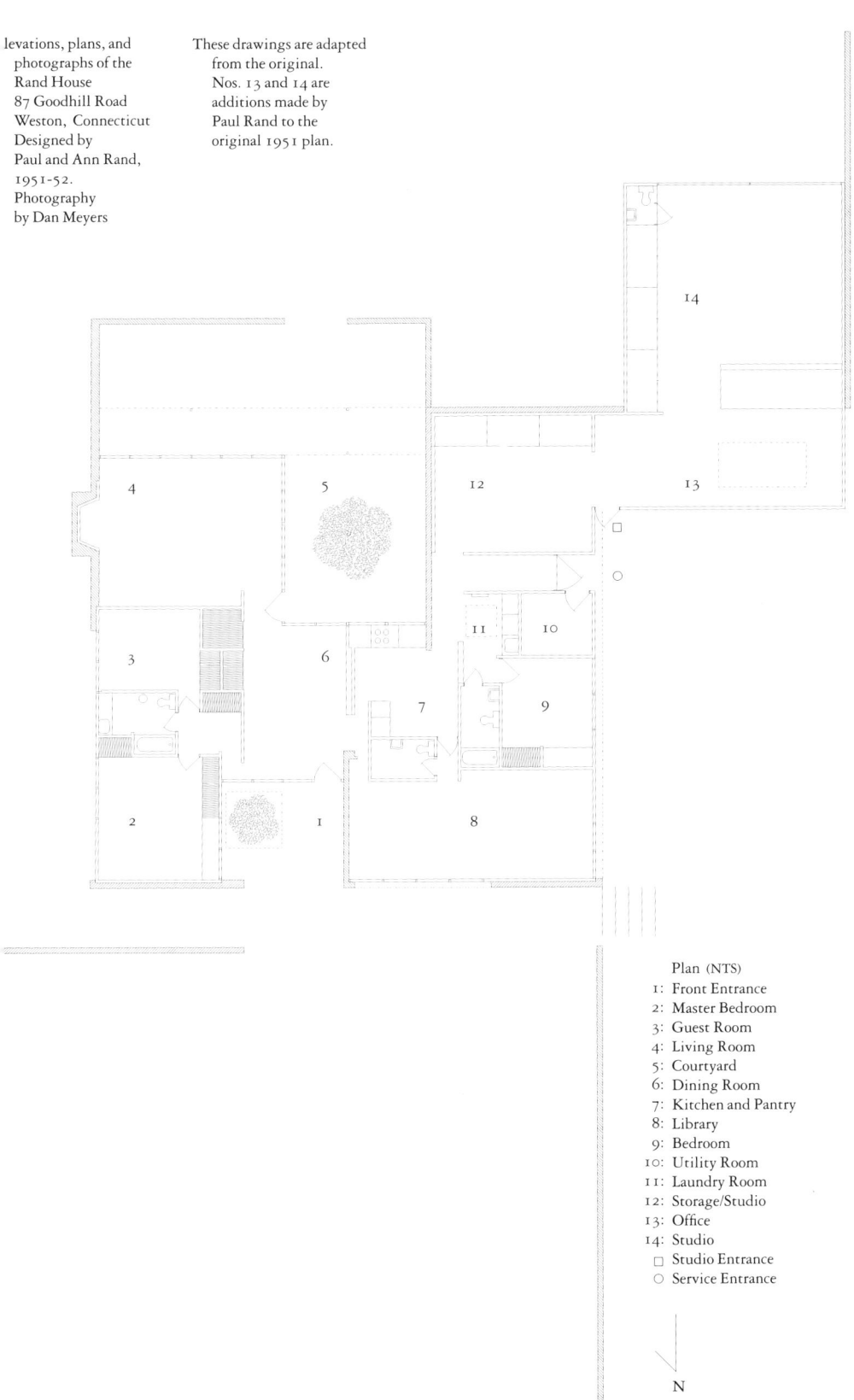

levations, plans, and photographs of the Rand House 87 Goodhill Road Weston, Connecticut Designed by Paul and Ann Rand, 1951-52. Photography by Dan Meyers

These drawings are adapted from the original. Nos. 13 and 14 are additions made by Paul Rand to the original 1951 plan.

Plan (NTS)
1: Front Entrance
2: Master Bedroom
3: Guest Room
4: Living Room
5: Courtyard
6: Dining Room
7: Kitchen and Pantry
8: Library
9: Bedroom
10: Utility Room
11: Laundry Room
12: Storage/Studio
13: Office
14: Studio
□ Studio Entrance
○ Service Entrance

N

○ □

2. Service and studio entrance
3. Front entrance

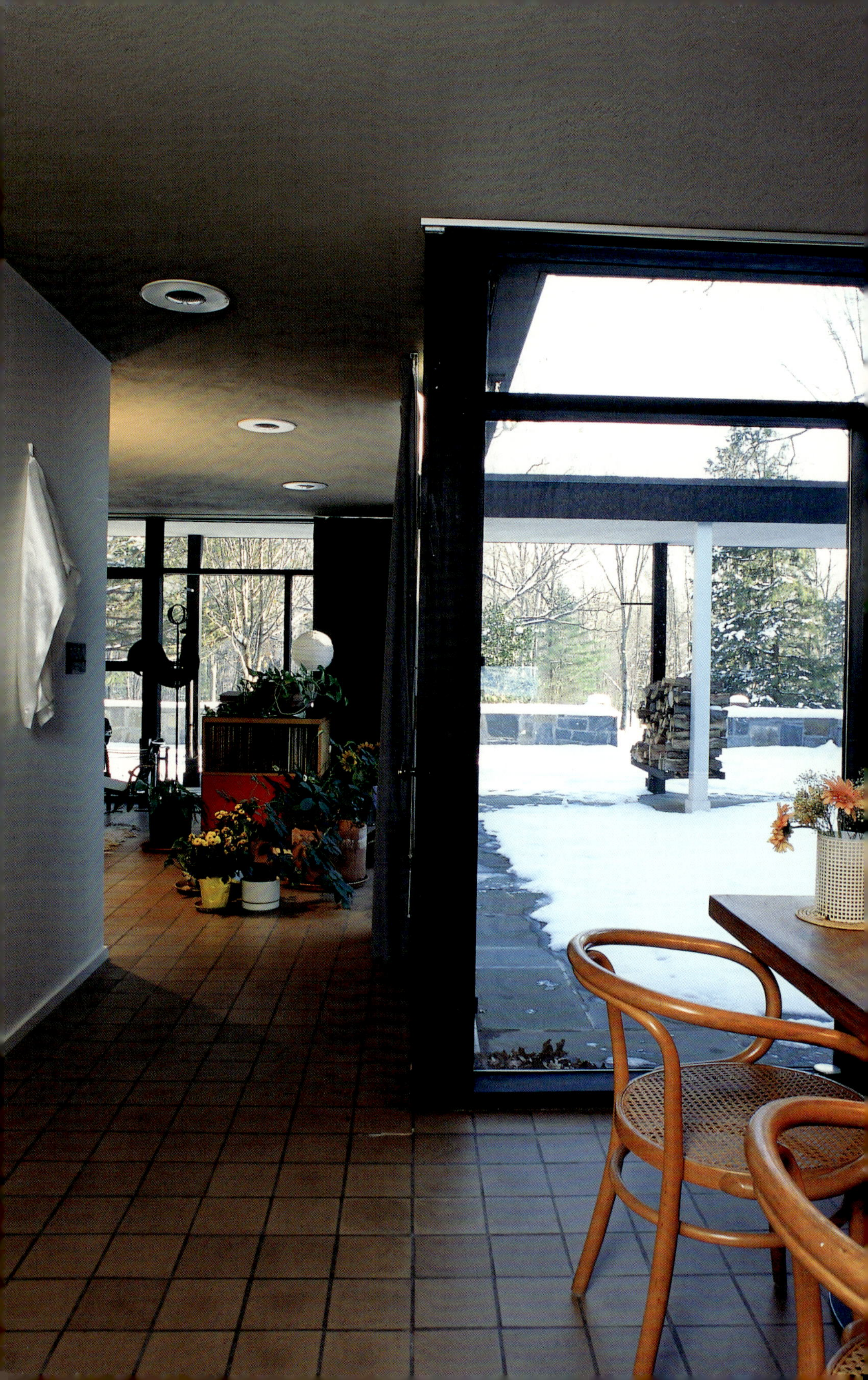

3. Dining room
 (opposite page)
 with a view to the
 living room and
 courtyard.
2. Living room
 with a view through
 hallway, dining room,
 and front entrance.
3. Library

4. Living room
 (next page spread)
 with a view looking
 west through glass
 walls to inner
 courtyard facing
 kitchen.

5. Inner and outer
 courtyard
 (next two page
 spreads)
 with a view looking
 north at living room
 entrance, dining
 room, and kitchen.

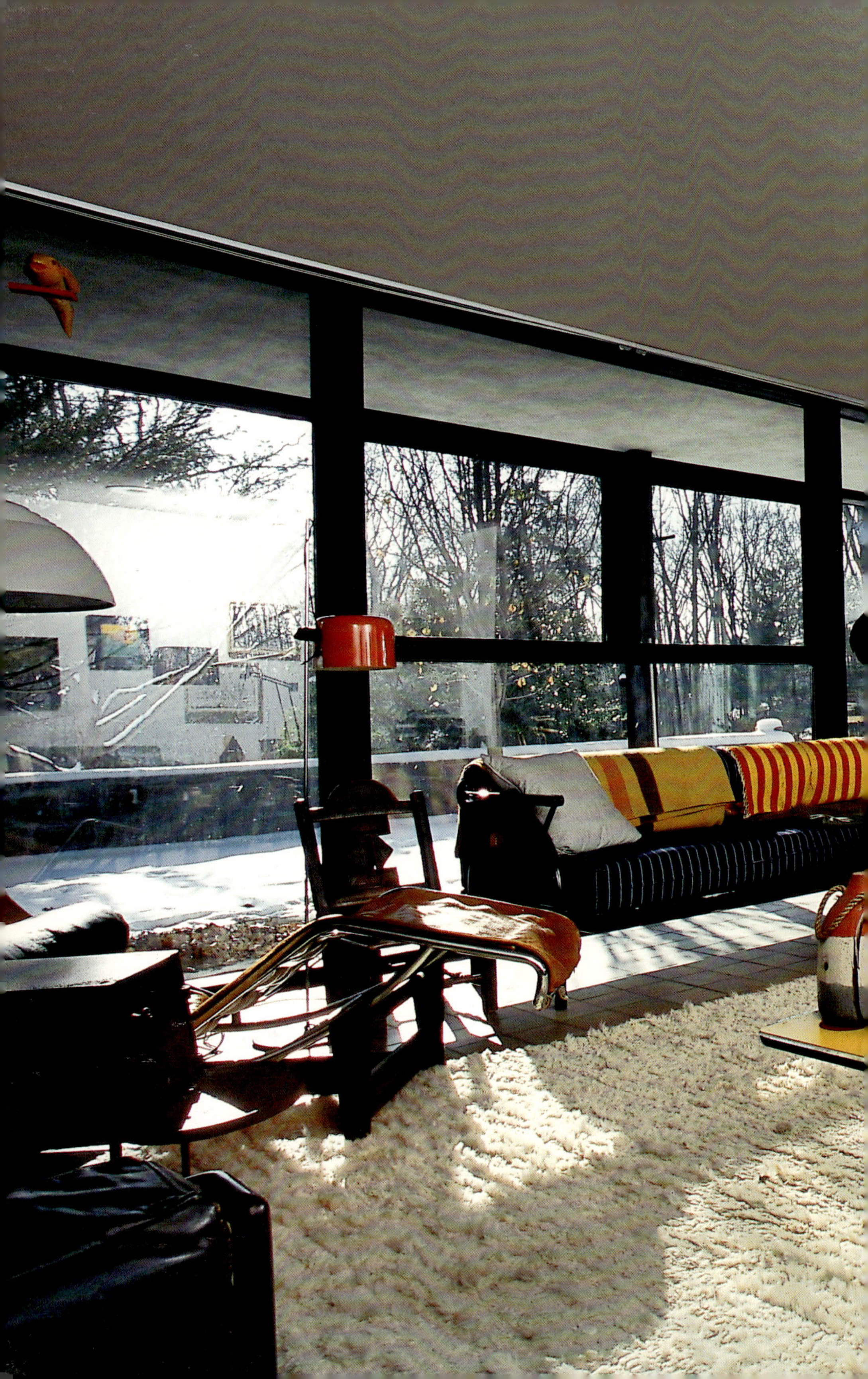

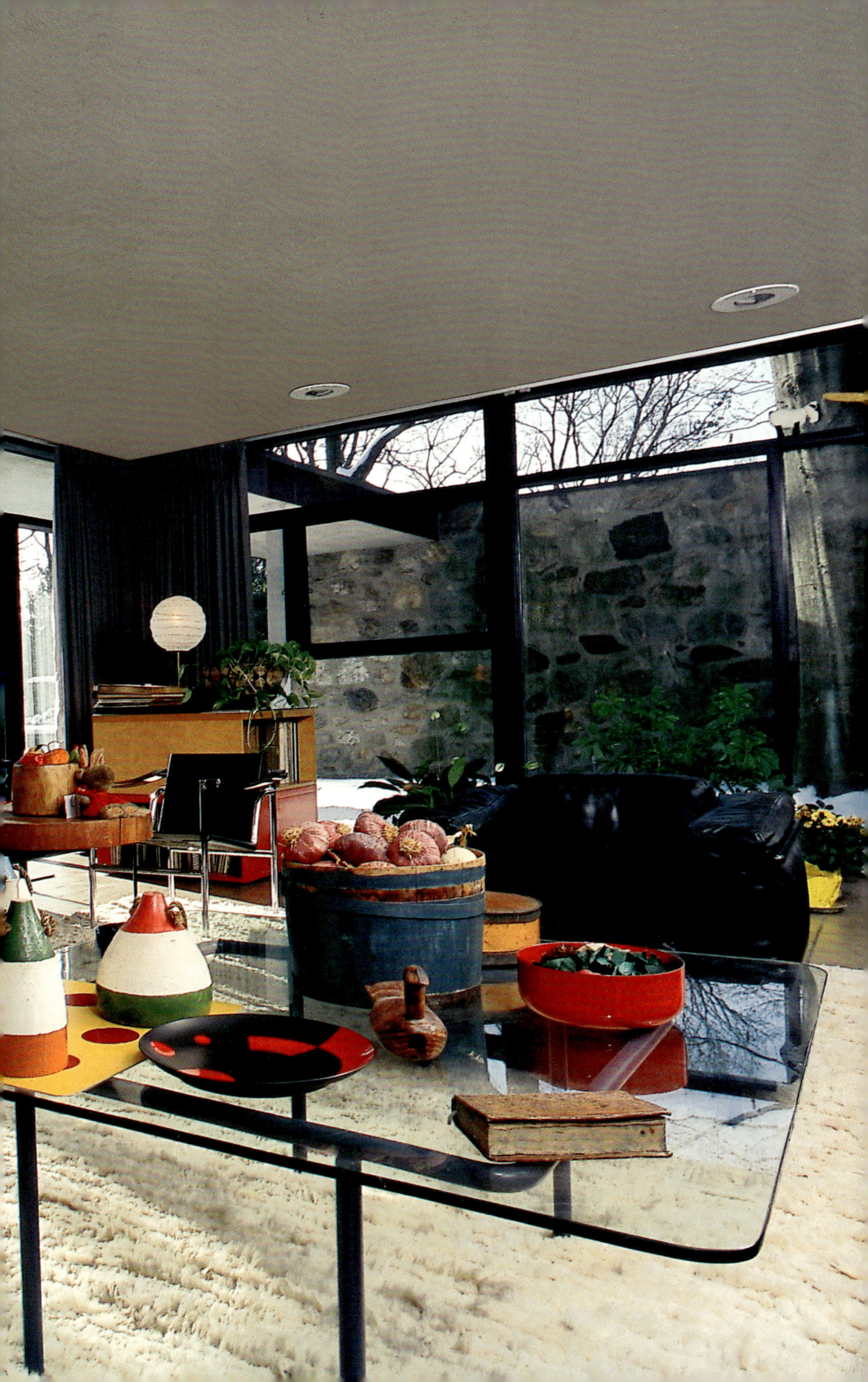

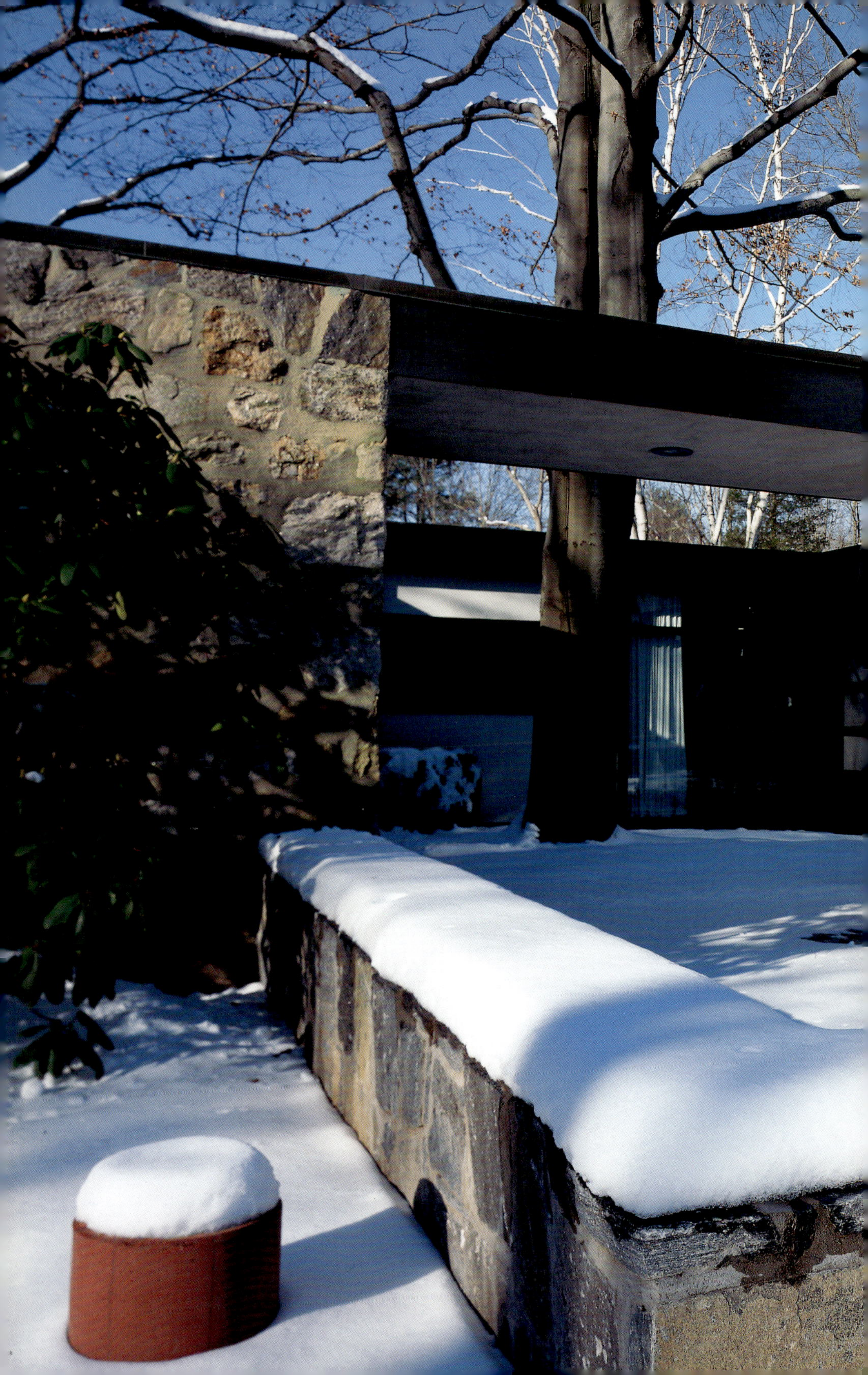

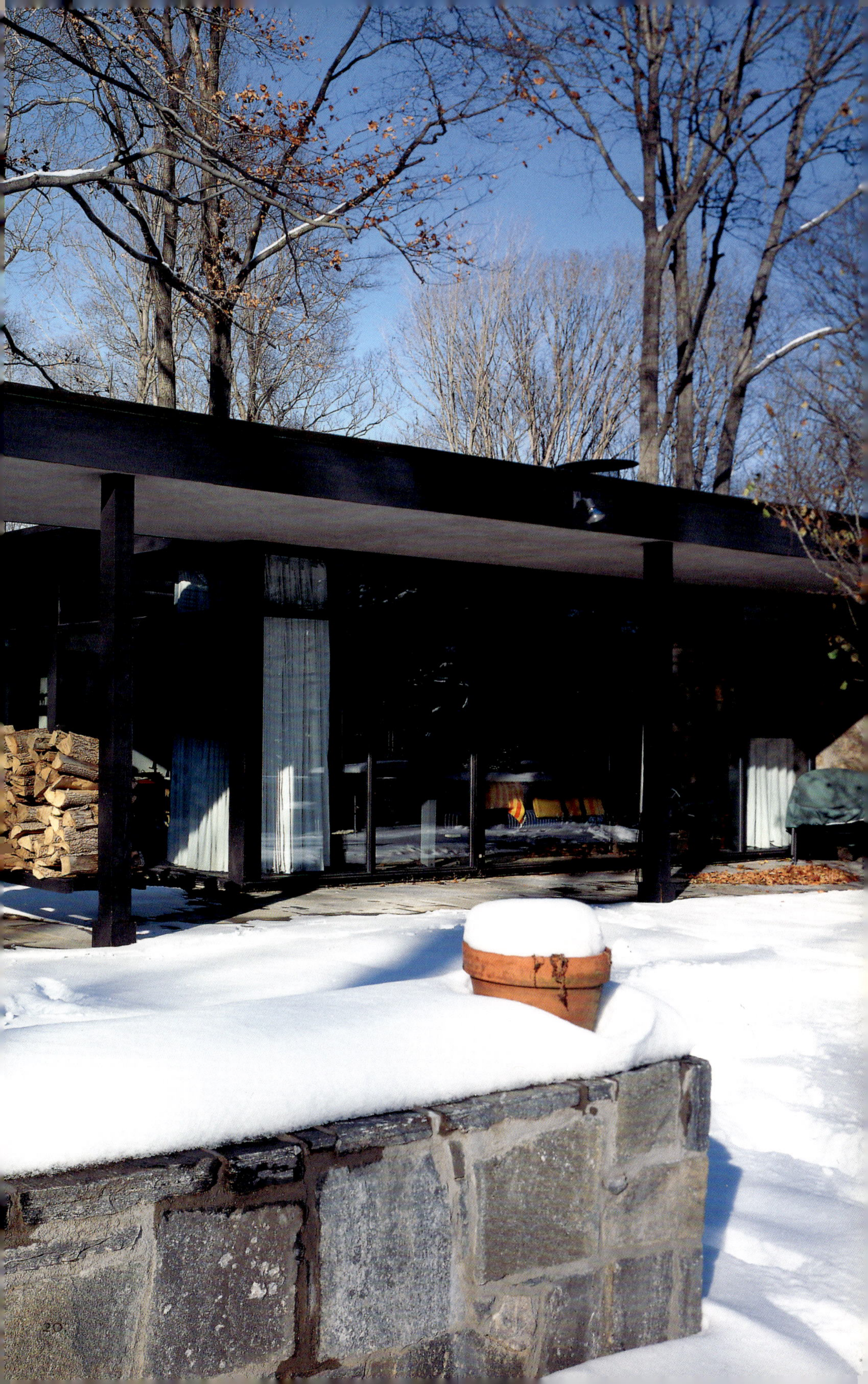

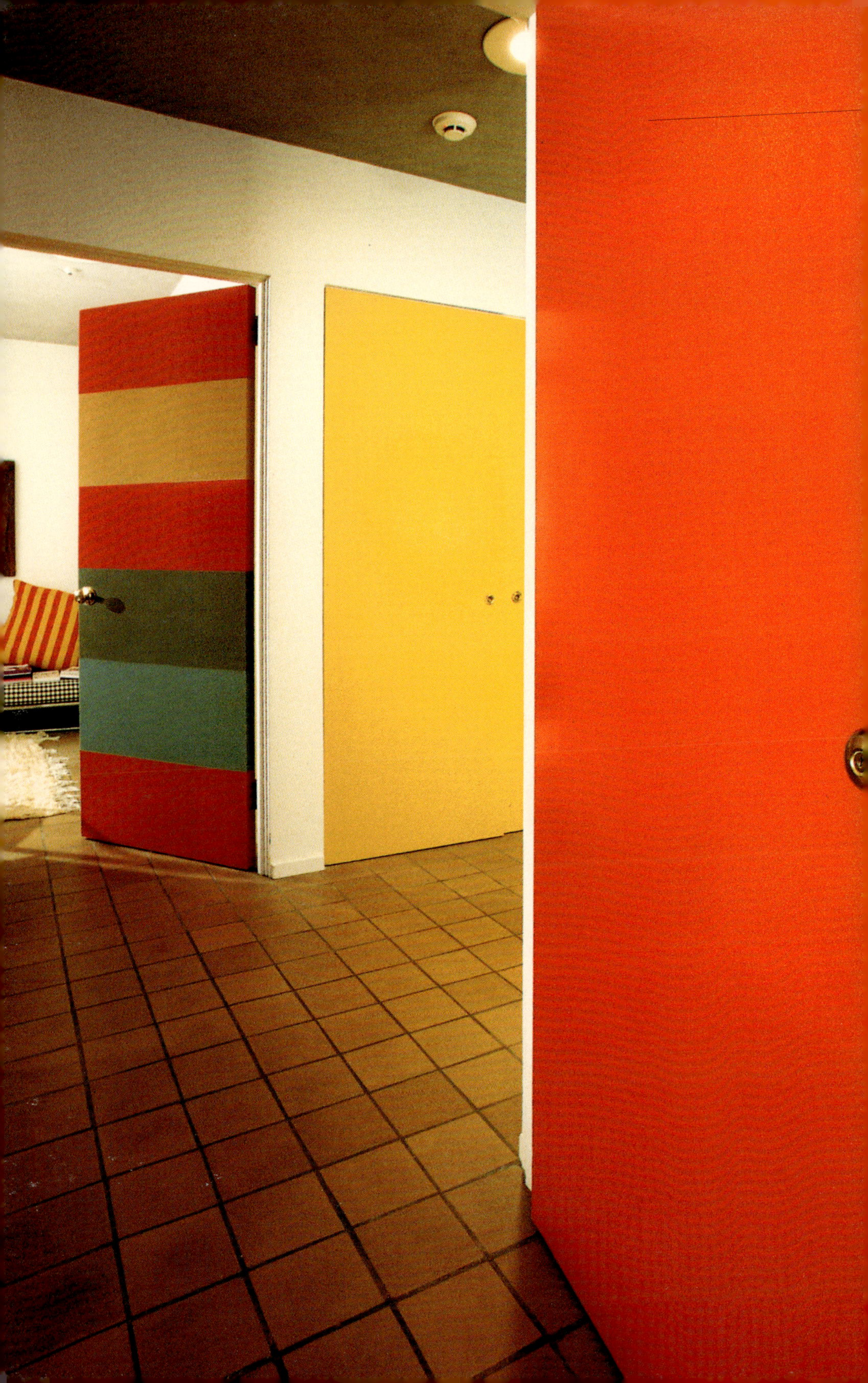

Guest room
Library

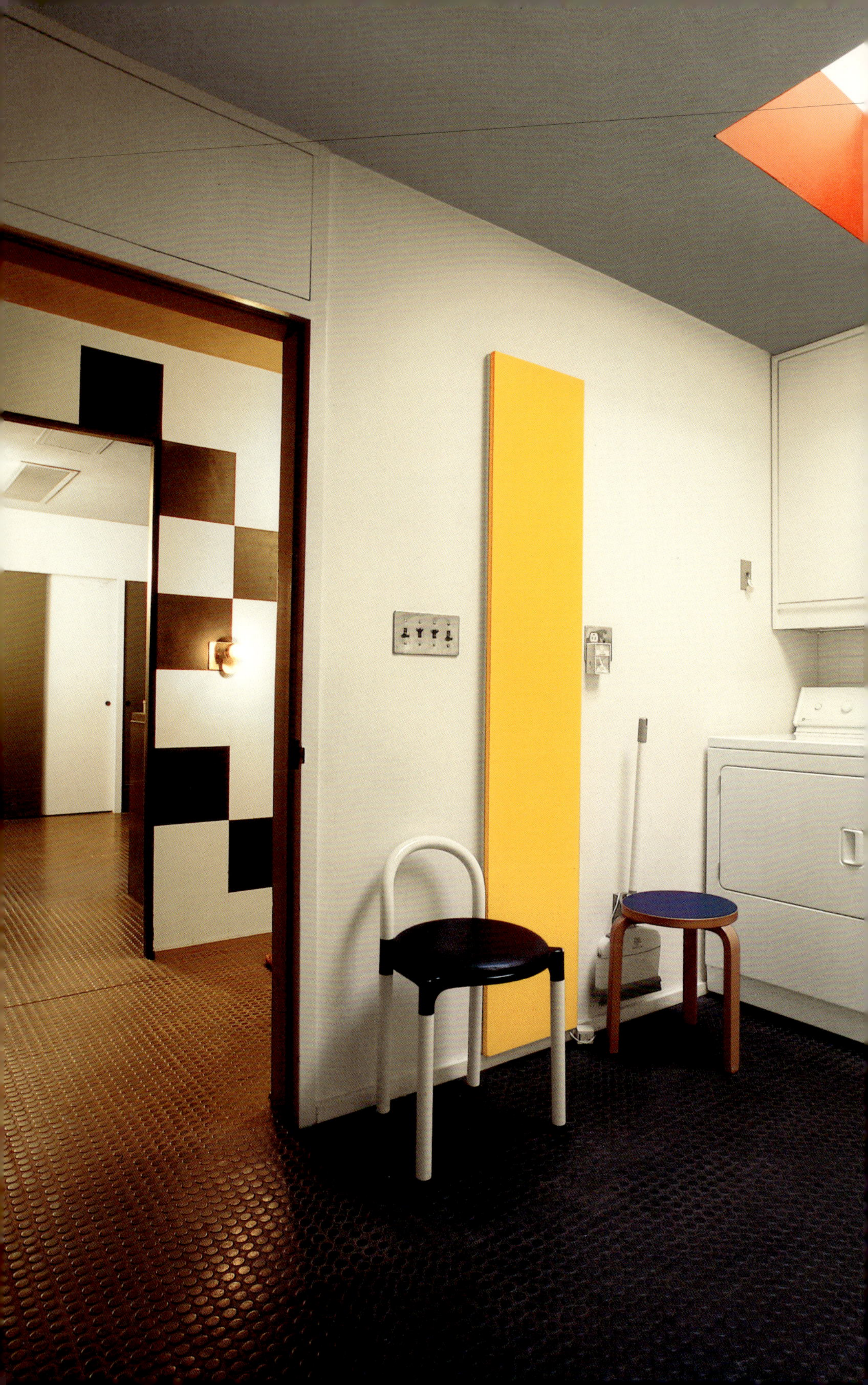

11. Laundry room with red-rimmed skylight and ironing board concealed with yellow door/panel
12. Storage/studio with view from side entrance hallway with checkered floor tiles on wall
13. Bedroom with view west toward garden and garage. In this room, Rand experimented with a William Morris *Fruit* print for walls and bedding.
14. Master Bedroom with view to the creek
15. Studio (next page spread) with a view south overlooking garden and a large portion of the property. Paintings are by Rand.

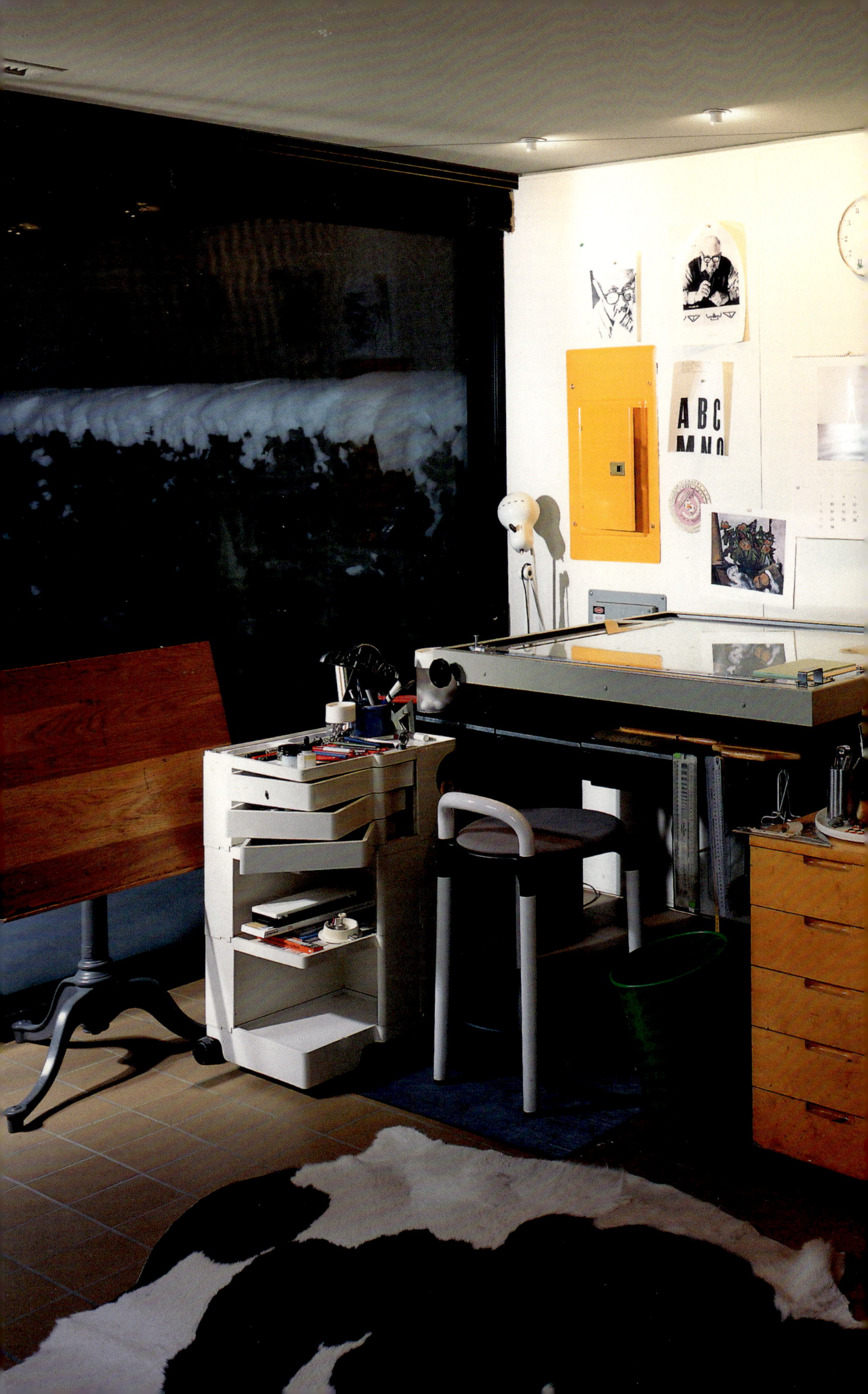
ABC

Ceci n'est pas une pipe.

356: 357:

Timeline:

Franc Nunoo-Quarcoo

The basis for the research and design of the following contextual timeline was inspired by the late American modernist designer Rudolph de Harak. He observed that time, in relation to history, should not only be sequential, but in fact, must be contextualized for a better comprehension and appreciation of any history.

References:
1. Rudolph de Harak, "A Contextual History of Graphic Design (unpublished manuscript)," 1980.
2. Georgette Ballance, *A Paul Rand Retrospective,* 1996.
3. Georgette Ballance, "Timeline," in Steven Heller, *Paul Rand,* London: Phaidon Press, 1998.
4. Paul Rand, *A Designers Art,* New Haven: Yale University Press, 1985.
5. Paul Rand, *Design, Form and Chaos,* New Haven: Yale University Press, 1993.
6. Paul Rand, *From Lascaux to Brooklyn,* New Haven: Yale University Press, 1996.
7. Edward Lucie-Smith, *Visual Arts in the 20th Century,* New York: Harry N. Abrams, Inc., Publishers, 1996.
8. *Communication Arts,* March/April 1999.

	1914:	1915:	1916:
His Life:	Born Peretz Rosenbaum on August 15 in Brooklyn, into an Orthodox Jewish family made up of twin brother, Fischel; father, Itzhak Yehuda; mother, Leah; and sister, Ruth. Father runs a small grocery store. Paul and brother Philip (Fischel) help in the store and study the Talmud at the local Yeshiva school. Attends Public School 101. Pursues interest in making art in the spirit of leading American illustrators J.C. Leyendecker and Norman Rockwell.		
His Work:			
His Time:	First traffic lights in the United States appear in Cleveland, Ohio. Panama Canal opens. Architect Antonio Gaudi designs Guell Park in Barcelona.	Assassination of Austrian Archduke Franz Ferdinand and wife by a Serbian nationalist in Sarajevo, Yugoslavia, starts World War I. James Joyce's *Dubliners* is published. Artist Robert Delauney paints *Homage to Blierot*. Alexander Samuelson designs the Coca-Cola bottle. D.W. Griffith directs *The Birth of a Nation*. Albert Einstein publishes *General Theory of Relativity*. First transcontinental telephone call is placed from New York to San Francisco. Ford Motor Company produces one-millionth car. Kasimir Malevich publishes Suprematist manifesto.	Dada is created at the Cabaret Voltaire in Zürich. Franz Kafka's *Metamorphosis* is published. First birth control center opens in New York. Writer Henry James, artists Odillon Redon and Umberto Boccioni die. Gabrielle Chanel establishes Coco Chanel. Frank Lloyd Wright designs Imperial Hotel in Tokyo.

358: 359:

1917: 1918: 1919:

Peretz (Paul), left, and his
brother Fischel (Philip).

Theo van Doesburg founds the group and journal de Stijl. Gerrit Rietveld designs red-yellow-and-blue chair. The Ballets Russes perform *Parade* with plot by Cocteau, music by Erik Satie, and sets and costumes by Pablo Picasso. Charlie Chaplin stars in *The Immigrant*. The October Revolution elevates the Bolsheviks to power in Russia. First jazz concert recording is made in the United States. The United States declares war on Germany.	General Motors markets the Frigidaire domestic refrigerator in the U.S. Kasimir Malevitch paints *White Square on White* Piet Mondrian paints *Composition No.2*. World War I ends. Austria becomes a Republic. First airmail service in the United States takes place. Tsar of Russia and his family are executed.	Under architect Walter Gropius, the Bauhaus at Weimar opens. Ernest Rutherford splits the atom. Observations of solar eclipse confirm Einstein's *Theory of Relativity*. League of Nations is formed. The Prohibition period starts. Civil War erupts in Russia. Artist Auguste Renoir dies.

                1920:   1921:   1922:

His Life:

His Work:

His Time: Le Corbusier and Amedée   Architect Mies van der   Picasso paints *Women*
             Ozenfant found the journal   Rohe develops a skyscraper   *on the Beach.*
             L'Espirit Nouveau.   project in glass, setting   Wassily Kandinsky and
             Photography is used to   in motion the birth of   Marc Chagall leave Russia
             demonstrate the structure   "curtain wall" construction.   for Germany.
             of the Milky Way.   Fernand Léger paints   The USSR is formed by
             French author Colette   *Three Women.*   a union of Soviet states.
             publishes *Cherie.*   Constantin Brancusi produces   March on Rome by Mussolini
             Mahatma Gandhi launches   first version of *Bird in Space.* leads to the formation of a
             civil disobedience campaign   Coco Chanel launches   fascist government in Italy.
             in India.   perfume No.5.   James Joyce's *Ulysses* is
             Nineteenth Amendment   The British Broadcasting   published.
             extends to American women   Corporation (BBC) is founded. T.S. Elliot's *The Waste Land*
             the right to vote.   Chinese Communist Party   is published.
             Italian artist Amadeo   is created.   Jazz musician Louis
             Modigliani dies.   United States stock market   Armstrong makes his first
             First electric hair dryers used booms.   recording.
             in the United States.   Albert Einstein wins   Vitamin E is discovered.
             First radio broadcasts begin in Nobel Prize in Physics.
             the United States and Britain. Insulin is discovered.
             Antwerp hosts Olympic Games.

1923:	1924:	1925:
Laszlo Moholy-Nagy joins the Bauhaus. Le Corbusier publishes *Toward A New Architecture*. Marcel Duchamp produces *The Bride Stripped Bare by her Bachelors, Even*. George Gershwin writes *Rhapsody in Blue*. Greta Garbo makes film debut. Economist John Maynard Keynes publishes *A Tract on Monetary Reform*. Adolf Hitler's coup d'etat in Munich fails.	André Breton publishes Surrealist manifesto in Paris. Gerrit Rietveld designs Schröeder House in Utrecht, The Netherlands. Sculptor Constantin Brancusi produces *The Beginning of the World*. E. M. Forster's *A Passage to India* is published. Fernand Léger directs *Mechanical Ballet*. Adolf Hitler writes *Mein Kampf* while in prison. Paris hosts Olympic Games.	The Bauhaus is moved to Dessau under the leadership of Josef Albers. New buildings are designed by Walter Gropius, and Marcel Breuer designs Wassily chair made out of tubular steel. Leica cameras go into production. J.J.P. Oud designs facade for De Unie café in Rotterdam. Sergei Eisenstein films *The Battleship Potemkin*. Charlie Chaplin films *The Gold Rush*. F. Scott Fitzgerald's *The Great Gatsby* is published. Franz Kafka's *The Trial* is published.

	1926:	1927:	1928:
His Life:			
His Work:			
His Time:	Alexander Calder makes first wire sculptures. Paul Klee paints *Neighborhood of the Italian Villas*. George Grösz paints *Pillars of Society*. Fritz Lang directs *Metropolis*. Franz Kafka's *The Castle* is published. T.E. Lawrence's (Lawrence of Arabia) *The Seven Pillars of Wisdom* is published. Kodak produces first 16mm photographic film.	Charles Lindbergh flies the Spirit of St. Louis from New York to Paris. René Magritte paints *The Murder Threatened*. Kasimir Malevich produces *The World Without Object*. Alan Crossland produces *The Jazz Singer*, the first film with sound. Duke Ellington's band plays at the Cotton Club in Harlem, New York. Hugo Häring produces publication on the reorientation of the applied arts. Fifteen million Model T Fords have been produced to date.	Richard Drew invents adhesive tape, marketed by 3M. William van Alen publishes *Surrealism and Painting*. Buckminster Fuller designs Dymaxion house. Gio Ponti founds design journal *Domus* in Italy. Alexander Fleming discovers penicillin. D.H. Lawrence's *Lady Chatterly Lover* is published. First performance of Bertolt Brecht's *The Threepenny Opera* with music by Kurt Weill. Erich Maria Remarque's *All Qu* *on the Western Front* published. George Eastman exhibits first color motion pictures. Amelia Earhart flies over Atlanti Amsterdam hosts Olympic Games.

362: 363:

1929:

Discovers British design magazine *Commercial Art*, German advertising, and the art journal *Gebrauchsgrafik*. Finds out about the Bauhaus and its proponents such as Laszlo Moholy-Nagy and other designers.

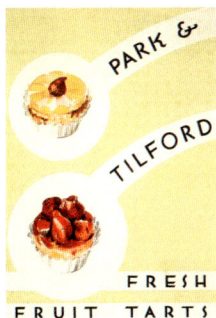

Alvar Aalto designs Paimio sanatorium in Finland.
Museum of Modern Art, first museum entirely devoted to modern art, opens.
Le Corbusier produces designs for *The City of Tomorrow*.
Salvador Dali and Louis Bunuel direct the surrealist fantasy *Un Chien Andalou*.
William Faulkner's *The Sound and the Fury* is published.
The term "science fiction" is first used in the United States.
Wall Street stock market crash on October 2 precipitates world economic crisis.

1930:

Mies van der Rohe designs Brno chair.
Grant Wood paints *American Gothic*.
Marlene Dietrich stars in *The Blue Angel*.
Human blood goups are identified.
First transatlantic airmail service occurs.
Planet Pluto is discovered.

1931:

Whitney Museum of American Art in New York opens.
Empire State and Chrysler buildings are completed in New York.
Alfred Hood designs Rockefeller Center.
Ezra Pound's *The ABC of Reading* is published.
Harold Edgerton applies the electronic flash to photography.
X-rays are used to investigate molecular structure.
Nazism rises in Germany.

	1932:	1933:	1934:
His Life:	Earns high school diploma from Harren High School and art certificate from Pratt Institute, both in Brooklyn.	Enrolls in art classes at the Brooklyn Institute of Arts and Sciences; the Art Students League, where he studies with German emigré artist George Grösz, a member of the Berlin Dada. Also enrolls in design classes at the Parsons School of Design in Manhattan.	Starts first professional job as an illustrator for Metro Associated Services, a resource company that supplied maps and stock illustrations to newspapers and magazines.
His Work:			
His Time:	Franklin D. Roosevelt is elected President. Frank Lloyd Wright organizes The Taliesin Fellowship Foundation for the study of architecture. Raymond Leowy, Henry Dreyfuss, Norman Bel Geddes, and Otto Kuhler design streamlined aerodynamic steam locomotives. Alexander Calder starts producing mobiles. Aldous Huxley writes *Brave New World*. First Venice Film Festival takes place. Mahatma Gandhi leads a campaign of non-violence in India. Vitamin D is discovered. Los Angeles hosts Olympic Games.	President Roosevelt's New Deal points way out of the Depression and economic crisis. Painter Edward Hopper exhibits at MoMA (Museum of Modern Art). Bauhaus at Dessau is closed by the Nazis, and many faculty flee to the U.S. Hitler is appointed Chancellor of Germany, starts the boycott of Jewish businesses, and begins the building of concentration camps. Max Braun becomes first to combine radio and record player.	Gerrit Rietveld designs Zig-Zag chair. *The Machine* exhibition takes place at MoMA. Ferdinand Porsche designs the Volkswagen (Beetle). Exhibition of graphic design work of Hans Schleger is held. In China, Chairman Mao and his partisans initiate the Long March. Scientist Marie Curie dies.

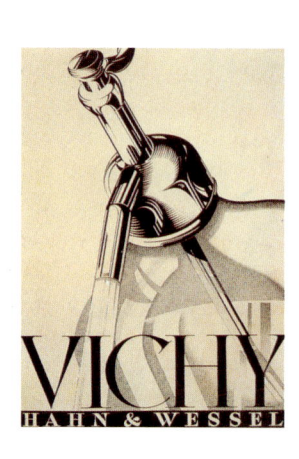

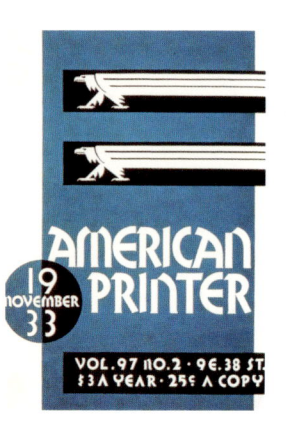

364: 365:

1935:   1936:   1937:

Starts freelance practice with *Glass Packer* magazine and other accounts. Interviews for jobs (without success) with European design emigrés Lucien Bernhard, Gustav Jensen, and others. Introduced to industrial designer George Switzer, for whom he starts apprenticeship, which helps improve his visual skills considerably. Changes legal name from Peretz Rosenbaum to Paul Rand, not unlike many children of immigrants who did so to gain access into an economic and social environment dominated by Protestant culture.

Starts the first phase of his career.
Hired initially as a freelance designer at *Apparel Arts*, a men's fashion magazine. Rises to the position of art director for both *Apparel Arts* and *Esquire* magazines. He produces modernist-inspired covers in the spirit of the European practitioners. Clearly, he was putting to practice and fusing for his own visual language the principles of the Bauhaus, Cubists, Constuctivists, and Dada. Rand's design contemporaries Lester Beall and Alvin Lustig also subscribe to the modernist aesthetics and principles.

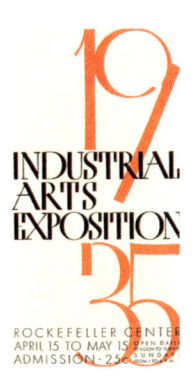

IBM markets first commercially successful electric typewriter.
First parking meters installed in the U.S., in use in Tulsa, Oklahoma.
Penguin launches first paperback-format books.
Sir Alexander Watson-Watt invents radar.
Richter scale for measuring earthquakes developed.
Rueben Mamoulian's *Becky Sharp* is first film in technicolor.
Braun builds first battery operated portable radio.
Italy invades Abyssinia (now Ethiopia).

Berlin hosts Olympic games; Jesse Owens wins four gold medals.
Frank Lloyd Wright completes Falling Water/Kaufman House.
Raymond Loewy designs Coldspot refrigerator for Sears Roebuck.
Walter Dorwin Teague designs the Kodak Brownie camera.
The BBC makes the first regular television transmissions.
Charlie Chaplin directs and stars in *Modern Times*.
Spanish Civil War begins.
China declares war on Japan.
King Edward VIII of Great Britain abicates the throne to marry American divorcee Wallis Simpson.

Walter Gropius is appointed Chair of Harvard Graduate School of Design.
Joe Louis defeats Max Schmeling for the heavyweight title.
Pablo Picasso completes painting *Guernica*.
Piet Mondrian publishes *Plastic Art and Pure Art*.
The Golden Gate bridge is opened to traffic.
Patent is granted for the manufacture of nylon.

	1938:	1939:	1940:
His Life:	Through the duration of WWII, designs covers for the anti-fascist magazine *Direction,* influenced by Dada, Constructivism, Surrealism, and the French satirist and artist Honoré Daumier, defining the first phase of his career.	Instructor at the New York Laboratory School. Designs New York World's Fair brochure, an insert to *PM Magazine,* for which he designed both front and back covers. His work is published in this same issue of *PM Magazine*. This is the first aricle written about his work.	
His Work:	 		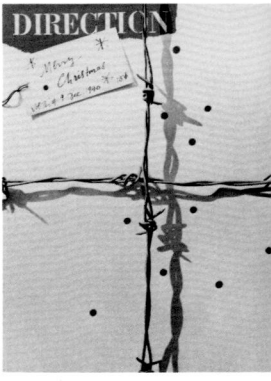
His Time:	Walter Gropius and Marcel Breuer begin working together. Frank Lloyd Wright completes Taliesin West in Phoenix, Arizona. László Biro invents the ball point pen. Marcel Duchamp completes *The Box.* Orson Welles's adaptation of *War of the Worlds* causes widespread panic. Walt Disney directs *Snow White and the Seven Dwarfs.*	Edward Durell Stone and Philip Goodwin remodel MoMA. New York World's Fair *Building the World of Tomorrow* opens. World War II begins. Britain and France declare war on Germany. Spanish Civil Wars ends, and dictator Franco assumes power. Igor Sikorsky develops helicopter. James Joyce writes *Finnegans Wake.* Victor Fleming directs *Gone With the Wind,* after the novel by Margaret Mitchell. John Ford directs *Stagecoach.* Sigmund Freud dies.	Charles Eames and Eero Saarinen win prize at MoMA furniture competition. Charlie Chaplin directs and stars in *The Great Dictator.* John Ford directs *The Grapes of Wrath,* based on the book by John Steinbeck, published in 1939. Walt Disney directs *Fantasia.* Commercial television services begin in the United States. Vivian Fry opens an office in Paris to arrange for the emigration of intellectuals and artists to the U.S. Winston Churchill becomes prime minister of Britain. Paul Klee dies.

1941:

Begins second phase of his career as art director of the William Weintraub Agency from 1941–55. In this span, designs groundbreaking work informed by modernism for Coronet Brandy, El Producto Cigar Company, Disney Hats, Dubonnet (adapted from the original design by the French poster designer A. M. Cassandre), Stafford Fabrics, Ohrbach's Department Store, Dunhill Clothiers, Kaufman Department Store, Olivetti, and *Architectural Forum*. Bauhaus proponent Laszlo Moholy-Nagy writes article about a young Paul Rand and his promising career in *AD Magazine*, an influential magazine on the design arts. Exhibition of work at the Katherine Kuh Gallery, New York.

German Expressionist painter Emil Nolde's work is banned by the Nazis. Siegfried Giedion writes *Space, Time, and Architecture*. Orson Welles directs and stars in *Citizen Kane*. John Huston directs *The Maltese Falcon*. Japan invades the Phillipines, attacks Pearl Harbor, Hawaii on December 7; the U.S. declares war on Germany and Italy.

1942:

Teaches at The Cooper Union for the Advancement of Science and Art. Designs advertisements for Stafford Fabrics, Ohrbach's Department Store, Kaufman Department Store.

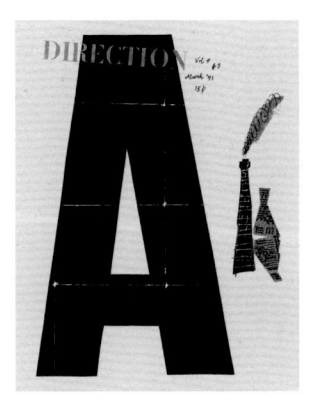

Mies van der Rohe designs Farnsworth House in Illinois, designs the buildings for Illinois Institute of Technology. Oscar Niemeyer and Le Corbusier complete Ministry of Education in Rio de Janiero, Brazil. Peggy Guggenheim founds Art of this Century Gallery in New York. Magnetic recording tape is invented. First electronic computer is developed in the U.S. First *Papers of Surrealism* published in New York.

1943:

Designs advertisements for *Architectural Forum,* Cresta Blanca Wine Company.

Piet Mondrian paints *Broadway Boogie-Woogie.* Jackson Pollock has first solo exhibition at the Art of this Century Gallery. Alexander Calder retrospective is held at MoMA. Philosopher Jean Paul Satre's *Being and Nothingness* is published. Allied Army invades Italy. Anti-Nazi revolt takes place in Warsaw ghetto.

	1944:	1945:	1946:
His Life:	Designs first book cover *The Cubists Painters* by Gillaume Apolinaire for publisher Wittenborn & Company's series *The Documents of Modern Art*. Designs trademark for Helbros Watch Company. Designs perfume bottle made with crystal and gold wire.	Designs first book *The Tables of the Law* by Thomas Mann for publisher Alfred A. Knopf, Borzoi Books. Redesigns Borzoi Books logo. Starts to design for *Architectural Forum* whose advertisements are aimed more at advertisers for the magazine.	Teaches at Pratt Institute, Brooklyn. Designs innovative advertizing for Ohrbach's Department Store. Designs a series of advertisements on the theme of Great Ideas of Western Man for Container Corporation of America. From 1946–49, designs arresting magazine advertisements for Disney Hats.
His Time:	Pietro Belluschi designs Equitable Life Insurance Building in Portland, Oregon. Picasso paints Charnel House in response to pictures from the death camps in Eastern Europe. Jean Dubuffet has first solo exhibition. Otto Preminger directs *Laura*. Edvard Munch, Piet Mondrian, and Wassily Kandinsky die.	Walter Gropius establishes the Architect's Collaborative. Mondrian retrospective held at MoMA. Picasso and Matisse both have retrospectives at the Victoria and Albert Museum in London. Billy Wilder directs *The Lost Weekend*. David Lean directs *Brief Encounter*. President Franklin Delano Roosevelt dies. WW II ends in Europe. U.S. drops atomic bombs on Hiroshima and Nagasaki, signaling end of WW II in the Pacific. United Nations is created by fifty nations when charter is signed on June 26 in San Francisco.	Charles Eames is the first designer to have his work exhibited at MoMA. Frank Lloyd Wright unveils Guggenheim Museum model. Henry Moore wins sculpture prize at the Venice Biennale. Jackson Pollock develops drip painting technique. Chester Carlson develops xerography process. Renato Piaggio designs the Vespa scooter. Jean Cocteau's *Beauty and the Beast* screened at first Cannes Film Festival. Frank Capra directs *It's A Wonderful Life*.

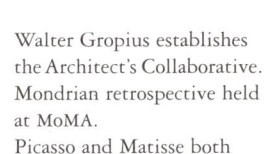

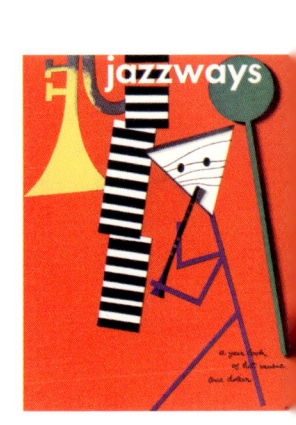

1947:

Writes his first seminal book *Thoughts On Design*, published by Wittenborn & Company.
Exhibition of work at the Composing Room, New York; National Museum, Stockholm, Sweden.
Designs advertisements for Kaufman Department Store in Pittsburgh, owned by Edgar Kaufman (who had commisioned Frank Lloyd Wright to design the Kaufman House-Falling Water at Bear Run in 1936).

1948:

Exhibition of work at the Philadelphia Museum of Art.
Designs a limited edition portfolio pairing writers and painters on the subject of Women for the Museum of Modern Art.
Commssions modernist architect Marcel Breuer to design a bungalow in Woodstock, NY, but the project is never realized.

1949:

Designs poster for the Museum of Modern Art, the subject of which is *The House in the Museum Garden* by Marcel Breuer.
Designs cover for *Modern Art in Your Life* for the Museum of Modern Art.
Designs catalog for the Arensberg Collection for the Art Institute of Chicago.
Commssions Marcel Breuer to design modernist house in Harrison, NY. During the early construction stages, Breuer and Rand part ways.

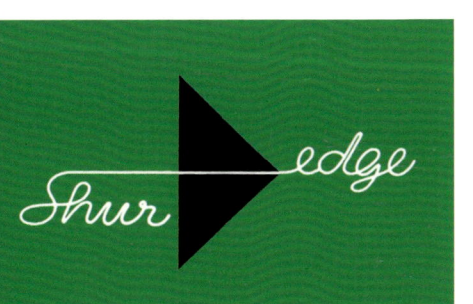

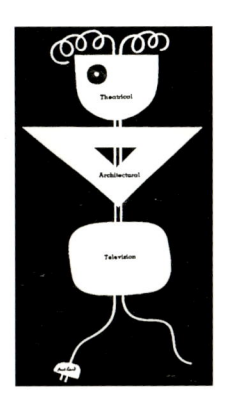

Christian Dior ushers in the modernist "New Look" in fashion.
Le Corbusier designs Unité d'Habitation in Marseilles, France.
Richard Neutra designs the Kauffman House in Palm Springs, California.
Clyfford Still exhibits first color-field paintings.
Albert Camus's *The Plague* is published.
Premiere of Tennessee Williams's play *Streetcar Named Desire*.
Marshall Plan instituted for the rebuilding of Europe after WW II.
India proclaims independence from Britain.

Le Corbusier, Harrison, and others design the United Nations Secretariat in New York.
Buckminster Fuller designs his first geodesic domes.
Edwin Herbert Land designs first Polaroid to provide instant images.
Orson Welles directs *The Lady from Shanghai*.
The transistor radio is invented by engineers John Bardeen, Walter Brattain, and William Shockley at Bell Labs.
In India, Mahatma Gandhi is assassinated.
The British organize the independence of the state of Israel.
London hosts Olympic Games.

Apartheid instituted in South Africa.
Mark Rothko makes first color-field paintings.
George Orwell's *1984* is published.
Arthur Miller's *Death of a Salesman* is published.
Republic of China is proclaimed under Mao Tse-tung.
Akiro Kurosawa directs *Stray Dog*.
First performance of John Cage's *Sonatas and Interludes* takes place.
Simone de Beauvoir's *The Second Sex* is published.
Cortisone is discovered.

	1950:	1951:	1952:
His Life:	Designs twenty-four-sheet billboard for the Twentieth Century Fox feature film *No Way Out* starring Sidney Poitier.	Designs Weston, CT, house with wife Ann, who had studied with Mies van der Rohe. The design of the modern glass and fieldstone house is influenced by Le Corbusier and Marcel Breuer. Designs book jacket for artist Robert Motherwell's book on the Dada movement in modern art, published by Wittenborn Schultz Inc.	Designs El Producto packaging for GHP Cigar Company, a striking departure from the traditional cigar box design, causing much discussion.

His Work:

| His Time: | Matisse is awarded the Grand Prize at the Venice Biennale. Franz Kline has first exhibition. Willem de Kooning paints *Woman 1*. Vincent Minnelli directs *An American in Paris*. Ralph Bunche is awarded the Nobel Peace Prize. First color television broadcasts take place in the United States. Korean War begins. Antihistamines are introduced against colds and allergies. | Le Corbusier is commissioned to design Chandigarh, India. Arne Jacobson designs the Ant Chair. Eli Kazan directs *A Streetcar Named Desire*, starring Marlon Brando. Picasso paints *Massacre in Korea*. André Malraux publishes *The Voices of Silence*. The supermarket cart is introduced in the U.S. Twenty-second Amendment limits U.S. presidents to two terms in office. | Sculptor Harry Bertoia designs the Diamond Chair in steel wire for Knoll. Louis Kahn designs Yale University Art Gallery. Dwight D. Eisenhower is elected U.S. president. Mass production of IBM computer 701 takes place. Stanley Donen directs *Singing In the Rain*. The Iron Curtain divides Berlin. Helsinki hosts Olympic Games. |

1953:

Designs covers for the journal *Perspectives*. Commissioned by industry leader Olivetti to design high profile advertisements. Rand House voted one of the ten best designed houses in America.

Headed by Swiss designer Max Bill, Horschule für Gestaltung Ulm Design School at Ulm, Germany, opens.
Scandal erupts over Picasso's *Portrait of Stalin*.
Stalin dies, is succeeded by Nikita Kruschev.
Francis Crick and James Watson determine molecular structure of DNA.
Samuel Beckett writes *Waiting for Godot*.

1954:

New York Art Directors Club votes him one of the ten best art directors. Exhibition of work at the Contemporary Art Museum in Boston.
Designs full-page RCA advertisement for the Weintraub Agency using Morse Code as main design theme. While successful and compelling, it did not help secure the account, but marks a seminal point in his career. Devotes time to painting, preferring abstraction over representation. Designs a series of posters for the Interfaith Day Movement.

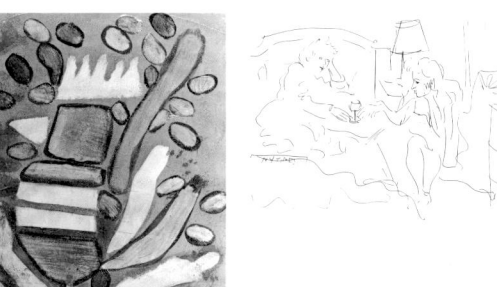

Push Pin Studio is co-founded by Milton Glaser.
Henri Matisse dies.
U.S. Supreme Court rules (Brown vs. Board of Education) that segregation by race/color in public schools is illegal.
Polio vaccine is developed at the Pasteur Institute in Paris.
Gregory Pincus, Min Chueh Chang, and John Rock invent the contraceptive pill.

1955:

Prolific design of bookcovers for publishers Vintage Books and Random House. Designs cover for the influential Japanese visual arts magazine *Idea*.

Le Corbusier's Ronchamp Chapel opens.
Eero Saarinen's design of the General Motors Research Center is complete.
Art critic and historian Clement Greenberg defines color-field painting.
Jasper Johns paints first 'Flag' painting.
Rosa Parks ignites bus boycott against racial segregation in Montgomery, Alabama.
Martin Luther King emerges as a Civil Rights leader against racial segregation.
First McDonald's restaurant opens in Des Plaines, Illinois.
James Dean stars in *Rebel Without a Cause*.
Albert Einstein dies.

	1956:	1957:	1958:
His Life:	Begins third phase of his career which involves consultations with leading American and international businesses, publishing, and financial institutions. Invited by modernist architect Eliot Noyes to redesign IBM logo as part of a visual identity team that included fellow modernist designers Herbert Matter, George Nelson, and Charles Eames. From 1956–91, he was the design consultant to IBM. Appointed Professor of Design at Yale University. Takes leave-of-absence from 1969–1974. Returns through 1993, when he was appointed emeritus professor. Starts designing book jackets for Bollingren Series and Pantheon Books. Designed and illustrated *I Know A Lot of Things,* written by Ann Rand and published by Harcourt, Brace & World.	Designed and illustrated *Sparkle and Spin,* written by Ann Rand and published by Harcourt, Brace & World.	Designs book cover for H.L. Mencken's *Prejudices: A Selection*, published by Vintage Books/Random House. For most of the book covers he designed from the 1940s through the 1960s, he used his handwriting in place of composed type, a practice he carried over from the design of the earlier *Direction* series. Awarded honorary degree from Tama University, Tokyo. Exhibitions at Art Directors Club, Tokyo; AIGA Gallery, New York.
His Work:			
His Time:	Oral vaccine developed against polio. Transatlantic cable telephone service inaugurated. Mies van der Rohe and Philip Johnson design the Seagram Building in New York. Frank Lloyd Wright designs the Guggenheim Museum in New York. Eero Saarinen designs TWA Terminal at Kennedy Airport. Jørn Utzon and Ove Arup design the Sydney Opera House. Eero Saarinen designs furniture collection for Knoll. Charles and Ray Eames design chair and ottoman for Herman Miller. Jackson Pollock dies. Melbourne hosts Olympic Games.	Le Corbusier designs Tokyo Museum of Art. United States passes Civil Rights Act. Independence of Ghana from Britain marks the beginning of decolonization in Africa. First satellites Sputnik I and II launched by the USSR. Leonard Bernstein records *West Side Story.* Sculptor Constantin Brancusi, singer Billie Holliday die.	Eero Saarinen designs Dulles International Airport. Paul Rudolph designs Art and Architecture building at Yale University. Artist Jasper Johns exhibits at the Leo Castelli Gallery in New York. Christo Javachev (aka Christo) begins first wrapping projects. Alfred Hitchcock directs the film *Vertigo*. Merce Cunningham choreographs *Arctic Meet* ballet to music by composer John Cage and stage design by artist Robert Rauschenberg. First Ikea shops open in Sweden. First stereophonic recordings made.

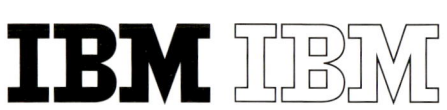

1959:

Designs trademark for Colorforms, a manufacturer of children's toys.
Invited by Eliot Noyes to consult with Westinghouse Electric Corporation, a role that lasts through 1981.
Designs book and book jacket for *Paul Rand: His Work from 1946 to 1958*, edited by his contemporary, Japanese designer Yusaku Kamekura, and published by Alfred A. Knopf and Zokuisha Publising, Tokyo.

Architect Louis Kahn designs the Salk Institute in LaJolla, California.
IBM launces the 401 computer.
Xerox introduces its photocopying machine.
In Cuba, Fidel Castro seizes power and the revolution in Cuba begins.
Playwright Lorraine Hansberry's play *A Raisin in the Sun* opens in New York.
Federico Fellini directs *La Dolce Vita*.
Hawaii becomes fiftieth state.
Frank Lloyd Wright, George Grösz die.

1960:

Designs Westinghouse trademark.
Authors *Trademarks of Paul Rand*, published by George Wittenborn, Inc. New York.
Exhibition at Pratt Institute, New York.
Begins design consultancy with Cummins Engine Company. This relationship lasts through his death in 1996.

John Fitzgerald Kennedy elected President of the United States.
Le Corbusier designs Dominican monastery in LaTourette, France.
Oscar Niemeyer plans and designs buildings for Brasilia, the new capital city of Brazil.
Reyner Barnham publishes *Theory and Design in the First Machine Age*.
Saxophonist Ornette Coleman releases album *Free Jazz*.
Massacre of black school-children in Sharpville, South Africa.
Rome hosts Olympic Games.

1961:

Designs United Parcel Service (UPS) trademark.

Artist Roy Lichtenstein creates his first works based on the comic strip.
The term "concept art" is coined by Henry Flynt.
Art of Assemblage exhibition opens at MoMA.
Russian cosmonaut Yuri Gagarin orbits the earth.
Berlin Wall is constructed.
The Republic of South Africa is formed.
Amnesty International is formed in London.
Joseph Heller's *Catch 22* is published.
MIT develops first time sharing computer.
Ernest Hemingway dies.

	1962:	1963:	1964:
His Life:	Designed and illustrated *Little 1,* written by Ann Rand and published by Harcourt, Brace & World. Designs American Broadcasting Company (ABC) logotype. Receives citation from Philadelphia College of Art (now University of the Arts).	Designs poster for the New York Art Directors Club, using the idea of a rebus to present subject and date in an integrated and compelling manner.	Exhibitions at Carnegie Institute, Pittsburgh (now Carnegie Mellon University); Carpenter Center, Harvard University, Cambridge; School of Visual Arts, New York.
His Work:	abc	design 63	IITRI / IBM / ATLAS
His Time:	Andy Warhol holds his first solo exhibition at the Ferna Gallery in Los Angeles. *Time, Life,* and *Newsweek* magazines cover Pop Art. Andy Warhol paints *Campbell's Soup Cans.* The art movement Fluxus is formed on the initiative of George Maciunas. Stanley Kubrik directs *Lolita* by novelist Nabokov. Seattle's World Fair, themed *Man In the Space Age,* opens. First black student admitted to the University of Mississippi.	ICOGRADA (International Council of Graphic Design Associations) formed. President John F. Kennedy assassinated in Dallas, Texas. Martin Luther King leads civil rights demonstrations in the United States. Under South Africa's apartheid policy, Nelson Mandela is condemned to a life sentence in prison. Sculptor Dan Flavin produces the first of his fluorescent light sculptures. Scupltor Claes Oldenburg produces *Soft Light Switches.* Stanley Kubrick directs *Dr. Strangelove.* W.E.B. DuBois, philosopher, and founder of the NAACP, dies in Accra, Ghana.	Architect and designer Eliott Noyes designs the modern gas pump and station for Mobil Oil. Robert Rauschenberg wins the prize for painting at the Venice Biennial. Martin Luther King awarded the Nobel Peace Prize. The United States gets involved in the Vietnam War. MoMA organizes exhibition *Architecture Without Architects.* Artist Carolee Schneeman performs *Meat Joy.* The Palestine Liberation Organization (PLO) is formed. Mary Quant launches the miniskirt in London. Tokyo hosts Olympic Games.

374: 375:

1965:

Authors *Design and the Play Instinct*, published in *The Education of Vision* by George Brazillier.

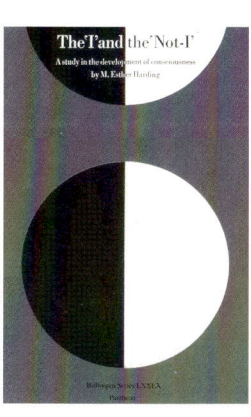

National Endowment for the Arts (NEA) established. Architect Louis Kahn designs the National Assembly Building in Bangladesh. Andy Warhol has first retrospective at the University of Pennsylvania. Noam Chomsky's *Aspects of the Theory of Syntax* is published.
Le Corbusier dies.
Malcolm X is assassinated. IBM introduces programming for Linotype machines. German type company Hell devises mathemathical formula for storing type in digital form.
Sir Winston Churchill dies.

1966:

Honored by the American Institute of Graphic Arts with the AIGA gold medal. Invited by Ford Motor Company to propose a new logo design, later rejected by Henry Ford II as too radical a departure from the original.

The new Whitney Museum of American Art building, designed by Marcel Breuer, opens.
Systematic Abstraction exhibition opens at the Guggenheim Museum. Andy Warhol films *Chelsea Girls*.
Truman Capote's *In Cold Blood* is published. Cultural Revolution begins in China.
Demonstrations take place against United States involvement in the Vietnam war.

1967:

Designs book jacket for painter Robert Motherwell's book on Dada in modern art published by Wittenborn & Company. The distinctive typographic solution shows Rand's deep vocabulary and knowledge of modern and contemporary art.

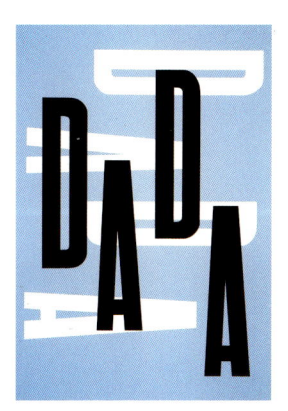

International Expo '67 in Montreal showcases pavilions by Buckminster Fuller and Moshe Safdie. Artist Robert Motherwell completes *Elegy to the Spanish Republic*.
South African Dr. Christian Barnard performs first human heart transplant. Cuban revolutionary leader Che Guevara leader is killed in Bolivia.
Six-Day War between Israel and Aran nations is fought. Surrealist painter René Magritte dies.

	1968:	1969:	1970:
His Life:	Exhibition of work at Temple University. Designs catalog cover and poster for the American Institute of Graphic Art. He uses humor and the rebus as effective tools of communication. Redesigns packaging scheme for Westinghouse Corporation. Designs mark for the U.S. Department of the Interior Bureau for Indian Affairs.	Exhibition of work at Louisiana Arts and Science Center, Baton Rouge.	Designs and illustrates *Listen! Listen!*, written by Ann Rand and published by Harcourt, Brace & World. Exhibition at IBM Gallery, New York; Virginia Museum of Fine Arts, Richmond. Designs packaging for IBM computer products.
His Work:			
His Time:	Horschule für Gestaltung at Ulm, Germany, closes *Art and the Machine* exhibit at MoMA. Martin Luther King, Jr. assassinated. Senator Robert F. Kennedy assassinated. Marcel Duchamp dies. Richard Nixon elected President of the United States. Mexico City hosts Olympic Games. Ban on TV ads for feminine hygiene products lifted.	Skidmore Owings & Merrill design the John Hancock Center skyscraper in Chicago. Major works by Picasso and Giorgio de Chirico are stolen from the Penrose Collection in London. Concorde makes its first flight. Woodstock music festival takes place. Stonewall riots ignite the gay rights movement. Apollo 11 lands on the moon, and astronaut Neil Armstrong becomes first human to walk on the moon. Writer Kurt Vonnegut's *Slaughterhouse-Five* is published. *Saturday Evening Post* magazine folds after 148 years. Public Broadcasting Service (PBS) begins operation.	IBM develops "floppy disc" to store computer data. Artist Judy Chicago organizes first feminist art course at California State University in Fresno. Aleksandr Solzhenitsyn wins Nobel Prize for Literature. Kent State University shootings over protests against the Vietnam war. Pelé and Brazil become first to win the World Cup three times. Artists Mark Rothko and Barnett Newman, General Charles de Gaulle die.

1971:

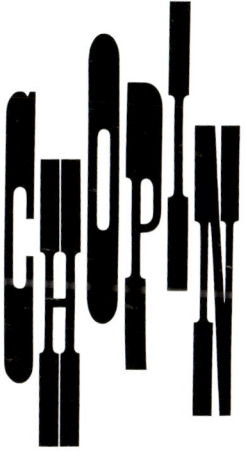

1972:

Inducted into the
New York Art Directors
Club Hall of Fame.

1973:

Awarded the Royal
Designer for Industry
Medal, Royal Society,
London.

Contemporary Black American Artists held exhibition at the Whitney Musuem.
Architects Richard Rogers and Renzo Piano design the Pompidou Center in Paris.
Artist David Hockney produces his California swimming pool paintings.
In Switzerland, women are granted the right to vote.
Stanley Kubrick films *A Clockwork Orange*.
China is admitted to the U.N.
Twenty-sixth Amendment gives eighteen-year-olds right to vote.
Intel invents microprocessor.
Nike "swoosh" symbol is designed by Oregon student Carol Davidson for $35.

Industrial designer Richard Sapper designs the iconic and best-selling Tizio lamp.
Texas Instruments introduces pocket calculator. Claes Oldenburg produces the first of his still-life sculptures.
Italo Calvino writes *Invisible Cities*.
Francis Ford Coppola films *The Godfather*.
Richard Nixon visits China.
Break in at the Democratic Party headquarters in Watergate complex in Washington, D.C.
First home VCRs are introduced.
Munich hosts Olympic Games. Eleven members of the Israeli team are killed by Arab terrorists.

Architect John Portman and his associates design the Hyatt-Regency Hotel in San Francisco.
Design historian Victor Papanek writes *Design for the Real World*.
Alexander Solzhenitsyn is exiled from the USSR.
Turkey invades Cyprus.
Barcodes are first used in supermarkets.
First color photocopier machine is marketed in Japan.
Roe vs. Wade decision legalizes abortion.
Pablo Picasso, President Lyndon Johnson die.

	1974:	1975:	1976:
His Life:	Awarded honorary degree by Philadelphia College of Art (now University of the Arts). Exhibition, 107 Grafici del AGI, Castello Sforzesco, Milan.	Designs Minute Man poster for the U.S. Department of the Interior.	
His Work:			
His Time:	Salvador Dali Museum opens in Spain. Joseph Beuys performs *Coyote* in New York, and *I Love America and America Loves Me*. I.M. Pei designs East Building of the National Gallery of Art in Washington, D.C. Charles Lindbergh dies. Hank Aaron breaks Babe Ruth's all-time home run record. Richard Nixon resigns presidency. Gerald Ford assumes presidency. Patty Hearst is kidnapped by Symbionese Liberation Army.	Architect Charles Jencks coins the term "Post-Modern." Roy Lichtenstein has retrospective in Paris. First personal computer (PC) is marketed. Bic disposable shaving stick is introduced. First warning of possible damage to ozone layer issued. Dictator General Franco dies and Spain becomes a democracy. Home Box Office (HBO) is launced by Time, Inc. Steve Jobs and Steve Wozniak design the Apple I, so named by Jobs after an Oregon apple orchard where he worked one summer.	Conceptual atist Christo builds the *Running Fence* in California. Los Angeles County Museum holds exhibition *Women Artists: 1550-1950*. Artist Carl Andre's *Bricks* generates controversy in London exhibition. Mao Tse-tung of China dies. Jimmy Carter elected President of the United States. United States celebrates bicentennial. Concorde supersonic airliner begins cross-Atlantic services. George Lucas films *Star Wars*. Montreal hosts Olympic Games.

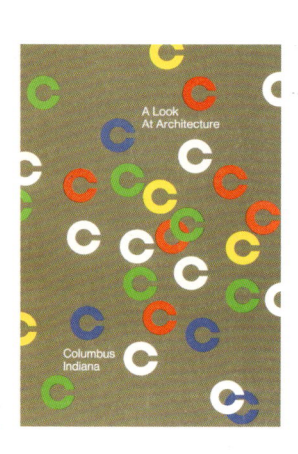

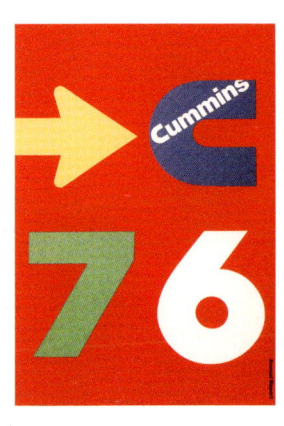

1977:

Starts teaching at the newly formed Yale University Summer Design Program in Brissago, Switzerland with colleague and friend Armin Hofmann. Taught in the program every year until he died. Exhibition of work at Pratt Institute, New York; Wichita State University, Kansas.

1978:

1979:

Awarded honorary degree by Philadelphia College of Art (now University of the Arts). Exhibition at Philadelphia College of Art.

Pompidou Center opens to the public in Paris. *Unofficial Art from the Soviet Union* exhibition held at the Institute for Contemporary Arts in London.
South African anti-apartheid leader Steven Biko dies in police custody.
Egyptian president Anwar Sadat visits Israel.
First democratic elections since 1936 held in Spain.
First AIDS cases are reported in New York.
Apple II microcomputer is marketed in the United States.
The television series *Dallas* premieres on television.

Anwar Sadat and Menachem Begin share the Nobel Peace Prize.
Louise Brown becomes the first baby born through in vitro fertilization.
Judy Chicago produces "The Dinner Party."
Nuclear accident occurs at Three Mile Island, near Harrisburg, Pennsylvania.
IBM presents first laser printer-copier.
Philips and Sony develop the compact disc.
Charles Eames, Giorgio de Chirico, and critic Harold Rosenberg die.

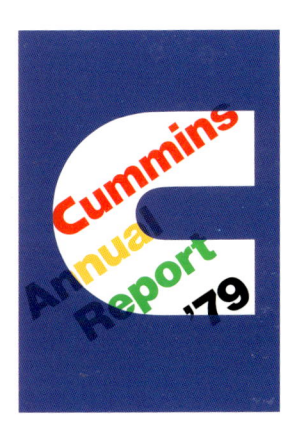

Germaine Greer's *The Obstacle Race: Fortunes of Women Painters and Their Work* is published.
Michael Graves designs Portland Public Service Building.
Woody Allen films *Manhattan*, and Francis Ford Coppola films *Apocalypse Now*.
Margaret Thatcher is elected British Prime Minister.
Artist Sonia Delaunay dies.

	1980:	1981:	1982:
His Life:	Designs trademark for real estate company Tipton Lakes Corporation. Designs poster for IBM on conservation.	Designs iconic poster for IBM using the rebus and play instinct. Interviewed by AIGA Executive Director Carolyn Hightower for the Design Archive Project sponsored by the National Endowment for the Arts.	Exhibition at Reinhold Brown Gallery, New York. Designs cover for the *Annual of the AIGA Graphic Design USA 3*.
His Work:			
His Time:	Robert Mapplethorpe's photographs *Black Males* series is exhibited in Amsterdam. Architect Richard Meier designs the High Museum of Art in Atlanta, Georgia. Ronald Reagan is elected President of the United States. In Poland, Lech Walesa leads strikes at the Gdansk shipyard and forms Polish trade union Solidarity. Italian firm Alessi commissions contemporary architects to design household products. Fax machines enter widespread use. Moscow hosts Olympic Games. CNN launched by Ted Turner.	Philosopher Roland Barthes publishes *Camera Lucida*. Maya Ling Lin, Yale University architecture student, designs Vietnam War Memorial in Washington, D.C. Sandra Day O'Connor is first woman to be appointed to the U.S. Supreme Court. President Anwar Sadat of Egypt is assassinated. François Mitterand is elected President of France. The U.S. Center for Disease Control recognizes AIDS as a communicable disease.	Swatch Watch is designed by Ernst Thonke, Jacques Müller, and Elmar Mock. First video art screenings at the Whitney Museum of American Art. Michael Graves designs Humana Building in Louisville, Kentucky. Britain and Argentina engage in Falklands War. Compact disc (CD) players go on sale. Fuji Corporation introduces the disposable camera. Steven Spielberg films *ET, The Extraterrestrial*.

380: 381:

1983:

Designs poster for the Art Director's Club Hall of Fame Awards.

1984:

Exhibition at the International Typeface Corporation Gallery, New York.
Authors *A Paul Rand Miscellany*.
Awarded the Type Directors Club Medal.

1985:

Authors the seminal book *Paul Rand: A Designer's Art*.
Honored with the President's Fellow Award by the Rhode Island School of Design, Providence.
Awarded honorary degrees at Yale University, New Haven, and Parsons School of Design, New York.

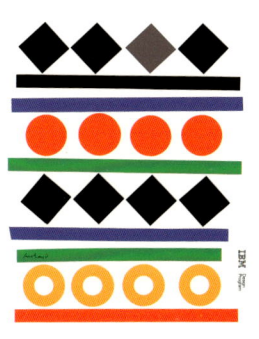

Architect I.M. Pei selected to design the Grand Louvre in Paris.
Artist Bruce Nauman produces *Dream Passage*.
U.S. invades Grenada.
Chicago elects its first black mayor, Harold Washington.
HIV/AIDS virus identified by American and French scientists.
Discovery of "genetic fingerprinting" in DNA.

Primitivism in 20th Century Art exhibition at MoMA, New York.
Milan Kundera writes *The Unbearable Lightness of Being*.
Ronald Reagan re-elected President of the United States.
Indira Gandhi, Indian prime minister, assassinated.
Los Angeles hosts Olympic Games; sprinter Carl Lewis wins four gold medals to equal his idol Jesse Owens (1936 Berlin Olympics).

Architect Peter Eisenman designs Wexner Center for Visual Arts at the Ohio State University in Columbus, Ohio.
Artist Cindy Sherman produces series of self-portraits.
Artist Barbara Kruger produces series of poster prints and paintings.
Mikhail Gorbachev is elected General Secretary of the USSR.
The luxury cruiser *Titanic* is detected by underwater robots.
Artists Marc Chagall and Jean Dubuffet die.

	1986:	1987:	1988:
His Life:	Exhibition at Pratt Institute, New York; the Design Gallery, Matsuya Ginza, Tokyo. Designs logos for NeXT Computers and Connecticut Art Directors Club.	Awarded honorary degrees by University of Hartford, Connecticut; Kutztown University, Pennsylvania. Work exhibited at the Universita Internazionale Dell' Arte, Florence, Italy. Receives prestigious Florence Prize for Visual Communication. Designs logos for Mossberg & Company, and PDR (Pastore DePamphillis Rampone).	Awarded honorary degree by the School of Visual Arts, New York. SVA honors him with a solo exhibition titled *The Master's Series* in the Visual Arts Museum.
His Work:			
His Time:	In Los Angeles, Museum of Contemporary Art is designed by Japanese architect Arata Isozaki. Artist Jeff Koons produces *Rabbit*. NASA Space shuttle *Challenger* explodes with seven astronauts aboard. President Ferdinand and wife Imelda Marcos flee revolution in the Phillipines. Iran-Contra scandal unfolds. First combination heart, lung, and liver transplant takes place. Chernobyl nuclear mishap in Kiev, USSR, occurs. First laptop computer is introduced. Conceptual artist Joseph Beuys dies.	Charles Jencks publishes *Post-Modernism: Neo-Classicism in Art and Architecture*. Architect Frank Gehry's Little Beaver armchair, made from pieces of cardboard, is manufactured. Mikhail Gorbachev introduces Glasnost and Perestroika. Iran-Contra congressional hearings take place in Washington, D.C. Compact video disc is introduced. Andy Warhol, André Masson die.	Computer art emerges as an art form. George Bush is elected President of the United States. Salman Rushdie's *The Satanic Verses* causes worldwide controversy. First world conference on AIDS. DNA fingerprinting revolutionizes forensics and paternity testing. Transatlantic fiber-optics become available. Spanish director Pedro Almadovar films and directs *Women on the Verge of a Nervous Breakdown*. Artist Louise Nevelson dies. Artist and designer Ray Eames dies. Seoul hosts Olympic games.

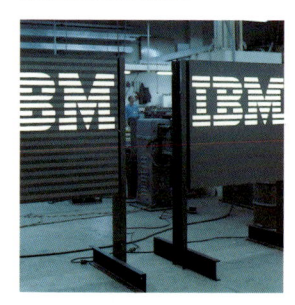

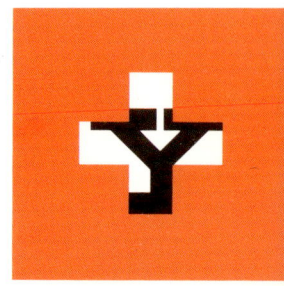

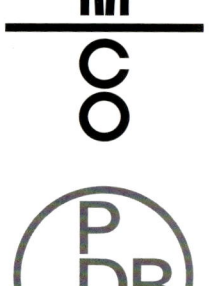

382: 383:

1989:

Designs logo for Monell Chemical Senses Center. Designs poster for the University of Hartford.

1990:

Designs logo for Irwin Financial Corporation. Designs mark, posters, and other supporting materials for Benjamin Franklin two hundredth anniversary celebration. Solo exhibition of work at the Joseloff Gallery, University of Hartford.

1991:

Designs logotypes for Morningstar Securities, Chicago; Okasan Securities Company, a financial brokerage firm in Tokyo; IDEO, a think tank organization in Palo Alto, California.

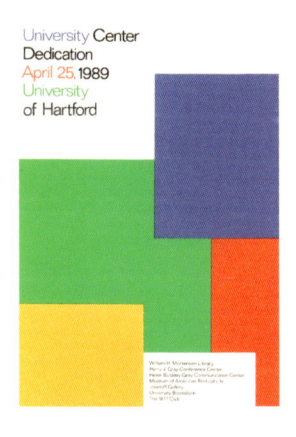

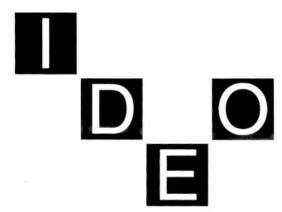

The Dallas Museum of Art organizes the exhibition *Black Art: Ancestral Legacy: The African Impulse in African American Art.*
Art historian Linda Nochlin publishes *Women, Art, and Power and Other Essays.*
George Bush and Mikhail Gorbachev declare end of Cold War.
In Czechoslovakia, poet Vaclav Havel is elected president.
The Berlin Wall is demolished; East and West Germany unite.
Pro-democracy students occupy Tiananmen Square in Beijing, but are violently dispersed.
Stephen Hawkins's *A Brief History of Time* is published.

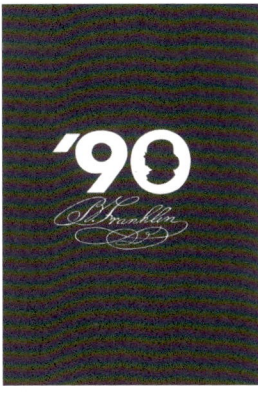

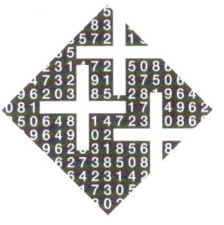

Writer Lucy Lippard publishes *Mixed Blessings: New Art in a Multi-Cultural America.*
In South Africa, Nelson Mandela, imprisoned for twenty-seven years, is released.
Boris Yeltsin is elected President of Russia.
Lech Walesa is elected President of Poland.
Iraq invades Kuwait, seizing oil reserves and setting off Persian Gulf War.
Hubble Space Telescope is launched.
Margaret Thatcher resigns as British prime minister.
First democratic elections held in Haiti.

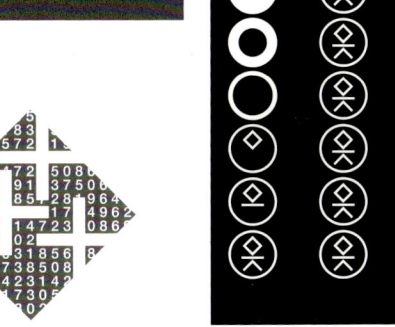

The USSR collapses.
End of apartheid policies in South Africa.
In India, Prime Minister Rajiv Gandhi is assassinated.
Yugoslav civil war breaks out.
U.N. forces triumph in Persian Gulf War.

1992:

1993:

1994:

His Life:

Solo exhibition at Ginza Graphic Gallery, Tokyo, Japan's premiere facility totally dedicated to the understanding and appreciation of graphic design and visual communications through presentatations, symposia, lectures and exhibitions.

Designs logos for Gentry Living Color in New York and EF English First.
Authors *Design, Form, and Chaos*, published by Yale University Press.
Named Professor Emeritus, Yale University.
Designs exhibition catalog on Leonardo da Vinci for IBM.

Designs logos for Accent Software International, based in Jerusalem.

His Work:

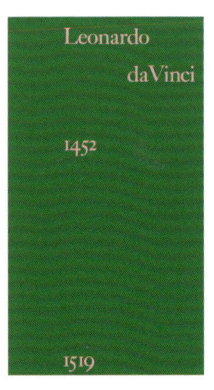

His Time:

Architect Frank Gehry designs furniture for Knoll.
Bill Clinton is elected President of the United States.
Los Angeles riots are ignited by police beatings of motorist Rodney King.
First Earth Sumit environmental conference is held in Rio de Janciro.
Spike Lee films *Malcolm X*.
Barcelona, Spain, hosts Olympic games.
Maastricht Treaty takes effect, creating the European Union.
The U.N. intervenes in Somali conflicts.
Hurricane Andrews ravages South Florida.

PLO-Israeli peace agreement takes place.
Concept of "Information Super-Highway" is promoted.
World wide web internet system links five million users.
NAFTA Treaty is signed.
Justice Ruth Bader Ginzburg is appointed to U.S. Supreme Court.
Toni Morrison wins Nobel Prize for Literature.
Israeli-Palestinian accord is signed.
Final episode of television sitcom "Cheers" airs on NBC.

First post-apartheid elections are held in South Africa; Nelson Mandela is elected President.
Massacre of Tutsis by Hutus in Rwanda.
Number of HIV cases worldwide is estimated to have reached seventeen million.
Northridge earthquake rocks California.
Major League baseball players strike. No World Series held.
Jacqueline Kennedy, Richard Nixon die.

384: 385:

1995:

Designs logos for USSB, a global satellite company, Computer Impressions in New York, and XGA for IBM.
Conducts student critiques and delivers lecture at the Arizona State University.

U.S. space shuttle *Atlantis* docks with Russian *Mir* space station.
Fighting escalates in Bosnia and Croatia.
Israeli Prime Minister Yitzak Rabin is slain by Jewish extremist.
Oklahoma City Federal building is bombed by terrorist Timothy McVeigh.
Kobe earthquake ravages Kobe, Japan.
Republicans take control of the United States Congress for the first time in several decades.

1996:

Designs logos for Enron and Norwalk Cancer Center in Norwalk, Connecticut.
Authored his last book, *From Lascaux to Brooklyn*.
Awarded honorary degree by Pratt Institute, New York.
Conducts his final class for the Yale University Summer Design Program in Brissago, Switzerland.
Retrospective exhibition of work at the Cooper Union for the Advancement of Science & Art, New York.
Delivers lecture at the Cooper Union, New York.
On November 14, Rand delivers his final lecture at MIT. John Maeda and Nicholas Negroponte initiate inquiries to offer Rand a teaching position at the MIT Media Lab.

Designs Cummins Engine 1996 annual report.
He approves final proofs in his hospital bed.
Dies of cancer in Norwalk, Connecticut on November 26.

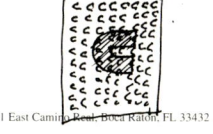

BOCA RATON RESORT & CLUB

501 East Camino Real, Boca Raton, FL 33432

Bill Clinton re-elected President of the United States.
Atlanta, Georgia, hosts Olympic games.
Britain alarmed by "Mad Cow" disease.
The English Patient sweeps the Academy Awards.
Jazz great Ella Fitzgerald dies.
On the evening news of November 26, ABC television News anchor Peter Jennings announces the passing of Paul Rand to world wide viewers.

Contributors

Guenet Abraham is assistant professor of graphic design in the Visual Arts Department at the University of Maryland, Baltimore County. She holds a Master of Fine Arts degree from the Yale University School of Art. She worked as a designer for Random House and W.W. Norton & Co. in New York City. Her consultancy with publishing houses in New York City includes Doubleday, St Martin's Press, Simon & Schuster, Random House, Viking, and Pantheon Books. Her work has been recognized nationally by the American Institute of Graphic Arts. Abraham is a 2002 recipient of the multiple-year Henry C. Welcome Fellowship.

Antonio Alcalá graduated cum laude from Yale University in 1983 with a BA in history. In 1985, after being named a Carl Purrington Rollins Fellow, he graduated with an MFA from the Yale School of Art. His work has been recognized by national and international design institutions. He has served as interim chair of the Corcoran College of Art and Design graphic design department as well as president of the Art Directors Club of Metropolitan Washington. His work is represented in the Library of Congress Permanent Collection of Graphic Design.

Georgette Ballance is a visiting lecturer at several universities and the curator of numerous exhibitions, including *A Paul Rand Retrospective*. Before starting her own business as a design consultant, she was design director at Pace Editions in New York. She has taught in Zambia and Ethiopia and worked at the Institute of Ethiopian Studies in Addis Ababa and the Museum of African Art in Washington D.C. She taught design history as well as interdisciplinary collaborative seminars at Cooper Union and was director of its Study Center of Design and Typography. The co-editor of *Graphic Design History* and *Paul Rand: A Designer's Words*, Ms. Ballance earned her MA in art history from American University and her MFA in graphic design from Yale University.

Derek Birdsall is one of the most distinguished graphic designers working in Britain today. Designer of the first Pirelli Calendar in 1964, his work has included the Monty Python books, a large number of Penguin book jackets, and *The Independent Magazine* (1988), The Georgia O'Keeffe Museum and the National Gallery of Art. His design for the new prayer book of the Church of England, *Common Worship: Services and Prayers for the Church of England* (2000), has been widely acclaimed.

Bob Burns studied graphic design at the California Institute of the Arts and at Yale University. He has directed and designed print, advertising and identity programs for several international corporations. Some of his clients have included Adobe, Apple, Compaq, Gartner, Hewlett-Packard, IDSA, Polaroid, Reebok, and Spinal Technology, Inc., as well as the U.S. Department of the Interior. From 1995-97 he was design consultant to the Polaroid Corporation, implementing their revised worldwide corporate identity initiative with design director Jon Craine. He has received awards from AIGA, Los Angeles Art Directors Club, and the American Center for Design. His work has appeared in *Print, Graphis,* and *Communication Arts,* and has been exhibited in the U.S. and Europe. He is a member of imPartners, design and marketing consultants specializing in strategic corporate communications, and is also on the faculty of Boston University.

Philip Burton received a Bachelor of Fine Arts in graphic design from the Philadelphia College of Art (now the University of the Arts) in 1968 and then attended the Weiterbildungsklasse at the Kunstgewerbeschule in Basel, Switzerland, between 1970 and 1975. He has held faculty positions at the University of Houston and the School of Art at Yale University. He was Coordinator of the Kent Summer in Switzerland Workshop between 1975 and 1981, which then became the Yale Summer Program in Graphic Design in Brissago, Switzerland, between 1982 and 1996. Mr. Burton combines theory with practice by remaining active as the designer of a wide range of projects including educational material, graphic identities, museum publications, and financial data. Since 1992 he has served a design consultant to Morningstar, Inc., a Chicago-based provider of financial data in print and electronic formats.

Ivan Chermayeff studied at Harvard University and the Institute of Design in Chicago, and graduated with a BFA from Yale University. In 1957, he helped found Brownjohn, Chermayeff & Geismar Associates, which became Chermayeff & Geismar Associates in 1960. Mr. Chermayeff is a past president of the American Institute of Graphic Arts, and was a trustee for the Museum of Modern Art for twenty years. He is a trustee of the New School for Social Research, as well as a national trustee of the Smithsonian Institution. He also has been on the board of directors of the International Design Conference in Aspen for over twenty-six years. His work has been exhibited widely throughout the United States, Europe, Japan, and the Soviet Union. His many awards include the Industrial Art Medal from the American Institute of Architects, the Gold Medal from the Philadelphia College of Art, and, with Thomas Geismar, the Gold Medal of the American Institute of Graphic Arts and the Yale Arts Award Medal. He was named to the New York Art Directors Hall of Fame and has received honorary doctorates from the Corcoran School of Art and Design, the University of Arts, and Maine School of Art.

Kyle Cooper received an MFA in Graphic Design from the Yale University School of Art, where he studied independently with Paul Rand. While at Yale, he was awarded The Calhoun College Resident Graduate Fellowship, created to generate undergraduate interest in the arts, as well as the Mohawk Paper Company Traveling Fellowship, which enabled him to do film research at the former Soviet Union's Sergei Eisenstein Kabinet. He has taught motion design at the Art Center College of Design in Pasadena, has been guest critic at Yale University School of Art, and was the Gerald Phillips Lecturer at the Cooper Union School. Cooper and The Imaginary Forces team's extensive feature film credits include main title designs for *Seven, The Island of Doctor Moreau, Mission Impossible, Twister, Dead Presidents, Quiz Show, Nixon, Braveheart,* and *Spiderman*.

Helen Federico was educated at the Parsons School of Design. During her professional career, she worked in advertising, editorial design, publishing, and music. She worked with and assisted famed designers and art directors Cipe Pineles, Alexy Brodovich, and Paul Rand. As a freelance consultant, she was a designer, illustrator, and art director for several national accounts. She has authored and illustrated children's books for Golden

Books, and cookbooks for Golden Press, Ridge Press, and Holt Rinehart Winston. She has also illustrated for publications such as *Mademoiselle, Seventeen, McCall's, Fortune, Glamour, Woman's Day, Gourmet, Redbook, Vista, Travel & Leisure, Harper's Bazaar, Better Homes & Gardens, Food & Wine,* and, many more.
A partial list of national and international companies she has provided illustrations and communications for includes Mobil, Westport Pepperell, Westvaco, Pitney Bowes, Standard Oil, IBM, Hennessey Cognac, *The New Yorker*, Lipton Tea, City of New York, Irving Trust, Savings & Loan Association, Ford Motor Company, Hertz, Bell's Scotch Whisky, and Corning Glass Company. She has also designed books, book jackets, and album covers for the Museum of Modern Art, Museum of Primitive Art, Arista Records, MGM Records, and Doubleday, Scribners, and Crowell. She is a member of the board of directors in charge of paintings in corporate and private collections and exhibits at the HHM Library in Pound Ridge, New York. A standing member of The Society of Illustrators, her work has been exhibited at Benton & Bowles, J. Walter Thompson Co., Inc., Society of Illustrators, New York Art Directors Club, HHM Library, and Fairfield University. She has been published in *Graphis, Communication Arts, American Illustrator,* and *Idea* magazines. A video of her work is housed at the Rochester Institute of Technology.

Shigeo Fukuda graduated in 1956 from Tokyo National University of Art and Music. His design work, which is characterized by illusion and humor, includes illustration, symbol-trademark, sculpture, environmental design, and ceramics. Since 1966, he has participated in major international graphic arts and poster exhibitions. He has had one-man exhibitions in New York, Italy, France, and Japan. Fukuda's work is represented in the Museum of Modern Art, New York, and collections in Colorado, Paris, and Moscow. He has taught at Tokyo University of Arts and Yale University.

Nathan Garland is a graphic designer whose work has ranged from annual reports to art books and from logos to marketing material. He serves both corporate and not-for-profit clients, and is based in New Haven, Connecticut. Originally from Chicago, he studied at Washington University (BFA), in The Netherlands on a Fulbright Scholarship, and at Yale (MFA). He has also taught and lectured. His personal work includes drawings, collages, and animation.

Milton Glaser studied at Cooper Union School of Art. On a Fulbright Scholarship he traveled to the Academia di Belle Arti in Bologna, where he studied with Giorgio Morandi for two years. In 1954, he was instrumental in founding Push Pin Studios. In 1968, Glaser became design director and chairman of the board of *New York* magazine, and in 1975, vice president and design director of the *Village Voice*. Since 1974, he has been president of Milton Glaser, Inc., a multidisciplinary office involved in signage, theming, packaging, and corporate identity programs. Mr. Glaser's graphics work includes the *I Love NY* logo, arguably one of the most copied graphic concepts ever created. He has designed hundreds of posters, most famously the insert for Bob Dylan's greatest hits album. An honorary fellow of the Royal Society of Arts, Glaser is represented in the collections of the Museum of Modern Art, The Smithsonian Institution, Washington, D.C., the Israel Museum, Jerusalem, the Musée d'Affiche, Paris, and the Victoria and Albert Museum.

Diane Gromala is associate professor in the School of Literature, Communication, and Culture at Georgia Institute of Technology, Atlanta, where she teaches in the graduate program in Information Design and Technology. She is also Director of Feral Computing. Her work has been performed and presented in Canada, the U.S., Europe, and the Middle East and has caught the attention of media networks such as Discovery Channel and the BBC. As a Senior Fulbright Fellow, Gromala created a new program in Human Computer Interaction Design at Wanganui Polytechnic and Waikato University in New Zealand, and performed cultural analyses of the use of technology and the embodiment of cultural difference at New Zealand's national museum Te Papa. Her undergraduate and graduate degrees are from the University of Michigan and Yale University, respectively.

Gerald J. Gross
After a career of thirty years in book publishing, from the mid-forties to the mid-seventies, Gerald Gross joined Boston University as vice president for arts and publications. There, until his present retirement, his responsibilities were wide-ranging: from dean-ad-interim of the School for the Arts to co-founder of the Huntington Theatre Company, now the foremost regional theater in New England.

Sarah Kerstin Gross lives and works in Weston and Westport, Connecticut. For twenty-five years she has run her own multifaceted catering and event planning business. Cabbages and Kings, for which Paul Rand created her logo. She is also an active painter of personal landscapes, both figurative and abstract, as well as a psycho-spritual healer. Many of Gross's paintings hang, on a rotating basis, at Kripalu Center for Yoga and Health in Lenox, Massachusetts.

Jessica Helfand is a designer, author, and critic. She is on the graduate faculty at Yale University School of Art, is a contributing editor to *Eye* and *ID* magazines, and is author of *Six (+2) Essays on Design and New Media, Paul Rand: American Modernist, Screen: Essays on Graphic Design, New Media, and Visual,* and *Reinventing the Wheel*. Her studio, Jessica Helfand/William Drenttel, focuses on editorial design and new media. She holds a BA and a MFA in graphic design from Yale University.

Steven Heller is senior art director at the *New York Times*. He is also editor of the *AIGA Journal of Graphic Design* and chair of the School of Visual Arts MFA/Design program in New York. In 1996 Steven Heller received the New York Art Directors Club Special Educator's Award. A prolific writer, he is the author or editor of more than seventy books on graphic design including *Graphic Style: From Victorian to Post-Modern, Grahic Wit: The Art of Humor in Grahic Design, Design Literacy: Understanding Graphic Design,* and *Paul Rand*. He is a contributor or contributing editor to nearly twenty-five magazines, including *Print, U&lc, Eye magazine, Baseline Typographics Journal, Communications Arts, ID magazine, Graphis, Design Issues,* and *Mother Jones*.

Ken Hiebert, a graphic designer, photographer, educator, and author, was the 2001 Nierenberg Professor at the School of Design at Carnegie Mellon University. He has held teaching positions at the Basel School of Design, Carnegie Mellon University, Yale University, and The University of the Arts in Philadelphia, where he served as founder and chairman of the graphic design department, and from which he retired professor emeritus in May 1999. Hiebert is the author of two books, *Graphic Design Sources* (Yale University Press, 1998) and *Graphic Design Processes* (Van Nostrand Reinhold, 1992). He received the Master Teacher Award from the Graphic Design Education Association in 1991. He received two individual design arts awards from the National Endowment for the Arts.

Charles Hillman was born in South Bend, Indiana, and graduated from DePauw University with a degree in business economics. He resides in South Bend with his wife, Anne. After college, he worked for McKesson Appliance Company of Toledo, Ohio, a manufacturer of anesthesia equipment, which he helped sell in 1957. He joined Mossberg & Company in South Bend, Indiana, becoming president in 1965. Under his leadership, Mossberg & Company gained a reputation for its advances and innovations in color separation technology and the ability to print complex four-, five-, and six-color projects with superior registration, accurate color and duotone reproduction, and unmatched quality control. It was because of Mossberg & Company's reputation and exacting standards that Charles Hillman and Paul Rand began working together in 1971. They developed a professional relationship, and personal friendship that lasted until Paul's death. The Cummins Engine Company annual reports were very important jobs, and won numerous prizes for design and print quality over the years. Other projects for venerable institutions such as IBM, Yale University, Westinghouse, and UPS were equally challenging and brought Charles Hillman and Paul Rand closer together as collaborators and innovators. Mr. Hillman retired in 1995, and today Mossberg & Company is under the very able direction of James Hillman, son of Charles. It is a rapidly growing printing and imaging company respected in the industry for the same superior quality and dedication to new ideas that it has had for the past seventy years.

Armin Hofmann was for many years principal of the graphics class at the Gewerbeschule in Basel, and, subsequently, of the advanced training course in visual communication at the Basel School of Design. He has been active as a guest lecturer at a number of American universities since 1955, among them the Philadelphia School of Art and the Graphic Design Graduate Program at the Yale University School of Art. From 1973 through 1996, he was the director of the Yale Summer Program in Graphic Design in Brissago, Switzerland. He has also been a guest lecturer and consultant to the National Institute of Design in Ahmedabad, India. His distinguished career has been celebrated with numerous exhibitions and awards, including an honorary degree from the University of the Arts, Philadelphia, 1987, and an honorary membership in the Royal Society of Arts, 1988, London. He received the cultural award of the city of Basel, Switzerland, in 1997. He holds a membership in the Alliance Graphique Internationale.

Allen Hurlburt (1910-1983) attended the University of Pennsylvania where, he graduated with a degree in economics from the Wharton School. Hurlburt started his career as an assistant art director at Robbins Publishing and within a year was overseeing all six of their trade publications. After a period as art director of the Bureau of Advertising, he went into the army, where he received a battlefield commission and the Bronze Star. After WWII, he became art director of NBC television. In his five years there, he had a significant impact on the development of television graphics and promotion, and received two Gold Medals from the New York Art Directors Club. This was followed by a year at the Weintraub Agency as administrative director, working with Paul Rand. In 1952, Hurlburt went to *Look* magazine as promotion art director and a year later became art director of the magazine, a position held for fifteen years. He never did a redesign of *Look,* but kept the magazine under continual and gradual change, creating some of the most beautiful and intelligent design in the history of magazine publishing. In later years, Allen was the author of several books: *The Grid, Publication Design, The Design of the Printed Page,* and *Photo/ Graphic Design: The Interaction of Design and Photography*. His many honors include The National Society of Art Directors Art Director of the year (1965), the AIGA Medal (1973), and the New York Art Directors Hall of Fame (1978).

Takenobu Igarashi graduated from Tama University of Fine Arts in Tokyo in 1968, and obtained a master's degree from the University of California in Los Angeles in 1969. He established Igarashi Studio in Tokyo in 1970. His widely honored work ranges from print media, corporate identity programs, and signage to environmental design and sculpture. He has taught and lectured at various institutions, including the University of California in Los Angeles, and Chiba University in Japan. His work has been exhibited at various universities and conferences, including the Smithsonian Institution. Igarashi's work is in the collection of the Museum of Modern Art and others.

Julie Klugman earned her BFA degree with honors from the School of Art & Design, University of Michigan, in Ann Arbor. She attended the Yale Summer Program in Graphic Design in Brissago, Switzerland. Her professional experience has been with some of Chicago's most distinguished design firms. Recently, she has taught at the School of the Art Institute in Chicago, and is currently teaching at the University of Illinois at Chicago.

John Maeda is associate director of the MIT Media Laboratory, where he is also Sony Career Development Professor of Media Arts and Sciences, associate professor of design and computation, and director of the Aesthetics & Computation Group (ACG). His mission is to foster the growth of what he calls "humanist technologists" — people that are capable of articulating future culture through informed understanding of the technologies they use. The ACG is an experimental research studio that was founded in 1996 as the successor to the late Professor Muriel Cooper's Visible Language Workshop. In the short time since its existence, individual experimental work in the ACG has received numerous awards and acclaim for a uniqueness in both concept and craft. A major component of the ACG's efforts involves outreach to the design and art community in the form of workshop and events that introduce the underlying concepts of computing technology, as exemplified in the ongoing *Design By Numbers* project. A 480-page retrospective of Maeda's personal work entitled *MAEDA@ MEDIA* has been published by Thames & Hudson in Europe, and Rizzoli in the United States.

Naoko Matsuzono is a recent graduate of the Graphic Design Program in the Visual Arts Department at the UMBC. Currently, she is involved in a number of independent projects. Her near future aspirations include writing, illustrating and designing children's books, working on a graduate degree in visual communications, and working in a multifaceted design practice environment.

Judy Metro is editor-in-chief at the National Gallery of Art, Washington, D.C. She was senior editor at Yale University Press in charge of art books, and also a critic in the graphic design graduate program at the Yale University School of Art.

Franc Nunoo-Quarcoo is professor of graphic design, and chair of the Visual Arts Department at the University of Maryland Baltimore County. He curated the exhibition, and co-authored with Cynthia Wayne, the publication of the same title, *Word + Image: Swiss Poster Design, 1955-1997* (1997). He also curated the exhibition and authored the publication *Bruno Monguzzi: A Designer's Perspective* (1998). Currently, he is preparing an article and a book on the eminent American modernist graphic designer Rudolph deHarak.

Bez Ocko is a graphic designer and partner in Hyland/Ocko Associates in Philadelphia. She has taught at Moore College of Art and Design and is currently a professor of design at Hofstra University in New York. In 2002 she curated the exhibition *The Swiss Poster: Art of Ten Masters* (with an accompanying publication) for the Hofstra Museum.

Mario Rampone is a typographer and printer. His interest in the graphic arts began with four years of study at the New York School of Graphic Communication. It was at that time that he and a team of ambitious friends attempted to start a weekly newspaper. However, their hopes were interrupted by the Korean War. Twelve years of post-graduate courses helped to round out his knowledge of design, typography, and printing. He established an impressive thirty-two-year career at Tri-Arts Press, a premier company in the graphic arts in New York City. In the mid-seventies, when new technology challenges began to mount, he established Pastore DePamphilis Rampone (PDR) in 1976 with two experienced partners. Rampone's greatest satisfaction in his practice was his longterm collaboration with Paul Rand.

Richard Sapper studied philosophy, graphic design, engineering, and economics before embarking on a career in industrial design. From 1956–58 he worked for Mercedes Benz until he moved to Milan, where he worked with Marco Zanuso for Brionvega. Other companies he worked for are Siemens, Fiat, Pirelli, IBM, and Alessi. His most famous design is the Tizio lamp for Artemide. He was for several years a professor at the Akademie der Bildenden Kuenste in Stuttgart. He received the Compasso d'Oro award five times.

Virginia Smith is a professor of graphic design and an author of design history. Her study of popular imagery, *The Funny Little Man: the Biography of a Graphic Image*, appeared in 1993 (Van Nostrand Reinhold). She has written articles for the *Journal of the American Institute of Graphic Arts, Printing History, Design Book Review, U&lc*, and various exhibition catalogs. She has worked at *Mademoiselle* magazine and CBS and for most major book publishers. She is an elected member of the Art Directors Club of New York, the Grolier Club, and the Association International des Critiques d'Art. She is the former national president of the American Printing History Association and board member of the Society of Publication Designers. She holds degrees from Yale University and Wellesley College.

Massimo Vignelli is the co-founder and president of Vignelli Associates and chief executive officer of Vignelli Designs in New York. His work includes graphic and corporate identity programs, publication designs, architectural graphics, and exhibition, interior, furniture, and consumer product designs for many leading American and European companies and institutions. Mr. Vignelli's work has been published and exhibited throughout the world and entered in the permanent collections of several museums, notably, the Museum of Modern Art, the Metropolitan Museum of Art, the Brooklyn Museum, and the Cooper-Hewitt Museum in New York; the Musée des Arts Décoratifs in Montreal; and the Die Neue Sammlung in Munich. Mr. Vignelli has taught and lectured on design in the major cities and universities in the United States and abroad. Among Massimo Vignelli's many awards: Gran Premio Triennale di Milano, 1964; Compasso d'Oro, awarded by the Italian Association for Industrial Design (ADI), 1964 and 1998; the 1973 Industrial Arts Medal of the American Institute of Architects (AIA); the Art Directors Club 1982 Hall of Fame; the 1983 AIGA Gold Medal; the first Presidential Design Award, presented by President Ronald Reagan in 1985, for the National Park Service Publications Program; the Interior Design Hall of Fame, 1988; the National Arts Club Gold Medal for Design, 1991; the Interior Product Designers Fellowship of Excellence, 1992; and The Brooklyn Museum Design Award for Lifetime Achievement, 1995. He has been awarded an honorary doctorate in architecture from the University of Venice, Italy, and honorary doctorates in fine arts from Parsons School of Design, New York, Pratt Institute, Brooklyn, Rhode Island School of Design, Providence, and Corcoran School of Art and Design, Washington D.C. In 1996 he received the Honorary Royal Designer for Industry Award from the Royal Society of Arts, London.

Wolfgang Weingart, born 1941, completed his typesetting apprenticeship in hand composition in 1963. He has taught typography at the Basel School of Design since 1968 and, invited by Armin Hofmann, was an instructor during the Yale Summer Program in Graphic Design in Brissago from 1974 through 1996. For the last thirty years Weingart has lectured and taught extensively in Europe, North and South America, Asia, Australia, and New Zealand. He is represented in the permanent collections of museums and private galleries, and has received design awards from the Swiss Federal Department of Home Affairs in Bern. Internationally exhibited, Weingart's publications and posters have been reproduced in numerous design references and journals. He was a member of Alliance Graphique Internationale/AGI from 1978 to 1999, on the editorial board of *Typographische Monatsäbtter* from 1970 to 1988, and contributed over twenty supplements for the educational series Typographic Process and TM/communication. A self-taught designer who fosters imagination and insight, Weingart teaches his students to teach themselves. His experimental work in typography has influenced the course of design history in the last decades of the twentieth century.

Bibliography

Books by Paul Rand
Thoughts on Design. New York: Wittenborn Schultz, 1946; London: Studio Vista/ New York: Van Nostrand Reinhold Art Paperback, 1970.
The Trademarks of Paul Rand. New York: George Wittenborn, Inc., 1960.
A Designer's Art. New Haven: Yale University Press, 1985.
Design, Form, and Chaos. New Haven: Yale University Press, 1993.
From Lascaux to Brooklyn. New Haven: Yale University Press, 1996.

Children's books illustrated by Paul Rand
Rand, Ann, and Rand, Paul. *I Know a Lot of Things.* New York: Harcourt, Brace & World, Inc., 1956.
Rand, Ann, and Rand, Paul. *Sparkle and Spin.* New York: Harcourt, Brace & World, Inc., 1957.
Rand, Ann, and Rand, Paul. *Little 1.* New York: Harcourt, Brace & World, Inc., 1962.
Rand, Ann, and Rand, Paul. *Listen! Listen!* New York: Harcourt, Brace & World, Inc., 1970.

Articles by Paul Rand
"Critique of the Fifty Books." *Bookbinding and Book Production,* April 1948.
"Too Many Cooks." *Art and Industry,* 1948.
"What is Modern Typography?" *American Printer,* 1948.
"The Story of a Symbol." *Type Talks,* May 1949.
"Black in the Visual Arts." *Graphic Forms.* Cambridge, MA: Harvard University Press, 1949.
Rand, Paul. "Impression of an 'Abacus.'" *New York Times Magazine,* 28 March 1950.
"Modern Typography in the Modern World." *Typographica* #5, 1952.
"The Trademark as an Illustrative Device." Chicago: Paul Theobald and Company, 1952.
"Guest Editor: Paul Rand." *Art in Advertising,* August 1954.
"Paul Rand: Ideas about Ideas." *Industrial Design,* 1955.
"The Good Old 'Neue Typografie.'" *Typography USA* The Type Directors Club, 1959.
Rand, Ann, and Rand, Paul. "Advertisement: Ad Vivum or Ad Hominem?" Kepes, Gyorgy, guest ed. *Daedalus: "The Visual Arts Today,"* Winter 1960.
"The Art of the Package, Tomorrow and Yesterday." *Print,* January/February 1960.
"Our Biggest Threat is Conformity." *Printer's Ink,* 2 December 1960.
"Modern Typography in the Modern World." *Print,* January/February 1964.
"A Mentor (Jan Tschichold: The New Typography)." *Print,* January/February 1969.
"Integrity and Invention." *Graphis Annual,* 1971.
"Politics of Design." *Graphis Annual,* 1981.
"Good Design is Good Will." *AIGA Journal of Graphic Design,* 1987.
"Observation on Intuition." In *Analysis and Intuition: Society of Typographical Arts Design Journal,* 1987.
"The Case for the Ampersand." *New York Times Book Review,* 10 September 1989.
"Logos, Flags, and Escutcheons." *AIGA Journal of Graphic Design,* 1991.
"Computers, Pencils, and Brushes." *IBM,* 1992.
"Confusion and Chaos: The Seduction of Graphic Design." *AIGA Journal of Graphic Design,* 1992.
"Object Lessons." *The New Criterion,* 1992.
"Typography: Style Is Not Substance." *AIGA Journal of Graphic Design,* 1993.
"Failure By Design." *New York Times,* Op-Ed Page, 5 April 1993.
Preface for *The 100 Best Posters from Europe and the United States 1945-1990.* Toppan, 1995.
"Wolfgang Weingart: from Mainz to Basel" in: *AIGA Journal of Graphic Design,* 1996.

Books on Paul Rand
Helfand, Jessica. *Paul Rand: American Modernist.* New York: William Drentell. 1998.
Heller, Steven. *Paul Rand.* London: Phaidon Press. 1998.
Kamekura, Yusaku, ed. *Paul Rand: His Work from 1946 to 1958.* New York: Alfred A. Knopf and Tokyo: Zokeisha. 1959.

Articles on Paul Rand
"A Designer Thinks." *Interiors,* February 1947.
"About the Designers." *Advertising and Selling,* September 1945.
Abrams, Jan. "Paul Rand." *ID,* September/October 1993.
"Ads With a Punch By Ohrbach's." *Fashion Trades,* 22 November 1946.
Ager, Shana. "Art is Like Digging Ditches." *PM,* April 1947.
"AIGA Medal Will Be Given to Paul Rand At '50 Books' Fete." *Printing News,* 16 April 1966.
"American Who's Who Taps Whopping 42 Area Dwellers." *Town Crier,* 5 August 1958.
"An Interview with William Bernbach." *Communication Arts,* vol. 13, no. 1, 1971.
"Art and Creative Thinking: Paul Rand." *Advertising Review,* November/December 1958.
Baule, Giovanni. "A Homage to Paul Rand." *The Tuscan Scene,* No. 6 1986.
Beirut, Michael. Book review: "Design, Form, and Chaos: Playing the Game by Rand's Borzoi Books." (*Borzoi Quarterly,* vol. 7, no. 4, 1958. Rules') *Eye,* October 1993.
Campbell, Heyworth. "Trends." *Art Director & Studio News,* December 1949.
"Contemporary Trends in the Evolution of Advertising Art." *Art Director & Studio News,* October 1952.
"Cigar Box – New and Improved." *Printers' Ink,* 19 December 1952.
"Code Followed Direct Mail." *Art Director & Studio News,* March 1954.
"Current Art and Typographic Examples Worthy of Note." *Art Director & Studio News,* December 1951.
"Design 84: On Beauty and Utility." *Adweek,* October 1984.
"Design '84: George Lois Talks with Rand." *Adweek,* October 1984.
Devree, Howard. "Art and Formulas." *New York Times,* 6 June 1948.
Dougherty, Philip H. "Advertising: Graphics Awards Handed Out." *New York Times,* 8 September 1972.
Dreyfus, Patricia Allen. "Paul Rand: Design in American Context." *Print,* January/February 1969.
"Effect of Advertising on Commercial Design." *Journal of the Royal Society of Arts,* 30 January 1948.
Esplund, Lance. "Rand the Magician." *Modern Painters,* 1997.
"Esthetic Ads." *Time,* 23 December 1946.
Ettenberg, Eugene M. "Variations on the Theme of Garamond Oldstyle." *American Printer,* August 1948.
_____. "What is 'Modern' Typography?" *American Printer,* 1948.
_____. "The Paul Rand Legend." *American Artist,* October 1953.
"Exhibition of Advertising and Editorial Art." *Advertising and Selling,* April 1949.
Fern, Alan. "In the Beginning Was the Logo." *New York Times Book Review,* 3 November 1985.
Ferris, Byron. Book review: "From Lascaux to Brooklyn." *Communication Arts Design Annual,* 1996.
"Fine Art in Industrial Ads?" *Industrial Marketing,* July 1962.
"Five Designers for Under Five Dollars." *Industrial Design,* December 1954.
Fletcher, Alan. "Getting Going." *Design,* 1978.
"Graphic Design: You've Come a Long Way." *Pratt Reports,* August 1975.
Grossman, Robert S. "The Work of Paul Rand." *Productionwise,* October 1959.
Helfand, Jessica. "Paul Rand: American Modernist" *The New Republic,* September 1997.
Heller, Steven. "Paul Rand" interview in: *ID,* November/December 1988.
_____. "Interview with Paul Rand. Friedman, Mildred, ed., *Graphic Design*

America, Walker Art Center/ Harry N. Abrams, 1989.

———. "Paul Rand: The Play Instinct." Anderson, Gail and Heller, Steven, eds., *Graphic Wit: The Art of Humor in Graphic Design.* Watson Guptil, 1991.

———. "In Defense of Rand." *AIGA Journal of Graphic Design,* 1993.

———. "Thoughts on Rand." *Print,* March/April 1997.

Henrion, F.H.K. "Paul Rand" *Printed Advertising,* November 1948.

"Honorary Degree Citations: Paul Rand." *New School Observer,* June/July 1985.

Hurlburt, Allen. "Paul Rand" *Communication Arts,* January/February 1979.

"IBM's New Look" *Print,* November 1960.

"IBM Annual Report Wins for Design/Typography." *Art Direction,* January 1961.

"IBM Image-Maker Paul Rand: "Design is a Forever Job." *Modern Packaging,* October 1965.

Imatake, Midori. "The Fiddler of Yankee Feeling." *IDEA Special Issue 30 Influential Designers of the Century,* February 1984.

"It's Colorful, It's Partitioned, It's a Cigar Box." *Packaging Parade,* February 1943.

Kaltenborn, Howard S. "New Seal – New Signature." *Sales Record,* June/July 1960.

Kamekura, Yusaku, ed. "Paul Rand: His Work from 1946 to 1958." Tokyo: Zokeisha Publications Ltd, 1959.

Kemper, Steve. "Conversations: Logos To Go, Paul Rand." *Hartford Courant Northeast,* 4 July 1993.

Kleinman, Kent, and Van Duzer, Leslie, eds. "Paul Rand and Rudolf Arnheim." *Rudolph Arnheim: Revealing Vision.* The University of Michigan Press, 1995.

Kraus, H. Felix. "Dubo-Dubon-Dubonnet." *Art and Industry,* October 1942.

"Leading Graphic Designer Speaks About Design and Then Some." *FIT Network,* Spring 1994.

"Little 1." *New York Herald Tribune Book Review,* 11 November 1962.

"Little 1." *Library Journal,* 15 February 1963.

Louchheim, Aline B. "Art Directors Show Their Work." *New York Times,* 1953.

Ludwig, Myles Eric. "'Document Rand' Art." *Direction,* October 1972.

Margolis, Sanford, H, and Silverstein, Morton. "This Week is Really Going to be Something."

Margolin, Victor. "More Than Meets The Eye." *New York Times Book Review,* 2 May 1993.

"Marketing Hot Spots for 1955." *Printers' Ink,* 31 December 1955.

Meggs, Philip B. *A History of Graphic Design.* New York: Van Nostrand Reinhold Co., 1983.

Miller, Arthur. "Art in Advertising Shown at Its Best." *Los Angeles Times,* 24 June 1949.

Miller, J. Abbott. Book review of *Design, Form, and Chaos* in: *Graphis,* June 1993.

"Modern and Traditional Typography in America." *Penrose Annual,* 1949.

Moholy-Nagy, L. "Paul Rand." *AD,* February/March 1941.

"More Upgrading in the Field of Light-bulb Packaging." *Modern Packaging,* March 1961.

"N.S.A.D. Nominates Twelve for 3rd Annual Award." *Art Director & Studio News,* March 1950.

Oeri, Georgine. "Paul Rand." *Graphis,* June 1947.

"Print That Matters." *Communication Arts,* June 1962.

"Paul Rand." *The Insider,* March 1939.

"Paul Rand." *The Insider,* September 1939.

"Paul Rand, Industrial Designer." *Interiors,* February 1947.

"Paul Rand, Advertising Artist." *Magazine of Art,* March 1947.

"Paul Rand." *Printers' Ink,* 2 January 1953.

"Paul Rand's Designs Exhibited At A-D Gallery." *Publishers' Weekly,* February 1952.

"Paul Rand Designs Cigar Album." *Art Director & Studio News,* December 1952.

"Paul Rand's Work, The AIGA's Show of the Month." *Publishers' Weekly,* 3 March 1958.

"Paul Rand." *AIGA Newsletter,* March 1958.

"Paul Rand, AIGA Medalist." *Journal of the American Institute of Graphic Arts,* 1966.

"Paul Rand." *New York Art Directors' Hall of Fame Program.* 1972.

"Paul Rand Awarded 1984 TDC Medal." *Gutenberg and Family,* vol. 1, no. 1, January 1985.

"Paul Rand." *HQ,* November 1992.

Poe, Randall. "The Old Gray Annual Report Ain't What It Used To Be." *Across the Board,* December 1979.

Poynor, Rick. "Rereading Rand." *AIGA Journal of Graphic Design,* 1993.

"Pratt Institute Honorary Degrees." *Commencement Program,* May 1996.

"President's Fellows Awards: Rhode Island School of Design Program." June 1985.

"Pros and Cons: Some Views of AIGA's Paperback Cover Show." *Publishers' Weekly,* 4 December 1961.

"Rand is Design Pioneer." *Pratt Campus,* vol. 4, no. 7, 8 December 1977.

"Rand: Thoughts on Design." *AIGA Journal,* June 1947.

"Rand Wins Florence Prize for Visual Communication." *Yale Weekly Bulletin and Calendar,* 6-13 April 1987.

Ransom, Will. "Problems in Book Design: No. 99." *Book Binding and Book Production,* October 1945.

Seitlin, Percy. "Paul Rand." *PM,* October 1938.

———. "Paul Rand." *American Artist,* 1942.

———. "Paul Rand, Advertising Artist." *Magazine of Art,* March 1947.

———. "Paul Rand, Commercial Artist: His Fantasy is Boundless." *American Artist,* October 1970.

Shepheard, Paul. "Grand Designs." *New York Times Book Review,* 24 March 1996.

Smith, Virginia. "Paul Rand" *Artograph* No. 6, 1988.

Snyder, Gertrude. "Profiles: The Great Graphic Innovators." *U&lc,* March 1977.

"Sparkle and Spin." *N.Y. Herald Tribune Book Review,* 17 November 1957.

"Spotlight on Airwick Advertising: Putting Our Products in the Eye of the Consumer." *Interface,* February 1987.

"Stafford's Stallion: A Case Study." *Tide,* 24 December 1948.

"Steve Jobs Turns to Big Blue." *Newsweek,* 23 June 1986.

"Ten Best Illustrated Books of the Year." *New York Times Book Review,* 17 November 1957.

"The Year's Work: Residence." *Interiors,* August 1953.

"The Story Behind: W[Westinghouse]." *The Kiplinger Magazine,* September 1963.

"Trademarks by Paul Rand." *Portfolio #1,* 1950.

"Tribute to a Designer." *Esquire,* December 1959.

"Two New Logos." *Industrial Design,* June 1964.

"Weintraub Bids for RCA Account in *Times* Ad." *Advertising Age,* 1 February 1954.

Weisenborn, Fritzi. "Adventure in Art." *Chicago Sunday Times,* September 1941.

Weiss, Eric. "Orchestrating Corporate Identity: Playing the Symbols." *M magazine,* October 1987.

"Westinghouse Redesign." *Printers' Ink,* 1 July 1960.

"Westinghouse Design Program." *Industrial Design,* August 1960.

"Workshop School." *Interiors,* February 1949.

Woudhuysen, James. "Hand Stand." *Designweek,* 16 August 1991.

Center for Art and Visual Culture Staff
David Yager *Executive Director*
Symmes Gardner *Director*
Maurice Berger *Curator*
Renée van der Stelt *Projects Coordinator*
William-John Tudor *Exhibitions and Technology Designer*
Janet Magruder *Business Manager*

Issues in Cultural Theory
Maurice Berger *Series Editor*
Antonia LaMotte Gardner *Managing Editor*

Editor
Antonia LaMotte Gardner

Design and typography
Franc Nunoo-Quarcoo
franc@umbc.edu
Design assistant
Naoko Matsuzono

Imaging, printing, and bindery
Mossberg & Company Inc.
South Bend, Indiana.
www.mossbergco.com.
Grateful acknowledgment is made to Mossberg & Company Inc., and the Mossberg Foundation for underwriting the printing of this volume, number 6 in the *Issues in Cultural Theory* series from the Center for Art and Visual Culture at the University of Maryland Baltimore County.

Paper
Cover:
Mohawk Superfine Ultrawhite
130 Double-Thick Cover
Text: Stora Enso Centura Silk
100 Text

Photography
©The Estate of Paul Rand
 pp. 16, 68, 201–216, 226–231, 246–254, 256–287, 290–331, 334–341, 356–385
©Hans Namuth
 pp. 130, 198, 356, 370–371
©Mario Rampone
 p. 7
©Peter Arnell
 p. 200
©Dan Meyers
 pp. 232–245, 255, 288–289, 331–334d, 342–355
©Georgette Ballance
 pp. 224–224
©Mitsumasa Fujitsuka
 and Ginza Graphic Gallery
 pp. 218–223
©Apple Computer
 Chiat Day Advertising
 and Peter Arnell
 p. 2

Paul Rand: Modernist Design is composed in Garamond 3. Garamond 3 was a favorite typeface of Paul Rand's. The typographical design of this book is inspired by a portfolio of broadsides he designed for the Museum of Modern Art in 1948. The content had to do with women and how and why artists historically found women to be the preferred subjects for paintings (see pp. 238–45). Each broadside paired a writer with a painter, resulting in a revealing document on the subject.

About Claude Garamond

- Born in Paris, France, in 1490, Claude Garamond started his career as an apprentice for the Parisian punch-cutter and printer, Antoine Augereau in 1510. It was during this early part of the sixteenth century that Garamond and his peers found that the typography industry required unique, multitalented people to produce fine books. Many of the printers of that time were able to master all or most of the artistic and technical skills of book production from type design to bookbinding. Claude Garamond was the first to specialize in type design, punch cutting, and type-founding in Paris as a service to many famous publishers.

- After a decade of success with the Garamond typefaces all over Europe, King François I of France demanded that Garamond produce a Greek typeface, which later became known as "Grecs du Roi." The three fonts were modeled after the handwriting of Angelos Vergetios, and cut the largest size first, on a sixteen-point body. All three original sets of Royal Greek punches are preserved at the Imprimerie Nationale in Paris.

- In 1545 Garamond became his own publisher, featuring his own types, including a new italic. His first book published was *Pia et Religiosa Meditatio of David Chambellan*. As publisher, Claude Garamond relied on his creativity, harnessed by reasoned discipline to produce superbly crafted products. He modeled his book publishing style after the classic works of the Venetian printers who catered to the absolute elites of high society. He admired and emulated the works of Aldus Manutius. Garamond insisted on clarity in design, generous page margins, quality composition, paper, and printing, which was always accentuated with superb binding.

- Because of the soundness of Garamond's designs his typefaces have historical relevance, and they are likely to remain the day-to-day tools of professional typographers. Reading a well-set Garamond text page is almost effortless, a fact that has been well known to book designers for over 450 years.

- Before Garamond's independent practice, men such as Jenson, Griffo, and Caxton played specific roles in the development of type. Jenson perfected the roman type, Caxton conceived a bastard gothic font, and Griffo developed italic. Although not the inventor of movable type, Garamond was the first to make type available to printers at an affordable price. Several of the fonts we see on our computers have evolved from the work of type founders of the fifteenth and early sixteenth centuries. Claude Garamond's contribution to typography was vast, a true renaissance figure in the history of typography and communication.